CREATE!

Eduardo Arroyo

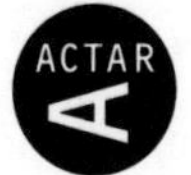

To the Creator, whoever you may be.

Summary

Preface

Prologue 1

Creation 2—11

Memory 12—22

Precision 23—32

Chance 33—41

Empathy 42—52

Events 53—63

Properties 64—73

Hybridization 74—83

Procedures 84—92

Cloning 93—101

Invisible order 102—110

Complexity 111—120

Gravity 121—128

Mutability 129—137

Mattergy 138—147

Epilogue 148—151

FINALLY, A MIXTURE OF PRECISION ALLIED WITH LIFE ^{82 : 10}

Amadeu Santacana

AN OCEAN OF POSSIBILITIES

SPEAK YOUR OWN LANGUAGE!

IN THE BEGINNING THERE WAS NOTHING... OR WAS THERE?

DECISION IS A PART OF PRECISION

DON'T MAKE TOO MANY PLANS! CHANCE ONLY HAS ONE

LOOK ME IN THE EYES!

OUR PASSIONS ARE THE MEASURE OF TIME

BE CAREFUL WHAT YOU CHOOSE!

THE FUTURE IS A MULTIPLE OF THREE

AN EGG IS FULL OF PROCEDURES

PRESENCE MARKS THE DIFFERENCE

ENTROPY IS AN INTUITION

THE ESSENTIAL IS INVISIBLE TO THE EYE

GETTING TO THE GROUND IS NOT A PRIORITY

DOES A MIRAGE EXIST?

MATTERGY ELIMINATES PREJUDICES

ENTHUSIASM AHEAD OF RISK

Preface

FINALLY, A MIXTURE OF PRECISION ALLIED WITH LIFE 82 : 10

AMADEU SANTACANA

"If comfort is all you expect to get out of life,
God help you."

John Cheever

Today we can state with conviction that the human race is positioned in an exaggerated condition of docility. We have become authentic house pets. This pleasant and calming comfort goes hand in hand with a suspicious pursuit of stability, which distances us from the disturbing questions about how we adapt our existence to an essentially savage world.

Doesn't this comfort, which is championed so staunchly by architectural discipline, act as a sedative, quelling some of the geniune elation that life can offer?

Is this sedative effect, which diminishes our nervous excitement and sinks us into a placid daydream, a tool for fomenting our current sedentary entrenchment?

Are the sedative and the sedentary ultimately two inseparable principles that lie dangerously hidden beneath the calm and safe solutions of commodity?

CREATE! takes an uncomfortable and stimulating stance; it is a plea for creation to take in all those things that spark an intensity of living. It sounds the alarm in the face of that feigned stability and lets loose a burst of energy to prevent a loss of tension. Chance, pleasure, vanity, fusion, individualism, empathy, cloning... are some of the themes that appear here, shaking up that state of pseudo-equilibrium. Just at the very moment when we had finally made some definitive decisions and had come to an accord about things that we didn't want to have to talk about again. Just as we were feeling serene, CREATE! pushes us to walk along the cliff's edge again; it is in this tension, on the brink of falling, that engaged creation appears – at just the right time. Like a watchman, attentive to this deluded comfort, it suggests a creative act derived from an intense relationship with the world around us, defining a non-dogmatic option that is aimed at a more authentic, honest kind of creativity; an effort to overcome that calm layer of superficiality to delve into the depths of the creative process.

The contents of this book are based on the capacity to eliminate as many prejudices as possible in order to put together a field of anti-paradigms, to activate creative processes from a position of uncompromising freedom. It shapes a territory full of unstable-seeming possibilities, which distances itself from the search for new truthfulness. There is the same intrinsic instability between Eduardo Arroyo and NO.MAD, between the person and the production, between a breaking out and a settling down. This imbalance between action and fact is inversely proportional. Arroyo's personal acts are disproportionate, imbibed with a strong desire to explore the limits. What NO.MAD produces is precise, moderate and controlled. Soul and precision. Integrity and relativism. A mixture that is as incompatible as it is inseparable. This unbreakable, apparently incoherent paradox is what builds a foundation for the desired intensity in spaces that we may end up inhabiting. This conflict emerges as the central axis of the contemporary creative process. It is the tool that allows for distancing ourselves from relaxing certainties in order to structure an apparently fuzzy position, which is still profoundly attuned to all the agents involved. A delocalized attitude; an escape from a safe territory, which allows for establishing a blurry stance. A gaseous atmospheric introspection in constant movement, with an energetic adaptive capability in the face of the structures of the world we live in.

This rootless stance is collected here in all its intensity, both in the texts and in the projects. In the words, which insist on preserving the power of the conceptual; and in the drawings, which resist in order to maintain their rigorous precision. The different formats come together, in this premature testament, into an invisible order that has emerged over the past 25 years of production. It contains a mixture of personal stories, travels, external references, conceptual reflections, projects and built work, generating atmospheric states for the positions that correspond to each chapter. Defining seventeen atmospheres that envelop NO.MAD's creative thought and map the migrating territory they travel across. It pieces together a story of invisible precision, the Dry Martini that Eduardo Arroyo chases after, in tireless pursuit. That transparent cocktail with fuzzy limits, a mixture of sophistication and action that activates an individual vital intensity and definitively soaks up the complex character of life.

AN OCEAN OF POSSIBILITIES

"Nothing looks so like innocence
as an indiscretion"

OSCAR WILDE ——————————————————————————

[1] At some point in our physiological lives, something inside each of us gets lost and our minds fill up with doubt. Any effort to return to the road we left behind us entails an acceleration that can lead to our own destruction. [2] Despite the inertia of the road we've travelled, stopping to look back with a sense of exploration can save something of our existence, carrying us courageously into unknown days. [3] Abandoning what we once were is understood as a betrayal by some and as weakness by others, but intimately it implies letting complex dreams evolve in the search for the essence that created them.

[4] This collection of texts and images lays out a thick web of atmospheres that condition the creative paths that I've walked, run and tripped along over the last twenty-five years. [5] They bring together origin and memory, soul and precision, chance and instability, the empathy of moments, the obligation to choose, hybridization and fuzzy systems, cloning and invisible order, complexity or the combination of matter and energy. This kind of kaleidoscopic perspective, though it may be driven by an indomitable excitement, has never been exempt from risk. [6] This journey demonstrates a critical view of the world and the voluntary obligation to attempt its transformation through creative independence, determination and bravery, which is this book's transparent message.

[7] And, if the reader cherishes any doubt about these intentions, let's make it clear before we begin: I definitively confirm that I belong to that minority of people who swim in a vast sea of naivety. And, that diving freely in the crystal clear ocean of possibilities, which borders on the territories of tribal obedience, I can finally fearlessly accept my total

inability to come back to shore. [8] Despite this tiresome evidence, I maintain my curiosity for the Last Judgment. At the administrator's table for the celestial state I may well meet Saint Peter in the company of a number of architecture critics who may reproach me,

"And you, Eduardo? What did you contribute to our system?"

Even naked, I hope I will be able to respond with this book under my arm.

SPEAK YOUR OWN LANGUAGE!

"To create one's mind is to create one's own language, rather than to let the length of one's mind be set by the language other human beings have left behind"

Richard Rorty ——————————————————

[1] A beautiful young blonde with blue eyes is staring at me from the front row. I'm nervous enough on my first day as a professor. I don't need any more risk factors in the mix. [2] It still feels incredible that I'm standing behind a podium when just a few weeks earlier I was using all of my energy drawing and thinking autistically about a little nursery school.

[3] A professor from the Design department in Madrid called to tell me that there was a professorship waiting if I was interested and that they would be delighted to have me on the university faculty. [4] After spending ten years away from Spain, I felt like my errant learning period was coming to an end and that I might have enough in my head that I could pass along to the next generation. It only took me two hours to decide to accept the new position and forty-eight more to get everything ready for me to leave Paris.

[5] In keeping with the tradition of giving university newbies a hard time, today I'll be giving the inaugural lecture, with no prior notice and no time to prepare. I begin talking and I feel like the words are working against me, they're coming out shy and nervous, falling into shameful incoherence. As I'm listening to my disconnected sentences, I'm thinking that we can only talk well and be convincing about things that really interest us.

[6] So, in a cold sweat, I manage to bolster some courage and I start improvising, expounding on the thermodynamics of V engines and the torsion they generate when mounted onto two-wheeled frames. A hundred students are listening, surprised and fascinated, but the smiles on their faces push me to continue. Almost without realizing it, I am talking freely about the fuel injection systems and asymmetrical

structures on certain Italian motorcycles. I continue with the fundamental difference between mechanical drum brakes with a sophisticated design, manufactured analogically, versus digitally controlled disc brakes with a coarser production technique.

[7] Out of the corner of my eye, I can see the other professors who are sitting in on my first class wondering whether they've made a mistake in choosing their latest young colleague. I have the feeling that nothing can touch me; the emotions of the words are running high, driving me to keep talking with intensity. [8] At the end of the class, the head of the department comes up to me discreetly and asks, carefully, if next time I might try talking about architecture. Without a trace of sass and with the security that comes from youthful audacity I reply,

"That's just what I was doing."

3   [1] There is no doubt that the ordinary man with a youthful air and somewhat disoriented is the preferred figure in democratic society. He was created as the reflection of a morality that attempts to repress independent action and thoughts that oppose prearranged conventions and the order of the moment. His faith in shared technology eliminates dissent, leading him toward a single mental attitude along with everyone else. [2] Brave people who cannot be controlled are automatically expelled from this dense network or, at best, they are pushed into a far-off corner. This independence comes at a very high price in countries where gregariousness is a survival mechanism, but it is a motor

for progress in other nations where the creative individual still inspires trust.

[3] The creator in rebellion appears as a demand for clarity and as an expression of the aspiration to defend who we are in a fight for the integrity of Man. He is born against the spectacle of inequity and in the face of injustice at a time when nothing is true and, as such, everything is permitted. [4] However, he may sometimes be confused with the media revolutionary, who is full of bitter resentment because he envies what he cannot be; so, he soon becomes a dedicated social climber, a slave to money in the service of all kinds of manipulators. He is the professional who embraces the slogan of the aesthetic of his time, bowing to the totalitarian order of a deteriorated world instead of making an effort to be discerning using independent criteria. [5] Creative courage knows no fear of failure; it is not concerned with appearing acceptable or realistic. Only true creation expects the victory of will and conscience over the temptation of falling into self-pity.

[6] There is no leadership in the present day, no clear sense of action; efforts are wasted senselessly in behaviors ruled purely by greed. [7] Creative thinking can only be active and communicable when it is motivated by feeling; that is why we need to recruit creatives to help make the society of the future attractive. Sooner rather than later, these new leaders will have to be responsible for taking the reins to steer us toward a Man without prejudices.

4 [1] Popular temperament expresses indiscriminate opinions about ideas like compassion, irreverence or creativity. [2] Compassion is the indicator of what is humanly upright and of what merits our aid. However, the increasing expansion of so-called citizens' rights which go hand-in-hand with lobbyist propaganda has tarnished that marvelous collective enterprise. They appear in the guise of multiple prohibitions, legitimized by all kinds of regulations. [3] Irreverence is the monopoly of the intelligent and the brave, the straight-talkers with malicious smiles. When nothing is revered anymore, irreverence stops being a sign of critical thought; it is absorbed by banality, isolating intelligence as mere wit. [4] Creativity is the product of genius, not ability, and it is bound for deception when it becomes a professional strategy promoted by mediocrity.

[5] In our society compassion, irreverence and creativity have been replaced by amusements decked out in colors and shapes, sex and violence to shake up the senses of dazed citizens. As a result, our public landscape has been filled with objects that are devoid of any aura, as though the world of the living has slipped away into something lifeless.

[6] Given this situation, independent judgment stands as the first step toward an attempt at transforming that devastating panorama. It can serve as the basis for escaping from systems of indoctrination, in a kind of rebirth toward a fascinating exterior light. [7] The comfort of not needing to differentiate guarantees that everything is equally valid because anyone's actions in an effort toward difference can be prejudged, without the need for understanding them. In

the faced of this group that is led by the nose, the seemingly primitive creative individual appears advancing toward an all too human humanity. [8] An uncompromising creative attitude proves to be the best antidote, toward a dynamic existence apart from social routine. Subversive anticipation, guided by critical ideas in the face of the world, makes him into a qualified and sophisticated agent capable of merging the divergent worlds of ideas and reality.

[1] The Association of Architects has asked me to design a **5** stand to sell the virtues of the profession to society at large. [2] I'm caught up in an internal battle between their expectations and my real opinion:

"Where has that first man gone, the father of the creative spirit, who, with a few of his friends, dared to raise an immense stone above the plain so that the heavens would look down upon him? And, what is left of that other man, the sorcerer's apprentice, who moved through the world by sensing how he could filter nature to protect himself? Thoughtless architects, how are we going to protect society from this nature if we don't even know what it means anymore?"

[3] Frustrated dreamers and domesticated technicians, we offer up fleeting life services like puppets in an irreparable techno-economic Punch and Judy show: $E=cm^2$. Everything has been reduced to a simple relativist equation, where the economic welfare of society is a function of the number of square meters that have been capitalized on. [4] Then, on an imaginary wall, I write the commandments that sum up the

violence that professional pragmatism wreaks on the creative imagination:

⁵ Pragmatism always masks opportunism.

⁶ The imagination is the least pragmatic of human abilities.

⁷ Once we have become pragmatic, there is no turning back.

⁸ We disguise pragmatism as imagination, in order to hide it.

⁹ Pragmatism is anchored in reality; imagination is anchored in the Real.

¹⁰ Imagination speeds up the world, pragmatism slows it down.

¹¹ Imagination knows no limits; pragmatism is a limit in itself.

¹² An imaginary pragmatism is incomprehensible.

¹³ A pragmatic imagination is unacceptable.

¹⁴ Pragmatism destroyed Gatsby's charm, and we've never gotten over it.

I realize that, soon enough, the criticisms will rain down.

6 ¹ Faced with Hegel's observation that nothing new ever occurs in nature, the rebellious man, freed from this powerlessness, understands that all creations are born from his own freedom. With his refusal of the archaic ideas of archetype, his will confirms his sovereignty. ² The absolute creator can only forge himself from the total vulnerability inherent in the choice between exile or existence in the subhuman evasion of a life manufactured for him by someone else. He has to find a path for every moment and a solution for every problem, figuring out why he does what he does through his own discovery of the world to improve the subjectivity of his life. Steering clear of borrowed dogmas and magic life solutions will bring him closer to new visions with wisdom, courage and honesty.

3 However, this uncompromising creative life includes the friendly head-on opposition of one's contemporaries. In attempting to look into enigmas like whether God shaves, creative determination comes up against manipulation, lies and false status although loneliness may tell us that we're in the wrong place, full of organized bandits. This creative inclination needs an independent will, social abilities and precise tools for transforming matter, all tied in with an exactness of vision. 4 The thrill of creating objects with a life of their own, without recurrences or occurrences, is the only thing that transmits a personal way of experiencing the world, undertaken with enough time to allow for reflection and development.

5 When time is lacking, creations appear with record-breaking speed by using uprooted projects in new places without adapting them, as an example of economic effectiveness. The language of personal profit prevails, at the expense of new and exciting ideas. 6 Massification erodes selectivity and electivity into reality-show competition systems that band together against the excellent life project. Just like the hero in "The Matrix" celebrates his mastery over the world when he can finally see bullets in slow motion, the power over expanded time can be used to judge situations in depth in order to perceive the values that connect us with things. 7 Ideas always appear with a clear and firm determination with respect to the words that describe the

creative experience after the fact, which are never of value on their own.

7 [1] Contemporary creative language has become a spectacle for the masses and imagination is counterfeit. When expectations are reduced to language as immediate communication, we find ourselves on the high-profile path of show business. [2] Creativity has been transformed into pure linguistic merchandise, flung into the free-market world where it is destroyed. The professional system has imposed its commercial relationships, repressing imaginative ability and making every effort to manipulate it from the realm of profitability.

[3] We are floating in an overdose of icons validated by the euphemism of a prospective imagination that is cut off from the present and which is ideally suited to a period of absolute shallowness. The ability to copy existing objects is the only thing the impatient market expects from the creator, a closed-circuit and forgetful reproduction for a world lacking in any authenticity. [4] These collective stylistic languages continue to betray what we ardently wish to convey because of their inability to precisely describe what defines Man. And still we insist on inventing sensationalist transmitters, which are paradoxically ineffectual and bordering on the incomprehensible, to bring us closer to the rosy immediacy of television. [5] Consequently, economic profitability and political strategy are the most valued qualities and are viewed as comfortable correctness. Overcoming this situation implies changing certain signs in the current

landscape, in the pursuit of harmony between our individual sensibilities and collective desires.

[6] Creation only has value if it represents the reflection of a common identity, associated with a personal style in its execution. It reaches its limit when freedom stretches out from us toward others, and not the other way around. [7] The oppression of liberal professions has created a strategic retreat toward the only thing that seems irrepressible: subjectivity. However, this poorly understood subjectivity no longer represents the collective will; it is the reflection of a fictitious expressive genius, strident and extravagant. It is camouflaged by languages that are cloned to hide its emptiness, underneath a false creative process. [8] In this guise it leaves the main value of creation behind, which is precisely to safeguard life and civil rights in an increasingly habitable space.

[1] In the desert that runs between Oman and Yemen there is an origin-object. A city that is astonishing for its resistance to time, isolated from any technological modernity, and yet intensely contemporary. [2] In its small central square I watch in fascination as a butcher carves up a lamb with immemorial skill. The blood runs across the large flat stone where I am sitting, under the cool cover of a straw lath house. [3] Set within a wadi that is subject to flooding in spring by several meters of violent current, the city sits protected atop a high pedestal. Hundreds of adobe skyscrapers are stacked in a network of streets that are only a few meters wide, creating permanent shade in the desert inferno. [4] As the

breeze runs along them, it cuts down on the thermal sensation by some twenty-odd degrees. Dozens of meters of human feces hang from random holes in the walls, drying in the sun. At the base, there are four walls that serve to store the waste once it has dried and detached from the vertical. They use it for fuel in their kitchens.

5 The butcher looks at me aslant, wary of the uncommon presence of a Westerner and, I imagine, somewhat concerned about my fascination with his hands. 6 In this original machine, born directly from the need to live with next to nothing, everything gets reused. Two minimal windows, one atop the other on each floor, are misleading about the real height of the city; they respond to the device that cools the houses using an adiabatic process. This trick creates a surprising perspective and I only become aware of the actual size when a child's head pops out one of the windows and just barely fits through.

7 Shouting in old Arabic, the child calls to his friends who appear running about the square. They stop, sure of themselves, about fifty meters away and, with an infantile battle cry, they pick up rocks to fling them at the stranger who has come to disrupt their fragile equilibrium. My admiration for their perfect machine for living close to the origin hasn't warmed them to my presence. The straight shot of a rock connects with my leg and the patient butcher turns toward the group, waving his bloody jambiya. 8 He makes excuses for the children's behavior, but I am embarrassed by my presence. In their closed-off universe of recycling, there is no room for outsiders. Standing up, I realize that I am not welcome in the world of Shibam.

[1] Bertrand Russell asserted that, without pleasure, Man never would have reproduced because it implies too much of an effort for a naturally lazy animal. And without vanity, he would never have created the great works that demand independence from an essentially gregarious ape. [2] Since there is something of pleasure in creation and a little vanity in sex, objects that prove to be close to the origin may serve as a defense of unpredictable reproduction and survival.

[3] The effort to slow down the unstoppable and to put order into the world through the use of formal and stylistic criteria, replete with passed-down inertia, only masks a fear of the magic whirlwind of the unknown. This obstinacy traces the thin line that separates a copy from an interpretation, creativity from creation, originality from origin. [4] Creation requires the highest degree of origin and is born outside its time with an atemporal presence. [5] What we recognize as original is always a child of its time, yet it tries to demonstrate that it is timeless. [6] A merely ingenious act is destined to exhaust itself and disappear in its own time. [7] The feeling of temporariness belongs to the realm of fear.

[8] The insistence on copying objects accurately and the perfection of simulacra never implicitly involve a creative process of personal growth. Nor do they entail the discovery or the amazement that is tied in with our existence as creators; ultimately, they represent a useless personal effort. [9] The interest in a copied image that requires no effort for its production cancels out any exchange of energy between the creator and the world. [10] It takes a lot of coldness to

recreate familiar objects and a little talent to propose something original, but both of these attitudes are on a different plane, far removed from the attempt to approach or even participate in the origin.

[11] In the face of this panic, objects appear that help us grow emotionally. They become part of our timeless points of contact with the origin by revealing a more transparent world. Once they have come into the world fully and have begun to interact with people, they no longer thrill their creator, or transform him and better him as a human being. Detached from the intense process of exchanging discoveries and resolving the uncertainties that inhabit their creation, they finally belong to reality as a whole.

10 [1] On the one hand, creative systems can respond to the phenomenon of self-referencing as a consequence of the power and expressive capabilities associated with a unique system that combines elements in an original way. [2] On the other hand, they can be based on the style catalog that pulls out recognizable elements that can be found in different objects over time, through the use of linguistic copies. [3] The first kind points to the origin as a primordial requirement for creation, whereas the second refers to the simulacrum, exponentially reducing the risk in the creative process. [4] The success of the simulacrum rests on an easy reading of a superficial image of expressivity, faced with the interpretation of memorized content. [5] The choice between what has received collective approval and an echo that forces us to think based on an effort of the imagination makes the pursuit of self-referencing less common than opting for the catalog.

[6] Creations close to the origin are born from instants that have to do with reminiscences of memory in movement. They are powerful references that inhabit our visual and conceptual memory in the form of visions, obsessions or hallucinations that serve as the embryo for the creative process. These imaginary triggers give rise to the specific vectors that each creation takes on in its friction with the reality into which it is introduced. [7] It is in this moment of intense contact between the abstract and the real that the work can become inhabited by doubt and uncertainty, in a tug-of-war where the rules of the game and its precise dimensions reveal the initial spatial realities. [8] Technology, energy and the alternative use of materials act as mediators in adapting the object to its constructive possibilities. This attitude is intimately linked with work that shies away from simulacra and camouflage, both of which can be attributed to the pragmatic professional.

[9] That is why moving beyond what we have been taught and abandoning the guilt that goes with feeling different is so necessary. Both acts, whether conscious or instinctive, are the foundation for the coherency of one's own voice. Without them, the assault on the heavens that Cocteau sought becomes a confused verbosity of linguistic transitions. [10] In the process of migrating toward a personal voice, creative anxiety becomes associated with the excitement that is awakened in the author by the unexpected encounters that occur as he walks without looking back or to either side.

11   [1] "I swear; nobody understands anything!" shouts the mayor, visibly upset.

"You have to do something right away!" he orders me, though he hardly knows me.

[2] The exhibition is a failure; our cryptic, encoded blueprints haven't succeeded in explaining the Plaza del Desierto to the public. On the train back to Bilbao I realize that the only thing people still understand are movies. So, enlightened by such a major discovery, I call the office and we dive into our first short film. [3] In the meantime, with the restless rattling of the train in the background, I feverishly write out the text for its public screening all in one go:

Letter to a Smiling User,

[4] "We recommend a random approach; meaning, come in from whichever direction you feel like. All roads lead to the square. [5] Let yourself be astonished, not frightened, by what you see. We promise that the surprises it holds carry with them some positive emotions. Above all, don't try to understand it instantly; enjoy the unfamiliarity. Sooner or later, you will inevitably enter into a dialogue with the square and its inhabitants. That's what we designed it for. [6] At some point you will notice that there is an underlying hidden principle beneath the apparent disorder; this order is similar to the one that we know exists in nature, though we can't see it. If you're thirsty for knowledge, climb up onto any one of the seven mounds that you'll see right away. We call them watchtowers, for keeping an eye out, you know. Up there, you'll find some answers; not all of them, of course.

[7] Turn your attention to the living rooms scattered around the space; they're the same size as the one in your house, with

benches made of concrete or warm wood, that are flexible or hard, with grass, clover or bushes, for each of the seasons. Use them to talk to your friends or, even better, your enemies if you have them. [8] Say something interesting to your wife in the lover's lounge; of course you'll have to find it first. You'll know it when you see it.

[9] As you're reading this your little boy will have run off a while ago to play boats with his friends in the aquatic systems. That's what they're for, don't bother them. [10] Your older son will be learning something about life with a girl from school but, of course, you won't see him. Although, on second thought, maybe he likes skateboarding and he's discovered that the square has an exciting topography. [11] If your daughter likes poetry, I can assure you that she's already in one of the silent rooms surrounded by fragrant plants and the rustling of nearby waterfalls. She's in a world of her own.

[12] But, above all, look at their grandfather. Although it may seem strange, he may be the only one who entirely understands what we were trying to do. There, where he's standing, with his silvered head resting on his cane, there used to be a steel mill; stainless steel tubes ran through the air, lit by night; there were overgrown bushes of all shapes and sizes, train tracks that carried carbon and stone, puddles that came and went with the tide. [13] All of it is still here; we've just rearranged it a little. Remember, we're architects,

"Enjoy it, man. Enjoy it."

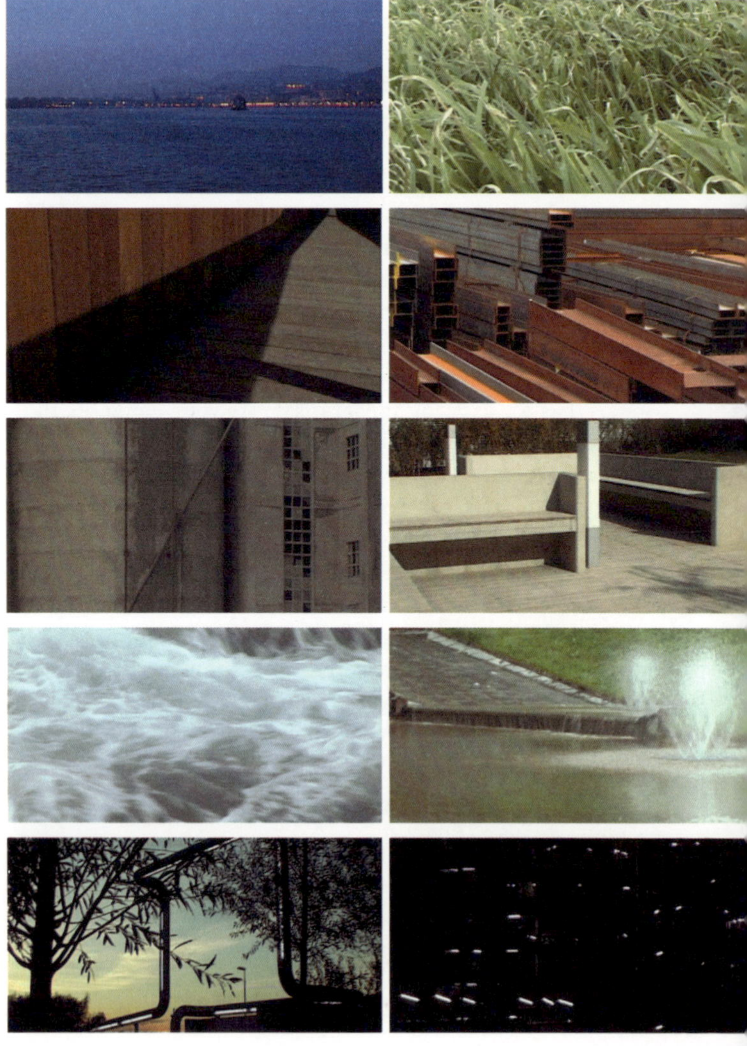

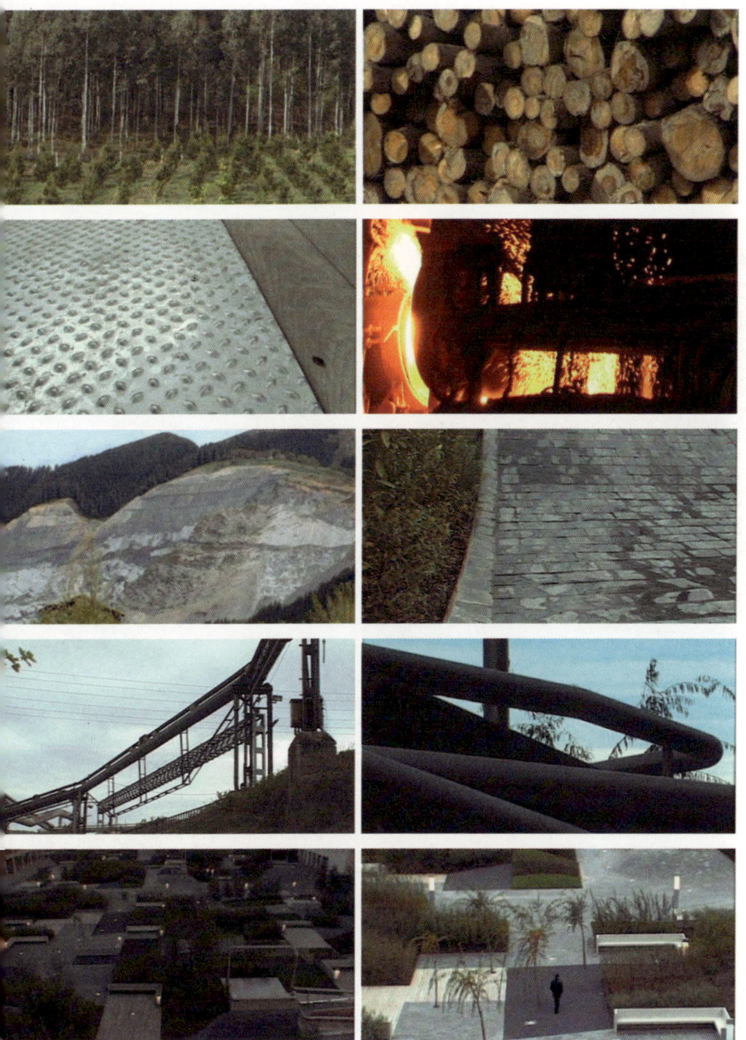

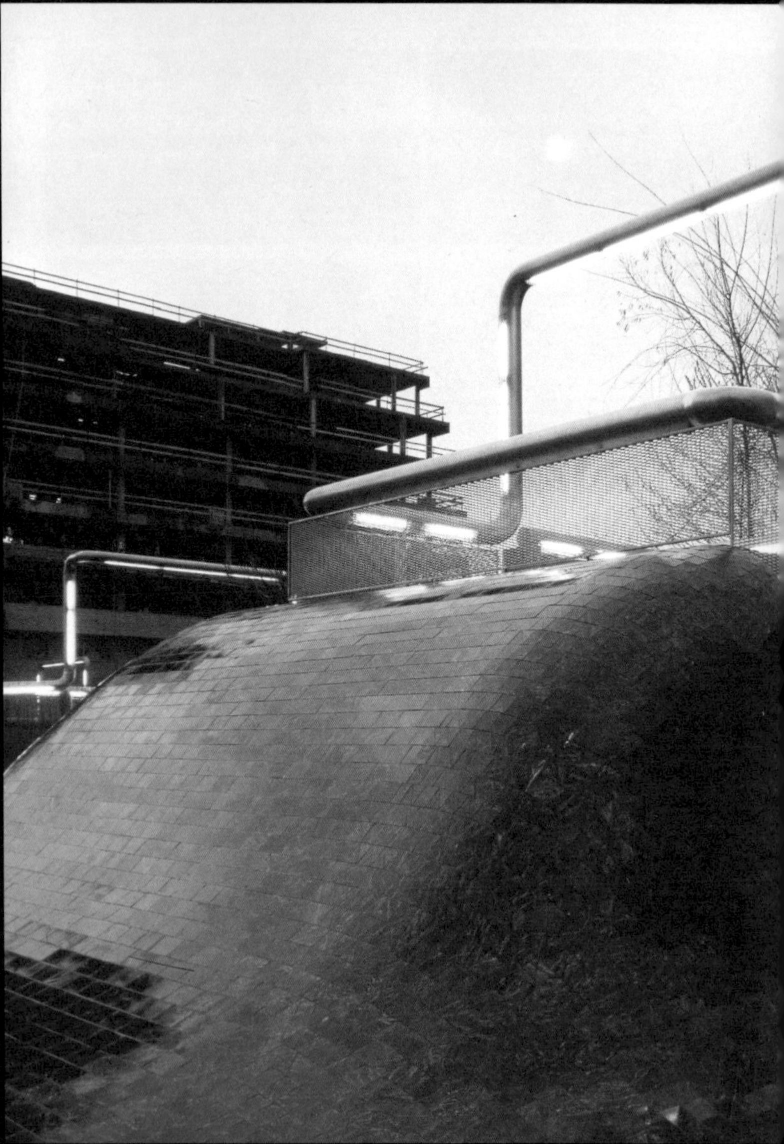

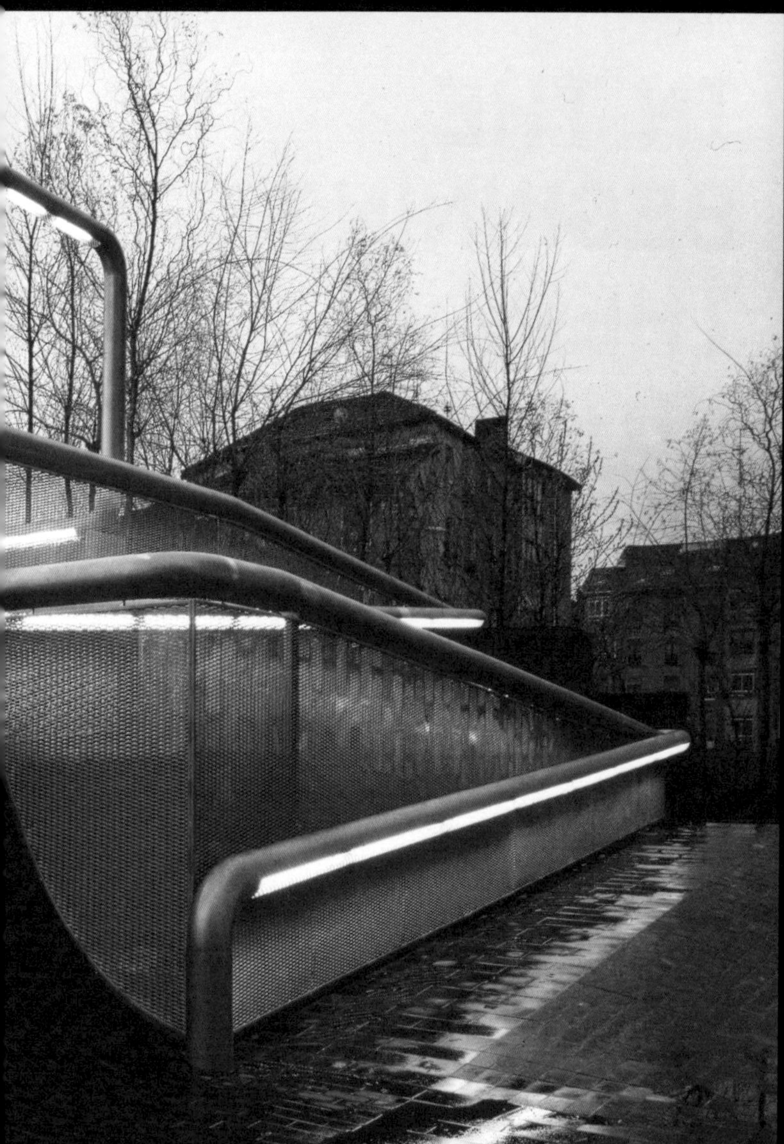

IN THE BEGINNING THERE WAS NOTHING... OR WAS THERE?

"And we will take heart for the future,
Remembering the past"

TOMAS STEARN ELIOT ————————————————

[1] The Rolling Stones' "Under My Thumb" is playing. The notes scatter hazily through the attic on the Quai des Bourbons transferring their rhythm into our surging bodies. The lyrics about lost love inspire us to put its message right, looking for a glorious accord between parts. [2] Lying in bed with a beautiful woman under my thumb, out of the corner of my eye I can see the rhythmic flashes of the Bateaux Mouches coming in through the window. Intermittently, their powerful spotlights take over the space, reflecting our bodies during fleeting moments. [3] The same unfinished fight from time immemorial continues with impersonal rhythms inherited from nameless ancestors. In unison with our movements, I hear disjointed fragments that go by in a time of well-earned happiness.

[4] Downstairs, the office is unfolding large sheets of paper printed with invented cryptographies. A subtle magic, still unproven, that makes up a message that is incomprehensible, even for its creator. It is the automatic writing of those who search for the origin of things beyond their own minds, even at the risk of losing themselves. Symbols that carry us into the past and slip away among the neurons in search of a little eternity.

[5] Suddenly, something breaks into the vague field of my thoughts; among the kisses and the sweat, my mind clouds over and splutters with strange meaningless visions. The fluttering notes, the disordered alphabet interspersed with incoherent moans, the dancing ancestral symbols and the stroboscopic lights. All together, they seem to work coherently and precisely toward uncontainable atavistic tension. [6] The chaos of meaningless nothingness takes on some kind of

emotional consistency that I don't recognize and which comes from the depths of time.

⁷ At the top of an encrypted peak, everything ends with the abandon men feel in their love for women. ⁸ Far away from my physical location, as skilful fingers run through my hair, I'm only thinking that there is something to be figured out, something to discover: The hidden meaning of what doesn't exist yet, what was never invited to reason's grand party.

13 ¹ Echoes from the past leave behind inert information in our thoughts and, hibernating, they wait for the moment when an emotional atmosphere will bring them back. Huddled like frightened prey, they take shelter in dark corners of the mind until reality disconnects for an instant and they find their way out. ² Memories tend to have a visual presence, which is nearly always associated with conditions of time, distance or physical qualities. Behind them, on a hidden level, lies the main feeling associated with a particular memory; it is the only long-lasting aspect, which is also entirely ungraspable.

³ Memory is a mechanism that blurs the clarity of concepts and smudges our reason for an instant conferring an unreal, unfinished and imprecise character on the creative process. Even though its influence is short-lived, the intensity of this intrusive and destabilizing memory can be detected in the object that is created. ⁴ The memory cannot be represented just as it occurred; it can only be handled through interpretation. If we do it formally, like reproducing its image di-

rectly, it quickly becomes an obsolete icon. Memories can only be recovered in the form of abstract ideas by capturing the sensible atmosphere they conceal. They are brought into the present using mechanisms that never have the same shape or image as the ones that initially supported them.

[5] This resonance of a recollection that we believe to be individual becomes visible when collective memory comes into play. A remembrance can reactivate what the collective is slowly trying to forget because it is out of date, detrimental or markedly unacceptable. [6] The memorized instant that is shared has the ability to touch a whole human group, exposing the fuzzy limits between what attracts us and repels us as a whole. The effect of this magic moment of memory increases the fuzziness of our sensitivity, which has already been diminished, even more. It destabilizes our reticulated existence by blurring the present in a bridge toward the past. [7] It is the diffraction of our life lines into a new reality pierced by invisible vectors of time, onto which we climb and we feel transported by the magic of creation.

[1] Mythologies are more than pretty stories, or terrible ones, **14** to be transmitted in strict order to our descendents. They constitute a commentary on the mysteries of the human mind and human existence from people belonging to a certain period and civilization. They act as a model for social behavior based on perceptions of its inner realities. [2] The metaphysical conceptions of the archaic world have not always been formulated using theoretical language;

symbols, rites and myths express a complex system of coherent affirmations about the ultimate reality of things.

3 For fifty thousand years Man has felt the need to explain his existence and his creations have not always been strictly functional, taking on informational beauty. 4 A forward-thinking primitive stonecutter, sitting in the setting sun, gazed at a colored stone in his hand that stood out among the grayish flint. How it was carved made him realize, in terms of a mystical order, that he was capable of going further. 5 The revelation of this initial animist conception, continuing through mythological religions and into modern day, resembles a path through time with a trajectory that constructs and oft-repeated story.

6 So it is that Man has always built according to an archetype as the representation of the original act of creation: the transformation of unpredictable chaos into an ordered cosmos. 7 In all mythology, before a territory is occupied the area first takes on a divine nature; only then can it be inhabited through the use of possession ceremonies that grant it a comprehensible form. The territory that is civilized in this way is not any more valid than the prototype that served as its model and confirms Man's obsession with the order of tangible reality. 8 This repetition of the creative act provides us with the security that our actions at a particular time are tied in with the mythical time of history, thus ensuring lasting continuity.

9 Although we cannot go back to mythical thought, we can recapture something of the extinguished power of that heroic faith through imagination. We can let ourselves go for an instant, carried away down the fuzzy road of inter-

pretations, allowing the echoes and the memories to penetrate into our minds. [10] Only then do we understand that everything we have built has to be independent of time and that, inevitably, one day it will have to disappear from the territory.

[1] Outside of everything, inside the world. Outside the world, **15** inside society. [2] A straight path shines brightly in the blinding sunlight. On both sides, meadows that look green and fertile. The ground is burning under the sun that heats the jagged rocks. It isn't easy to walk over, but something pushes me to keep going, to see where it leads. [3] I forget about the fruit trees and their useful shade. I see people lying in the fields, singing, as they smile, inviting me to come join them in their routine tasks.

[4] But the road is stronger and commands obedient progress. Under thousands of curses, I leave behind the happy rustics who have never thought that this road might lead somewhere productive. [5] Suddenly, the surface becomes brighter and polished, like it's been crafted to perfection from ancestral times. Among the stones, green plants begin to show, with tiny golden flowers as the pastures begin to dry out, becoming wasteland. There aren't any farmers anymore, there aren't any smiles. The road has begun to disappear into mosses and wildflowers, blurring its fuzzy limits with the barren land. [6] A fresh breeze blows through this magic corridor and even so, I can feel the drought and the dryness of death on its sides. Strangely calm and tireless, my agile feet walk across the thousand-year-old carpet.

[7] Suddenly, I can make out a magnificent silhouette in the distance, getting bigger by the moment. My stride lengthens and, without knowing why, I'm running. It grows bigger and bigger, clearer. [8] The air is still and smells don't exist anymore. I don't need my senses, because I'm already here. Finally it's before me, the Tree of Life...

[9] At the same time, without knowing it, somewhere nearby under the faint blue light a sensitive Viking is carving the runes of the pantheon of Norse Mythology into a stone:

Yggdrasil	The tree of life in the virgin territory
Ymir	The creation of nascent power
Thor	The protective thunderbolt
Freyr	Cultural prosperity
Njord	The sea that inspires movement
Loki	The enigma of uncertainty
Fimbulvetr	The end of the world restored

[10] And, with its exorcism, it conjures the process of the regeneration of the universe: Discovery, Creation, Protection, Culture, Movement, Uncertainty, Destruction and a new beginning.

16 [1] Operatinging in places where memory and the legacy of bygone eras carry a lot of weight should not imply blind obedience to preexisting conditions. Preserving memory does not limit each period's right to transform the world on the basis of its own beliefs and its own languages for creative expression. [2] An attempt at camouflage or invisibility with respect to the world that has already been built implies the prevalence of what has been handed down over the present, which halts the flow of evolution. That kind of attitude only detracts from the importance of what is to come by assuming that what has been accepted historically is always original. [3] By no means can the creator believe that this kind of action implies moving closer to the origin. From this point of view, when we act within the heavy baggage of inherited architecture, we can introduce living elements that are coherent with the present, which add new urban properties to what is functionally obsolete.

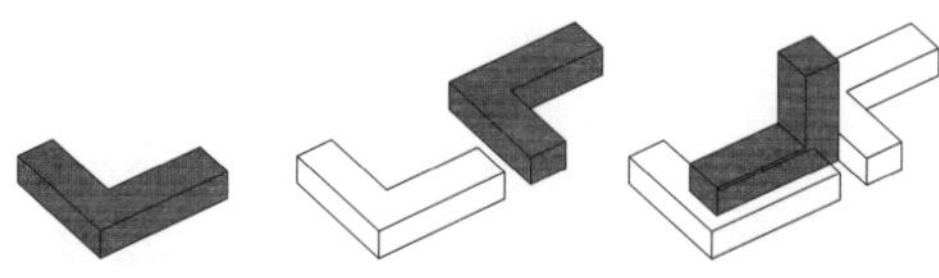

[4] The Bilbao Fine Arts Museum (1997), with its historicist style, is shaped like an L along one edge of a park. It has a bold extension built in the sixties, also in an L-shape, raised on pillars that leave the ground level free. We inserted a new L-shape into this complex situation, vertically this time between the existing buildings, adding the possibility of looking out over the park and the city from a privileged height. [5] Like a mythical graft from the Tree of Life, it serves as a symbol of the vital and economic regeneration of a city in decline. The base and the trunk of this intrusive tree transport the flow of visitors and their feelings that increase in intensity as they climb. It houses all of the public services, freeing up the other buildings for use as exhibition space.

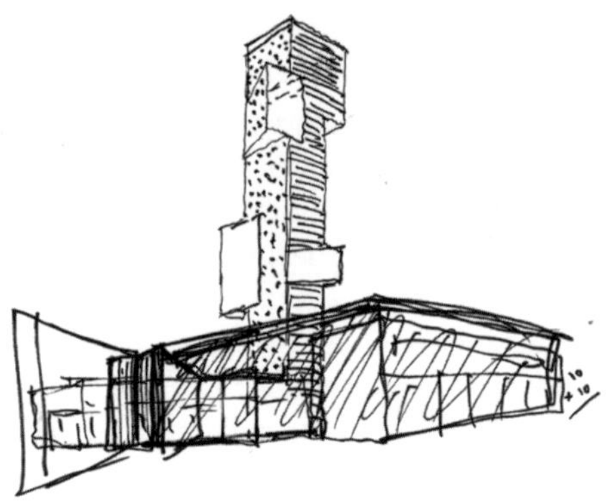

⁶ Spatial outgrowths designed for recreational use spread away from the trunk, pointing toward different landmarks in the city and the landscape for the perceptive pleasure of the users. ⁷ The bark of this artificial tree is adapted to the environmental pressures and the energetic requirements, showing different material sensitivities adapted to each orientation. ⁸ The whole, with its obvious chronological complexity, precisely represents the vocations of each time period, from a place of mutual respect and acceptance, without falling prey to the stylistic sentimentality that suggest that the past is capable of representing the present.

17 ¹ At times when everything is flowing and nothing is permanent, individuals fight desperately to preserve their own identities, independently of the fluctuations in their surroundings. That is not the case with inanimate objects, which fall prey to constant changes in the world around them. [2] Biology accounts for the fact that, when a species is endangered due to the deterioration of its habitat or food shortages, self regulation occurs through the inhibition of the reproductive drive. It leads males to pair up with other males and females to become infertile.

[3] Our new consciousness of the threat of extinction has led us to want to preserve the dignity of objects before they succumb to the passage of time. Today, everything can be recovered before it reaches a corrupt old age, avoiding an inevitably familiar deterioration. Our age-old desire for rebirth, in an eternal return without fleeting finales, pushes us to revive everything that we throw away like lives that have ended, with the hope of some kind of cosmic redemption. [4] We find it touching that an old washbasin has the potential to become a new toothbrush. Although everything tends to return to the earth, our frightened minds are capable of transforming decadence into some kind of strange beauty by preventing its return to the origin. [5] It is a contemporary collective artifice, which stimulates memory and recollections, and forces the reinvention of the concept of waste as well as the mechanisms for its resurrection. Trash dumps have become mystical places of purification, like soccer stadiums, where consciences can be recycled during a Sunday catharsis.

[6] This evidence of reuse results in a certain hindrance to evolution and imposes some well-known creative restrictions. It is true that, from the strict point of view of survival, in this thinking environment creating could well become an obligation. [7] However, the suspicion remains as to whether a world of reduced material consumption in the first place

might solve part of the problem. [8] As such, many of the objects that are reused that don't have any creative or emotional value for society could be disposed of definitively to be substituted by other objects with more relevance to their time. [9] The political veneer attributed to salvaging everything that already exists, at any cost, should be backed up by a selective consideration of which things are actually worthwhile. Otherwise, any present time will be emptied of content.

18 [1] History is full of moments when salvation has been the most important problem facing societies in decline. In many cases, the solutions that are applied are upheld by the mythical vision of a figure with growing influence and the power of persuasion over the majority. [2] The land and the weather emerge as the enemy to be defeated, understood as the causes of famine, wreckage and economic devastation.

[3] This situation can only be transformed through an exciting manipulation on the part of the population, aimed at creating a saving consciousness. [4] So it is that the myth of the flood is resolved by the idea of Noah protecting the animals, as the only person who was capable of carrying out the act of building the arc. [5] In the creation lore of the Aborigines, survival is guaranteed through the domestication and appropriation of specific places. The mere act of naming the particularities of the territory tames any potentially aggressive object. The nomenclature as a whole, the famous songlines, draws a lexical map of mythical

command over the Australian continent. [6] For his part, Ulysses represents the archetypical hero who manages to save the Pleiades though a titanic effort, despite the ever-present threat of death. His journey demonstrates the power of control over multiple dangers, which makes him worthy of saving the society that initially rejected him from its own decadence.

[7] However, the most surprising mythical accounts are the ones that are capable of mobilizing an entire society toward unknown horizons. [8] At the beginning of the fourth century, an imminent rise in sea level threatened to submerge the entire population of a Polynesian island. Their leader, Hotu Matua, had a vision in which he was asked to send a canoe, manned by seven warriors, toward the rising sun. From the dream to reality, they sailed toward the Pacific East, where they came across Easter Island. To commemorate that legendary act, they built the seven Moais of Anakena as a future reminder that there is always a possibility of survival.

[9] The collective unconscious of current societies continues to use similar methods in a number of guises. Many of them are camouflaged as heroic constructed appearances that are capable of instilling economic optimism and social self-esteem.

[1] During historic moments of increased tension and social **19** upheaval, urban structures have also responded from the point of view of symbolic renewal. [2] Given the deluge of values and the decadence of society, proposing mythical

1	INDIVIDUALISMO	——	ASOCIACION
2	SEDUCCION	——	CONVICCION
3	INDIFERENCIA	——	PARTICIPACION
4	NARCISISMO	——	ACEPTACION
5	PARODIA SOCIAL	——	CONSCIENCIA ETICA
6	VIOLENCIA	——	PAZ
7	SUPERFICIALIDAD	——	INTENSIDAD

and emotional possibilities capable of introducing the message of a new, hopeful urbanity seems necessary.

[3] As such, the hydraulic modification of the floodable areas of Zorrozaurre island in Bilbao (1994) generates a new floating city that uses the wind and the tides as systems for creating a variable urban structure. It proposes unexpected transformations of physical space in terms of orientation and organization. [4] The inhabitants occupy floating arcs of different sizes and variable uses, the captivating symbol of a new society. [5] In this urban context, space is slowed to a maximum, disconnected from vehicle traffic, which allows individuals to decide on their own encounters. As such, it offers inhabitants the possibility of exercising an extreme freedom, raising the anchor on their living space in search of new life relationships.

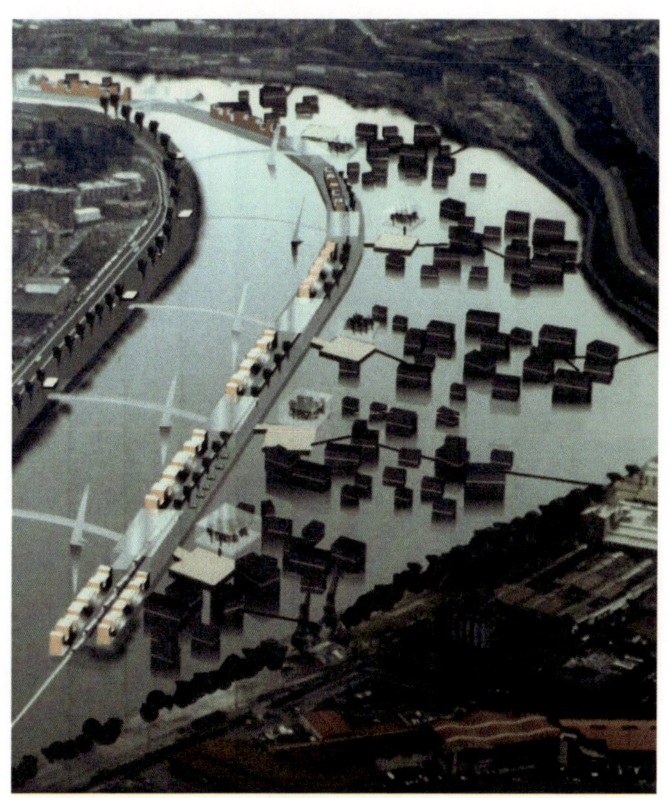

20 [1] With the persistence of collective memory, there is an accumulation of recurring images of primitive monolithic alignments that can lend new meanings to an insensitive overcrowded world. This type of structure guarantees a certain mystery in the city; something apparently trivial, but which inspires us to lift our heads.

[2] Absorbing the hard and incoherent limits of deindustrialized areas along the Nervión estuary, a series of new public spaces provides differentiated responses to the river and the structure of the city. [3] This creates a several-kilo-

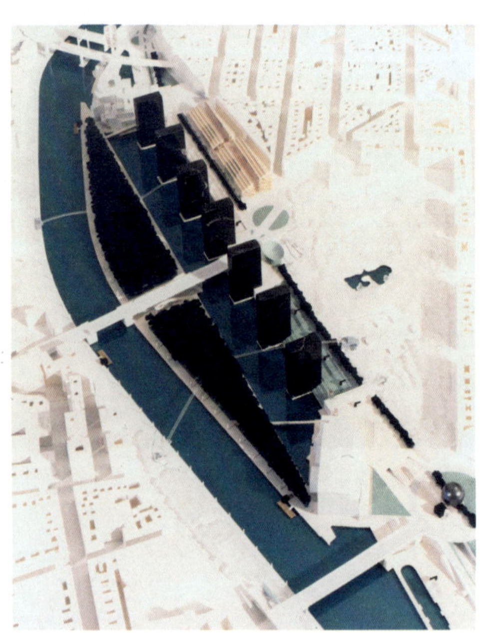

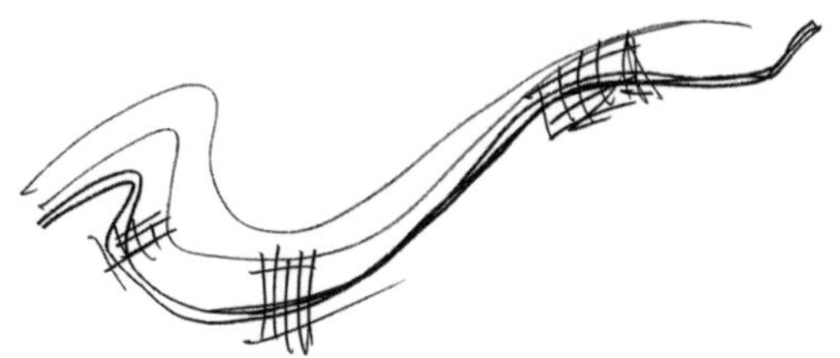

meter-long buffer that masks the frenetic movement of cars and provides for their storage under a static surface covered in vegetation. In the Abandoibarra Business Center in Bilbao (1993), generic high-rise buildings are lined up to create a visual memory in motion. [4] This metropolitan axis runs along the estuary, colonizing the large empty postindustrial areas. The city's pleasant approach toward the river is made more gradual through the use of artificial aquatic layers and large wooded areas for public use.

[1] The Austrian was entirely incompetent. His mocking smile **21**  hid an arrogance that didn't bode well. [2] During the dive to view the SS Thistlegorm near the Sinai Peninsula, a breathtaking school of hammerhead sharks appeared. I turned back to look at the group I was leading, studying their faces so I could anticipate any fear. The hammerheads began to circle above us and I gave everyone the signal to descend quickly toward the sunken ship. [3] At a hundred twenty feet, the compressed air was being consumed alarmingly fast by all those hyperventilating tourists.

4 In an instant, the heavyset Austrian panicked and rushed toward the surface. I knew that without a safety stop he would be in trouble and I followed him closely, watching the depth gauge. He wasn't going to make it. When he was at fifty feet, he spit out his regulator and I stopped seeing bubbles. I pulled him to the surface, motionless and heavy. 5 The nitrogen was banging at my brain and I dove down again to pick up the rest of the group waiting obediently at the anchor line. When we finished the dive, a helicopter had already transported him to the hyperbaric chamber in Sharm el-Sheikh.

6 The crew and the group of inexperienced divers looked like attendants at a funeral foretold, in their black neoprene suits. All the same, I managed to convince them to do a second dive, despite a lot of complaints and underlying fear. 7 The best medicine for something that has you paralyzed is getting back on the horse to restore the confidence you've lost. 8 The second dive ended with smiles and expressions of thanks; the elegant manta rays had accompanied us, flying liquidly around the group and restoring the beauty that had been disrupted by unchecked panic.

9 When we got back to the port I took a taxi to the hospital. 10 Cristoph had spent an hour in the recompression chamber, between life and death. When I saw him he was conscious, ashen-faced, his girlfriend beside him. I made my way over and took his hand gently. He smiled weakly and thanked me for pulling him to the surface. He didn't remember anything. 11 There wasn't a trace of arrogance left in his smile; it was all pure and transparent humanity.

22

[1] Throughout history, Man has built spaces that have been used for spiritual transformation, in the form of chambers that prepared him for understanding the inexplicable. In most cases, access to those spaces was restricted and reserved for the well-to-do or the mystic elite in each respective society. [2] Whether in primitive caves, cathedral halls or the first museums, the meaning of the mysterious was preserved in places that could only be accessed via a transitional route. After passing through, one could exercise the right to epiphanic contemplation of the objects held inside. [3] In the same way, ultra-democratic contemporary Man still needs mental anticipation in order to carry out the proper per-

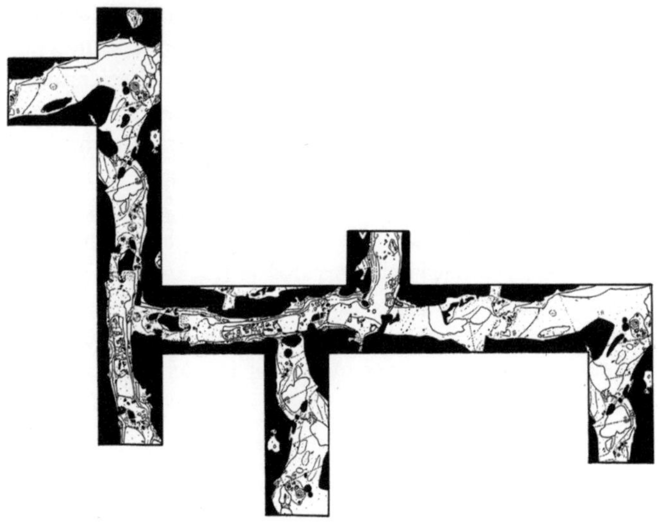

ception of the artistic experience. [4] As a result of the diverse specificity in the spaces along the preparatory route, the mind breaks free from Cartesian routine, entering into resonance with the surprising properties of difference.

[5] From this standpoint, the extension intended to join together all of the buildings at the Prado Museum in Madrid (1995) links a series of spatial events to act as transformative phases. Each one entails a different rhythm of initiation into the mysterious within a linear system of connections that manages and processes the flow of visitors. [6] The spatial variations are adapted to the sensible intention of each use through the creation of decompression chambers that prepare visitors for viewing the collections. [7] Through the use of variable geometry and different types of materials, all exterior references are eliminated, leading to another state of perception. All of these chambers are accumulated in a large half-sunken infrastructure ditch that connects the buildings where the collections are housed.

[8] Their luminous energy is released in the shape of cryptic writing on the urban surface, symbolically translating what is happening inside. This new urban path, traced in light-symbols, hides a secret meaning that enters into dialogue with the unique buildings around it. [9] Running between historic buildings and the museum's new library-periscope, it connects the Retiro Park and the Botanical Gardens through a contemporary system that is anchored in ancestral emotional meaning.

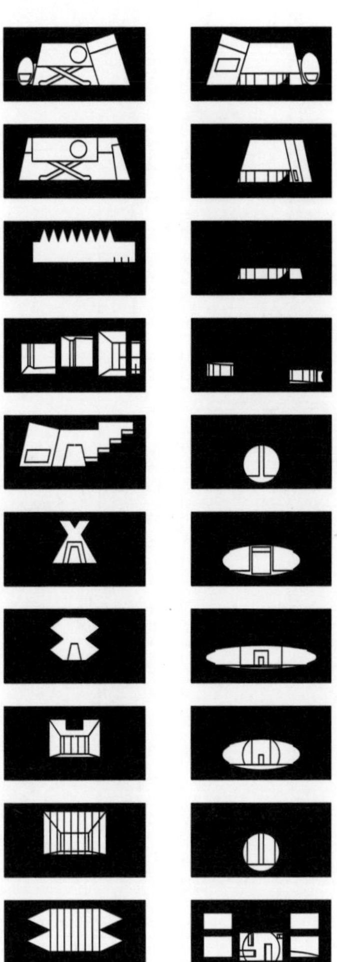

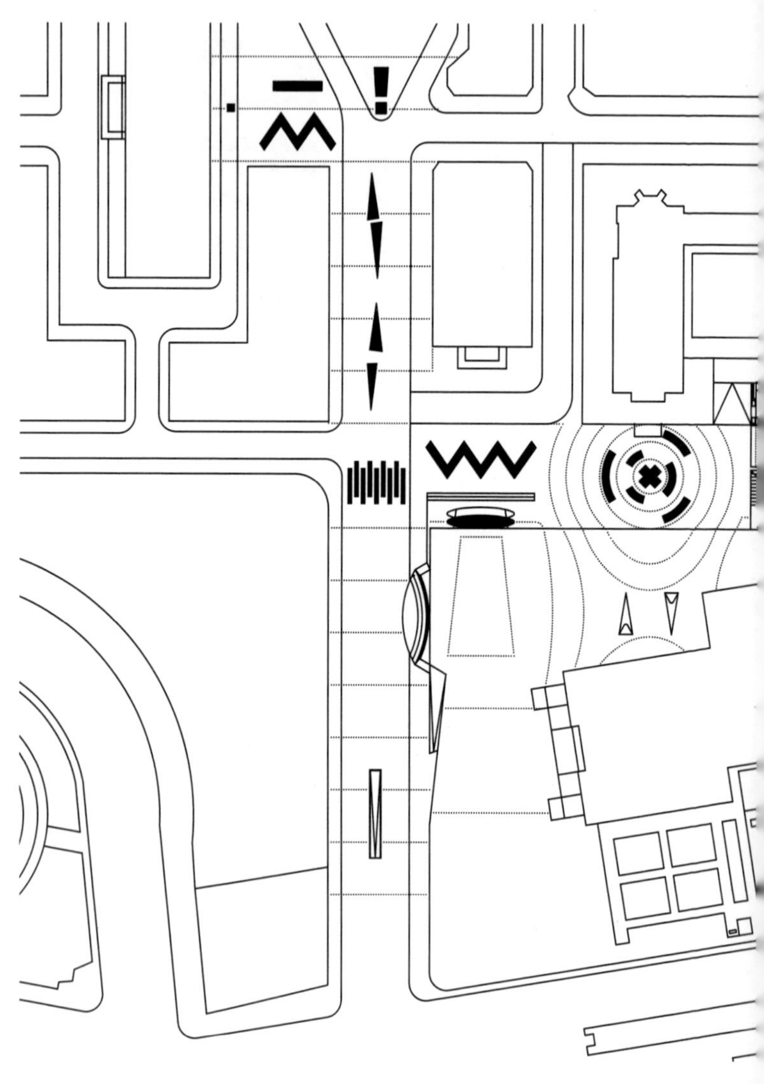

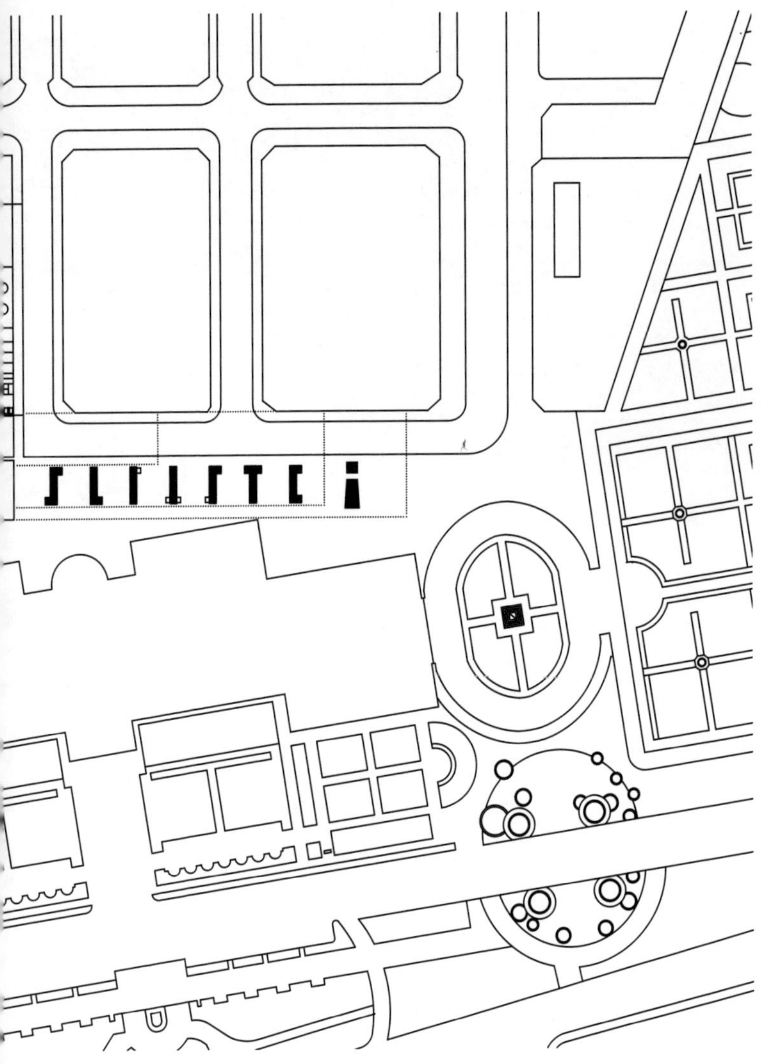

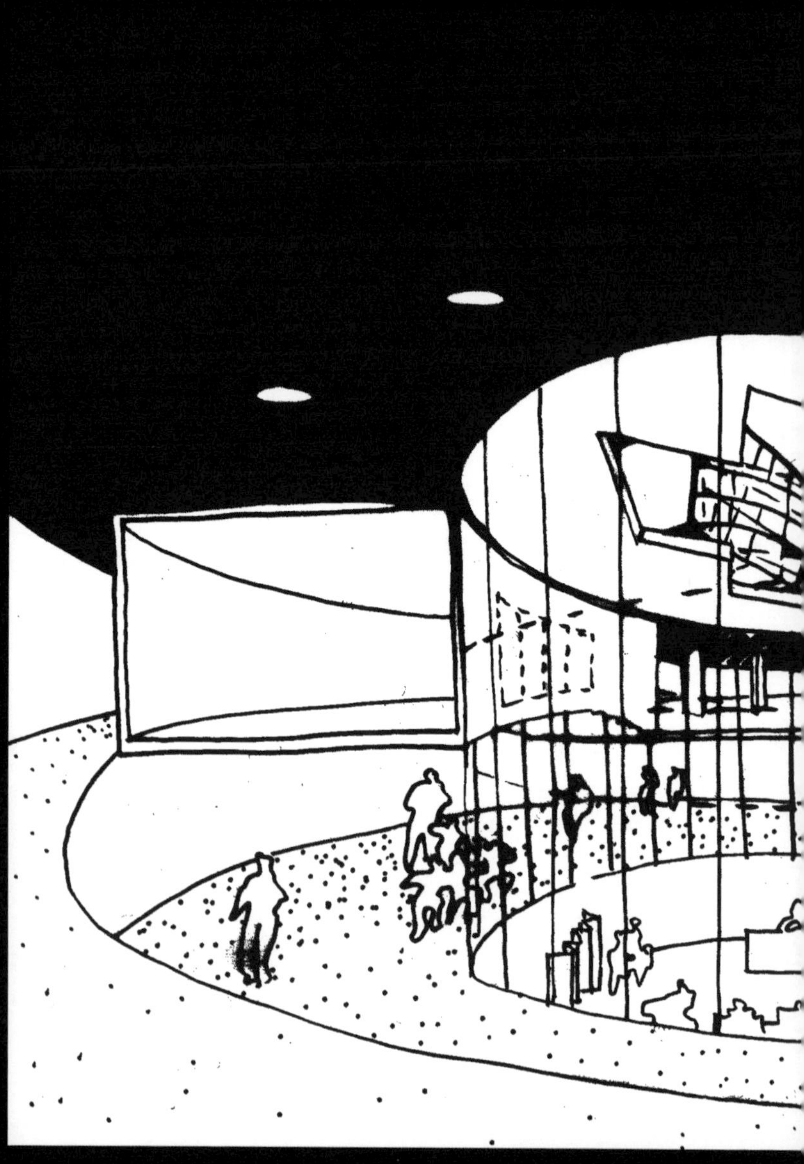

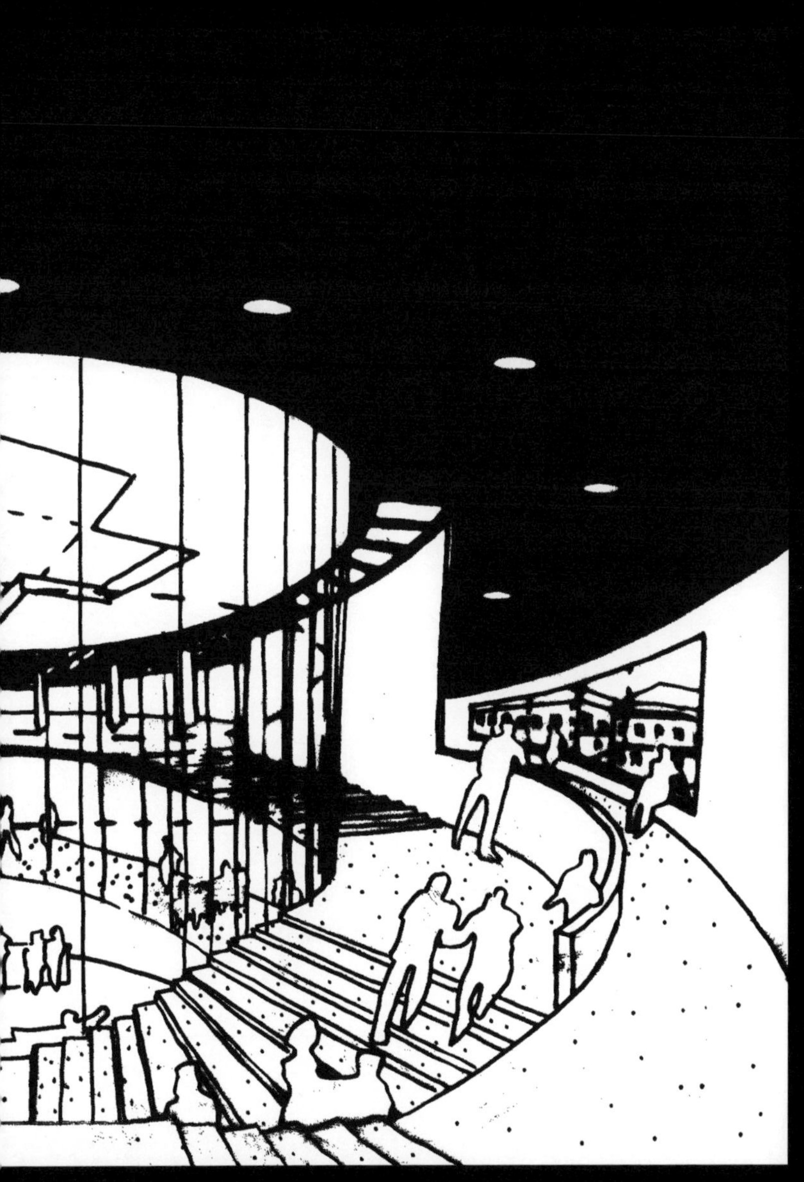

DECISION IS A PART OF PRECISION

"Scientific truth and moral truth need to be understood together, the assurance of the irrefutable with the excitement of our passions"

Henri de Poincaré ——————————————————

23

[1] Four Japanese engineers are here to film a movie about their Komatsu machines. One of them tells me that their idea is to use the machines to return the seven Moias of Anakena beach back to their original platform.

"The film will be a success; the strength and precision of our cranes, in the service of beauty and history," he says smiling.

[2] I've been in Hanga Roa for a few months and these are the first visitors from the outside world to this far-away island. They look at me quizzically from the Toyota they've brought from Tokyo, because I'm sitting bareback atop a horse. It is a source of pride because the horse won last year's race during the Tapati Festival and it was a gift from Marco as a symbol of our friendship. [3] With Western courtesy, I invite them to come tuna fishing the next day, before they begin work.

[4] At five a.m., Marco and his brother have prepared a boat with a small, unsteady motor. As the sun comes up over the curved horizon, we set out toward an unknown destination. After a few hours of travel across gentle seas, Marco stops the motor.

"We're here," he says distractedly.

[5] The Japanese look at me in astonishment at the exactness of the location, out in the middle of nowhere, but they recover quickly enough and begin throwing out their hooks, forgetting that we have lost sight of the island in the distance. I wonder how we'll get back. [6] A short time later, we pull up a tuna amid cheers from the Easterners and perplexity from the islanders. [7] Before my eyes, Yushi pulls out a black leather case and unrolls it to reveal a dozen shining knives and a

tube of wasabi. In silence, the men feverishly slice up the animal, using a different knife for each specific piece and type of cut. I imagine they won't be able to use all twelve, but I'm wrong. [8] Out there in the middle of the ocean, without a guide, except for the sun as it changes position, we devour the raw tuna, amid smiles and stories. We make short time of the tastiest bits, selected with precision by the engineers, along with a case of beer. The salty, spicy taste wakes up our senses. After smoking a few unfiltered cigarettes, we fire up the halting motor and set off across a featureless sea.

[9] Unsure about the trust we've put in our sailors, we applaud when we recognize the peak of the volcano Rano Raraku as it slowly rises before us. [10] When we arrive at the port, I ask my friend how he found the way back. He looks at me surprised and says:

"From the color of the sea, obviously."

24 [1] At the end of the 1930s, in his book *The Man Without Qualities*, Robert Musil proclaimed the creation of a General Secretariat for Soul and Precision as a way of certifying the separation between animist and scientificist readings of the world in early 20th-century society. [2] Based on this distinction, the currents in each historical period cause most of the disasters we see by confronting religions, philosophies and other areas of knowledge. According to him, the combination of perceptions through these two vortexes of the soul and precision, resulting in love and force, generates an elevated degree of humanity without restrictive attributes.

³ The perceptive efforts of the soul pinpoint a feeling that there is always something missing, along with the intuition that there is no total system that can guarantee external peace. This emptiness reminds us of the trust that we have placed in certain periods of our lives, when we make preparations for the great changes we have been promised, which never come to pass. ⁴ That is the logic of the soul, incapable by itself of carrying out the transformations that are necessary to incorporate us into reality. ⁵ On the other hand, precision can only be achieved by using forces that apply one-sided pressure on the surroundings in a centrifugal, inflexible way. It is the law of clear thoughts and deeds, guided by skeptical and objective behavior as the definitive conclusion of the logic of reason, when faced with the pressure of the necessity for survival. ⁶ Precision is tied in with the spirit, though there is no evident a priori connection; it creates a bridge between reality and thought. Its representations in scientific form are a system of the subconscious to control the devastating disorienting effect of pure sensibility on our existence. ⁷ It complements the soul and it completes the indeterminacy of our feelings, making them transmissible by specifying their dimensions.

⁸ A full life cannot be lived with just the action of the soul; it must be complemented by the precision of our actions, so that reason and life, and the spirit and thought can come together. ⁹ At some point in history, Man was afraid of his potential and, forcing himself to look outside himself, he took to measuring the exterior world, instead of measuring what was inside him.

25 ¹ Creating cities requires a strong mind and an iron will at the service of an original point of view on life and the world. ² Without mixing them together, the city reflects two images of Man set before his living space and his existence. ³ On the one hand, as a representation of his scientificism, there is the inclination toward what is economically inflexible, toward vigilance and coercion. ⁴ On the other hand, in tension and in a condition of inferiority, his animism is characterized by a lack of confidence and the need for leadership.

⁵ If the creation of cities is given a meaning in terms of sensibility, it results in dreaming and art, but between them and real life there lies an abyss. ⁶ If it is given a reasoned, economicist meaning, truth and science are obtained, but feeling is destroyed. ⁷ Just as certain species of bacteria divide the organic substances that they attack into two parts, the human species separates the vital elements of its cities between the solid material of artifice and the crystalline atmosphere of belief. ⁸ The combination of both generates a higher degree of urbanity, without restrictive attributes, where emotional satisfaction is an essential requirement for maintaining social stability. That kind of city multiplies the power of Man and magnifies it, despite reducing it numerically, allowing for a heroic epic which private life still maintains.

⁹ The creator of those cities is a critical pessimist who watches as the true strength of his love for others is destroyed by the opulence of the pragmatic society which he is attempting to provide with a physical space. ¹⁰ Contemporary society, with its politics held hostage by economic

gain, has changed everything; it is manipulated by a merciless few, who are disguised as leaders. The kind of urbanity that represents them dissolves social ties and crushes the individual, through isolation.

[11] Diffuse and vacillating public opinion, always poised for competition, replaces the individual with independent criteria, whose conclusions are transformed into intellectual dust that is scattered all over, never to be reassembled. [12] In this organizational fight, we have come to a point in time where the univocal has won out over the allegorical and where emphatic economic conclusions have prevailed, for the time being, over the dreams of the logic of sensibility.

[1] In the nineteen sixties, during a high-precision low-altitude flight in a military fighter plane, an Austrian pilot buzzed past a glacier with the engines at full throttle. Having dinner with a surgeon friend some time later, he talked about the beauty of the icicles as they exploded from the noise of the plane's reaction engines as he passed. [2] Inspired by that image, the doctor imagined the possibility of breaking up solid objects from a distance using acoustics. The next day, he had his entire research team begin experimenting along those lines. As a result of that chance conversation, invasive surgery was never again used for kidney stone removal; since then, doctors have used ultrasound.

[3] Contrary to what many critics attempted to dictate not so long ago, knowledge and disciplines have currently proven themselves to be permeable. [4] Rational and sensory approaches to understanding the world are closer together

than ever, behaving asymptotically. No one should be surprised to hear an astrophysicist talk about mysticism, or a mathematician about philosophy. [5] This nomadic thought runs across different fields of knowledge, taking advantage of the optimum relationships from each. It picks them up in random conversations or loose threads, as Rilke would say, which build up the awareness of what interests us. [6] We can talk about wormholes, quasicrystals, antimatter, or multidimensional space in the context of nearly any discipline. [7] This plea for permeability and the cross-pollination of fields of knowledge goes hand in hand with rejecting a defensive isolation of professions. [8] This sheds light on the lack of understanding of the ultimate reality of certain concepts that sometimes seem foreign, but which we consider to be fundamental pillars of creativity, and which we use as the foundation for building theories and objects.

[9] Ecology, science, genetics or advanced mathematics no longer deal with states of balance; they talk about change and express change because they have accepted that nothing remains the same. [10] An uncertainty principle in any discipline raises doubts about convictions with respect to space, matter, time and energy which are merely different definitions for the same thing as well as experimental guides to asking the right questions in any creative discipline.

27   [1] In a world of fuzzy limits and given the awareness that precision does not lie only in measurements, we are faced with asking ourselves which parameters can help us achieve it. [2] On the other hand, however, the control regulations

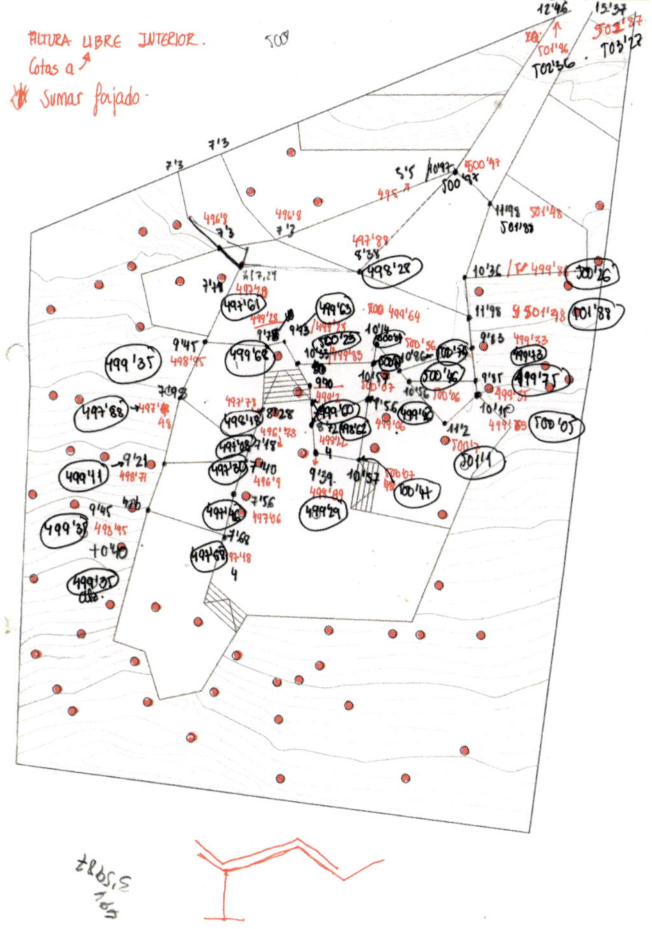

applied to matter and energy always have a measurable numeric character and rarely originate in sensitivity toward them. [3] As such, living in nature with precise respect depends on uncovering mechanisms to prevent the energetic sustainability from remaining merely superficial, as an abstract system that is isolated from the senses.

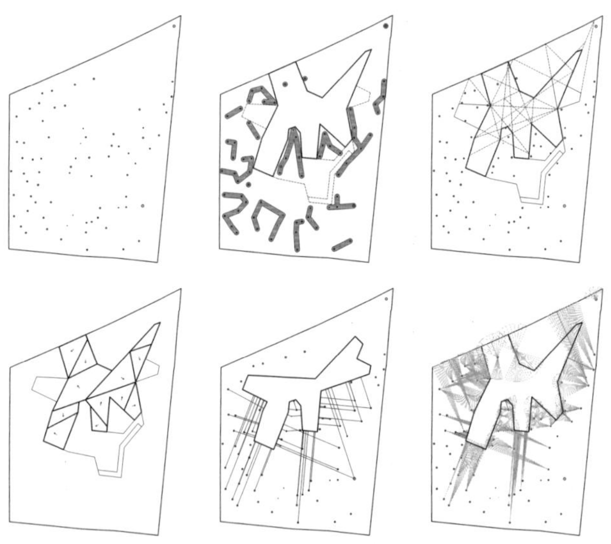

[4] In keeping with this vision, our work in a hundred-year-old forest with a large topographical slope is based on a perceptive system that describes symbiotic complicities among the characteristics of the trees. The groups of trees that result from this process are overlapped with the reg-

ulations concerning dimensions and occupiable surface areas that apply to the specific site. [5] On the one hand, the selection system creates a residual space between the areas where there are similarities among the groups of trees. [6] On the other hand, applying the regulations to this empty space generates a three-dimensional geometry that is produced by negotiating all of the required parameters at each point. [7] As such, the volumetric possibilities for occupying the site for the Levene House in El Escorial (2002–2005) are revealed, together with certain sensible indications as to how it should be inhabited.

[8] The configuration of the volume is defined using inclined planes in successive attempts until the necessary conditions are achieved all along the perimeter. The non-Euclidean geometry that results is then precisely adapted both to the sensory demands of the landscape and its topography, as well as the planning requirements. [9] The special volumetric

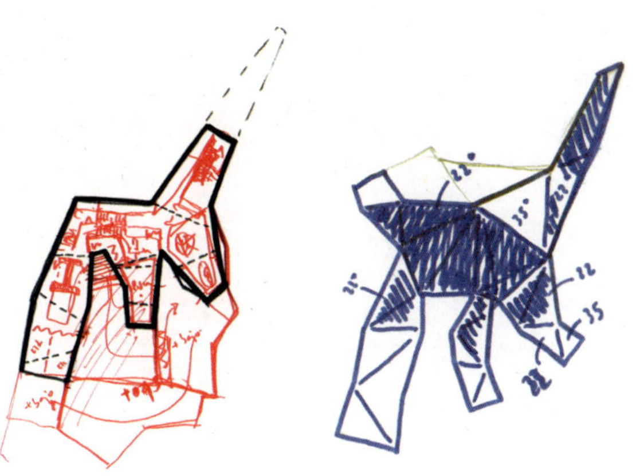

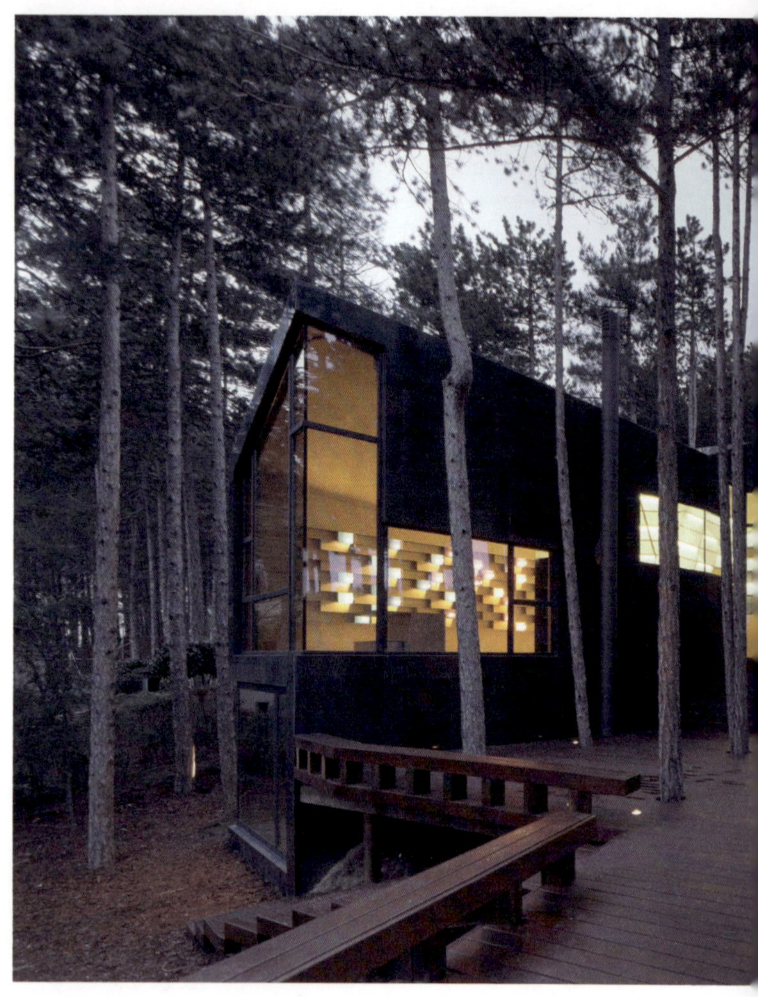

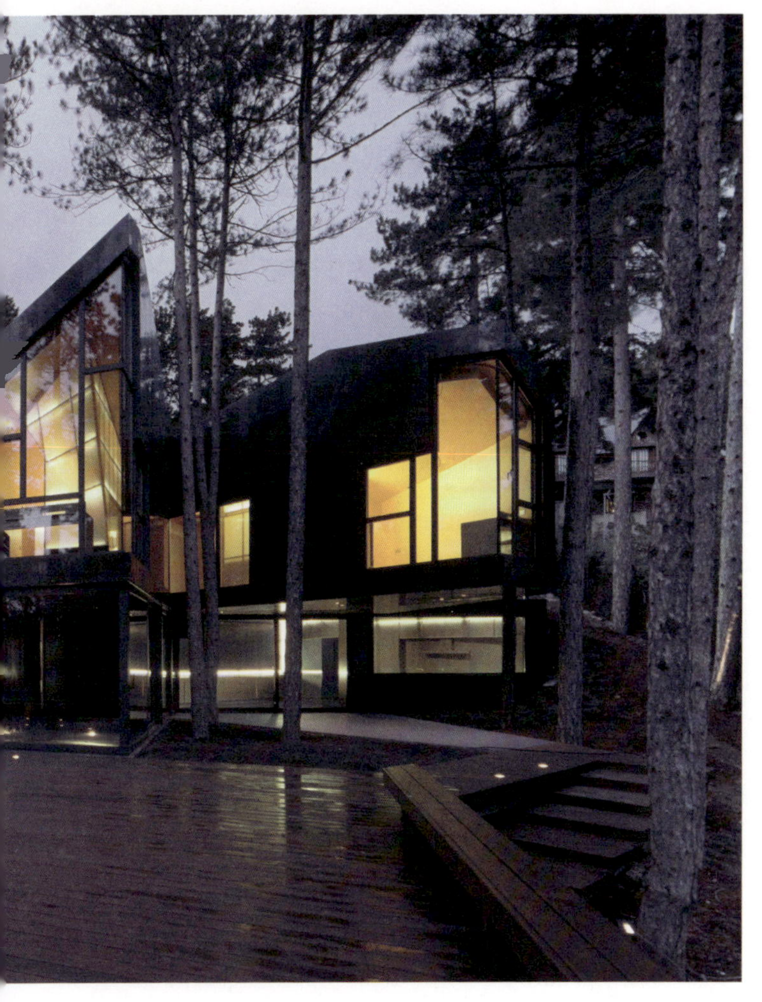

characteristics provided, in the form of arms that reach between the trees, maintain a similar character although the dimensions vary. The interior spaces they enclose encourage seeking out their function in the relationship between the spatial conditions and the views toward the landscape oustide. [10] Ways of inhabiting the object are revealed in a fruitful and unexpected relationship that is generated based on a respect rooted in sensibility combined with abstract urban regulations.

28 [1] The cornerstone of Saint Augustine's natural philosophy is his distinction between sensibility and intelligence. [2] Human beings share with animals the ability to perceive the material world using our senses. Our sensory perceptions help us create representations of the sensible world and physical objects in our minds. [3] We use these representations, which appear in the presence of objects or are recovered from memory, to situate ourselves in time and space. [4] That is how we acquire consciousness of our surroundings. However, if our understanding were limited entirely to our sensory perceptions, we would have very limited capabilities for judgment. It is true that we would be able to decide whether or not the material conditions were favorable to the satisfaction of our needs or desires. But we would be incapable of determining whether those desires, born from a series of circumstances, were appropriate or worth satisfying. [5] In order to make value judgments, we need more than representations of the sensible world alone; those representations have to include some aspect of good. Mental representations of what we perceive through our senses, i.e., the intelligible world, inform us with a type of understanding that animals do not possess.

⁶ Using our intelligence, human beings are capable of perceiving the physical world in its vileness or beauty, its evil or good. ⁷ And this basic sense of goodness, which can be found in all of us, is built up spontaneously on the ruins of mystical and religious ideas, never on scientific conditions. ⁸ That is why the primitive morality of practical selfishness derives solely from the instincts and is founded on common sense. That morality sees life itself as the only certitude and understands sickness and poverty as the only real evils. It is only capable of perceiving irreducible good in health and wealth, understanding that all other realities, either fortunate or unfortunate, are ultimately derived from them. ⁹ Because it does not allow any impositions, the conscience has no objection to selfish movements and their triumphs in that moral state, which many people never move beyond.

¹⁰ Accessing a higher degree of morality than this common one requires ridding oneself of inherited concepts in order to construct a shared perception between sensibility and science. ¹¹ It demands moving one step beyond the egoism of one's own life toward a place where reason and emotion can accept the needs and uncertainties of others as one's own.

¹ I aspire that our protection from the world will become **29** increasingly intuitive, adaptable and precise.

² I aspire to let time help finish things, to leave them open-ended so that use can shape them.

3 I aspire to the precision of thought, filtered through sensibility.

4 I aspire to formal appearances and their adaptation to necessity.

5 I aspire to colors, all of them.

6 I aspire to the maximum possible particularity, to that limit where things belong to others, yet the ties that bind them to us remain intact.

7 I aspire to memory as a creator of sensations as opposed to images, to memories as trampolines as opposed to chains.

8 I aspire to respect for our elders if their knowledge is not corrupt, for their wisdom if they have known how to use it.

9 I aspire to a life without restrictions, merely the ones that are derived from our own understanding.

10 I aspire to learn even when the person in front of me does not realize that they are teaching.

11 I aspire to a moral universe that is applicable to everything, both living and inert, to a life without prejudices.

12 I aspire to be able to create, to follow the inertia of origins.

13 I aspire to what I don't know how to do, trusting that, at some point, I will do it unexpectedly well.

14 I aspire that the moose won't run away when they see me.

15 I aspire to be able to achieve some part of what I aspire to, just some part.

30   1 In 1850, Riemann defined the zeta-function in the imaginary space created by a four-dimensional topology that was based on the distances between the prime numbers. He conjectured, at the age of thirty-eight, that the solutions

for that function where its complex topology intersected with the horizontal would be located on a straight line, where they would line up according to the rhythm of prime numbers. [2] All of it was abstract and impossible to calculate due to its complexity, until the advent of computation and Selberg's contribution. That Norwegian enthusiast dedicated his entire life to calculating three million solutions to the equation, all of which fell along Riemann's critical line, just as he had predicted.

[3] That world full of uncertainties would get a big surprise in 1996 from a group of quantum physicists at MIT, working outside the realm of pure mathematics. While comparing their studies on the location of energy levels in the atom and its quantum-scale particles, they were literally stupefied when they realized that the vibration frequencies of matter coincided with the intervals of the prime numbers along Riemann's critical line. [4] They had demonstrated that matter and energy, in the world we live in, with all of the chemistry underlying our sensations, are intimately related to that vibration which they called the quantum drum. [5] Its essence involves strange and ungraspable numeric frequencies of an energetic nature, which our sensitive minds pick up on unconsciously, leading to our different states of mind: happiness, anger or sudden love.

[6] From this vantage point, to which we have been raised by those confident scientists so we can contemplate ourselves, like in Niels Bohr's dream, a whole world of possibilities unfolds that is vaster than the ground where we stood just moments ago. [7] Living up to this revelation implies the need for precise, more responsible choices, with no support in

the face of the imminent danger of the unknown. [8] Any wager in this lofty territory of sensibility carries an associated risk, where slippery words like beauty, rules, precision, chance or discovery get mixed together. [9] It is a delicate world where measurements become abstract, fertilized by our sensory awareness of the real.

31 [1] Man's interest in controlling nature and anchoring himself to it has always lain at the root of the invention of systems of measurement. [2] That implies abandoning the emptiness of an imprecise existence in the sensible world and moving toward one that is ruled from the perspective of enlightened reason. This path provides evidence that the senses were never a convincing metronome for Man as he moved forward. [3] However, Man on his journey toward contemporary science is also like a hand dealing cards onto the table from an unknown deck, full of uncertainties. [4] In those cards, we see that a meter is no longer a precise entity but a fluctuating one, or that a second is defined approximately by the jump of an electron between two states of caesium. [5] Similarly, we catch a glimpse of how the universal time we use to regulate ourselves is out of phase with our planet's fluctuating time, which varies as it interacts with the tides.

[6] As science perfects the precision of its readings of matter, it becomes increasingly ungraspable. [7] Quantum physics certifies that any experience of measurement depends on the observer who carries it out and, as such, the limits of its precision are individual in nature. Thus, it appears before

contemporary Man as a new world of changing dimensions, born from the confirmation that exactness is not altogether possible.

[8] We should ask ourselves, then, what lies in the vague space that remains between what Man manages to measure and the ultimate reality of things. Perhaps it is in this final stretch between science and the real where the causes of our sensations lie. [9] From this point of view and faced with the order of an aseptic reading as accepted by physics, we can imagine that there is another invisible order that links our perceptions to that ultimate reality. [10] An order of sensations that allows for meshing sensibility and reason, soul and precision. A combined structure, which completes the words written in the language of rational thought with parametric letters that have their origins in the sensible world. [11] This universal linguistic code, imperfect by nature, is demonstrated to be variable and continually subject to discovery. [12] Why go on pretending that there is stability in the real if we are capable of letting our understanding flow into something unpredictable, which encompasses both enlightened reason and the illumination of the universe?

[1] In a world governed by a material and energetic pragmatism of a financial order, sensitivity to our surroundings becomes a high-risk creative factor. [2] However, objects that are set into the landscape based on sensory conditions can be more precisely adapted to the reality where they are introduced. That requires prior independence from the

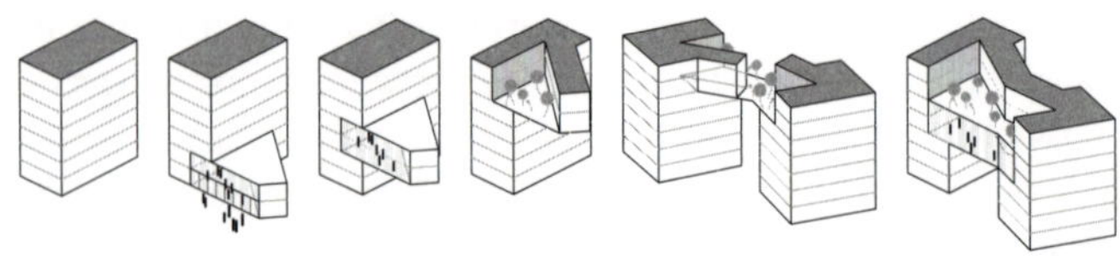

formal prejudices that are always associated with a strictly functionalist outlook.

[3] From this point of view, in the interest of the correct operation of the university campus that includes the WU Executive Academy in Vienna (2008–2013), the educational uses are condensed by grouping them according to specialties. [4] These autonomous, generic vertical structures distribute the accesses and visitor services on the ground floors, the faculty departments on the intermediate floors and the

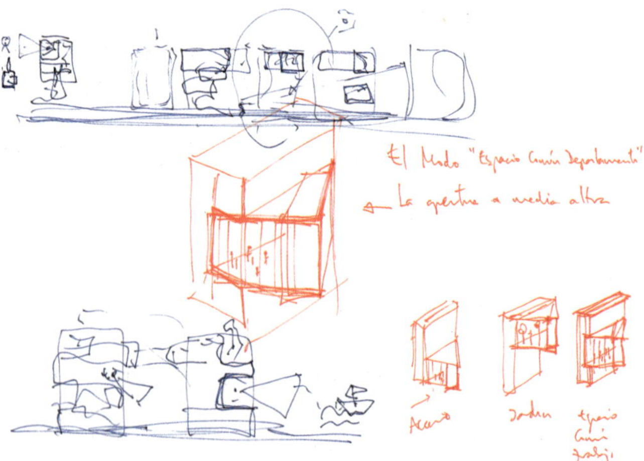

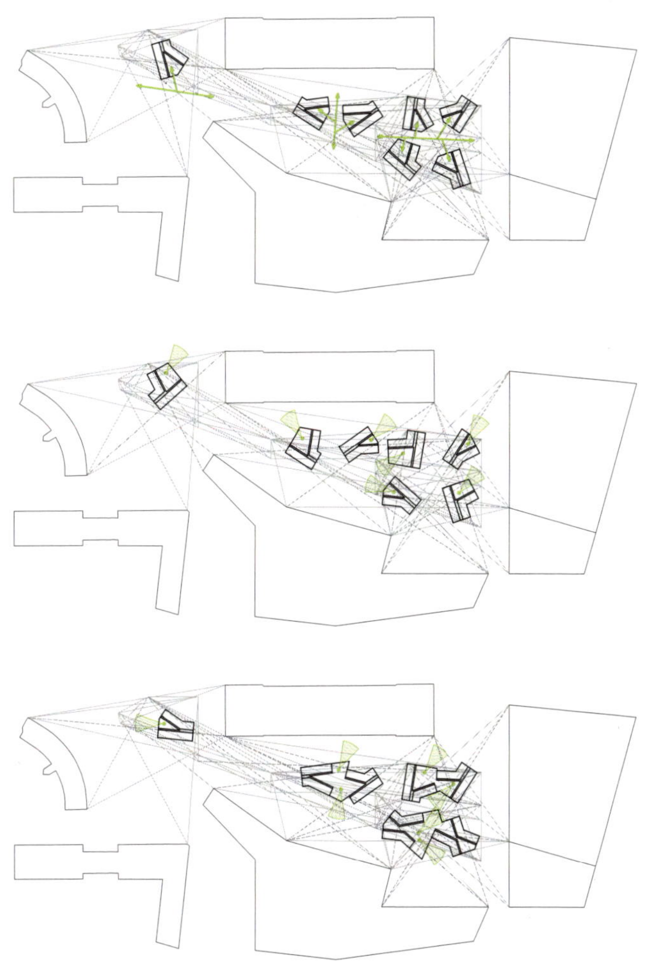

PRECISION — 32 : 4

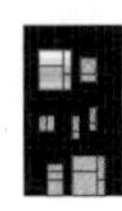
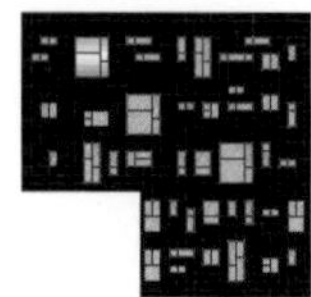
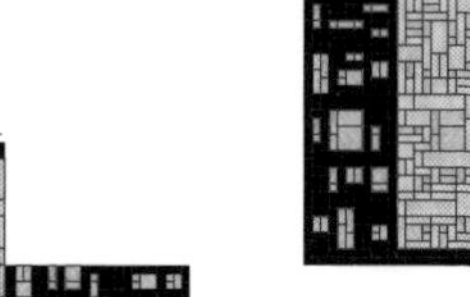
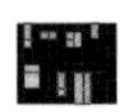
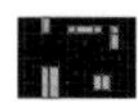
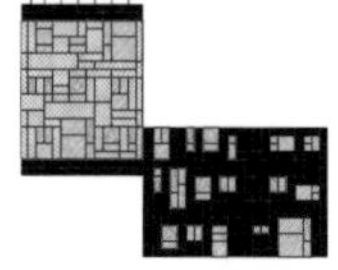
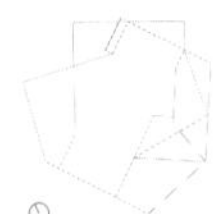
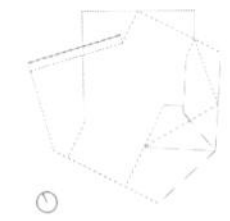
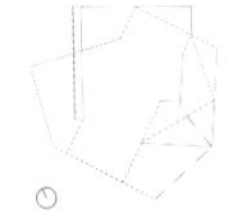
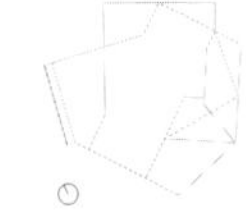
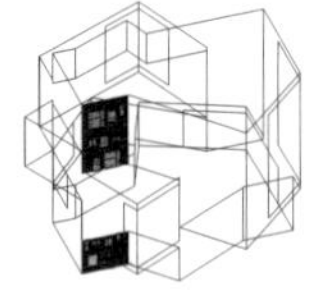
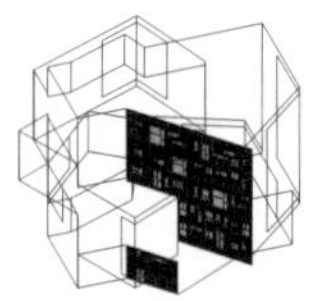
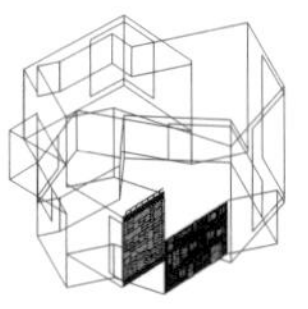
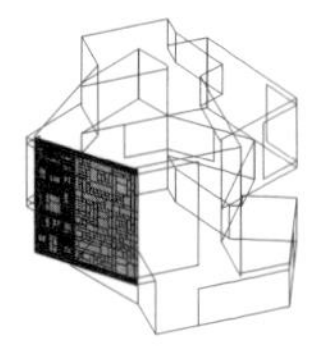

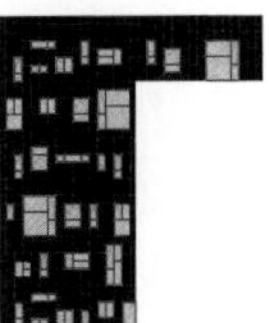
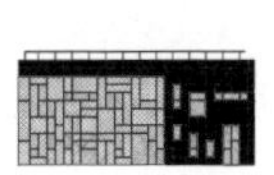
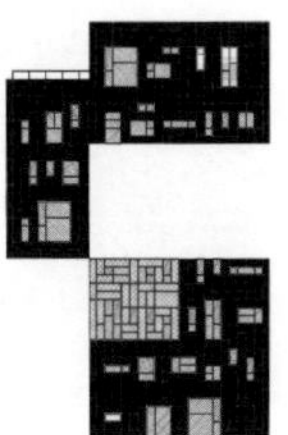

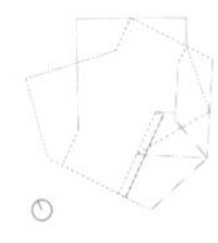
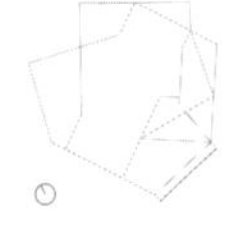
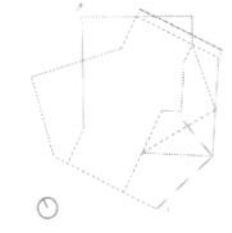
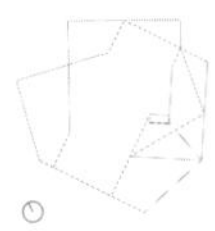

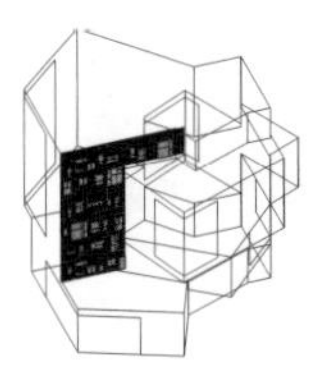
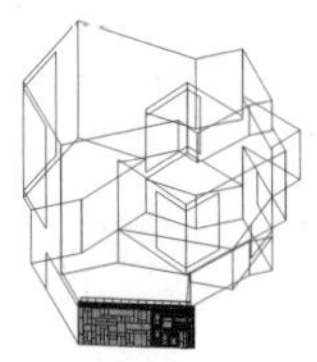
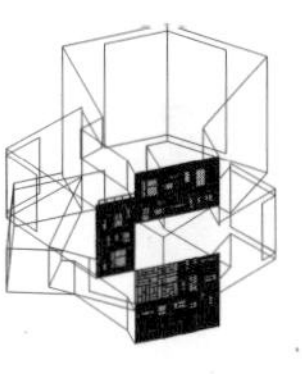
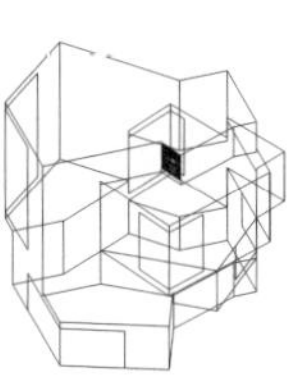

classrooms on the upper floors. In this way, the students can benefit from the surrounding landscape on the higher levels, with views over the Prater and the historic city. [5] Uncovering the spatial qualities of the general arrangement of the campus provides a geometric relationship between the different buildings; the compact structures are then synchronized on top of it.

[6] Once they are situated, each bland volume is subjected to different adaptations of its shape as the position of its internal program comes into contact with the immediate surroundings and the distant landscape. These deformations generate new spaces to house the public entryways, the interdepartmental lounges and the mixed educational areas, each of which is provided with optimum views toward the exterior. [7] The need for connection between the different departments leads to the appearance of common areas be-

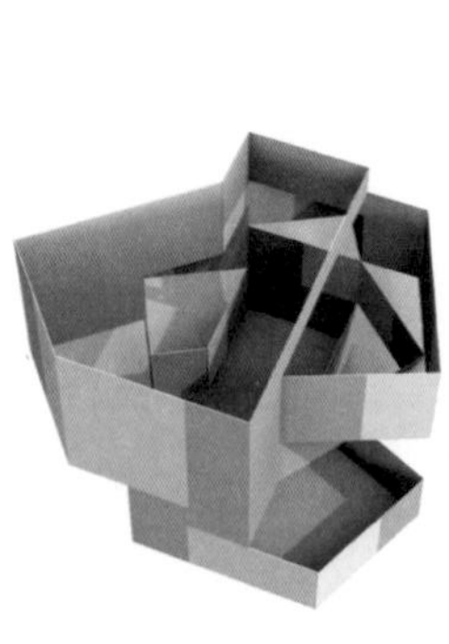

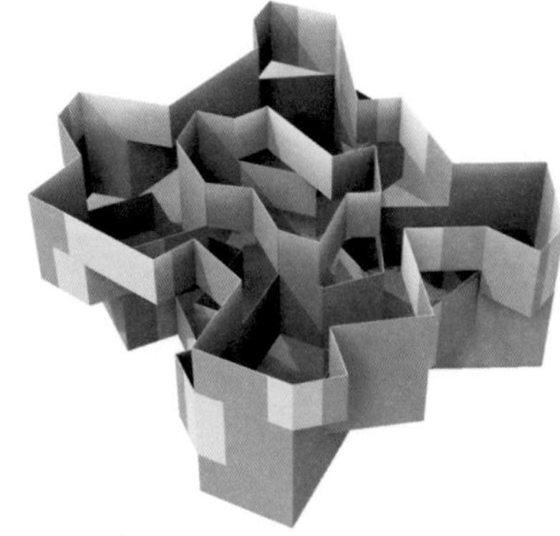

tween the generic volumes, defining an exciting secondary adaptation with a marked connection with the landscape and an exogenous nature.

[8] The choice of how theses spaces relate to the exterior, free from visual obstacles, creates a vertical imbalance between the deformations corresponding to each floor. [9] This non-coinciding geometry generates the final volume, coordinated by a structural envelope that transfers the load. [10] The compact structure of the perimeter also acts as a control system for temperature and light, allowing for the existence of large panoramic windows on the spaces that emerge during the adaptation process.

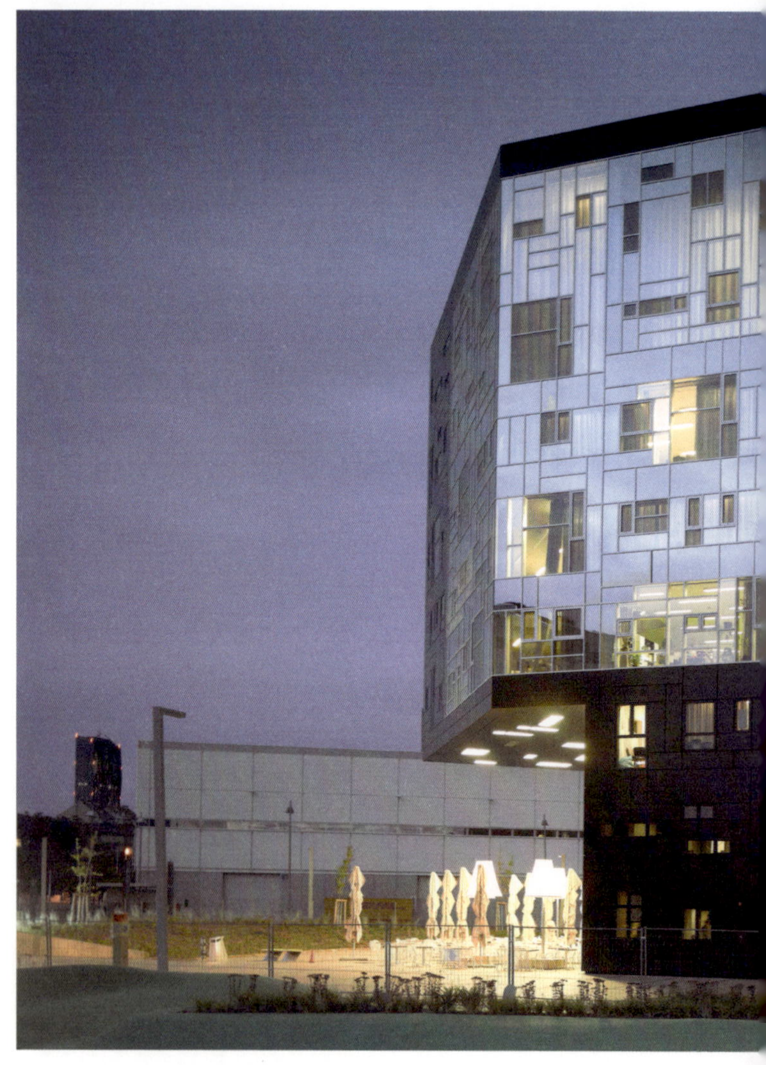

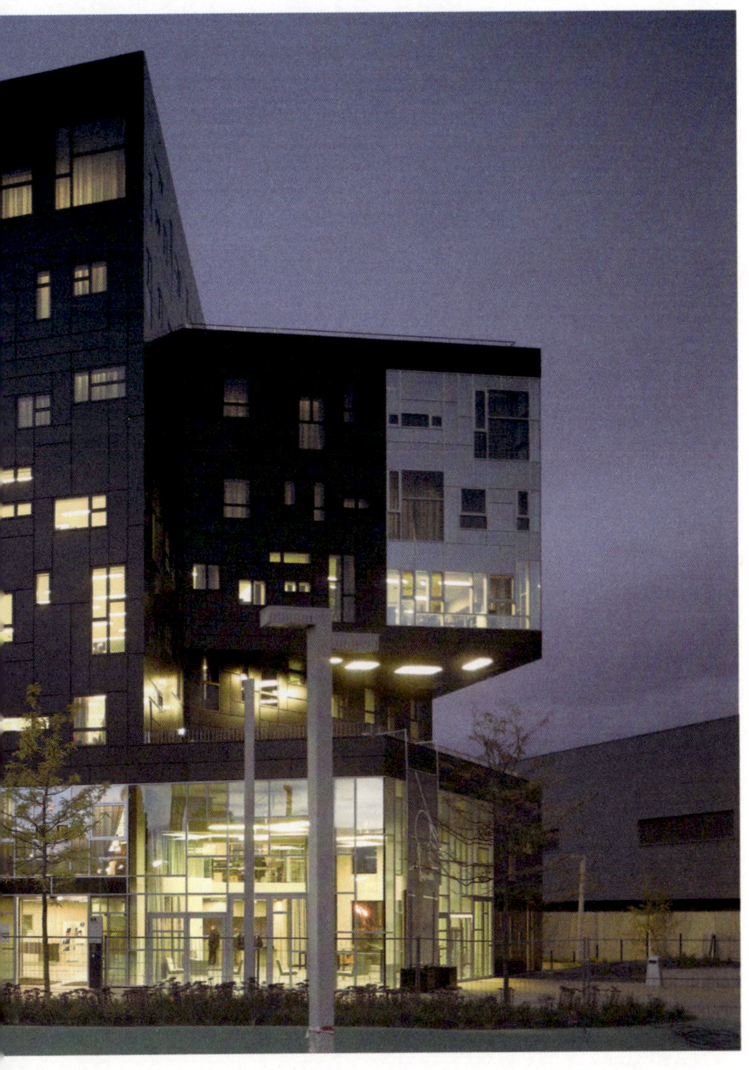

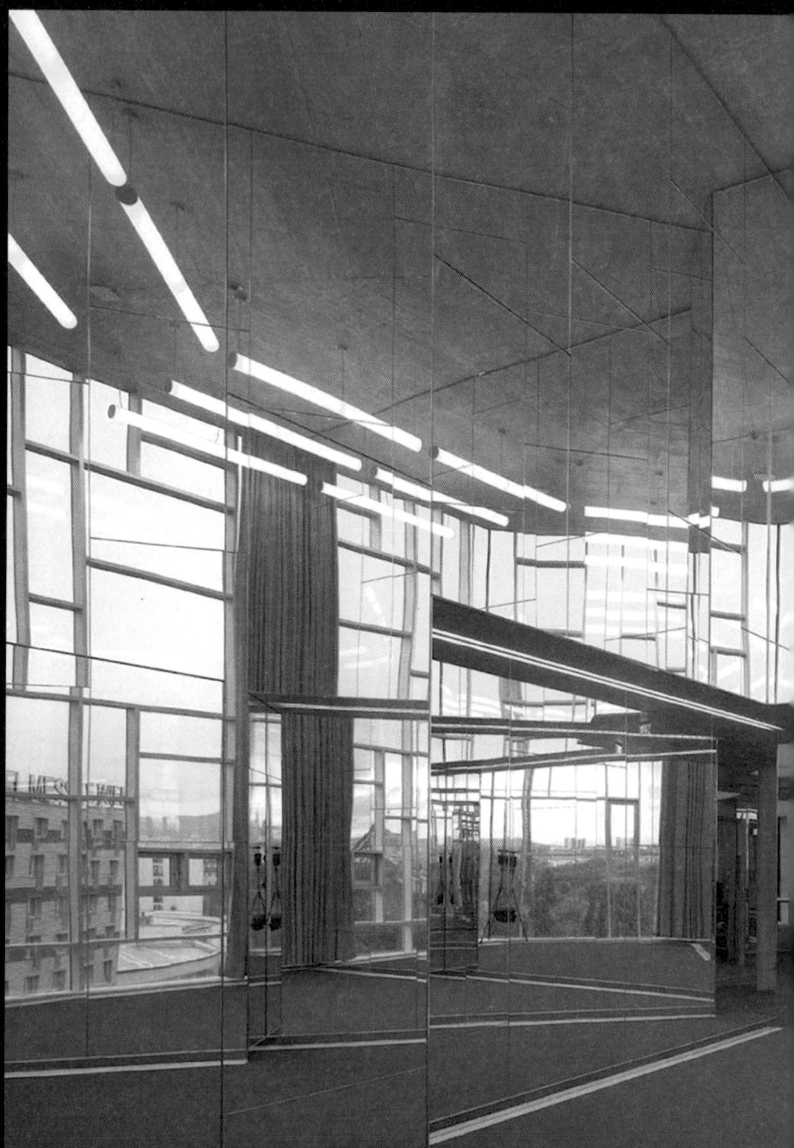

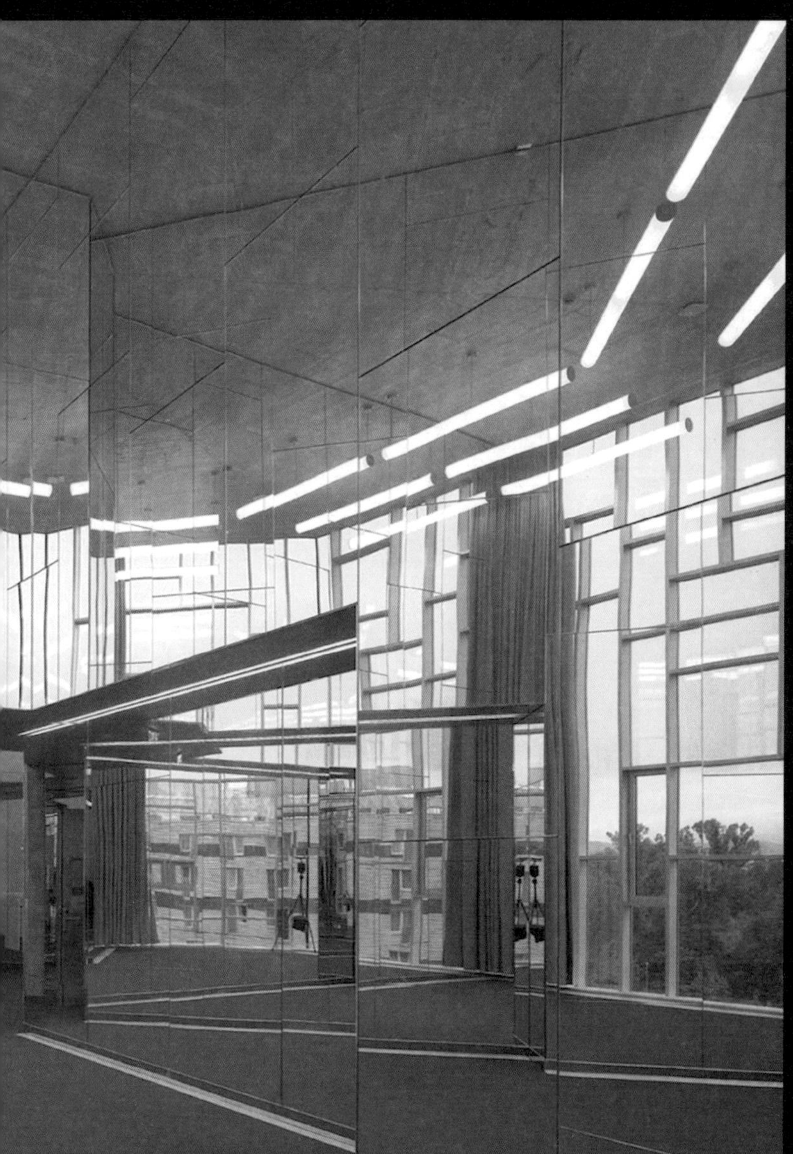

DON'T MAKE TOO MANY PLANS! CHANCE ONLY HAS ONE

"Although men pride themselves on their noble deeds, these are seldom the outcome of a grand design but simply effects of chance"

François de la Rochefoucauld —

¹ KLM is flying me to Yemen. ² The plane's radar points toward Mecca, instead of the traditional North. I imagine distractedly that it is a courtesy on the part of the developed Dutch world to Muslims who need to pray during the long plane ride. I suppose, both amused and condescending, that after a while I'll see some bearded men in djellabas genuflecting in the aisles.

³ To pass the time, I start flipping through the airline magazine and I pause for a while to look at the map of European flights. I've always been interested in the kind of cartographic projections they use: Peters, Mercator, Behrman, or cylindrical, because I sincerely believe that it reveals a lot about the company. Today's map corresponds to the more traditional Mercator projection and, all things considered, it is a bit surprising in the context of such a forward-thinking country.

⁴ My eyes slide alternatively over the European cities where I have lived intensely: Madrid, Paris, Amsterdam... Oslo. I have memories from each of them, of the chance meetings that couldn't be accounted for statistically, without which I wouldn't be able to live now. ⁵ Suddenly, a strange hallucination startles me as I realize, time and again, that they all seem to line up. Using the airline safety card, I trace an imaginary line between them and, to convince myself of what I'm seeing, I draw over it with a pen.

⁶ There's no doubt about it. My erratic wanderings through Europe, swept along by women and spatial reveries, glide precisely along a straight line, round trip. ⁷ Taken in by this discovery, I turn the page to the complete fold-out world map. I realize that it's based on a more sophisticated cylin-

drical projection, which restores my tarnished image of the Netherlands a little.

[8] I draw the line through Europe again and it occurs to me, like a clairvoyant faced with the unknown, that I might be able to catch a glimpse of my destiny if I extend the line across the rest of the globe. So I draw the bottom end, cutting across the Atlantic and then up through the South Pacific, and then the top end, crossing the polar region and down through the North Pacific. [9] I'm beginning to imagine that my future existence lies sunken beneath featureless oceans when both ends come together in an unexpected location: Wellington. I smile, relieved,

"Something or someone is definitely waiting for me in New Zealand."

34 [1] Avoiding chance leads to a determinism against the very foundation of time and attempting to control every parameter of creation stops it short, creating a regressive effect. [2] Chance is the product of our ignorance in that incidents can occur to affect the creative process that we cannot foresee.

[3] Many creations are chance encounters with objects, laws or events during the working process, which belong to the realm of the unexpected. [4] Defined in these terms, the flow of creation is not entirely stable and it includes factors that redirect and alter the paths that we may have marked out ahead of time. These factors shape fields of probabilities where the information we manipulate ricochets off toward unknown places. [5] Chance, the gaze, matter and energy, order and geometry direct how the creative process proceeds

linearly, where chance is the first tool and all of the others act on it.

[6] Chance is contingent on the acceptance of an interior freedom and it lends autonomy to the creative strategy, leaving part of creation in the hands of unpredictable relationships. [7] A haphazard gaze can be trained by learning to recognize events that break with routine, by being attentive to the flashes of brightness that converge at a particular moment. Controlling this situation and working to focus it can help us recognize the positive and useful moments of chance where ideas take shape.

[8] In genetics, saltations are an example of moments when there is a rupture in the logical evolution of inheritance, followed by radical change. Natural history recognizes these leaps as a line of instructions for the creation of life which, though it is already ordered, recreates an unpredictable mutation within its own laws of behavior, resulting in the appearance of new properties in a species.

[9] The ways of working with the discovery of the world that cannot be remembered demonstrate the value of the unexpected, when we don't know its rules. [10] The possibility of encounters through the use of innovative instructions lets us harness chance without leaving our creations entirely under its control. In this search, our consciousness acts as an active cerebral mechanism at the quantum levels of the neural tubes and its statistical operating system is disconcerting. [11] Resolving its uncertainties will be possible once we are capable of establishing a language of consciousness that brings sensitive perception into resonance with action in the world, without formal prejudices getting in the way.

35 [1] After confirming the failure of classical physics to arrive at a definition of our universe, in the wake of the surprising introduction of the arrow of time and the postulates of General Relativity, in the twentieth century ideas took a statistical turn. [2] It is more comfortable to try to live in a world of cause-effect conditions, where we can trust that when we do x then y will happen. But we know that there is only a small percentage of probability that something will see the light exactly as we have imagined it. [3] The world is not predictable, as religions and philosophies have tried to convey throughout history, but probable according to a statistical quantification.

[4] Despite our determination, creative work will still consist of a series of approaches that are padded with security coefficients, exaggerated tables and sensitive egos. This only hides an incapacity for precision in the face of a growing shortage of causal relationships and a fear of the improbable. [5] There is no one solution for a specific problem. Yet, among all of the possible solutions, there is always one that is the most adapted to the host of conditions involved. [6] Creative systems, then, are organized as fields of probabilities where intentions can only represent a percentage of the approach to the final outcome. Their responsibility with respect to the future ends at that point.

[7] For a long time, the creation of infinite languages to define the world has kept us from realizing that they might all be trying to explain the same thing, assuming that it is just one coin we are looking at and that we can see either heads or tails, and not both at the same time. [8] We know that matter behaves like a wave of energy and that energy

behaves like a material particle but we are incapable of finding a language that will allow us to join those two conditions together simultaneously. [9] In the case of the smallest and largest of elements, it is impossible to define their position in space and their impulse or energy at the same moment, and attempting to do so generates situations of instability.

[10] These two ways of defining the same thing allow for a satisfactory presentation of creations that can be explained through processes that deal either with material variables or energetic parameters. [11] From this point of view, architecture can no longer be defined as the play of volumes under the light, since light and volume don't provide complementary information; rather they are different languages which express the same thing.

[1] Reflection and self-confidence are out of place in a society **36** that has turned the individual into a passive observer, yet they appear in the context of certain events, such as sports-performances. This system of indoctrination from a position of power feeds into the most antisocial aspects of human psychology, at the limits of primitive passion. [2] Its spatial representation is a fascinating, disorganized visual experience and this kind of gathering is always defined by the numerical dimensions of its occupation. [3] From this perspective, the crowds that make stadiums visible end up eliminating the presence of the players through a random combination of multiple groups in artificial spaces. As a result, a stadium that houses them can be treated in a frag-

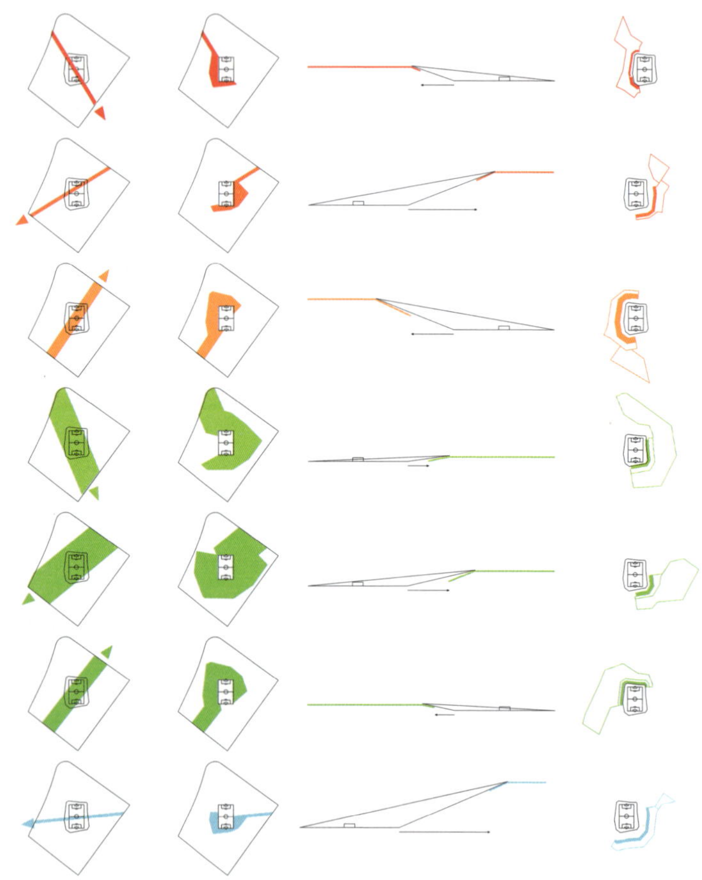

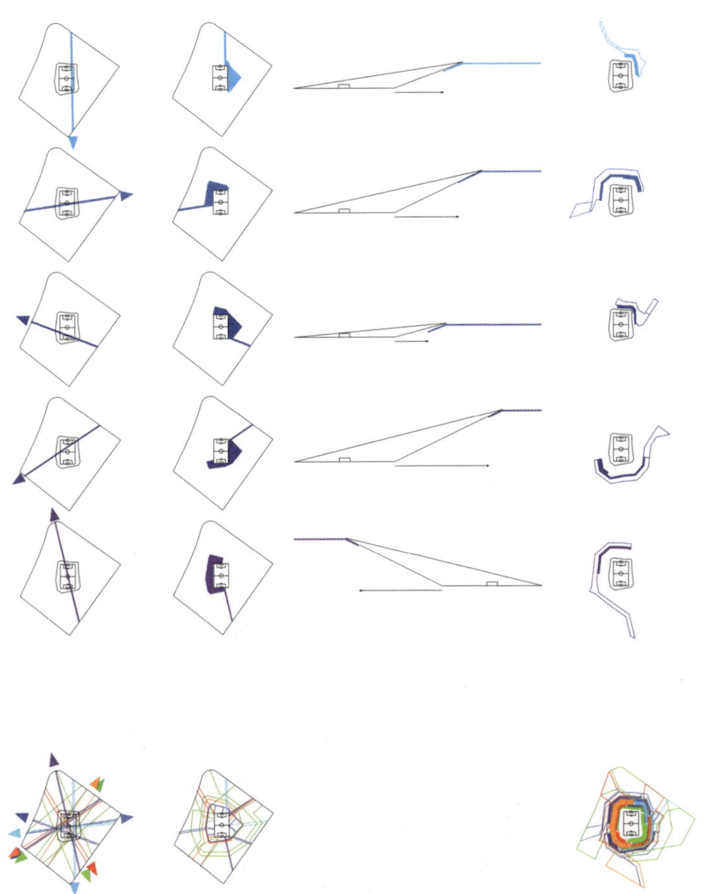

mentary way, creating a variety of arrangements for spectators.

⁴ In the case of the Zaragoza Stadium (2002), the layouts respond to controlling the dynamic forces of each specific flow of arrivals from the city: pedestrians, buses and other vehicle traffic. ⁵ The number of people who engage in a specific behavior in terms of movement are grouped together into entrances, parking areas and control stations, which are made independent through their spatial organization. ⁶ This serves as a catalyst for a reaction in which different morphological, non-coinciding arrangements appear. The virtual playing field is created from the apparently hap-

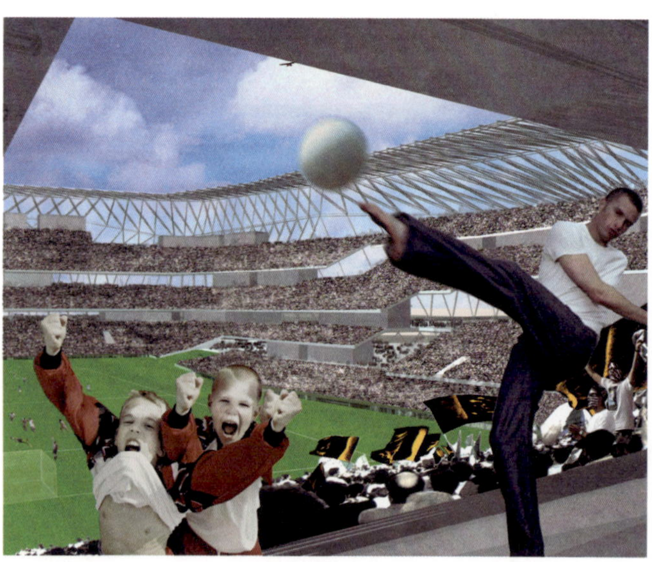

hazard accumulation of these organizations. [7] It is represented by a geometry that is revealed as each major group is adapted independently around the playing field.

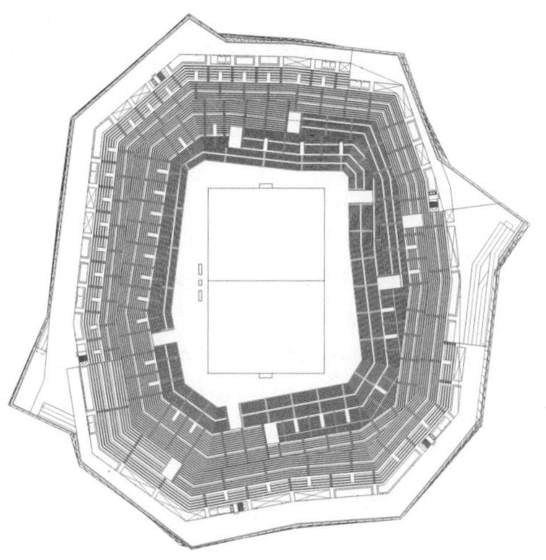

[8] The location and slope of each group of bleachers is characterized by optimum visibility depending on the distance and elevation above the stadium floor. This implies that the overall shape appears a posteriori, with the compilation of the different crowd-selection rings that have been defined using geometries belonging to a single family. [9] The stadium becomes an element that is permeable along its entire perimeter, allowing for the city's residents to make use of the large-scale covered passageways on non-game days. The building is transformed into a large, vertical urban park

that can be used any time in any weather. [10] The use of shallow ramps, oriented in different directions to create visual perceptions of the immediate and more distant surroundings, ensures the interior continuity. This public space around the perimeter adds a centrifugal experience to the building's uses, along with its habitual more centripetal use during sporting events.

37 [1] The beginning of this century has left an unsettling question hanging in the air about the future of creativity. We are witnessing the birth of a freer discipline that is not limited to simplified situations and that has set itself up facing the complexity of the real world. [2] What has been passed down to us is now placed in doubt for its immutability and what emerges is situated between two alienating representations. [3] On the one hand, a determinist world where the only option is accepting what has been imposed based on collective approval and, on the other, a totally arbitrary world subject to uncontrolled free will.

[4] Between these two poles, a new situation appears, defined by the use of systems that are capable of incorporating chance into the creative equation. They are represented by a series of instructions expressed using fields of probabilities, in the style of Heisenberg, associated with unstable behaviors in the surroundings. [5] These rules for the creative process give way to a flexible and reliable working system for acting under the current conditions, where the weight of the unexpected is always greater than what can be predicted.

[6] This instability, with its changing nature, is a creative capability that is based on an open and conscious lack of definition with respect to formal properties, which makes it possible for objects to take on a more adaptive relationship as opposed to one of imposition. It emerges as an uninterrupted transformation, where versatility allows for coupling objects with users' timeframes and with the variable energy of the city. [7] In this way, what may initially seem to be incidental or uncontrolled becomes a part of the process, creating mutations in use and in form that weren't initially expected.

[8] This unstable and variable world responds with an amazing capacity for adaptation in response to other formal properties from the collective imagination, which can be absorbed into the system. [9] These processes stand in direct opposition to the alleged autistic flexibility that attempts to make a single object valid for any number of functions. These objects, which allow for multiple future transformations that have not been accounted for in the process of their generation, are always prefigured by a hollow and aseptic neutrality. [10] Faced with this primary determinism, camouflaged beneath a multifunctional appearance, the objects that appear have the ability to absorb any future uncertainty using pre-established rules that have been implanted into their genetics.

[1] Equilibrium is not a normal state in the world; on the **38** contrary, it is strange and precarious in its duration and its pursuit as a promise of stability creates temporal mirages

in our surroundings. [2] Let us consider the lack of equilibrium as the norm that governs our lives, assuming that matter, energy, space and people display unusual behavior when they distance themselves from their routine. [3] Most states implicated in everyday life are entropic situations that tend toward disorder, such as the natural environment and transportation, or they are unstable systems of exchange, like the economy or geopolitics.

[4] Imagine a system that is far removed from a state of equilibrium and lacks any specific organization. Using active properties, creative actions can transform it into an organized, persistent system that is stable over time, although it may maintain a disordered appearance. [5] Organization requires the use of a quantity of energy in proportion to the desired degree of order. Even more energy is needed if the goal is to maintain a latent order over time, since that implies working against entropy. [6] There are other more active types of order, which express their properties through less energy-hungry functions because they allow for variation and adaptation to unstable states. [7] Bearing in mind that we have knowledge of only a very small portion of what exists and that we can only predict what we already understand, we can deduce that unpredictability is infinitely more important from a creative and progressive point of view.

[8] The tendency to exaggerate stability and security as a firm belief in equilibrium stands in opposition to the kind of thought that feels the need to fill up the holes of the unknown. That is why any object with a highly ordered appearance and organization will be more likely to lose its

internal stability than one that was created without the search for order as a central factor. [9] Objects that incorporate the unexpected into their production rarely seem familiar to us, since they carry something of the discovery of the creative process in their presence. [10] In those objects, each new thread leaves the following one with a possibility for pursuit. This contributes to finding those moments when new human needs begin to resonate with the chance of the space and the time that they inhabit.

[1] The presence of nature in cities is usually very localized and controlled. Its association with public space is always understood as closed off and it rarely participates in the built world. [2] The intentional isolation of nature in the urban environment means that, in order to enjoy it, we always have to go out toward it, and we never come into contact with its presence by surprise. [3] One of the opportunities for bringing about this situation comes in the form of public buildings which, from this standpoint, can

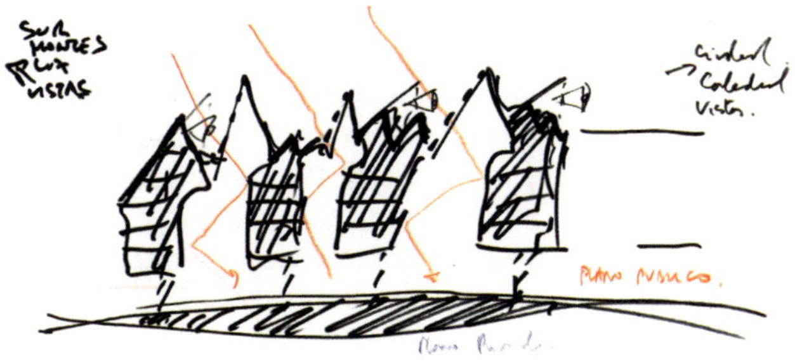

be organized as possible absorbents of nature in a more fragmented state.

4 In the creation of the new City Hall in Bolzano (1999), a landscape is generated from internal functions that include the presence of green space for public use, among others. 5 As opposed to using a horizontal distribution logic for the working areas, the organization is vertical, compact and self-sufficient for each specific administrative area. This creates a functional public-private gradient beginning at the entryway and continuing as we ascend, until we reach the observation decks on the roof.

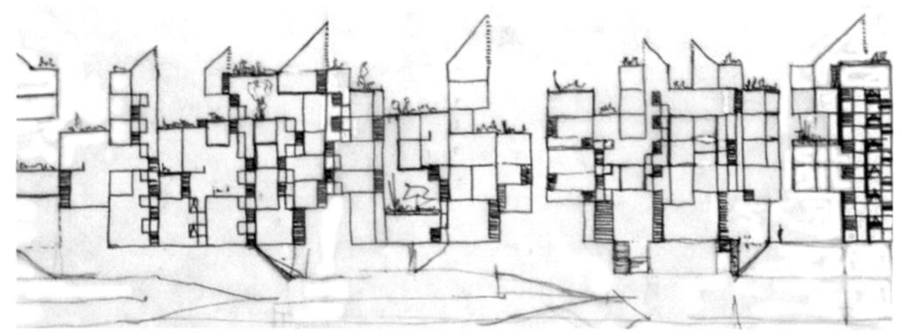

6 The different structures are organized into eighteen layered volumes which operate independently. Coupling them together horizontally generates a comb shape with a number of intermediate empty areas with different characteristics, in keeping with a familiar yet unpredictable geometry. 7 This hollowed-out compactness, based on internal relationships, leads to an independence from contextual conditions and rules out the possibility of a pre-established shape and order. 8 These emptied sections house the circu-

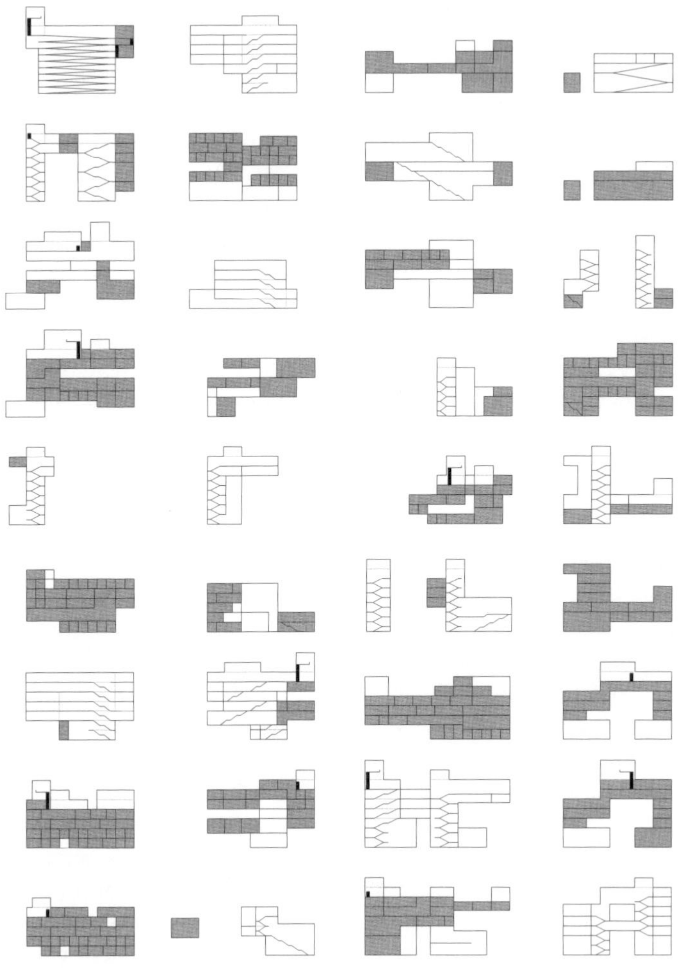

lation areas and the public interior gardens, taking advantage of the natural light. Their independent accessibility means that the public can enjoy the landscaped areas of the interior regardless of the normal administrative opening hours. [9] The urban system of green areas is reinforced, harkening back to the organization of the nearby medieval city with its small scale spatial compressions and decompressions. The system of vertical public accesses to the roof decks, through the gardens, transforms a habitually private use into a system for public viewing of the natural surroundings and the medieval city. [10] This "Naturfice" appears as a group of aleatory spaces that allow for discovering the richness of the unexpected in an endless catalogue of connections between the natural and the artificial.

40 [1] As I'm looking over at the Ferrari dealership on Rue de Lausanne, a pair of soft hands comes up over my eyes. [2] Startled, I hear a familiar voice that takes me back to the distant past,

"You again? This is impossible!"

I turn my head, taking hold of those hands, and I see Nancy's face, framed by a colorful silk scarf. I haven't seen her in ten years and we spend a long while bringing each other up to date on our nearly parallel lives.

[3] "I came to pick up my car," she says suddenly and she adds, "It's a wedding gift from my husband, a '64 330 GT. Red!"

[4] Hiding my somewhat jealous surprise, I look to change the subject, reminding her of the last time we met unexpectedly, high up in a Mafraj. That was when she told me about the

legend of the five thousand travelers who, straying from the tourist routes, always ended up running into one another by chance in the most unexpected places. [5] Since that was the third time we had met, we decided then, under the Sana'a sun, that we were part of that select global group of professional nomads. [6] Somewhat stunned, I also remind her of the first time we met, in the Chilean desert.

"You aren't going to start up with that again, are you?! she says, furrowing her brow.

[7] After a long and uncomfortable silence, she tugs fondly at my arm and invites me to come inside. As the doors close behind us she whispers in my ear,

"Come take a ride with me! Pretend like you're my husband for a few hours."

[8] I smile at her, saying that I still believe in chance and that it's a hidden order that we don't have access to. She bursts out laughing and, a little hurt, I let fly,

"You were the one who believed in impossible encounters, or don't you remember?"

And I continue, just a bit angry,

"Nancy, we've met four times by total chance. What more do you need?"

[9] Then I tell her that I'm surprised to see her in Geneva. Her face falls when she hears that and, somewhat solemnly, she replies,

"Every phase comes to an end; it's a global world and the five thousand are a dying breed."

Standing there, as she distractedly runs her hand across the luxurious vehicle made the year she was born, I don't dare ask about the audacious documentaries she used to dream of directing. [10] Looking at her affectionately, somewhat dispirited, I sense that we won't be meeting again. [11] At that moment, I have the feeling that some people can all too easily eradicate the element of chance from their lives. And it's all a question of the price.

41 [1] Combining objects according to a series of rules for joining them together or piling them up creates random organizational structures that are independent of a pre-established form. [2] From this point of view, the search for personalization in contemporary collective housing leads to built presences that dissolve the innocuous appearance created by simply stacking up similar dwellings.

[3] In this sense, the Social Housing Building in Durango (2005) separates domestic functions that require connections to the vertical facilities networks from the others. These uses, associated with utilities, take on an introverted character that does not vary as the building rises, creating a series of small-scale functional chains related to the size of each housing unit. [4] The spiral arrangement of the different-sized units around the building's core results in an apparently random internal organization. Taking into account the number and the type of units, each of the utility chains is twisted around the central infrastructure core. [5] They make up a genetic structure without a fixed length; the necessary length can be cut off according to the heights that are permitted by regulations.

[6] Positioning this utilities chain on the site is the first step in a process intended to appropriate the landscape

(1) Unidades "autosuficientes"

Viviendas con "elementos servidores (25% de la superficie de la viv. aprox.). Son elementos vinculados al suelo (conducciones,...)

(2) Secuencia genérica funcional.

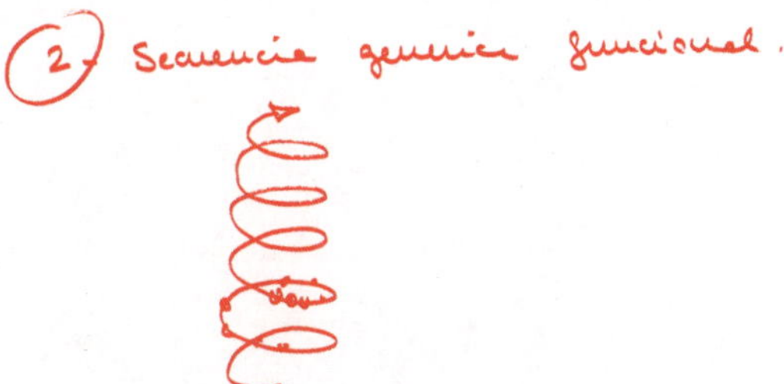

(3) Selección del fragmento de cadena en función de las necesidades requeridas.

- sup. const. ——— 11000 m².

- Total sup. cadena funcional : ≃ (25% de la sup. total).
- Nº viv. →90

18	70 m²
6	80 m²
36	110 —
30	115 .

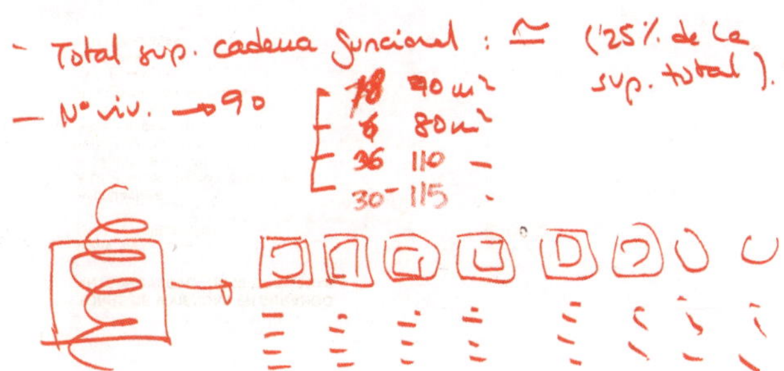

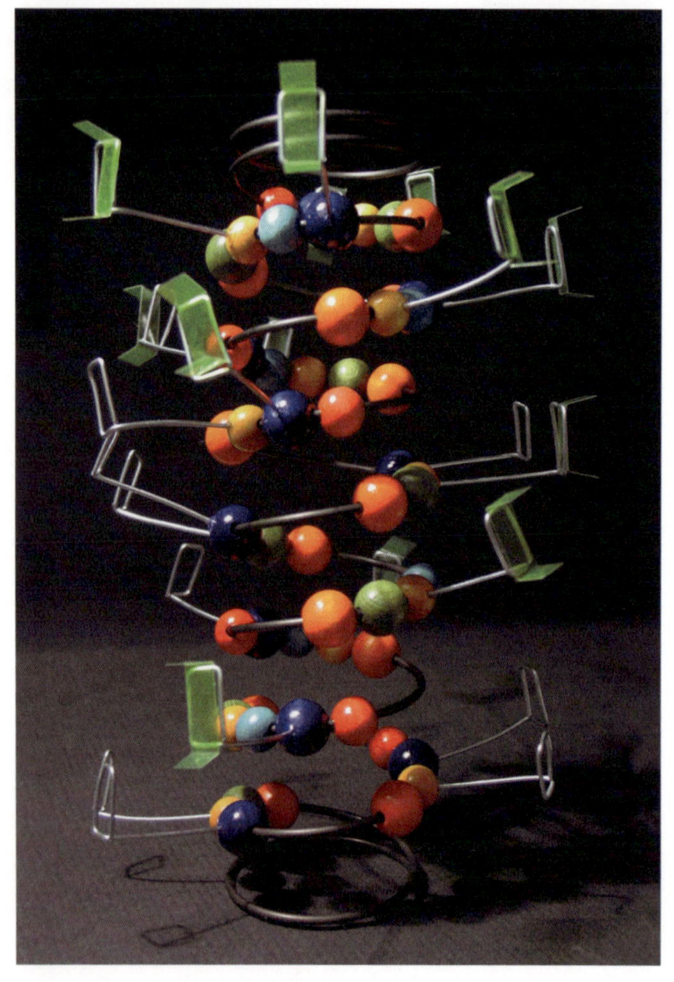

using the rooms with a more extroverted character, stimulating the exterior skin. These relationships materialize in a catalogue of openings determined with respect to where each room is situated along the height of the building, its type of use and the built obstacles that exist in the nearby surroundings. [7] The areas of the façade that relate to the far-off mountains are perforated with open observation areas; their depths are also determined by their orientation and interior uses. The areas with less private views, or where the sightlines are blocked by adjacent buildings, are fitted with smaller openings. [8] This appropriation process is undertaken for each floor independently, in response to the orientation and the stimuli from the landscape.

[9] Once this has been carried out, the building's equilibrium shows an apparent overall, yet compact, disorder resulting from the strict rules for stacking the different units and their precise sensitivity with respect to the surroundings.

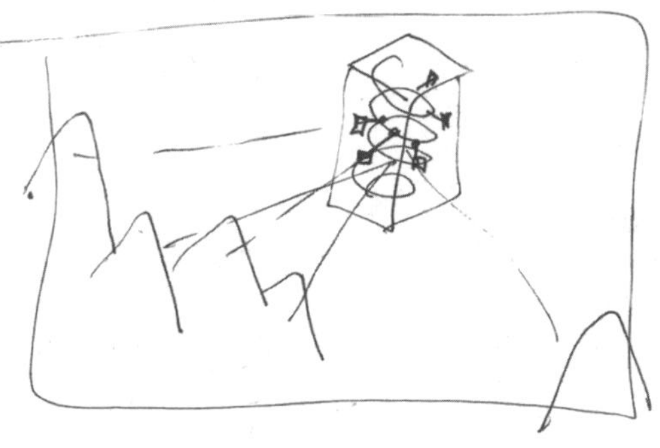

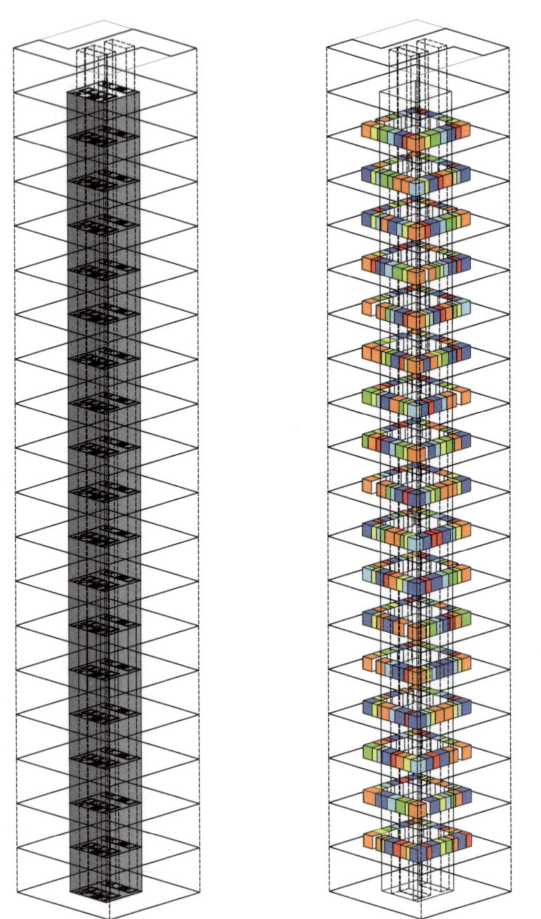

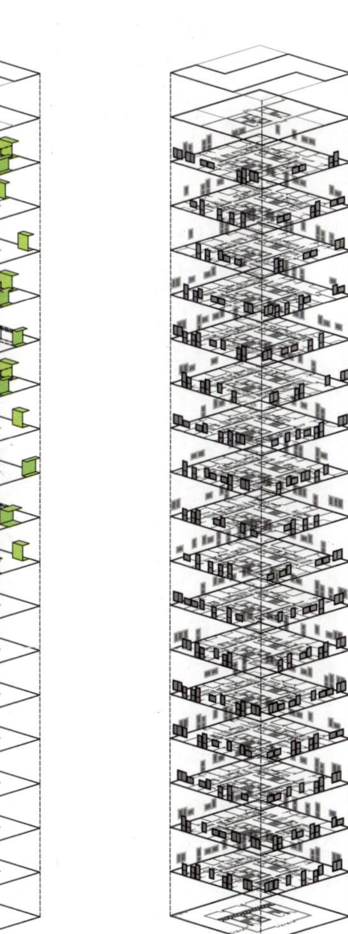
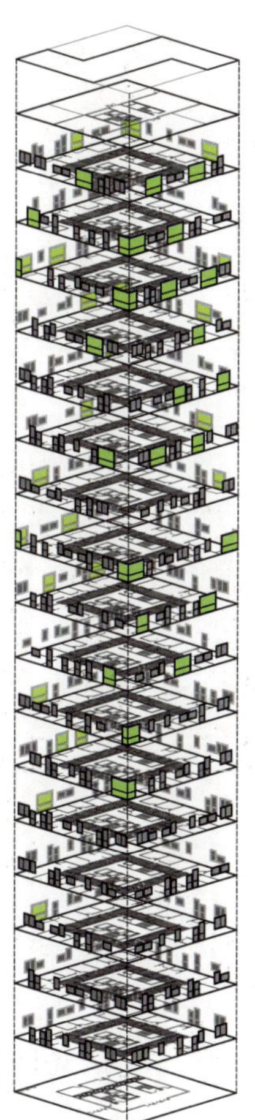

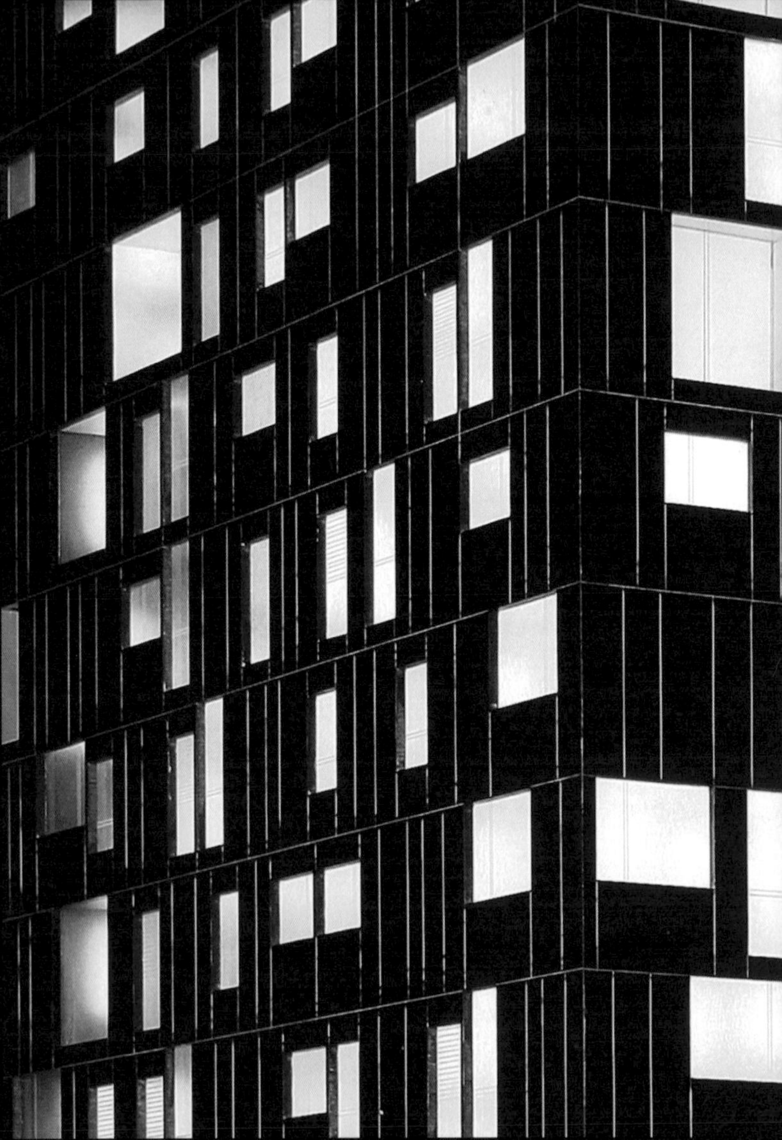

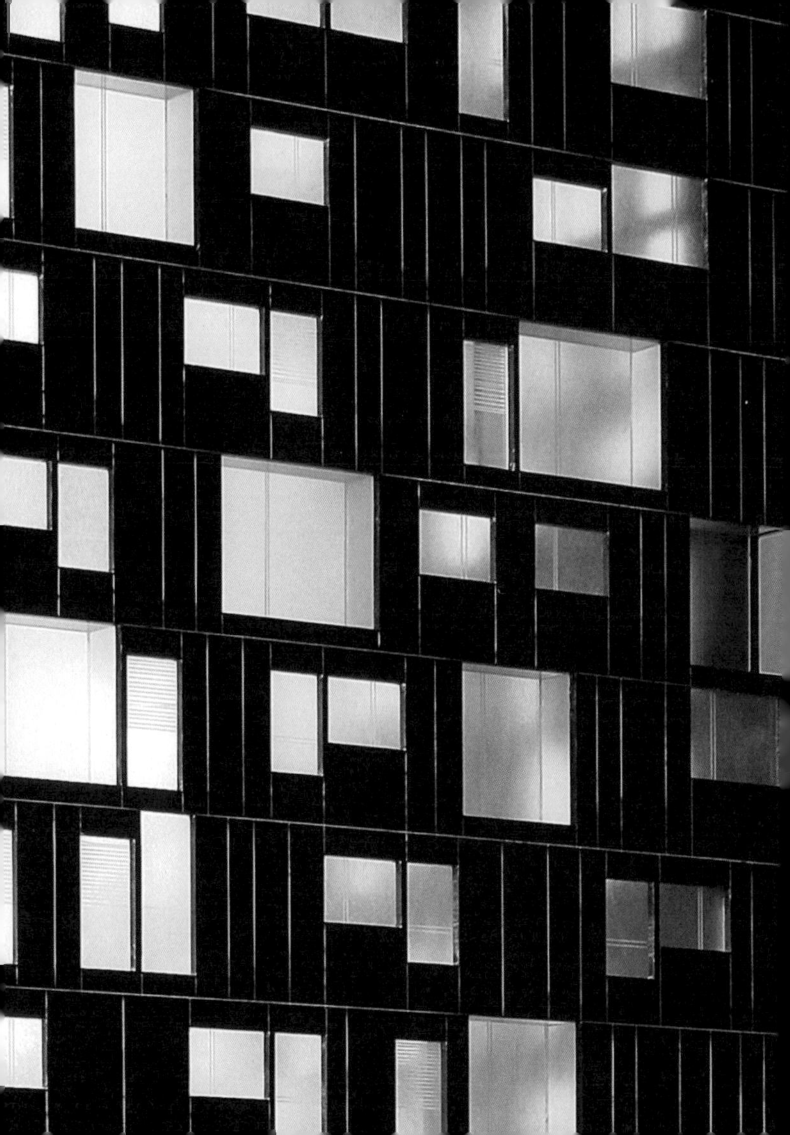

LOOK ME IN THE EYES!

"The skin is the deepest thing there is"

Paul Valéry —————————————————————

[1] The Autodrome in San Sebastián is full of the aromas of all kinds of compounds. [2] I came to the Stranglers concert, but I secretly want to see Wendy O. My friends have gotten lost and I find myself surrounded by a leather-clad crowd. [3] Amid the smoke and the impossible loud background music, we pile up in the front row like starving animals. I see faces that I recognize on people I don't know but, looking at each other, we share the dark pleasures that connect us wordlessly. We are members of the night family, restless minds who won't settle for routine and who have come together once more for their dose of otherness.

[4] On the stage, full of inquisitive darkness, silence falls suddenly, drawing howls from the eager crowd. Light shadows move like ghosts from a world that doesn't belong to us, and where we try to make out hidden figures. [5] With a dry blast of guitar, the first chords of "Butcher Baby" ring out. The uncontrollable shoving begins, the act of communion among that brainless kin.

[6] In a red flash, my secret love appears and disappears, her yellow mohawk shining. She's wearing a tiny monokini with two sharp studs over her nipples and she's bounding like a cat in heat, yowling wildly. Her presence alone fills the gigantic arena. In her obsessive hallucination she grabs a chainsaw, which she starts up violently to cut a guitar in half. [7] The sound of the body splitting and the strings flying apart seems to be in perfect accordance with the rest of the Plasmatics pack. [8] She still has the neck, like an ax, raised in her arms. With an unexpected twist of her athletic body, she starts smashing a television to the beat of the drums. Half naked and wild, I feel my blood pressure rising out of control.

9 I see myself bouncing around with the rest of them, all of us following the rhythm of the priestess of destruction. Her conscious and coordinated insanity discharges images, concepts and tremendous sensations that beat at our neurons like quantum hammers. She is the origin. Mother to everyone watching. 10 We have been reduced to little apes who unprotestingly obey her extreme and unattainable creative power. I am under her spell. I adore her.

43 1 Wittgenstein made his students look and refrain from acting, giving preference to an attitude of superiority on the part of the observer as opposed to the activist. He advocated for connecting with all of the exciting objects, colors, glimmers, movements, forms, ideas, discourses, silences, gazes and gestures that impress and inspire us with their nature.

2 In the contemporary city, thousand of complex events take place, yet hardly anyone is capable of relating with them anymore in an abstract life spattered with restrictive appearances. 3 If we distrust this superficiality, however, we can keep hold of a magic key for deciphering the world: our own way of looking at things, which we can share with others through a common semantics of sensations. 4 An interpersonal empathic relationship that brings about a close, immediate and tangible feeling of concretion associated with places and their shared use. This spatial sense brings us closer to a creatively written geography where our consciousness and the materiality that enfolds us are shown as radically different forms of existence, taking on multiple ways of life.

[5] Individual consciousness needs freedom and an active inhabitant's life involves the incorporation of this freedom into the collective need for survival. [6] This generates a way of classifying people that can be found everywhere: professions and social classes that differentiate decent and indecent people according to the degree of generosity in their gaze. The neoliberal mobs repeatedly confuse this with simplicity of character.

[7] A generous gaze, understood in this way, disengages itself from speculative space in search of new places and possibilities. It catches a glimpse of a subjective space with a latent potential that is susceptible to transformations that are not permitted by the laws and the functions of space in the pragmatic city. [8] The new geographies promote a regime of permanent attention to the territory without incorporating urban references in terms of use. They are alternative places for saving anesthetized minds that are addicted to geofinances and cyberspaces, organized as no-man's-lands but with a highly personal sensitivity. [9] These spaces are in a continuous state of discovery, due to their multiple sensory possibilities, and they transform each moment into a time where no one has been before, creating a dynamic personal understanding.

[1] Contemporary urban public space is a place where experience is unpredictable; it is full of mediation, coincidences, transitions, misunderstandings, indifference, secrets, confidences and doublespeak. Because it belongs to a complicated human community where hybridization is

generalized, it requires a certain amount of incongruity as fuel for its vitality.

[2] The unknown loiterer who uses this space is its great hope and the last bastion of resistance to functional control. His disobedience as a spontaneous passer-by allows him to leave off acting in order to perceive. [3] The space he discovers is made up of micro urban events in the form of arbitrary accidents, incidents and spectacles of emergence, the origin of which he never knows. [4] He puts together a personal psychogeography that reproduces a dynamic vision of multiple circumstances which are unpredictable and in constant transformation. Through his disorientation, he brings about the appearance of his own territories of passion. [5] The urban environment is thus configured as a process involving the dissolution and coagulation of specific experiences in cycles that are different for each person.

[6] In this expanded time of discoveries, our amazement is mingled with that of the Other; it is in that very intersection where shared collective empathy appears through the reading of the territory. [7] This feeling of emotional transference is a spontaneous act of love. Every culture and civilization recreates its own way of understanding security or the economy, but interpersonal empathy is the only unified global system unified common to all. The energy that is given off in this relationship between people and places belongs to the realm of the deepest humanity.

[8] In order to predispose the population in this direction, the earth needs to become blurred and let its hidden properties show through. [9] The creator reveals his material

graphics in an exploratory journey inspired by his curiosity for a world he does not know, but which comes alive before his eyes. Those lines, which create new landscapes, help to emphasize what is latent in the territory, turning the geography of time into a landscape. [10] Any unstable artifice, then, will form a second space-time skin where the centimeters above the crust are more important than the symmetrical ones toward the interior. Only an artificial transformative intention can allow for putting together a powerful message that can give rise to that shared empathetic amazement.

[1] Contemporary urban space is open both to the calmest **45** of citizens and to the most daring; it is where they can engage in all kinds of actions, from the contemplation of others to the most difficult of urban acrobatics.
[2] Playing an active role in the social life of the city, Pamplona's Congress Hall (1998) is defined as a variable topography of vegetation that can be used twenty-four hours a day. The exciting variations in elevation due to gentle inclines transport the population effortlessly from one viewpoint to another. [3] This sensible vibration in the ground is a reflection of the internal activity of the building's program and comes across as a collective space that has no specific instructions for use. [4] It is organized as a large-scale urban vortex that absorbs the flow of pedestrians and the views of the city along its perimeter. Depending upon how you approach it the multiple topographies have entirely different readings, from the gentle roof gardens for leisure purposes

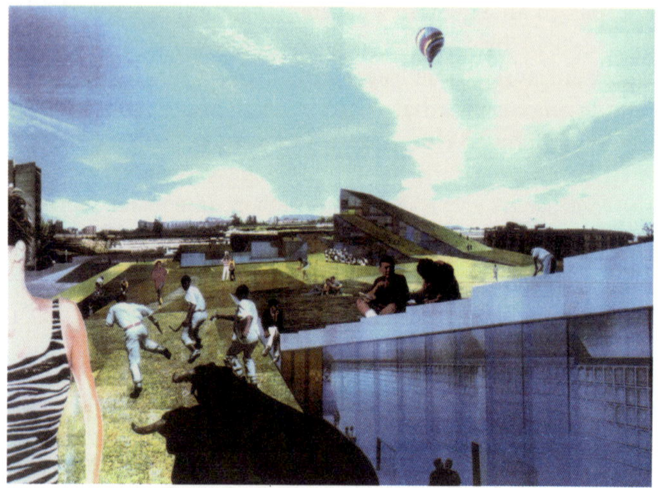

to the steeper slopes for sporting events. [5] In support of its public roof-square, the building is accessed from above through a fluid penetration that blurs the limits between inside and outside.

[6] The interior pursues the same idea of topographical vibration as the square above it, creating continuous itineraries with gentle slopes. [7] This allows for gradual discovery and recognition of the spaces and uses, filtering the surroundings through a series of chromatic crystalline formations. The chromatism reflects the internal uses on the outside, using an encrypted code that varies when the interior functions are activated, giving the building a changeable image. [8] The variation in colors on the façade generates a continually changing vision from the public space. As such,

the visual experience is never the same, maintaining the focus of attention and creating an empathetic relationship with the inhabitants.

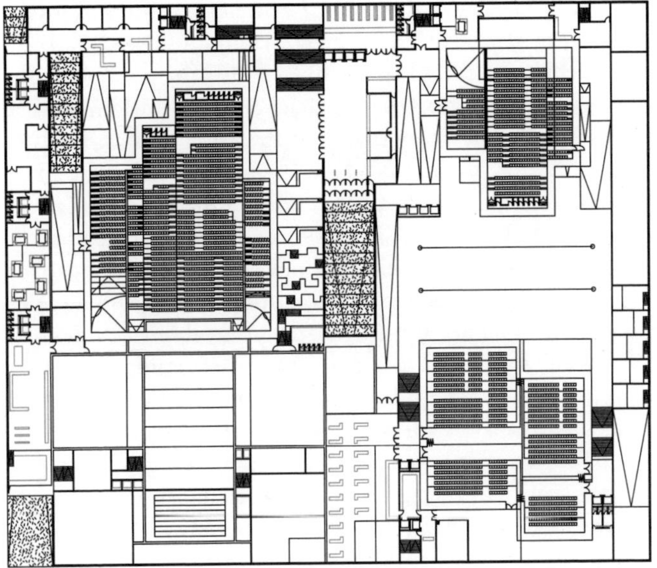

⁹ As we enter into the building, the presence of vegetation decreases and there is a progressive increment in the rigidity and hardness of the materials in response to depth, which has an effect on the sensibility of the user. The colored windows are still present, filtering the views toward the exterior, whereas the floor solidifies, commenting on the growing hardness of the underlying earth.

46 ¹ Societies in decline no longer provide the tranquil life they once promised, but a miserly one; they look to rapid and sensationalist architecture for an image to represent them. Having gone about planning with the idea that centrality is always somewhere else has resulted in a dissolution of the collective space of communication. ² Oversized densities and infrastructures recall the omnipresence of opaque power and the ever-clearer prohibition against finding and expressing the drive toward a passion for life. ³ The territory is urbanized under an aura of legality, but that is no longer a sufficient condition for society to experience gains in terms of living space or collective empathy.

⁴ In the same way, housing is pulled into a metamorphosis toward homogeneity and banality, the common denominator of common people. By virtue of an absence of details, this banalization pursues speed in construction and a lack of reflection in the decision-making process as a reflection of modern society's thirst for profit. ⁵ Habitable space drags the paradigm of the traditional family along with it and suffers from sad nomenclatures like four bedrooms, three bathrooms, etc. This reduces the inhabitants' choices to a simple selection of decorative elements from any furniture store catalog worldwide. In this vital trap, the creative possibilities of the individual decline and he ends up looking into the mirror of the Other instead of turning his gaze inward. Then, the individual loses himself and repudiates the roof over his own head, beginning a compulsive hatred for architecture from the inside out.

⁶ Faced with this situation, the creator can only deploy all of his social responsibility that is founded on safeguarding

people's dignity. As a producer of empathy he has to move beyond the function of protection against the elements to incorporate the production of the possibility for social relationships. [7] He even has the duty, like music does, to work toward curbing our unconsciousness of animality. [8] Peter Sloterdijk tells us how we, as frustrated animals, are condemned to be humans; this dignity is the specific value of those who have experienced a conscious awakening toward the Other. Its application to habitable space is society's best tool for motivating the functions and capabilities of reunion and relation. [9] We cannot forget about the interests of the innumerable anonymous men and women who strive day after day toward intense freedom.

[1] People who have decided to live in the same place rarely **47** know one another beforehand. But there are hidden characteristics, interests and shared economic situations that underlie that choice. [2] Far from signifying a classist selection, it can lead to the discovery of a common denominator, which can spark its development and joint social evolution. The space of their desires acts, then, as a powerful mediator for their empathic relationships. [3] As such, all space should tend to emphasize the sociability of its users with dream-like possibilities for relationships among the people who share it.

[4] From this point of view, the principal virtue of living up high is the possibility of seizing on far-away horizons that activate places of calm and daydreaming in our lives, separating them from the grey moments of routine.

5 A series of common squares, located at different heights, bring different horizons into the Social Housing in Valencia (2006) corresponding to each position and orientation inside the building. The nearby landscape of vegetable gardens, the historic city, the port or the sea on the horizon on sunny days are absorbed for their shared enjoyment. 6 These semi-public elements are allocated specific uses and activities, making up a mini vertical city with an avenue of elevators that connects the successive squares together. The building's directional volume and its different orientations mean that none of the spaces have the same lighting or thermal qualities.

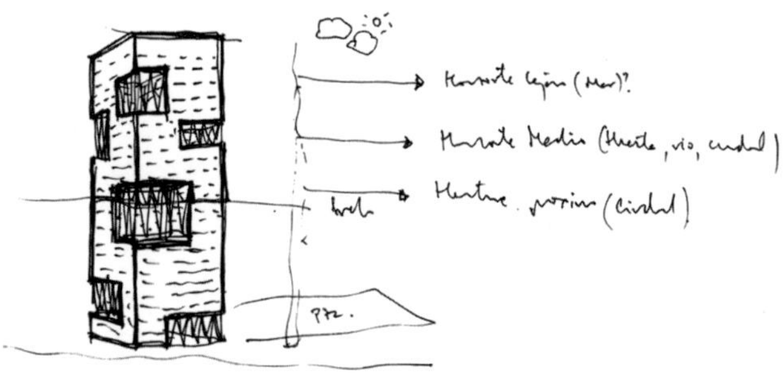

7 The program and the times of use assigned to each space are varied and characteristic. There are different moments for socializing in the beach solarium, the games for children and for seniors, or on the miniature golf course, establishing an empathetic promiscuity among the inhabitants. 8 The use of these spaces as meetings places and for keeping track

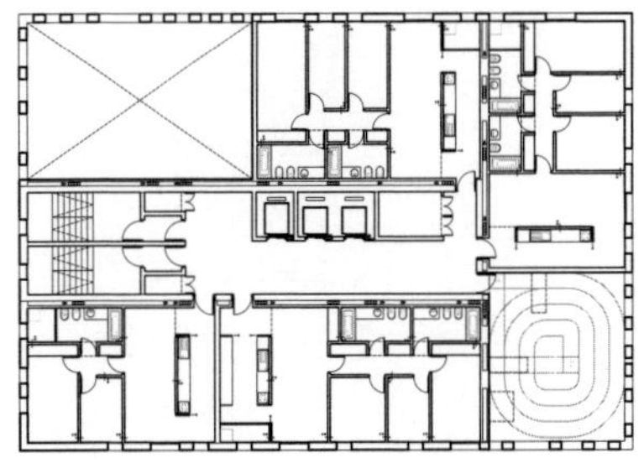

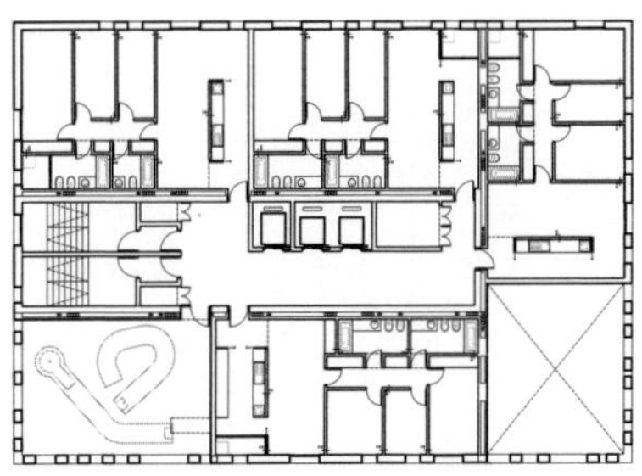

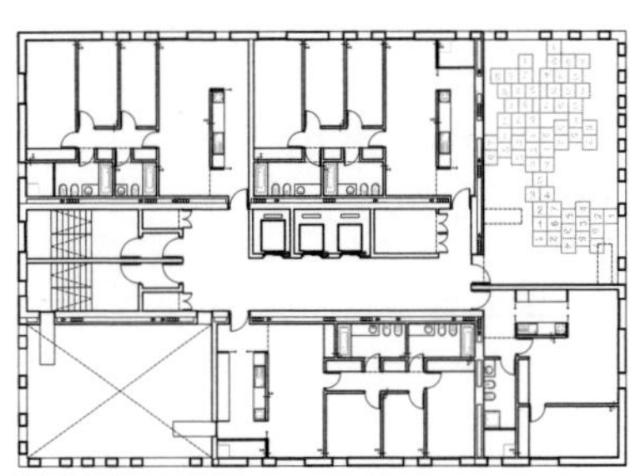

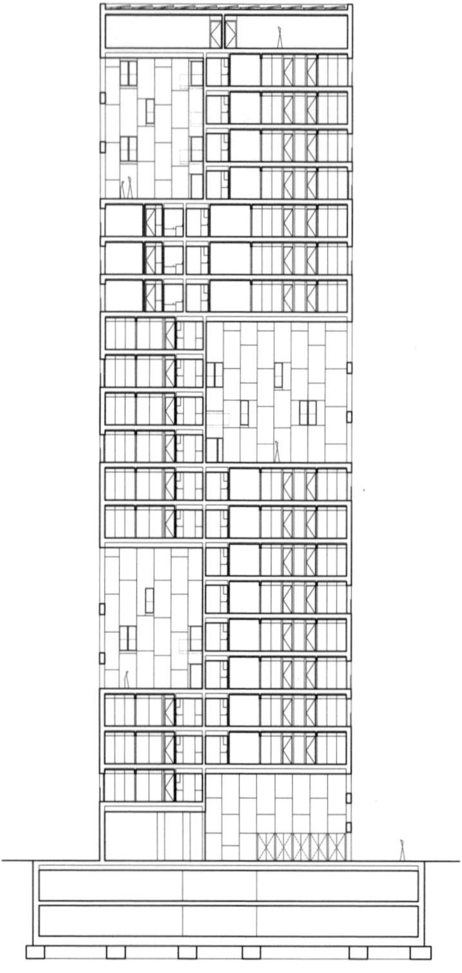

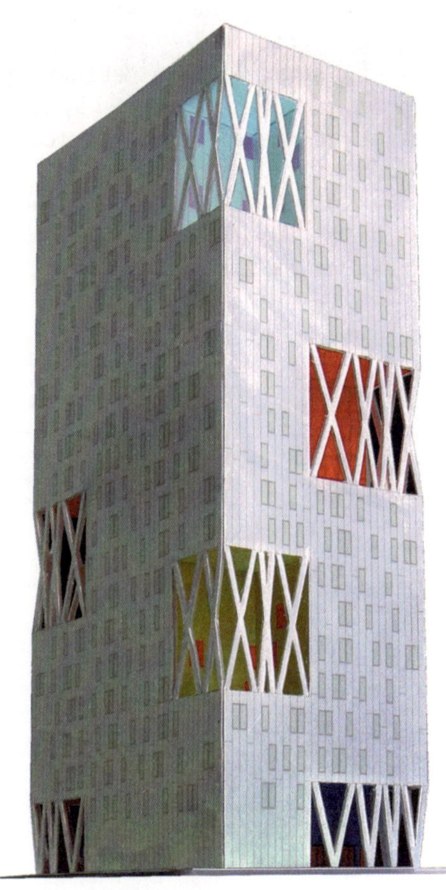

of children is broadened by the presence of the interior apartment balconies which look down over them. [9] Each empty space has two structural sides that filter the distant landscape and two sides that are marked by the presence of spaces that jut out from the dwellings, creating visual relationships in all directions. [10] The result of this axial-centrifugal organization with respect to the landscape creates an image that manages to dissolve the domestic scale of the dwelling in favor of an understanding of the building as a space for collective relationships, beyond the scope of predefined formal values.

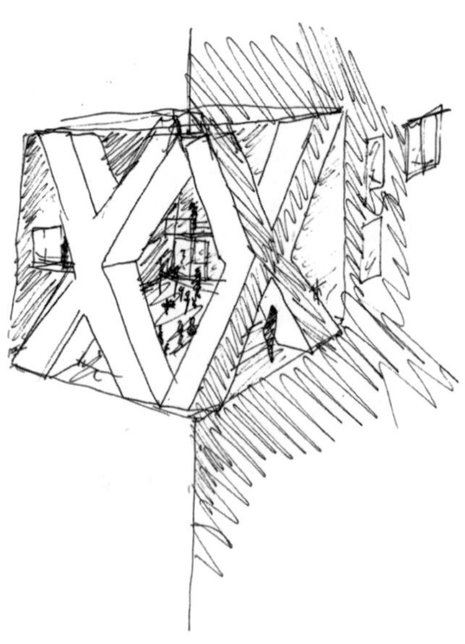

[1] "Hey, it's my flashlight" I say to nobody, still half asleep. I pick it up, smiling, imagining who must have left it on the table. Sitting on the cabin terrace, I look out at the crystal clear waters, remembering how it was stolen the night before in an embarrassing way. [2] Since my arrival in Romblon, the howler monkeys have accompanied me everywhere, always present among the trees, moving closer then shying away. Over a period of days, I've managed to recognize a braver male, with a black back, who forays in among the people. He steals food and has a good time startling the adults. Last night it was my turn.

[3] While I was quietly drinking a beer, the monkey sprung rapidly onto the table and stole my Maglite. Before I could even react he was up at the top of a palm tree. For some strange reason he knew how it worked, because I could see intermittent flashes shooting back and forth among the trees. Each burst of light was accompanied by rhythmic howls. [4] After I'd tried to chase him for a while, the owner of the place told me I might as well give up.

"Nobody can catch Rico," she exclaimed, smiling.

[5] This morning I'm making guacamole, using the avocados from a tree in the garden, to go with some packaged nachos, as I watch Pía floating magically over a nothingness tinted light blue. [6] As I'm mashing the avocado I hear a rustling in the reeds above my head. Keeping a safe distance, Rico climbs down one of the posts, looking at me insistently. He moves toward the table with his head down, like someone who knows he's done wrong, and pushes the flashlight toward me with his fingers.

"Yeah, I saw that you brought it back," I say.

I offer him a corn chip piled high with avocado and, after doubting for a second, he grabs it quickly and puts it in his mouth. As he chews messily, he moves closer, casually. [7] Without really knowing what I'm doing, I open my arms and, with one agile move, he leaps up against my naked chest. Following a behavior acquired from his ancestors, though he probably doesn't even know what it means, he begins to remove invisible insects from the hair on my chest and my head. Every now and then, he pretends to put something in his mouth and then looks up at me for a moment until I nod. We go on like that for a long while, trading insects and guacamole, until he considers that we've made our peace. [8] Then he pushes away violently and, standing on the table-top he lets out a savage shriek that makes me shudder. Immediately, he runs his hand across my cheek with an unsuspected gentleness and I think,

"I get it. We're friends, but you're stronger than I am."

49   [1] Our brain has two hemispheres with well-defined abilities. The information we receive from the outside world is treated selectively: the left half controls rational processes, whereas the right half deals with animistic and emotional perceptions. [2] Their collaborative struggle determines our personal character and the way we take on the world. [3] Both sides of the brain work simultaneously although at present, with knowledge guided by scientificism, the right side has been relegated to an inferior situation and along with it our most primitive creativity and intuition.

⁴ The right hemisphere governs our relationship with words and the definition of emotion and it is what helps us to interpret the immaterial elements hidden in reality. It is the part of our body that develops and understands our empathetic relationship with others. ⁵ That makes it an expert in controlling how we move through space and our relationships with the people we meet there. It is a kind of internal GPS that instantaneously detects what is occurring around us and how we integrate into that whole. ⁶ It controls how we read empty spaces in reality and can fill them up with the powerful force of creativity and invention. In short, it is what gives us the courage to take on the unknown, beyond the reach of reason.

⁷ On the opposite side, the left hemisphere is in charge of producing fear as a detector and limiter of our recklessness. It is entrusted with the combination of words through the reasoned complexity of language and it handles logic problems. ⁸ It stores our capacity for memory where it can be safe from the creative and emotional digressions of its twin. It is the part where nothing ever occurs without prior confirmation and where every act is ordered pending demonstration by virtue of laws and objective data.

⁹ In a new era, where sensitivity toward the planet and a focus on the adversity suffered by our fellow men have again become a powerful social motor, it seems evident that the right half should dominate brain function. ¹⁰ As a result, our decision-making will not be allied exclusively with personal benefit and we can leave behind our selfishness in favor of a more empathetic reading of the people before us. This generosity seems somewhat strange to us in a statis-

tical world of market laws that has left it fatally exposed to extermination.

50 ¹ One of the pursuits of architecture is the power to solve problems of a social or psychological nature, like abuse or drug addiction, helping to redirect socially excluded individuals. ² A creative system that extends beyond space and materials can allow for incorporating an analysis of future inhabitants' personal problems.

³ Evaluating and assimilating them gives rise to the characteristics for planning the Therapeutic Housing in Valencia (2003), directed at creating specific situations intended to improve empathy and social adaptation. ⁴ The problems corresponding to each type of inhabitant are classified by determining their Physical, Economic, Mental and Social information which, in combination, provides a given

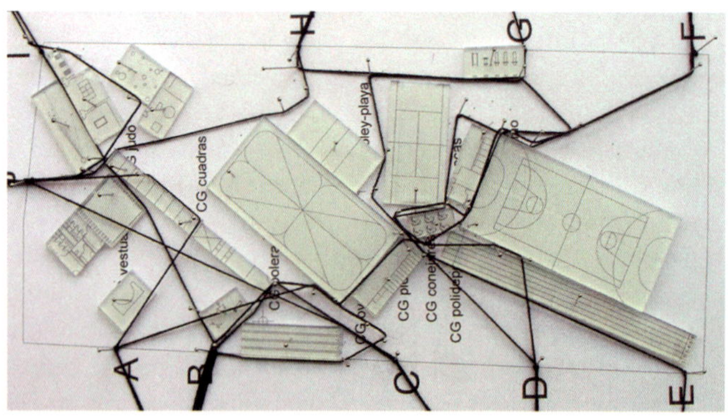

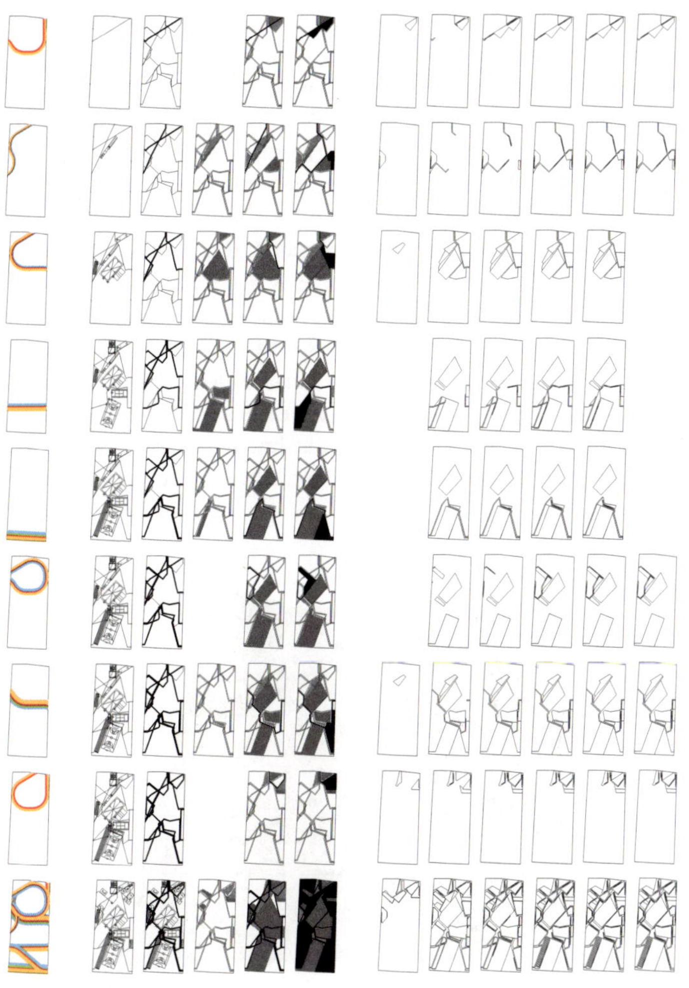

P.E.M.S. coefficient for each user. [5] Then users are associated with specific programs and spaces that allow for supplementing their shortages with occupations directed at improving their quality of life and their positive empathy toward others. This collective structure of relational morphology and precise programming acts as a decanter for their personal problems.

[6] In order to establish how these therapeutic dwellings will be lived in, each inhabitant is allocated a vegetable garden, a productive animal or a pet, and a system for moving around the habitable surroundings where the maximum incline is eight percent. The surface area of the dwelling is also defined, making it equal to the area of the associated productive garden. [7] The accompaniment program includes a variety of animals and the installations necessary for

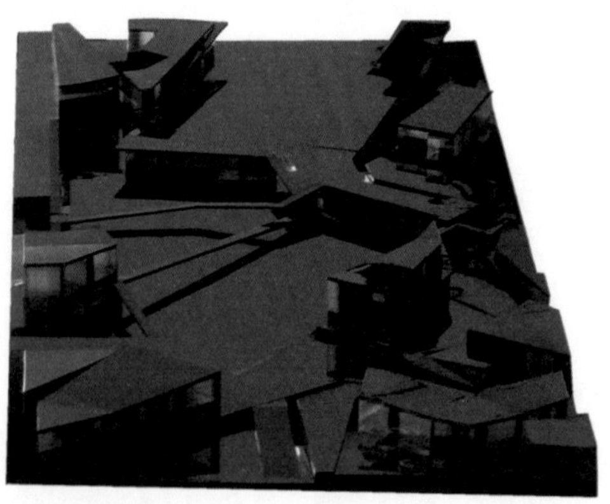

their care, as well as a series of shared playing fields to provide a quality of life in accordance with the expectations for improvement.

[8] The planning establishes a geometric layout of channels that connect with the rest of the city of Sociópolis, activating a number of different directions. The relationship between the P.E.M.S. characteristics associated with each use and the characteristics of the channels in the master plan is used to adapt generic dwellings and their associated exterior spaces. [9] This geometry around the sports activities defines the optimum locations for each group of dwellings and their access routes. [10] The resulting urban space proposes multiple possibilities for community activities and for relationships among inhabitants, aimed at promoting of their shared empathy.

[1] Among the types of large accumulations of people, an **51** audience is an example of a distribution in which people want to be near a specific idol. To that end, they move from one place to another in flows that group together characters with similar interests. [2] These are nearly closed-off systems with intrinsic variables that can have an influence on dissuading specific individual conduct. [3] A critical mass with a shared sense of empathy is the starting point for a dynamic reaction that can generate spaces for interaction, by grouping together individuals and increasing their social presence.

[4] Swarm theory effectively explains the combinatorial analysis of all of the elements that generate an artificial form

of intelligent space. Fragmentary knowledge about these groups explains their behavior without having to rely on the complexity of the inhabitant, who appears decentralized and with no leadership capability. [5] Positive feedback associated with a specific behavior generates the automatic organization of the group, absorbing its random fluctuations, which create multiple unexpected interactions, into the grouping process itself. The swarm understood in this way possesses a collective empathy, in that each settler maintains his conduct; in turn, that influences the organization of the colony, due to the high connectivity among the settlers.

[6] In the case of mass performances, the guidelines for social behavior lose their usefulness and take on their own language as the condition for a symbolic group. Group members are trained in the obedience of the passive observer, preventing them from reflecting on truly important social issues. [7] This collective attitude gives rise to an irrational loyalty as training in the subordination to power and it feeds into antisocial aspects of human psychology.

[8] From this point of view, the famous Solomon syndrome shows that societal pressure conditions us more than we imagine. It demonstrates that when it comes to individual decision-making, given specific behavior within a group we tend to avoid standing out or attracting attention as a protective measure. [9] And, in the same way, we sabotage ourselves in order to stick to the routine road of the majority. But that only reflects a lack of personal self-esteem in the belief that our worth depends on how other people see us. [10] The decision between Solomonic masses and the empathetic group does not have to do with social class, but with the

type of people involved; those who are content in their vulgarity and those who aspire to break away from it through shared sentiment.

[1] When incorporating an artificially manipulated nature **52** into space, it is difficult to preserve the emotional message that it transmits to man in its wild state. [2] But, this degree of lost empathy can be resolved using unexpected spatial or lighting properties that activate the user's emotional perception of the new nature. [3] From this standpoint, a place that looks to give soccer back its primitive character of a sport played in nature has to incorporate those properties with an emphatic presence.

[4] In a rectangular plot defined by a master plan without any self-esteem, a system of visual-emotional behavior is established between the user and a number of manipulated natural values. The Lasesarre Stadium in Barakaldo (2000–2004) lays out a continuous space between the grandstands and the playing field that allows for seating that is surrounded by grass, blurring the disciplined limits between

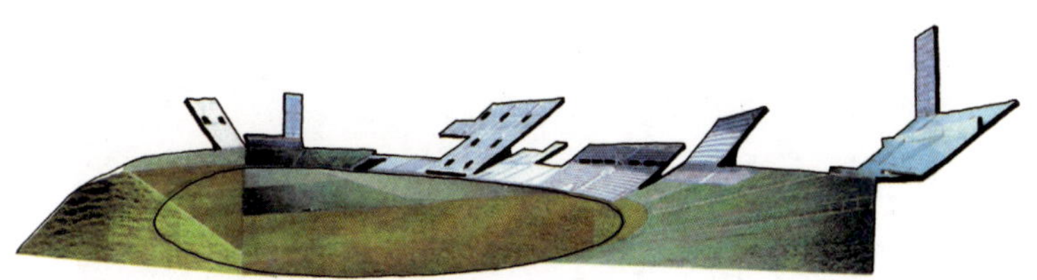

the active player and the obedient spectator. [5] The multiple angles for watching from above and from a distance, along with the distribution of spectators into controlled groups, shape the bleachers into different folds and inclines. [6] The particular inclusion of grass in each one generates a catalogue of autonomous mini-buildings, which house their own services and accesses. [7] Grouping them together creates a random set that functions as a space for catharsis on the weekends, but which can also be rented out partially by inhabitants for group meetings.

[8] In order for the spectacle to maintain social fascination at all times, a chromatic mirage based on the combination of seven colors peoples the bleachers with silent spectators, giving off a message of an unreal fullness. [9] The apparent

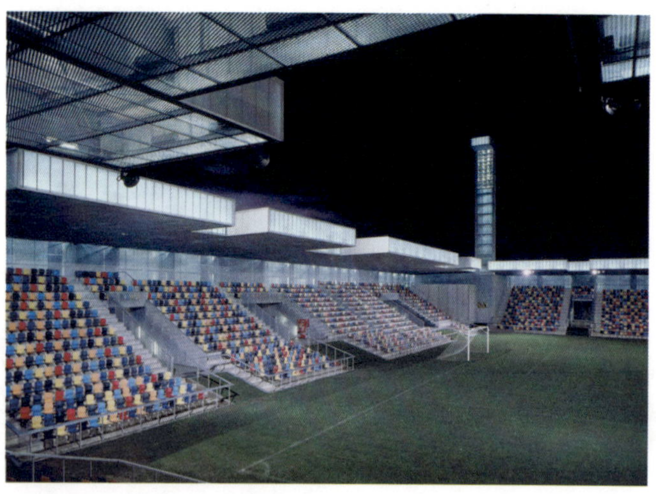

unity is provided by the roof, which lets light through and is the direct reflection of the internal organization, cut away so that rain can fall into the interior gardens. It stretches out toward the exterior, protecting the street and the stadium exits with arrhythmic folds that are the translation of the independent operation of each set of bleachers. [10] Under it, a counter-vandalism skin reproduces the luminous variations of a dense wood, warning passersby that they are entering into an atypical geography.

[11] At dusk, the translucent volume is transformed into wrinkled energy and constitutes a new luminous topography with a high level of collective empathy. It becomes an object with varying lighting conditions that acts as a beacon in the darkness, while it broadcasts its significance as a new exciting emblem.

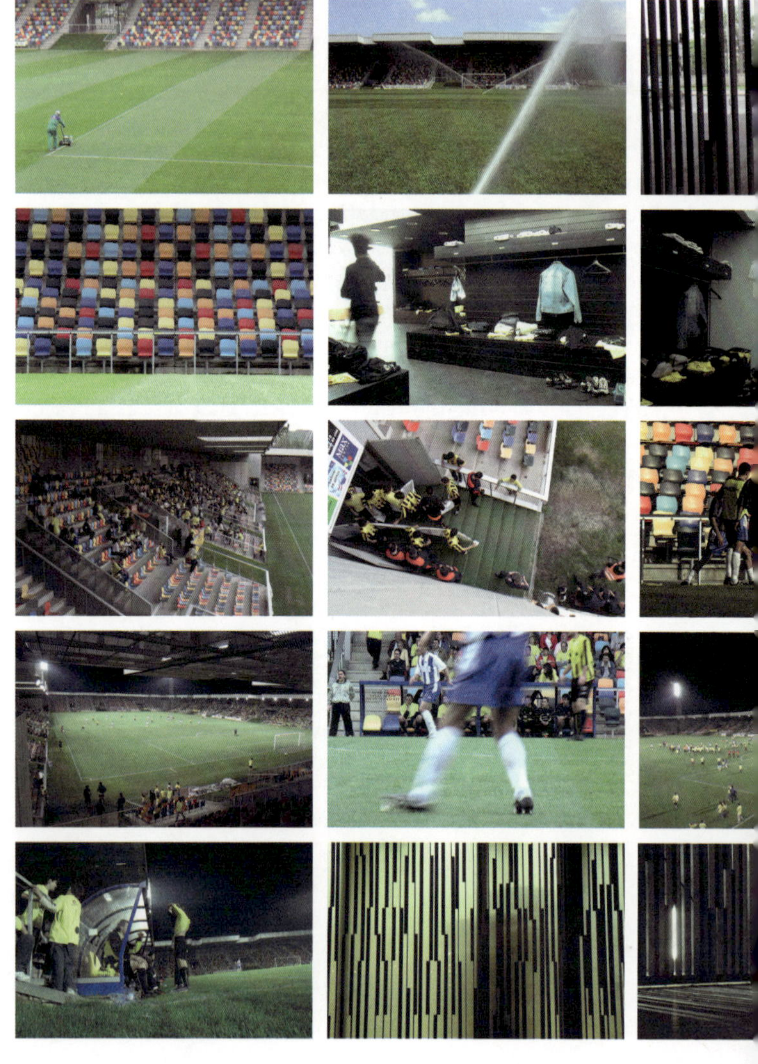

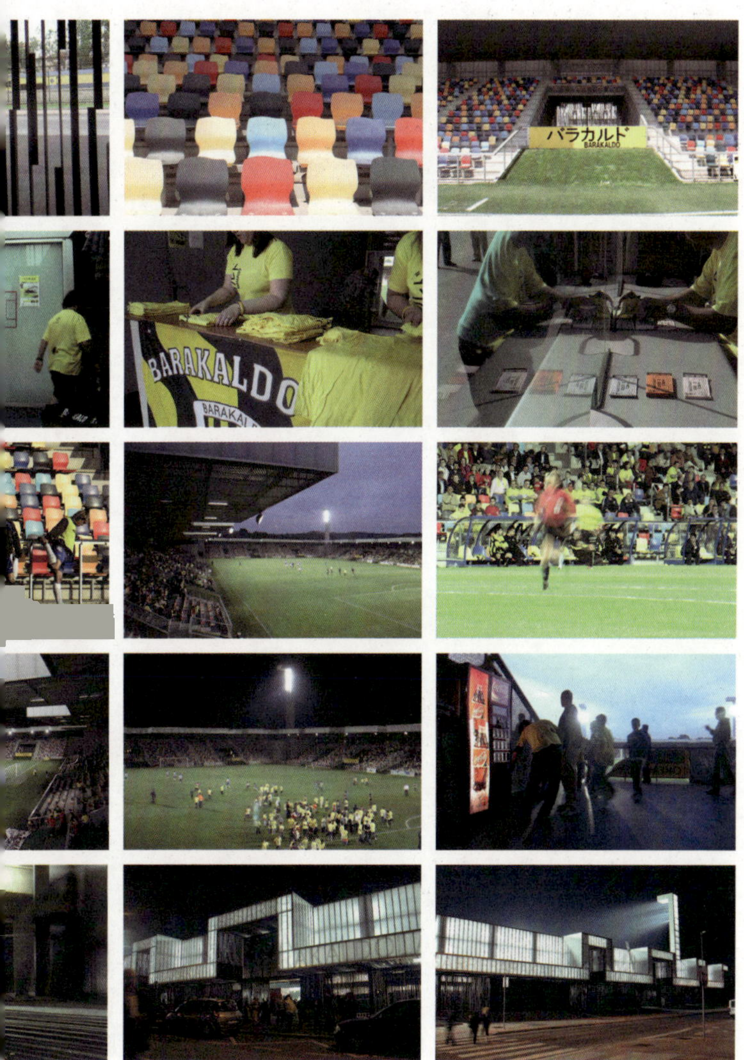

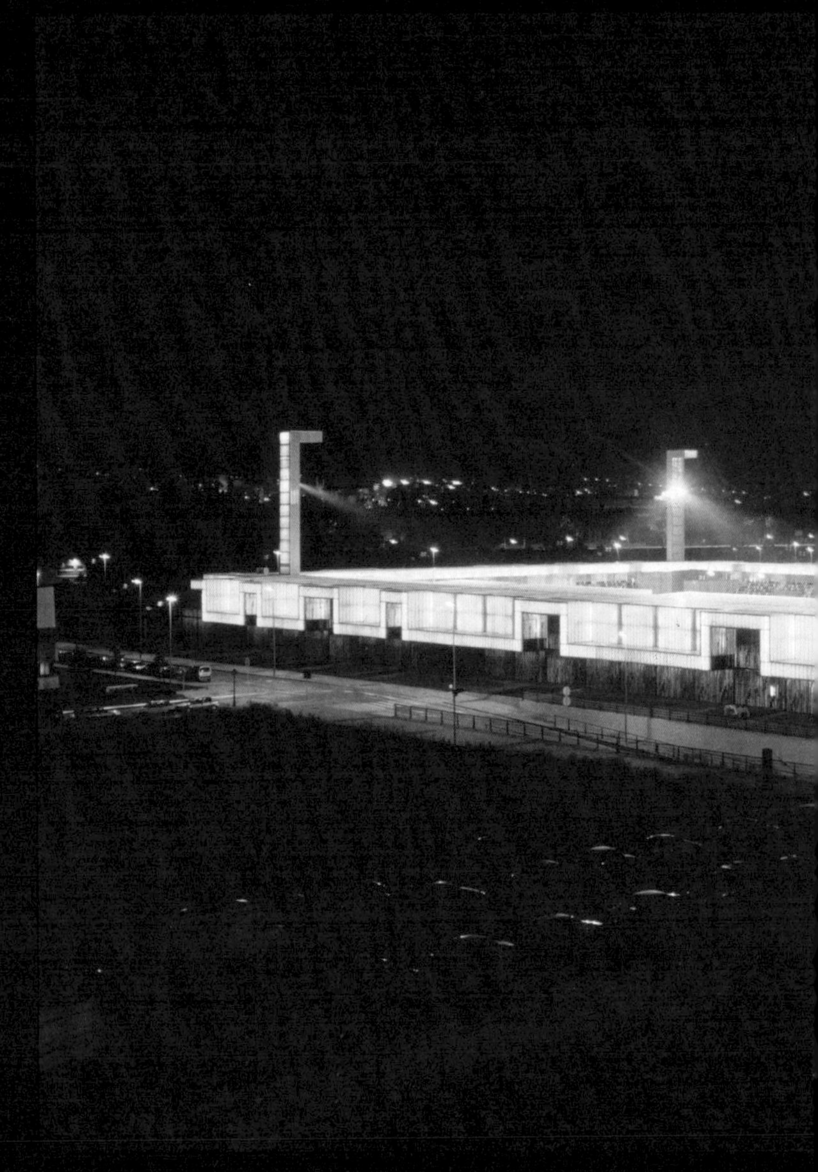

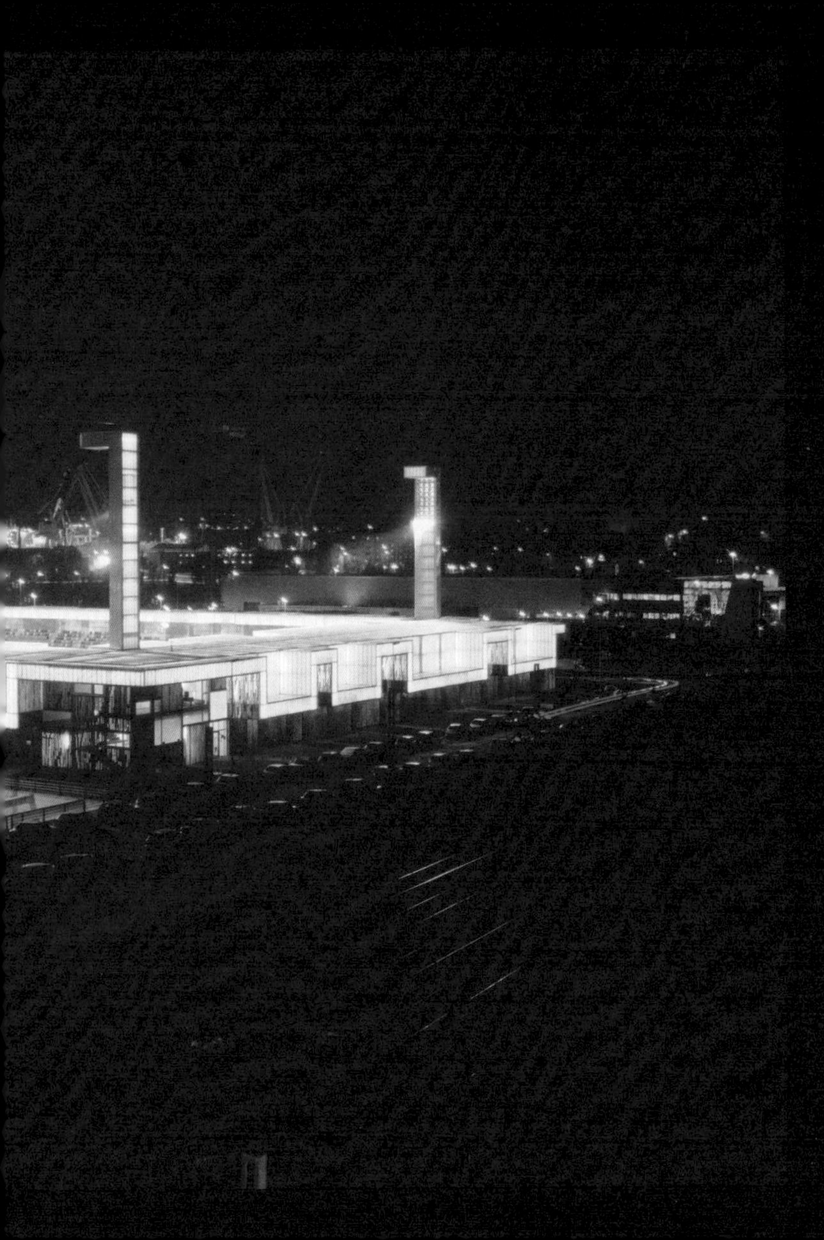

OUR PASSIONS ARE THE MEASURE OF TIME

"Distances used to be greater because space is measured in time"

Jorge Luis Borges ————————————————

¹ They've closed the airport in Lhasa and it seems like I'm going to have to spend the winter in Tibet. ² Walking through the dusty streets, I run into a Frenchman and we smile at one another, knowing we're in the same situation. At a bar near Norbulingka we share our stories. ³ Philippe is an engineer who carries a heavy weight on his conscience:

"You know, I design the computer systems used to guide the weapons on Leopard tanks."

Unfazed, I let him continue, sensing that there is another confession under the surface.

"So I'm responsible for thousands of deaths each year, all over the planet," he says, hanging his head.

Then he murmurs that he escapes to Tibet three months out of every year to cleanse himself of his job perfecting algorithmic artillery,

"My time here is enough. It's so in depth that the period I spend in Paris flies by. I miscalculated and the Amdo plain took me longer than I thought," he says, making excuses.

⁴ I tell him that after weeks touring monasteries I'm tired of eating tsampa and drinking buttered tea. I'm in a hurry to get to Kathmandu, the closest airport.

⁵ "But you'll have to cross the Himalayas!" he exclaims.

I tell him that I've talked with some mountain guides who are willing to lead me over and I ask if he'd like to come along for the crossing.

⁶ After three days of intense cold our jeep arrives in Tingri, the base used by mountaineers to climb Everest. The easy part of the trip is over. From there, it's seven more days in a yak caravan until we cross through the pass. At night, the thick-furred animals huddle against our tents, which makes

the extreme temperatures easier to bear. [7] During the sunny days, above the clouds, our smiles light up. The vision is brightened by the sight of the white peaks pointed to by the colored scraps printed with Tibetan prayers, chanting in the wind. [8] The shining horseman in the lotus flower. When we arrive at the border, an ATV takes us to Kathmandu, in what feels like tropical heat, and we move off eagerly in the direction of the hotel.

[9] The ten days of the crossing, however, feel like a much longer beautiful time. My companion looks content, but I can read the hidden sadness in his eyes as he draws closer and closer to his Leopard. With our dirty beards and stinky clothes, the clerk only decides to give us rooms after we've shown him our credit cards and Western passports. [10] Soaking in a hot bath at the Sheraton, time relaxes and returns to its usual rhythm.

54 [1] Marcel Proust finishes off the final volume of his extensive work with a defense of the importance of man's passage through space and the intimate union of that act with the unfolding of his days on Earth. [2] The importance he awards to the Man's size with respect to a place is something that we understand intuitively but which we exercise very seldom: the priority of people over objects and, by extension, the priority of days stitched together in time over existing material space. This vision puts forth an obvious mechanism for differentiating between what belongs to the thread of time and what only participates in the moment and then disappears when it has passed.

[3] Detecting atemporality has become a forensic task requiring the scalpels of skeptical criteria sharpened by distant reflection. Objects that relate with time in an aseptic way are recognized as the ones that still stir up passions after the fleeting moment of their actuality has passed. Once the reasonable period of creative surprise has elapsed, the message they carry survives even after the social conditions that surrounded them have disappeared. [4] This symptom of a continuous contemporaneity is what lends proximity and admiration to those things that are never and yet always in fashion. The heavy veil of affected languages that correspond to each moment fogs our understanding of the concept of actuality, carving away at its independence and enslaving it to the redeeming platitude of belonging to our time.

[5] In this sense, Zygmunt Bauman points to the introduction of consumer logic as the explanation for the volatility of everything, devaluing durability and eliminating the perseverance of skeptical individuals who fling themselves into that fleeting spectacle instead. [6] Applied to the pragmatic professional who belongs to his time, he becomes an illusion full of volatile and homogenizing productive routines, as opposed to the timeless concretion of true creative will. [7] Despite the sophistication of image-rich media aimed at concealing this creative non-existence, the give-away always comes when the built spectacle reveals its disconnection from timelessness. [8] This makes it easier to distinguish between unpretentious craftsmen who believe in the transcendence of their work and professionals who are only focused on media emphasis.

55 [1] A Ducati 986 is a near-perfect machine with a V-twin engine, yet its homogeneous and constant power would be unusable without its sophisticated gearbox. [2] The six gears make up a system that adapts the constant gradient of the revolutions to the capacity for creating a variety of sensations and types of perception. Each gear is associated with a range of speeds determined by the development of its geometry. The interval depends directly on the absorption of the motor's revolutions as it releases more or less power. [3] The margin offered by each gear constitutes its variation in emotional intensity, which increases along with the amount of horsepower that is consumed. Control over the situation, and therefore over the exterior reality, follows the same proportional progress. [4] As such, taking a curve at high speed requires a clear mind and heightened instincts, since the driver's life can hang in the balance.

[5] With a more focused mind, however, we realize that an increase in passionate intensity does not lie only in the speed of movement; meaning that the time our perception requires is not compressed the faster we move. Just the opposite, this intensity is seen with the need for paying immediate attention when there is an increase in the concentration of events that have to be controlled. [6] Travelling along a mountain road that has a series of curves with different intensities demands a complex variation in the gears in order to adapt to the variability of the terrain using an expanded range of revolutions. [7] Within these margins, concentrated time acts as a motor for our senses, sharpening our sensations into an essential point. [8] We can see, therefore, that speed, although it may be the most direct rela-

tionship between space and time, is not the ultimate generator of passion. There are other factors related to our internal sensory perceptions that are the real compressors of time. The counterpart to that perceptive self-control is the revolution of our sensitivity.

[9] Increased risk makes our perceptions of the world more productive, creating lasting images and sensations that draw their power from the creation of a new altered state of consciousness. [10] As the instability of the world is revealed, routine time is neutralized and it transforms us, pushing our minds toward a different, more elastic kind of time.

[1] There is a functional time that can be measured quantitatively and another emotional time that can only be measured qualitatively. [2] Objective time is expressed in the hours during which a specific space is used, whereas subjective time is expressed in the emotional intensity with which we use it. [3] The combination of the two produces a statistical time which lets us evaluate the subjective parameters that correspond to built spaces. [4] The representation of this statistical time, which brings together the first two, presents a clear difficulty in terms of measurement, since the two times in question consist of a measurable period and an emotional aspect that cannot be quantified. The times of use that correspond to each space in the Pamplona Congress Hall (1998), combined with the emotional intensity of those uses, provide us with the statistical size of the object.

[5] Reading a distribution using traditional systems of representation is always fascinating for its sterility in transmit-

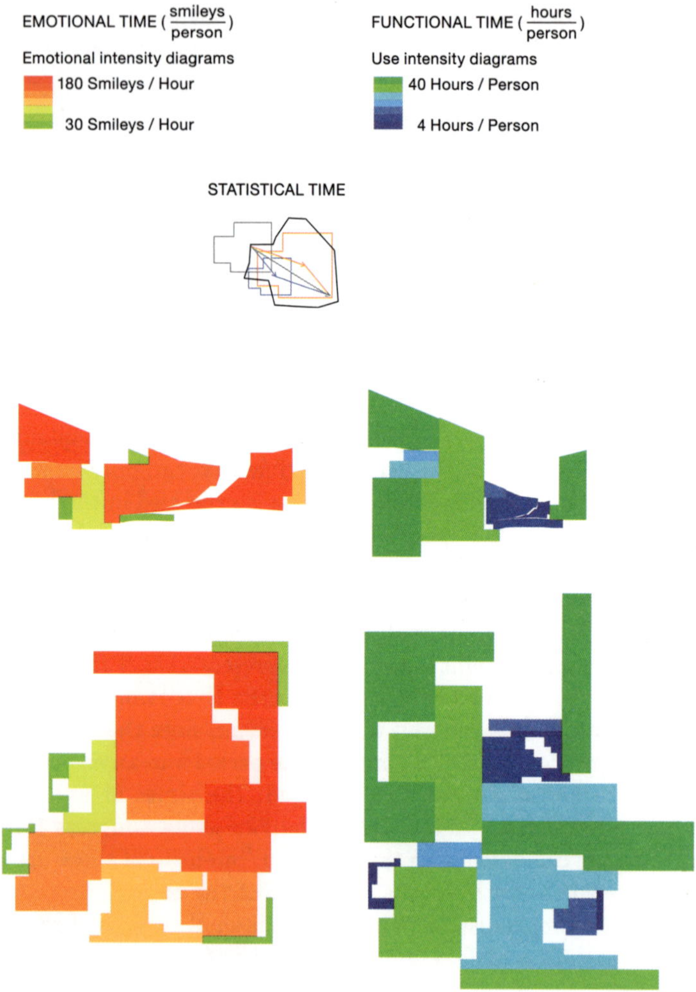

EMOTIONAL TIME ($\frac{smileys}{person}$)

Emotional intensity diagrams

180 Smileys / Hour

30 Smileys / Hour

FUNCTIONAL TIME ($\frac{hours}{person}$)

Use intensity diagrams

40 Hours / Person

4 Hours / Person

STATISTICAL TIME

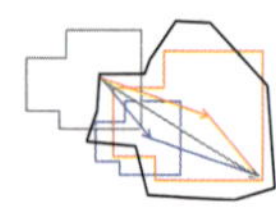

ting the emotional intensity of the space in question. The graphics do not include time directly in their expressions, much less the specificity of the spatial seduction. [6] These systems of representation can, however, be enriched by the incorporation of information that includes both the times of use for each program and the intensity produced by their contemplation. [7] Blending together these two series of functional and emotional data leads to a diagrammatic series that relates the initial space with each of the times described. This leads to a deformation of the traditional information

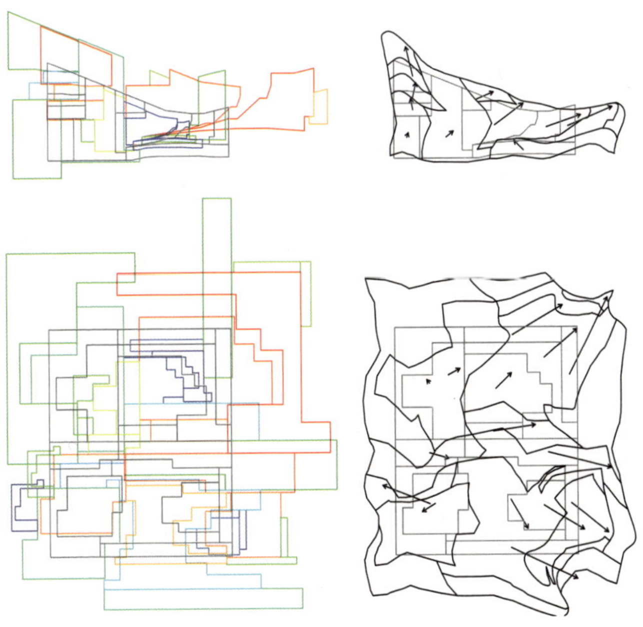

through a range of transformational units. [8] In one case, the hours of use per person for each space and, in another, the "emoticons" or units of spatial amazement.

[9] However, the fusion of these two times cannot be undertaken as a simple addition because the systems use two different units; it has to be the product of the forces as they operate simultaneously in each space. As such, a vectorial result, and not a dimensional one, unifies the two types of time in order to represent the statistical time. [10] By applying each vector sum to the original information, in a process that modifies it, a new system of representation is determined in which each space provides a simultaneous reading of the physical characteristics and its temporal and sensible uses.

57   [1] Einstein confirmed that space and time are modes that we use for thinking, as opposed to conditions that we live under. [2] As such, they do not exist as we understand them; there are only events as a conjunction of both. [3] It is strange to accept that the universe has many dimensions, some of which are closed off to our direct perception. It also takes a serious mental effort to imagine a space with so many dimensions, where time is just one more, perpendicular to the space that we are used to dealing with. [4] It is hard to comprehend that time is not linear, underneath the compact appearance of history, and that the future only exists once all other possible futures have been tested out by vibrating matter, settling on the most useful option from an energetic point of view. [5] The evolution of our understanding of space and time occurs faster than our consciousness can adapt to its increasing abstraction.

⁶ And, if time only has one reality, in order to construct a complex instant and nourish a number of simultaneities on top of it, the perception of time as a chain of events should be eliminated. The gaze that travels across space provides the illusion of a topography and of distance, but if it is not informed by sensible information, it can end up getting lost. ⁷ As a result, speed seems like the most comprehensible relationship between space and time, since before we get somewhere we are in a different intermediate place without hardly being conscious of it. Thus, the arrow of time is defined that runs between history and the future with multiple links between simultantaneous presents.

⁸ Therefore, static spaces do not exist and given some attention they are revealed as dynamic and fluctuating in their use. Understood in this way, a place absorbs a number of functions that interact with it and transform it. These transformations may not be immediately discernible but, over time, a space breaks up into places that are colonized in different ways as a result of their different temporalities in terms of use. ⁹ Apparently neutral objects are charged by programmatic crossings that qualify them in time.

¹⁰ The creator's work is reinforced by the use of this fourth dimension, although it may carry with it the feeling of being poorly adapted to a much more complex reality. Despite the fact that we are living with a relatively crippled creative discipline, we can be content that its evolution is currently leading us toward a new, more open and indeterminate one.

58 [1] Reading time in urban space depends on a refined attention to the temporal fragments of the uses that occupy it. From this point of view, there are places that tend to slow us down because of the way they are physically put together and others, on the contrary, that speed us up.

[2] The urban introspection of the historic city, with its structure of landscaped and cloistered courtyards, creates a relaxed and intimate urban atmosphere. Walking through it leads to the discovery of hidden places with a static character, in contrast to others that are tied in with movement. [3] The characteristics and the dimensions of this structure are reproduced in the new National Hotel-Parador in Alcalá de Henares (2002), equating the importance of the new buildings to be built with the existing historical ones. [4] The proportion of each of these two conditions within the organization establishes different uses, leading to the appearance of a series of chronological lines that encompass both the new and the old.

[5] In order to situate the different programs, the historic buildings are associated with the values of absorption, contemplation, stillness and permanence; in short, what is intensely slow. On the other hand, the newly built areas are associated with the concepts of dynamism, surprise, variability and transience; in short, what is immediately fast. [6] The intersection of the different lines that correspond to varying times of use, forming nodes, results in a coupling and a subsequent adaptation of the lines into a grid, which then serves to define the definitive speeds of the overall diagram. [7] Each program is situated by relating

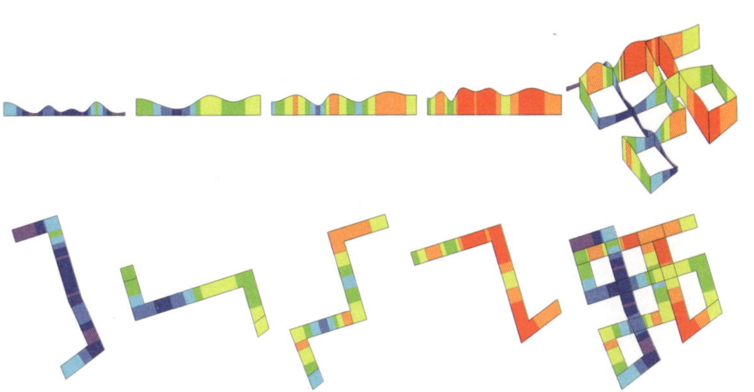

the temporal use conditions that are assigned to each one with the speeds given by the time line diagram. The correspondences between them allow for optimum positioning of the hotel rooms, the lobbies and the common areas.

[8] This temporal conception of the building provides users with a range of opportunities linked with different ways of experiencing the interior. Users will find static spaces associated with contemplation and relaxation, as well as more dynamic places for leisure or entertainment, both inside and outside the building. [9] It all signifies the desire to represent different paces of life within a consistent whole; the immediately fast and the intensely slow are combined for the benefit of users. [10] This diversity of tempos ensures a rich awareness of variability as opposed to the temporal homogeneity of a static environment.

SISTEMA DE PROYECTO — (LA DIVERSIDAD
(TIEMPOS CONT

1 = La condición urbana introspectiva o
accesibilidad
2 = La ~~contradicción~~ realidad concreta del lug
3 = El tiempo de uso y permanencia
4 - La posición y acumulación de uso
5 - La privacidad determina la pla
6 - La energía define los sistemas
7 - Aparición de la ~~tiempo continuo~~ dirección del tiempo, el m

mismo)

- Antiguo y nuevo el lo mismo) .

- la estructura conceptual.
.... transforma la estructura.
... los programas.
termina el volumen.
... al exterior y del exterior.
...tección.
... la ... de lo variable.
... antiguo, el ensimismamiento, la
... la lentitud, lo estático y permanente,
... nuevo, la diversidad, lo sorpresivo,
... lo inusable, lo rápido

④

← a Ronda
+ Por abajo.

⑦
LA DIVERSIDAD DEL TIEMPO

59 ¹ "Today we'll be playing 'A Love Supreme'," says Otto, my saxophone teacher.

² We're locked up in the sound proof room in my attic in Amsterdam. It's made with thirty centimeters of foam and egg containers from the flea market in the Pijp. I painted it all a deep IKB and when you walk in, it's like climbing a little ways into the sky. The cone-shaped bumps give it the atmosphere of a sophisticated cave, ideal for forays into intense music.

³ Facing the wall, I start to play the main notes on the lowest keys. John Coltrane wrote it over a period of three days, locked up in his American garret. When he emerged, worn out and wild-eyed, he called his musicians to meet him at the recording studio. Bewitched by the notes, they recorded the piece all in one go as though they'd been playing it all their lives.

⁴ Otto stares at the floor, his head swaying, holding his trumpet. His notes in the key of C pile on, a fifth above my tenor sax in B-flat, like a cotton cloud crossing dark mountains. ⁵ During an immeasurable stretch of time, we overlap and I feel my fingers move along the Selmer MK IV all by themselves. Pressing and letting up, high and low, the reed vibrates precisely between my lips.

⁶ Then his low voice comes in with the love supreme mantra way down below my lowest key, like a descent into a familiar abyss. He says that's the part that stops time. Looking fixedly into my eyes, we continue with every known note toward an unknown place. ⁷ The depths of the room have turned orange in the corner of my eye. My fingers and lungs are on the receiving end of a powerful force

that doesn't come from thought. There's no air between us. [8] There are only a few bars left when I'm gripped with an irrational fear and the magic ends. At that very moment he lets go of the trumpet furiously and, looking angry, he blurts out,

"You broke away; you ruined it at the end! It was coming out perfect!"

I let loose the Rico mouthpiece, half bloodstained, and I look at him with a questioning glance. [9] I figure he's picked up on my anxiety, but he reassures me ironically,

"Don't be afraid, anxious Spaniard! Everything in its own time!"

[1] One of the pioneering and most intuitive efforts at visualizing space-time was made by Karl Schwarzschild. During his service in the German ranks during the First World War, he came close to the now famous vision of the space-time curvature around a spherical body. [2] The image of a very heavy sphere placed on top of a sheet of foam rubber can help us better understand something that is foreign to our everyday perceptions. The deformation the sphere creates is similar to what happens to time when it approaches an object of tremendous mass. [3] The lines produced on the surface of the sphere, geodesic lines, serve to guide the dilation of time. [4] Schwarzschild's geometry represents the deformation of space as it fluctuates in time, something like the effects of lunar gravity on the tides. [5] As a consequence of this curvature in the vicinity of a massive element, the objects that rotate closer to the sphere rotate at a higher

velocity than the ones that are farther away. As such, the slowness of an object does not depend on the force of attraction, but rather on the geodesic line of space-time where it is located.

[6] The conclusion is exciting; the movement is not a consequence of gravity, but of the space-time geometry that houses it. [7] However, on a sufficiently small scale, space-time is no longer considered continuous; it is more like a foam composed of events, called the Planck scale. In it, space-time becomes discontinuous, pointing to the idea that on that nanoscale geometry no longer exists. [8] There is a minimum threshold for the duration of those microevents, defined by Planck as ten to the forty-third per second.

[9] Although there is no clock that can measure beyond this dimension, there are microscopes that use lasers with individual accelerated electron beams that can handle wavelengths in billionths of a meter, which are capable of measuring the variation of these structures over time. [10] The increase in the spatial resolution of the perception of three dimensions and its simultaneous variation with the fourth dimension supposes a major advance in our knowledge about the behavior and the resistance of matter. [11] Understanding the variation of its spatial properties over time can bring us closer to a vision that was heretofore impossible.

61 [1] There is a type of morphogenesis that makes decisions at each instantaneous bifurcation, while maintaining the memory of the preceding unstable form during each transition phase. [2] The organization created in this way emerges from leaps during which the appearance of a new phase of change, resulting from the introduction of program or volume conditions, demands the delineation of a precursor for the new form. Each piece of information introduced into the working system qualifies and classifies initially generic parts into something specific, which makes them irreplaceable.

[3] Applied to the case of the creation of the Durango Train Station (2004), the organization emerges from a temporal staging of the surrounding landscape for its collective use and enjoyment. [4] The geometry that ties together the time of use with the space that is being used is uncovered using a creative system based on defining the movements of perception and their combined temporal and spatial representation. [5] The urban structure that appears is the result of mixing a number of different perceptions based on new uses of the place, an observation in motion from the train, another more static observation from the point of view of tertiary programming and, finally, the observation of random pedestrian movements in public space. The perceptive movement from the train is represented using acceleration and deceleration graphics for the arrivals and departures from the new station. [6] The temporal vision of the landscape depends, therefore, on the velocities at each moment and their duration.

[7] In order to define the space-time of perception, we determine the sections and durations of the journey during which a specific icon in the landscape can be seen. Each stretch of vision will have a different duration depending

ACELERACION TREN = $2 \, m/s^2$

PRIMERA LEY DE INERCIA :

Todo cuerpo permanece en su estado de reposo o movimiento rectilíneo o uniforme a menos que otros cuerpos actúen sobre él.

VELOCIDAD MAXIMA   120 Km/h

ACELERACION DE ARRANQUE   ~~1,00~~ $1 \, m/s^2$ – DECELERACION NORMAL $1 \, m/s^2$

ACELERACION   0 · 60 Km/h $0,75 \, m/s^2$

               0 · 100 Km/h $0,60 \, m/s^2$

               0 · 120 Km/h $0,50 \, m/s^2$

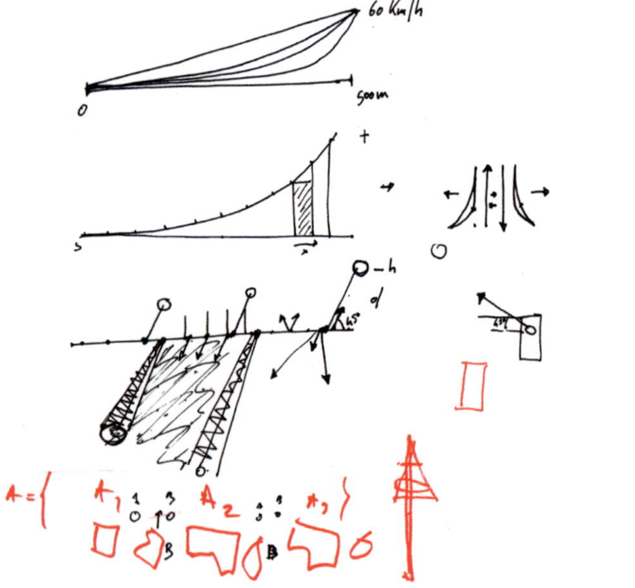

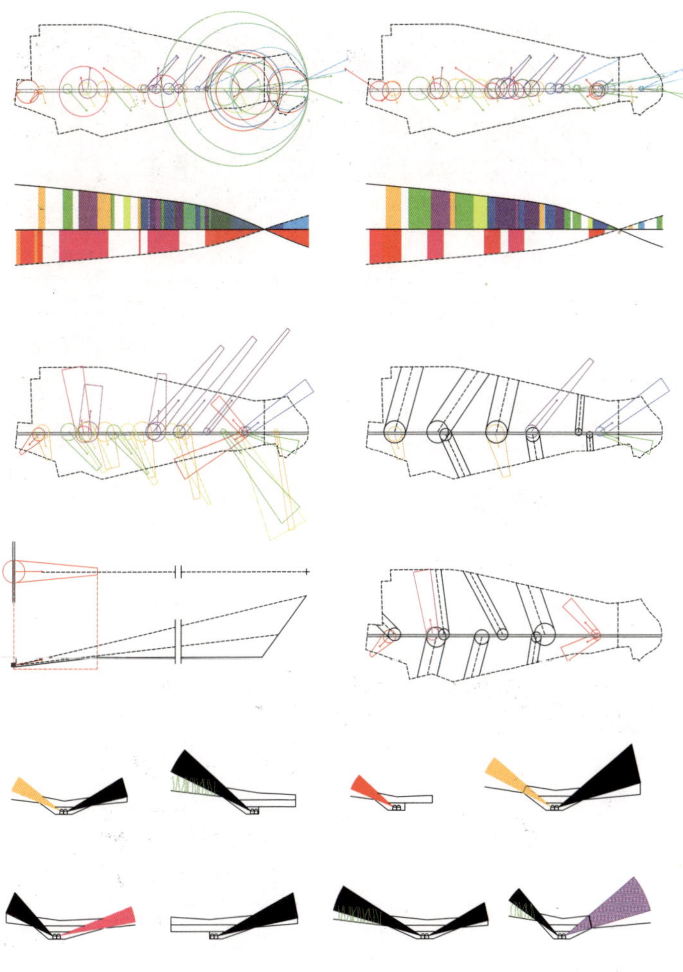

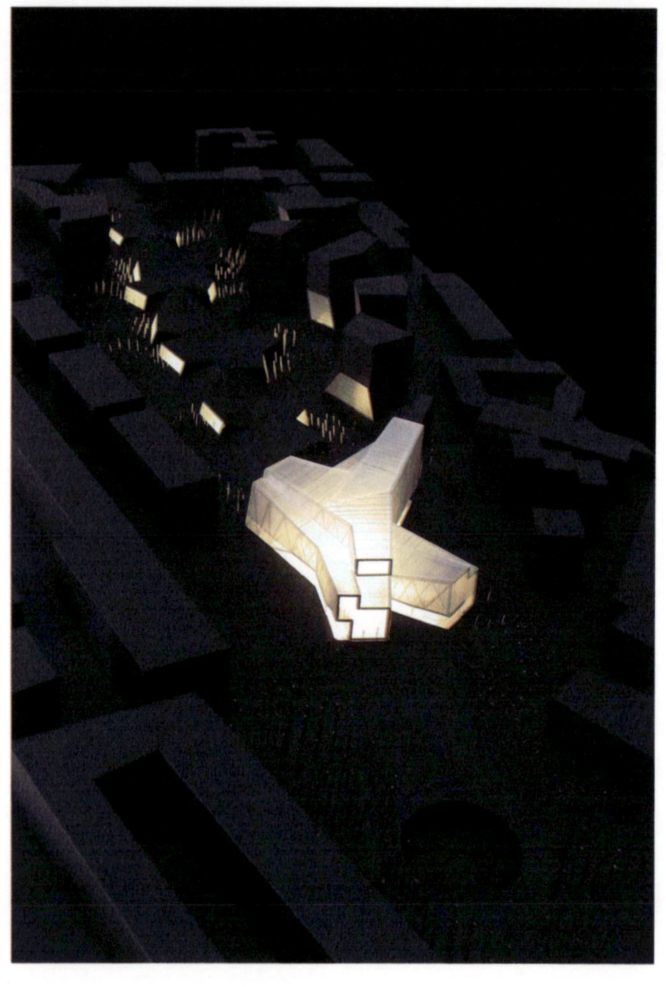

on the direction in which we are moving and our acceleration. [8] The new space-time rhythm provides each element in the landscape with the same temporal fragment in the itinerary. [9] This translates into the production of still shots that structure the city by way of an invisible order of sensations. [10] The representation of the visual cones for each still shot results in a geometry that is a function of the distance and the relative position from each point along the route. [11] The geometry that appears allows for putting together a family of objects that provide a representation of the mechanism behind the relationship between fragmented space and instantaneous time.

[1] The moment when the inherent sensibility of an object **62** enters into a dialogue with the creator, and later with the user, generates an emotionally intense linear time. During this interval, physical barriers disappear and the values we once thought were stable totter before a transcendent force. [2] The moments that relate us with creativity conspire so that the limits of our beliefs are blurred, transgressing the accepted virtue at each period in time.

[3] History shows that the consciousness of good is in constant temporal expansion and it is in this passage where sleeping souls wake, enter into dialogue and enrich one another. [4] The smiles of the people that inhabit a particular space are interesting for the naturality with which they are capable of making it their own and sensing that everything around them is intended for their benefit. [5] Between Man and his time in the world lies the space he inhabits

as he recreates himself in his dreams and hopes, made up of moments brimming with sensations. Let us look intuitively, walk in enjoyment, let us sit and listen and take in the scents elegantly, creating intense relationships like free animals in the woods contemplating one another.

[6] Transforming the traditional condition for the physical design of space into an area for individual action depends exclusively on the creative perception of the user. [7] This creates a place of times where the physical structure recedes into the background as a generic support for activities of connection that are excluded from the obvious rhythm of cities. A changing environment, detached from the static perspective of urban composition, begins to depend exclusively on the action and perception of the individual.

[8] This geography of moments is appears as a space that is shaped by times that are different from the discourse that attempts to homogenize the city. It serves as an atypical foundation for generating movements and actions that are free from the restrictions of ultra-designed space. [9] This exploratory personal journey is inspired by the curiosity before a new world that we don't recognize, although we are still a part of it, through a fragmented temporary space similar to that strange place where the stars unfold their universal relationships into infinity.

63 [1] Our images of cities end up being defined by the emotional intensity we experience there. Those moments tend to be associated with spaces which are most often charged with spatial or iconographic forces. [2] As a result, each personal vision is built up from fragments that define a place, which we never come to know in its full scope. [3] The urban horizon takes on a discontinuous character made up of perceptive instants involving far-away objects that blur the continuity of time. [4] The obstacles between us and the far-off distance establish stable personal relationships between the user and the existing objects that constitute what is permanent in the city and what is meaningful in the flow of reality. [5] As such, we can associate each different fragment of the horizon with a meaning related to its use for enjoyment, seclusion or productivity, assembling groups of thematic icons that are visible in the distance.

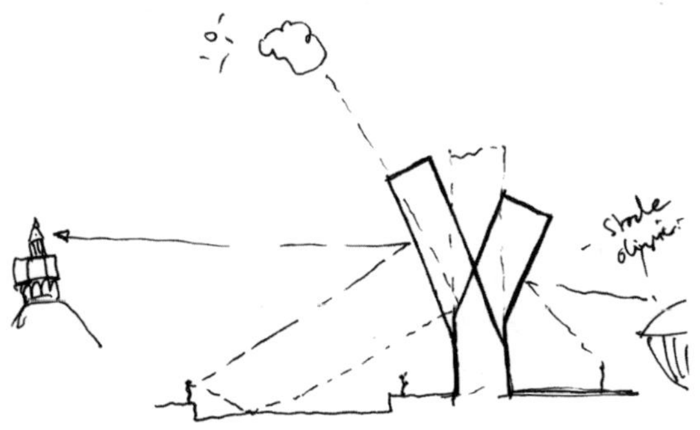

[6] All of these images are drawn into the new Saint-Denis Olympic Village in Paris (2000), through a mechanism that reflects them on angled buildings so they become visible from their associated public spaces. [7] This generates an urban structure with collective uses tied into the topic associated with each object on the horizon in a series of

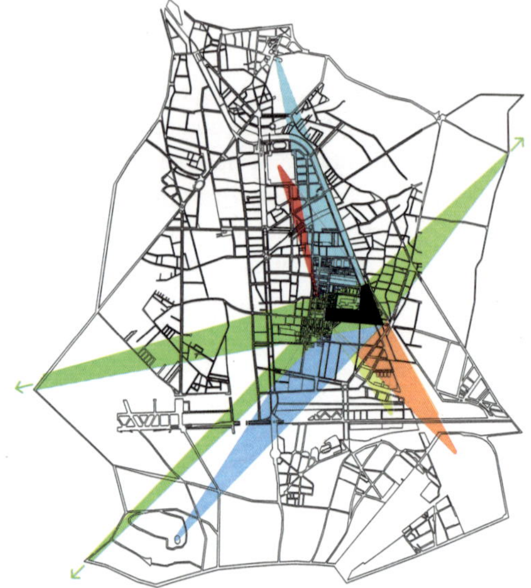

moments for contemplating the city. [8] The precise geometry is generated using visual parameters as a guide in order to control and direct the process of situating and formalizing the buildings.

[9] Within this system, with its zero degree of initial order, the new structure is organized by controlling the relationship between directions, distances, angles of reflection and the duration of visibility for each far-off icon. [10] The resulting structure is organized in four dimensions, creating a landscape of moments with a hidden order that depends on the factor of time for its experience and comprehension. From

precise locations near each building we can enjoy the views that draw their themes down into the public space itself. [11] In this way, the more intimate areas will look toward Sacre Coeur and the training areas will have views of the Stade de France, and so on. From this point of view of temporal use, the Olympic housing will also have a mechanism so that inhabitants can choose from among different internal uses, tying into the same perceptual horizons and defining types of habitation: leisure, seclusion and productivity.

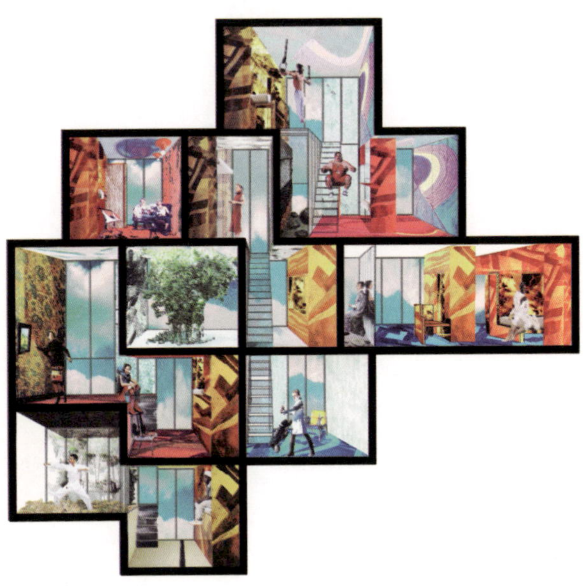

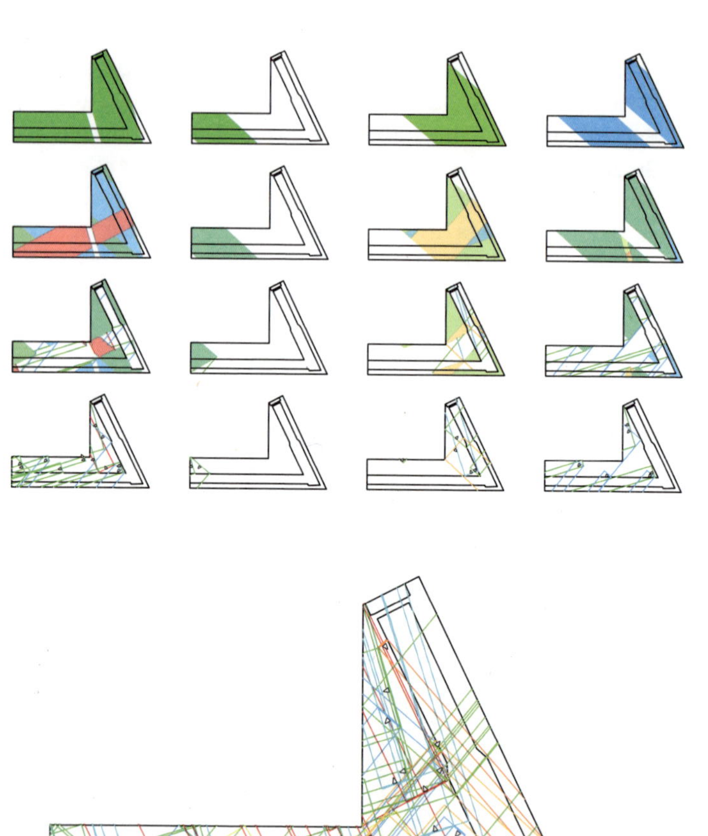

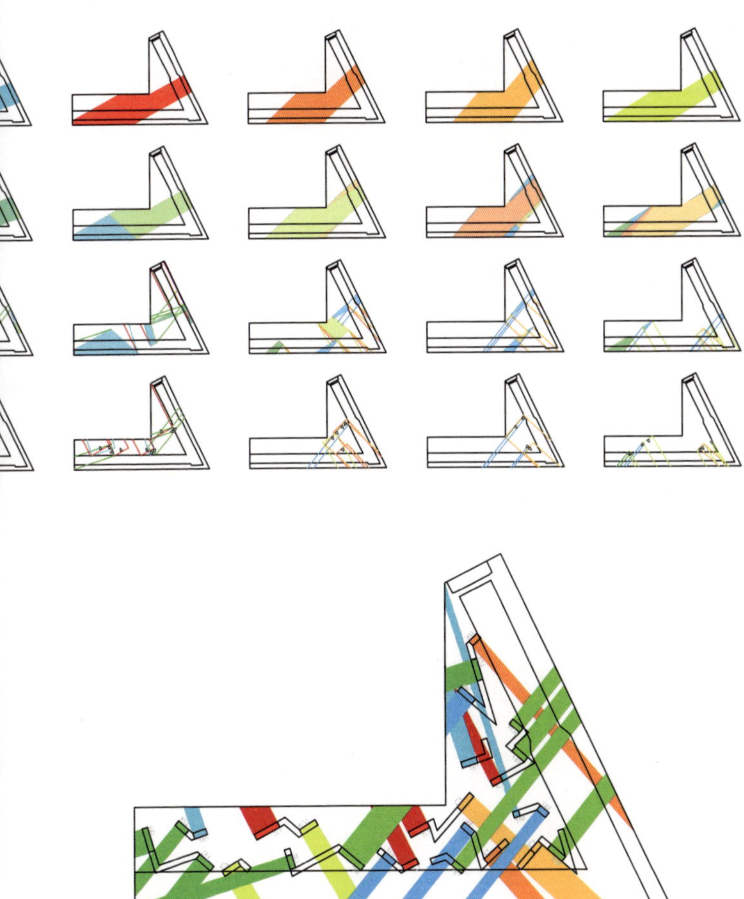

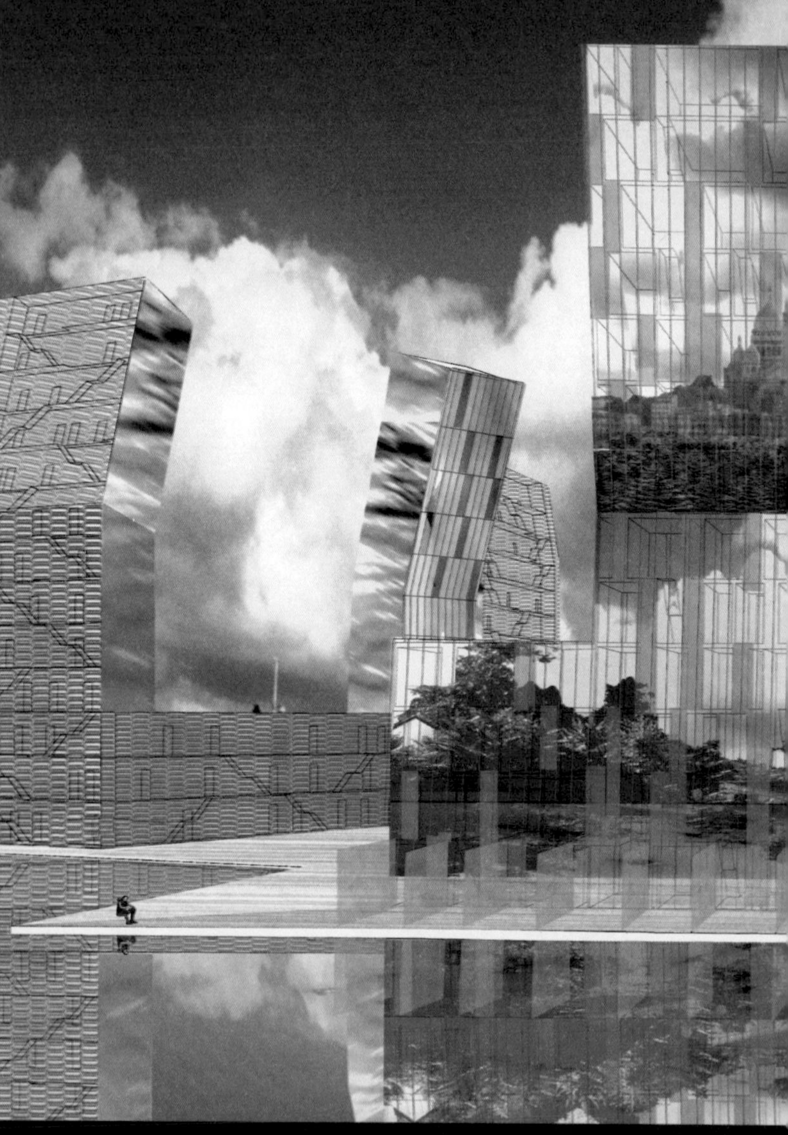

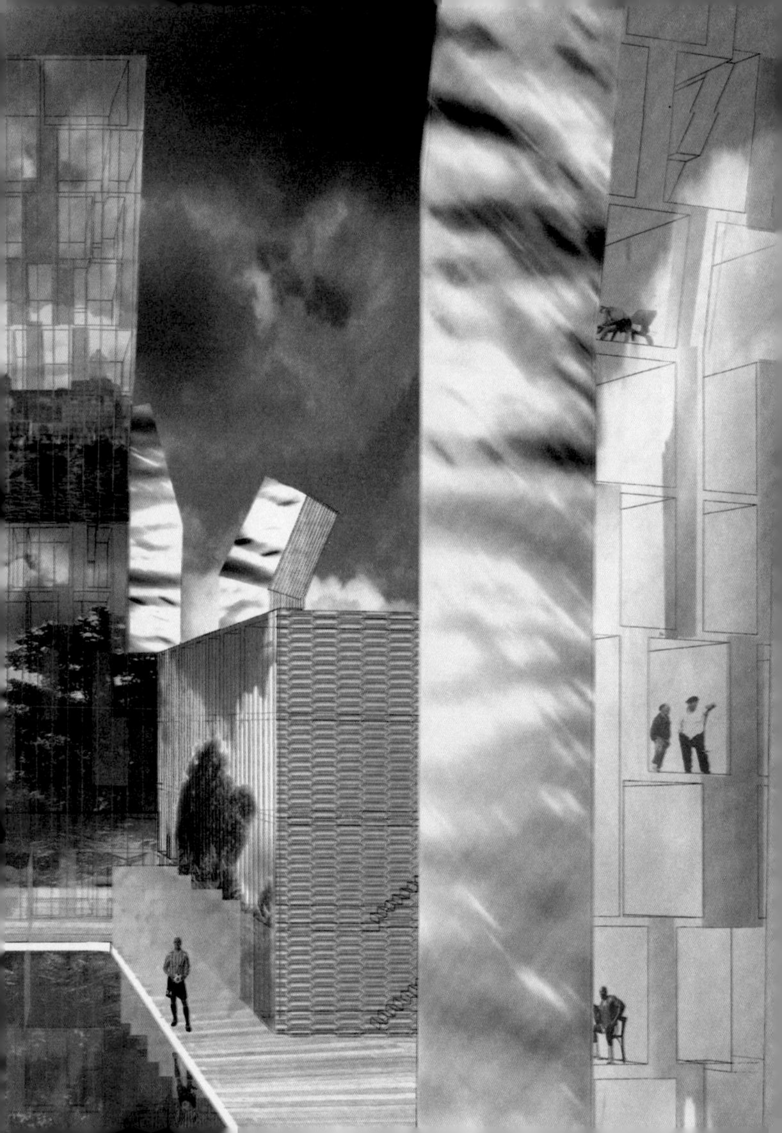

BE CAREFUL WHAT YOU CHOOSE!

"Having studied clocks, we should now study clouds"

Ilya Prigogine ————————————————————————

¹ Don't go back on your word now!" Pete exclaims, a bit **64**
angry.

² This is the moment of truth, where we'll find out whether we're courageous enough for what we've wished for. It looks like my travelling companion has no shortage of courage, as is evidenced by his attire. He's a member of the Black Widow Motorcycle Club from New York and he's walking around China wearing the trappings of his lifestyle.

³ We've finally come to the legendary plank walk. After three thousand stairs carved into the rock face, the path up the mountain has become a completely vertical wall of granite. There are wooden planks anchored to it, hanging weightless, challenging the intellect. A thick chain runs along the surface of the rock, like a banister, a meter and a half above them. There's nothing to prevent us from falling. ⁴ The monks who hoped to enter the order of Shaolin had to demonstrate their mental strength by crossing the planks. It's fifty meters of well-planned recklessness.

⁵ Some days earlier I'd met the biker in a small village in a remote area, where it isn't common to run into travelers. The proximity to the sacred mountain of Huangshan meant that we asked each other about the reason for our trip.

"I'm a student of kung fu and I promised the master that I would climb to the monastery on the mountain," Pete says in an arrogant tone.

I reply that I don't know anything about martial arts and my reason for making the climb is to prove something to myself. ⁶ Sitting on the edge of the road, we talk about the three paths up to the summit and that, according to legend, it is our choices that are the mark of our courage. Without thinking too much about it, we reject the routes that only demand physical fitness and we decide to opt for danger.

[7] Pete has crossed over in the blink of an eye and he's shouting to me from the other side,

"Whatever you do, don't look down!"

I realize that I don't have to do this, but I grab onto the chain and I start to feel the planks vibrate with each step. I try to think about something pleasant, something else, but it doesn't work. [8] I come to a standstill half way across. My hands are sweaty and I feel like I'm going to slip.

"You can't turn back now! I'll buy you a sake when we get down!" he shouts, to cheer me on.

Then, I start laughing hysterically and my legs start to move through some unconscious force. [9] When I get to the other side, we embrace in the face of our stupidity, but I notice that I'm just that much taller.

"You know, I think we should come back the same way," he says, smiling.

I shudder in that instant, knowing that I'll be doing it again.

65   [1] Our habitat has succumbed to the confrontation between construction that is governed by pragmatic and deterministic legislation and uninformed individuals. [2] This prevents a short-term reconciliation of human creativity with financial forces in order to create an exciting description of the space of our future. [3] This economic determinism drives the distinction between a coherent world of predictable facts and the elimination of unpredictability.

⁴ Karl Popper was ahead of his time when he demonstrated the incongruity of this position, showing that we are capable of understanding the internal laws of clouds, which have an indeterminate nature, to the same extent that we can understand deterministic clocks. He revealed that clocks are not as reasonable as we might think and that, when we study them, we find that there are properties connected with the dissipation of heat or mechanical resonance which affect the supposed infallibility of their precision. ⁵ Two identically manufactured clocks will never tell the same time indefinitely and the adjustments that will have to be made imply that they will no longer have the same appearance for us. ⁶ The determinist machine definitively loses its image as a device that is subject to predictable mechanical laws and becomes a physical system of energetic properties, bringing it closer to the variable and unpredictable world of clouds.

⁷ Something similar occurs with any alleged stability when the linearity of the cause-effect relationship is broken, and random appearances are generated. One example of this is turbulence, which has been used as a symbol of disorder for decades, yet which maintains a high degree of interior organization at an invisible level. ⁸ This type of order does not reside in properties that our senses can recognize and it requires deeper knowledge. Nor can it be contemplated by aesthetic systems based exclusively on appearance.

⁹ The definition of indeterminist and interrogative thought, based on specific questions and the choice of concrete properties as a response, determines the precision of our actions for the common good. ¹⁰ In this situation, the creator can

develop an individual starter protocol through the selection of a sophisticated catalyst system when faced with the emptiness of creation. [11] If he works with an idea of pre-established order, the process will be simple and sure; but dealing with risky questions from the beginning can lead him to surprising discoveries.

66 [1] Sometimes places appear before us as untouchable and complete, giving us the feeling that interfering in the rhythm of that world can only lead to disaster. Their appearance of stable emptiness can even lead to aborting the search for a way of colonizing them. [2] However, a thoughtful and empathetic reading of any territory can allow for finding hidden properties that we can relate to. Through them, we can produce enough connections to be able to move on to manipulating them. [3] These interventions, which consist in making the invisible visible, reveal properties that stimulate certain sensory aspects.

[4] Using the senses, our brain function qualifies the conditions that are present in the territory and classifies them instantly. Each part of the brain, specific in controlling our different senses, produces the relationships between those conditions, grouping them into related sets independently of their proximity to one another. [5] In this way, the unfocused fragments of a golden wheat field come to form a complete landscape that can be detached from the rest. [6] Isolating each sensory reading from the others strengthens its specific properties and maximizes the user's perception from places that have been selected beforehand.

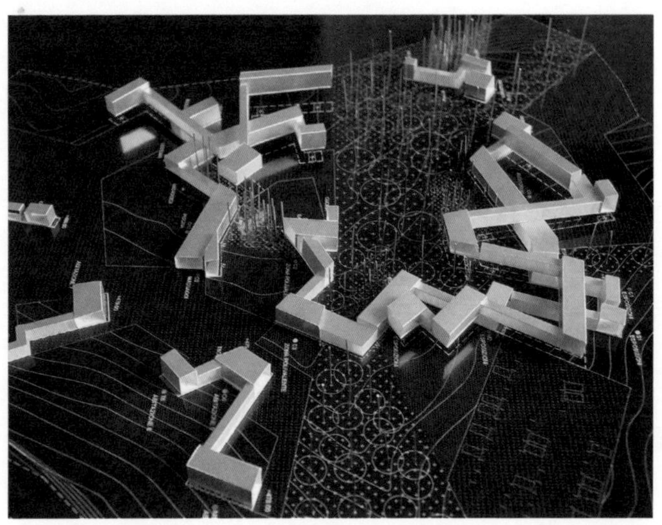

⁷ As a reflection of this condition, the organization of the Fabriano Visitors Center (2003) is born from the distances and positions relating to each of the independent fragments of the landscape which stimulate the interior of the area that is to be transformed. ⁸ The built elements are distinguished through a specific geometry in keeping with each sensation that has been evaluated, though they all belong to a common familiar set. ⁹ In order to increase the strength of each territorial section, the materials that are used activate their sensory properties, considered independently in terms of color, touch, sound, smell or changeability. This increases the power of existing elements by way of a filtering process.

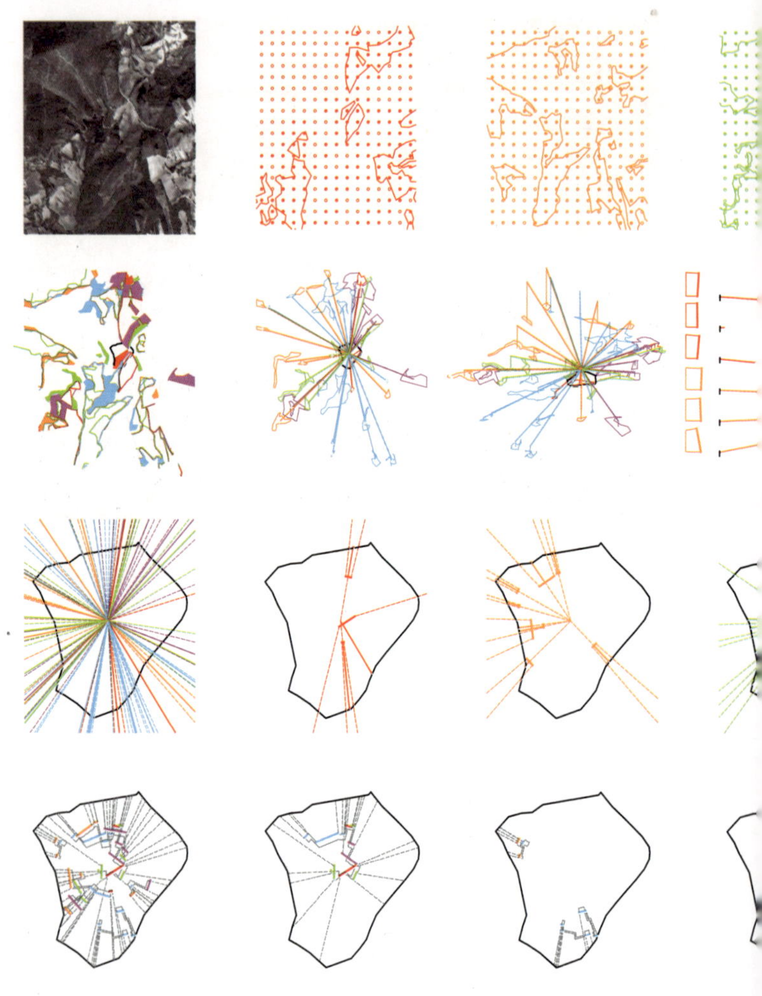

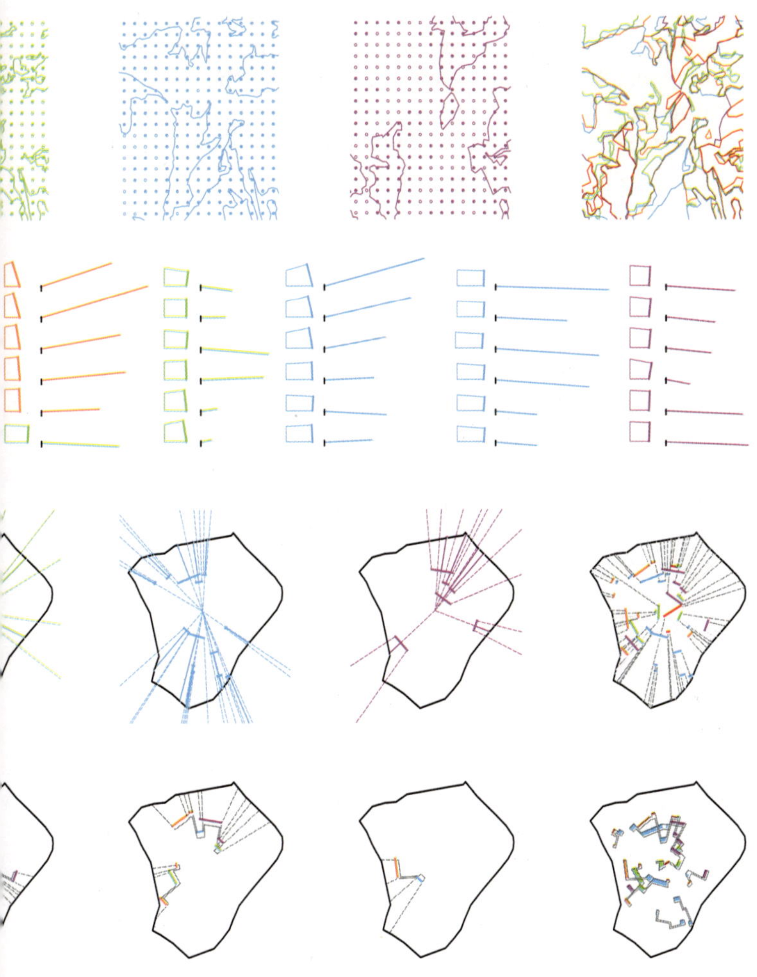

[10] The centrifugal organization of the program allows for absorbing all of the territory while recreating a directional spatial system from the community areas to the small villas intended for relaxation. This sensory expansion toward the landscape encourages increased intensity among visitors and generates the necessary mood for sophisticated understanding.

67 [1] The excesses of modern reason and its axiomatic method have led us to think that theories have to be formulated without ambiguities, based on a coherence that implies the non-existence of contradictions. As such, a thing and its opposite cannot exist at the same time, encouraging a superficial pragmatism that defines and accompanies all imposed formalisms. [2] On a more relaxed level, consistency proposes a state of affairs in which all components form harmonious groups. This allows for multiple connections and relationships as well as a gradient of variation within the creative system. [3] The responses that, evading coherence, seek out this consistency presuppose an equality of importance between the improbable and the probable, the impossible and the possible or the unreal and the real.

[4] The global explanation of the world attempted by the avant-garde has not led to a better understanding of it and the informational obscurantism of the dilettante new politics drives the need for new questions. [5] In order to formulate them, the objects of thought are classified on the one hand into those that refer to phenomena of human life, systematized via general laws based on the techniques of

science. And, on the other hand, into creative propositions in the form of acts of fiction from the imagination. [6] This grouping is not clearly defined and both systems can be mixed in a blurry field of thought where facts, laws and fictions alternate their development in the search for questions and their particular responses. [7] Creative fictions are formed through acts of passion or logic and both stand out for the premeditation of their execution, some with the excuse of expression and others based on the use of irrefutable rational thought. [8] Timidly situated between this duality, there is another type of understanding in the form of a frothy passionate and unexpected logic that is very effective in these diffuse times.

[9] From this point of view, there is a clear difference between a closed-off system of creation that pursues a process of relaxation and resemblance with what has been approved of collectively, and a synergetic method that allows for analyzing the evolution of complex structures when they tend toward a less probable and unpredictable state. [10] The first implies working with known orders, whereas in the second we can only access a gradient or a parameter of order that defines the state and the variation of the fluctuations and their instability at any given moment.

[1] By relating the transitions between fluctuating orders, **68** topology considers objects that can be obtained one from the other without breaking to be equal, including those that are inscribed in the Poincaré conjecture. In order to recognize an object of these characteristics, some of its properties

have to be deformed, like mathematicians do with partial differential equations. [2] This manipulation is always undertaken in the direction of the homogenization that is considered to be the most beautiful. This means that the analysis of the characteristic properties of the objects implies a distancing from the strict axioms of reason when the subjective condition of sensibility is introduced into the process of recognizing that homogenization.

[3] Given the perplexity into which the impossibility of choosing the most convenient option sinks us, because of the difficulties presented by the facts and the circumstances surrounding creation, the risky option is taking the side of the most honest one. [4] Some questions about the properties of the objects can help us in this selective search by revealing the honesty in those processes that resolve uncertainties using exogenous and homogeneous principles which generate complex informality.

[5] Is it uncertainty or certainty? In his work on the production of geometries using random systems, Benoît Mandelbrot referred to uncertainty as a powerful mechanism for creativity. He defined it as a process of gradual affinity with what we find as we go along. He associated the ballast in his vocation for discovery with the recurring and involuntary appearance of certainties concerning the things he was already familiarized with. [6] New questions can only be resolved precisely by way of unknown creations.

[7] Is it a principle or a metaphor? Albert Einstein differentiates very clearly between principles, which for him represent a superior degree of understanding of the world, and metaphoric occurrences, which are born from a pragmatism

that lacks a desire to understand reality and has dangerous pretensions of truth. [8] Principles lead to the presence of variable meanings in creative systems, whereas metaphor is a simple appearance that is closed off in itself and does not vary when faced with different contexts.

[9] Is it exogenous or aseptic? James Clerk Maxwell and his famous demon indicate the informative nature of everything that exists in the world through a continuous exchange of information, which causes the necessary imbalances toward evolutionary systems. [10] The exchange of conditions with external elements supports the transformative intention and allows for the definition of the limits of creativity without taking part in an aseptic conformism.

[11] Is it homogeneous or discontinuous? Karl Popper warns us of the need to study clouds as opposed to clocks, because the variations in their form possess homogeneous and constant properties. This confers them with energetic characteristics that are closer to how reality works than the mechanicist ones that have been used up to the present day. [12] Creative objects appear when a void is stimulated; where previously there was nothing, there are properties and tension, continuously and consistently, between the enveloping surface and the volume.

[13] Is it informal or complicated? Ilya Prigogine reminds us that when there are phase changes in nature, adding information to a specific system, there comes a point when it enters into a new unexpected working regime, altering its energetic qualities, form and presence. [14] The complexity discovered in the creative process is instinctively close and its presence stirs up a resonance with what already exists inside our being.

69 ¹ Objects that break when you deform them with respect to one of their internal characteristics are not among those that pursue the above-mentioned properties. This implies that their properties are not variable, or that they are dependent on form. ² However, there are objects that maintain their properties during transformation, because those properties are independent and have the same level of importance as form.

³ We call the first group clocks, in which a minimum deformation alters their precise operation, leading to incorrect readings of the reality they measure. ⁴ The second groups cloud-like objects, for which any deformation that is applied does not produce any incoherence in operation. Sometimes other properties appear, beyond those that it already possessed. ⁵ This classification requires refined attention since there are objects that, despite their shapeless appearance, are camouflaged clocks with a principal property that resides in the aesthetic condition of their form, which is lost during the testing transformations. ⁶ As such, we can establish that those creative objects that tend toward the homogenization of their properties throughout their volume are closer to clouds, whereas those that relate autonomous parts with different properties tend to be clocks. ⁷ Moving a little further along in the classification, some are energetic and others are mechanical.

⁸ The type of object that is most interesting for its effectiveness keeps a strange relationship of distance with the two former categories, moving away from the clocks in its search for the homogenization of properties and moving closer to clouds for its distance from an agreed upon and conventional equilibrium. ⁹ In this manner, in some in-

termediate place, "cloucks" begin to appear as a product of this thought foam, which can be deformed in the direction of some, but not all, of their properties. This lends them a directional importance and their characteristics take on a selective gradient of superiority. [10] They prove to be more attainable in terms of their management, letting us center our attention on a specific response to a particular place-question by abandoning generic or de-territorialized thought.

[11] These "cloucks" are traversed by a surprising dynamic equilibrium which directs the transformation of one working system into another and one object into another familiar one. [12] In some unspecified place, a promiscuity of thought occurs constantly, removed from stylistic formalism. It would be creative irresponsibility to wander around these states with inherited or referenced manners. [13] The reflection they produce with their diversity is enough to remind us that in states of equilibrium matter, people and their creations become inert and impede their own opportunities.

[1] An urban void occurs when the time flowing in the city **70** comes to a halt. The inhabitants' lives continue around it, unconnected to this strange abandoned structure lacking in energy or living matter. [2] In order to take over a place of this kind, without internal conditions, we uncover the forces that act at its perimeter, originating in the city. [3] These synergies, cut short by the physical and psychological limits, are chosen beforehand according to the importance of their

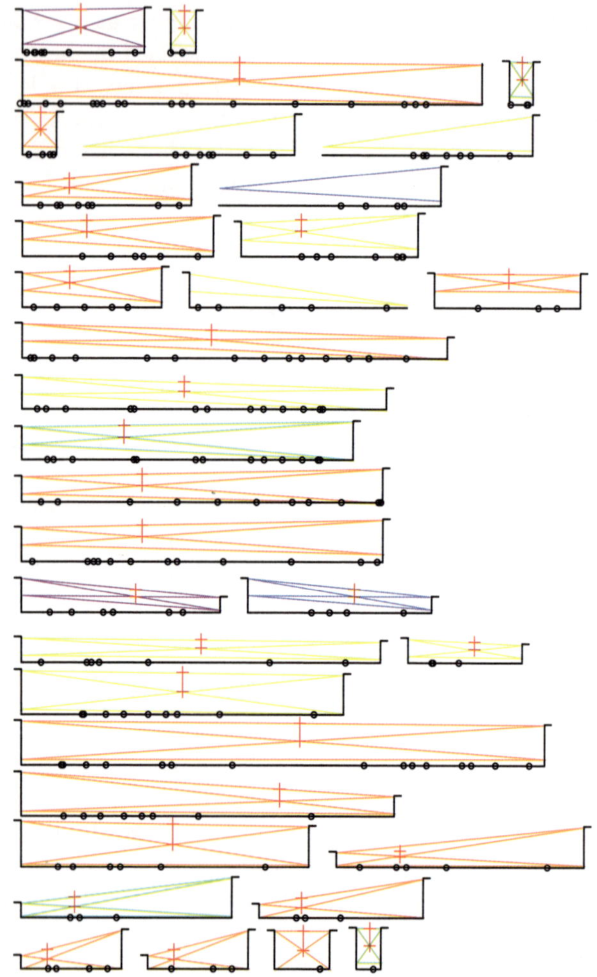

influence on the final objective. Once they have been selected, they are incorporated using an elastic appropriation
that allows for organizing the occupation as readings of the
different data are added. [4] The flexibility of a system understood in this way allows for structuring objects and
altering them in successive phases, steering clear of a
pre-established vision.

[5] From this standpoint, in order to guarantee the continuity of the new Isla Chica Urban Center in Huelva (2004)
the personal stories that inhabit the active perimeter are
incorporated into the site. [6] Their influence is classified according to stories with neighborhood rhythms that enliven
the topography of the streets, urban stories about unknown
people and their anonymous rhythms tied in with ways of
crossing the city, and far-off territorial stories wrapped up
in ways of perceiving the landscape.

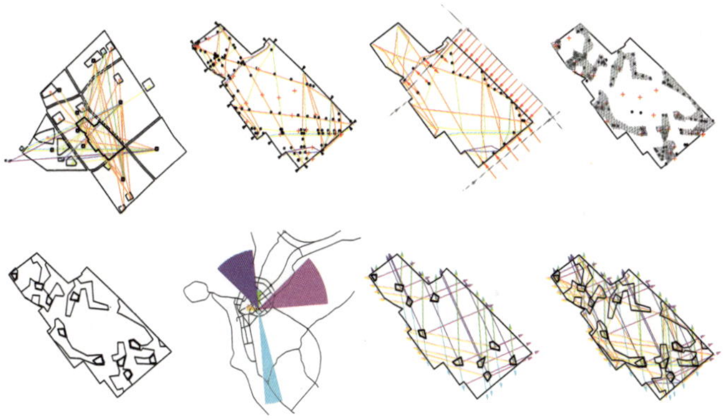

[7] From the study of these differentiated vital rhythms, a system is born that generates vectors of continuity in the shape of a three-dimensional web crossing over the site. [8] The social universe of the surrounding neighborhood and its uses are absorbed into a topography that produces continuity and fluidity at the ground level. [9] The urban-scale world, built vertically, is absorbed through the refined transitions of the existing volumes through the perimeter. [10] A third, territorial world proposes the creation of elevated public programs associated with the interested and directional contemplation of specific distant landscapes.

[11] Using these invisible and transversal rhythm lines, we define the intersections into groups with greater or lesser density. These groupings occur at different heights, creating the optimum location for each program and the embryonic envelopes for future constructions. [12] A new city appears, in which uses and volumes respond to preexisting rhythms displayed by inhabitants, absorbing them through the continuity of topographic, programmatic and temporal properties.

71 [1] "I feel a bit better now, thank you," I tell the doctor in a faltering voice.

In a sweet tone and a lovely Peruvian accent she responds,

"We'll be discharging you tomorrow. This is a marvelous country. Make the most of it, and don't get into any more trouble."

I thank her for her advice and for her care during the week I've been there and I promise that as soon as the border is reopened I'll be making way to the Caribbean. ² Fujimori's coup has had me stuck in Peru for a couple of months and I've taken the opportunity to travel to remote areas.

³ I met a crazy Danish woman in Lima and she convinced me to go as far as Amazonia, which wasn't part of my plan. Lying in that bed, twelve kilos lighter, I think back, finally smiling, on our meeting in the Plaza de Armas:

"You have to try it. It's the most incredible thing that's ever happened to me," she said, her eyes wide.

And she continued, in amazement,

"It's like floating, tied to your body by an energy cord."

⁴ A few days later I was on my way to the lost fortress of Kuelap. No one knows who built it and there is talk of a yellow-haired tribe with eyes the color of the sea, probably some reckless Vikings who sailed up the Amazon way before Columbus. At the lonely summit, a group of tupamaros at their camp, far from robbing me blind, offered me a cheerful morning cup of coffee. ⁵ After passing through Cajamarca and Chachapoyas I arrived in Bagua, crossing vertiginous canyons on the first bus that ran through the area. According to the driver, they made the trip at night so that no one would see the drop-offs, hundreds of meters high, next to the highway cut into the side of the mountain. ⁶ When I finally got to the Marañón River, a canoe took me jerkily toward Nazareth.

"You'll have to talk to the Jivaros," the boatman told me contemptuously when I asked him about Ayahuasca.

I didn't have any trouble finding someone in one of the huts to put me into contact with them. ⁷ I feel like gagging all over again as I remember drinking the liquid made from hallucinogenic vines, while the little shaman smoked his mapacho to protect me. Next to him in the half-light, I started to feel dizzy and throw up; I saw sounds as luminous waves and I heard colors emit jarring sounds. I managed to see with my eyes shut while the pressure of the small man's fingers on my body activated or blocked my hallucinations.

[8] After a few days losing weight, I ended up in the hospital. Sitting sluggishly in bed in Chiclayo it occurs to me that, at some point, I'll have to establish whether all of this has been an inspiring passage through another dimension or just a trip to hell and back. Right now, I can't decide.

72 [1] The exchange of information between what already exists and what we wish to introduce implies processes that involve the divergence and transfer of data. [2] The Platonic mental object can be diverted in its material, through spatial transformation or through the disposition of its use, as long as sufficient energy is provided. [3] The primary object of thought cannot remain unaltered when it is introduced into a specific site since it must avoid remaining alien to that place and to its exterior conditions.

[4] The creative work of dissipative structures in the territory (non-equilibrium processes, geometries that are excited over time, or fields of probability) pursues urban states that respond precisely to the conditions of space and time in which they are carried out. The system used for their configuration brings together linear processes that hybridize and mix together concepts of a temporal or a spatial nature, or both simultaneously, depending on the selected properties.

⁵ Most of these processes end up behaving like gelatinous or foamy systems, with a semi-rigid approach which allows for their confrontation with experience. We use them to produce the ability to adapt to the network of abstraction and reality that constitutes the spider web of urbanity. ⁶ These systems are like a kind of plasma that is stimulated from time to time in contact with the specific properties of a particular context, giving rise to forms, uses, materials and energies that are different in each case, and which can only be expressed through their own distinct language. ⁷ Some of the responses may seem to originate in other fields of knowledge, but they are upheld by the serenity of knowing that our questions were also asked from within the confines of territories that may seem disconnected from traditional creation.

⁸ The definition of new complex statistical paradigms using a thought process that shies away from equilibrium allows for rethinking our creative methodologies. ⁹ We can take up structures other than the ones that are governed by convention, stepping away from the eternally tidy image that propaganda and publicity put forth as the waterline of existence. ¹⁰ That is the only way to safeguard concepts like beauty, chance, instability, stimulus, exchange or quest from their violence and manipulation. The exquisite precision of their meanings will create a solid common front against the retrograde order that disregards them.

¹ The interested reading of the territory using properties **73** that are recognizable within it can produce surprising ho-

mogenous configurations. The selection of properties related to topography, composition, color or permeability results in different maps that, nonetheless, represent the same place. [2] The study of a territory's variability over time also creates readings that behave dynamically due to the appearance of gradients of variation. Acting on the basis of an overlapping of a number of these parameters leads to a flexible system of probabilities in which equilibrium only appears at the end of the process.

[3] In this way, a complex geometrical structure can be obtained from the parametric reading of the territory, which takes on greater relevance and meaning in its interaction with the new properties that we introduce and its subsequent transformation. [4] Thus, a process of self-organization emerges which takes over the place based on the insertion of new elements. The structure that results from the development of the geometric embryo takes on its dimensions, organization and properties after the introduction of the quantities from the program. This mutation process leads toward an unpredictable state of pre-established non-equilibrium and non-form.

[5] From this standpoint, our intervention in the natural environment in Seoul focuses on light, sound and speed as the properties for use in filtering the site, in order to generate the new Nam June Paik Museum in Seoul (2003). This information, hidden in the territory, indicates places where movement is slow or rapid, areas that are shady or bright, and zones where there is quiet calm versus others where the urban racket can be heard. [6] Based on this selection, a series of geometries and topological groups appear, into

which functional quantities of the museum's program settle. Looking at how their properties coincide with the ones revealed on the site, their optimum locations can be determined. [7] The parameters used in the reading define the speed of interior circulation, the variable control of light according to the different aspects of program and the qualification of the interior and exterior acoustic qualities as motors for the formal evolution.

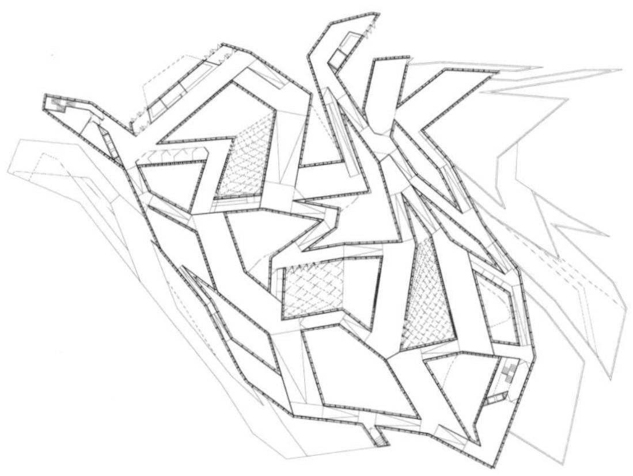

[8] The homogeneous construction system, however, allows for specifying the properties for each space by adapting the structural parameters. [9] The nature that is captured inside this blurry space promotes the disappearance of limits, where art is a part of nature and nature, finally, imitates art.

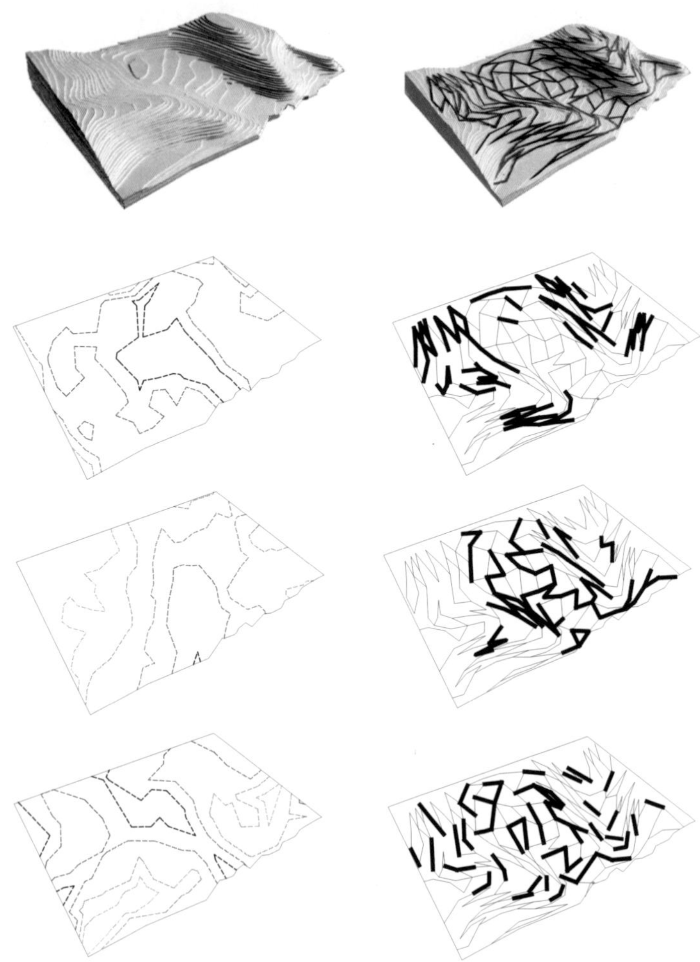

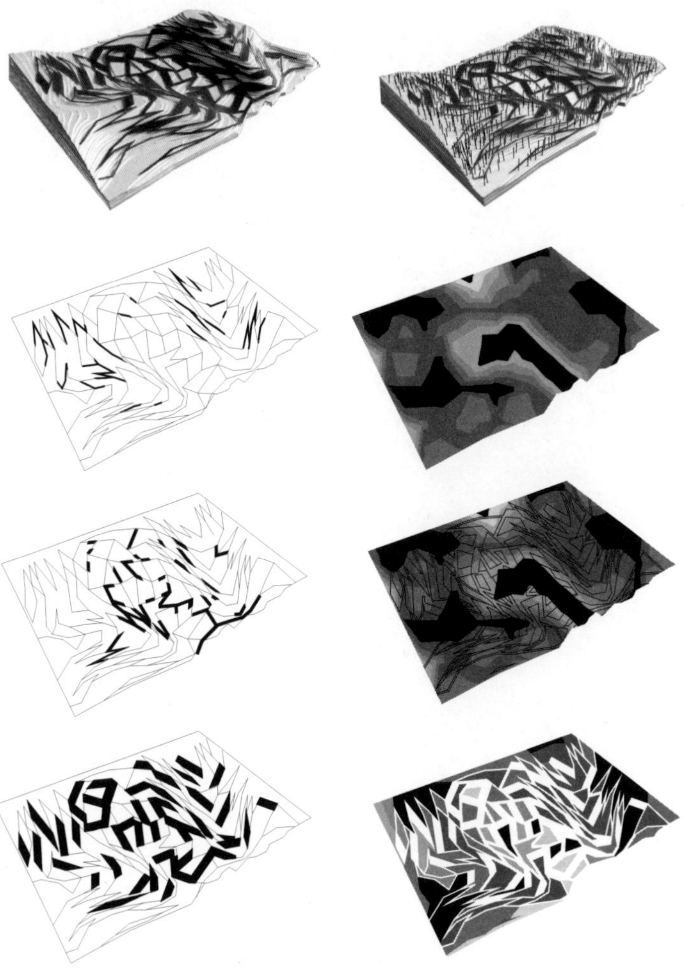

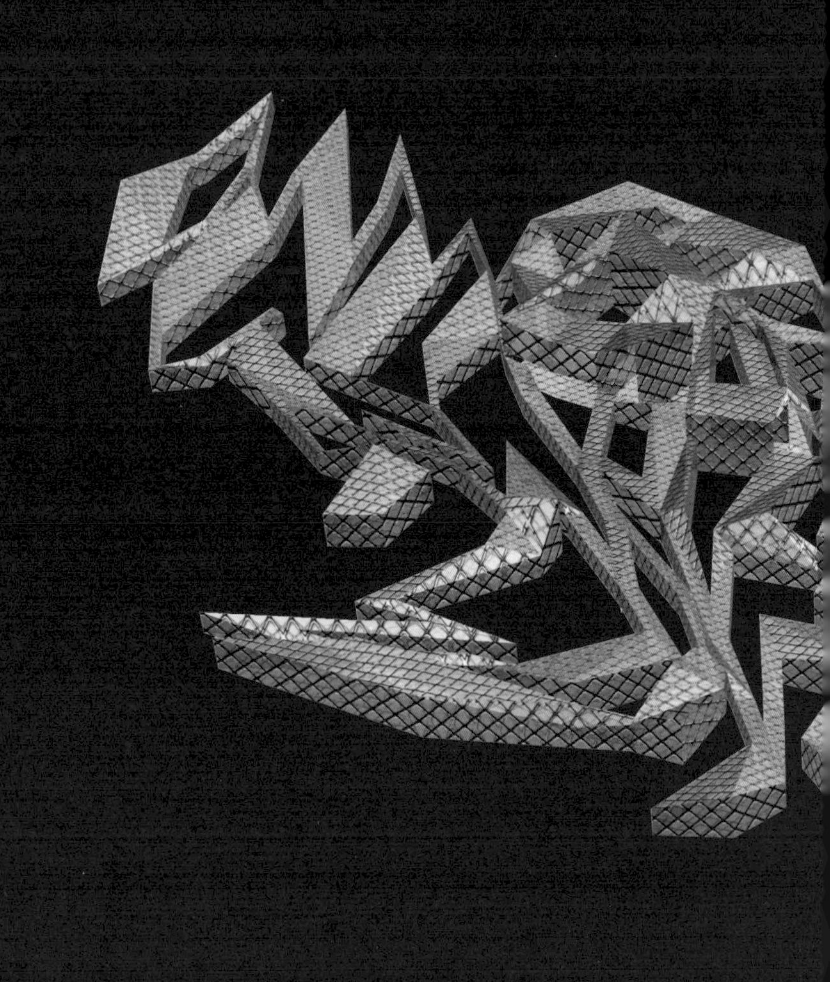

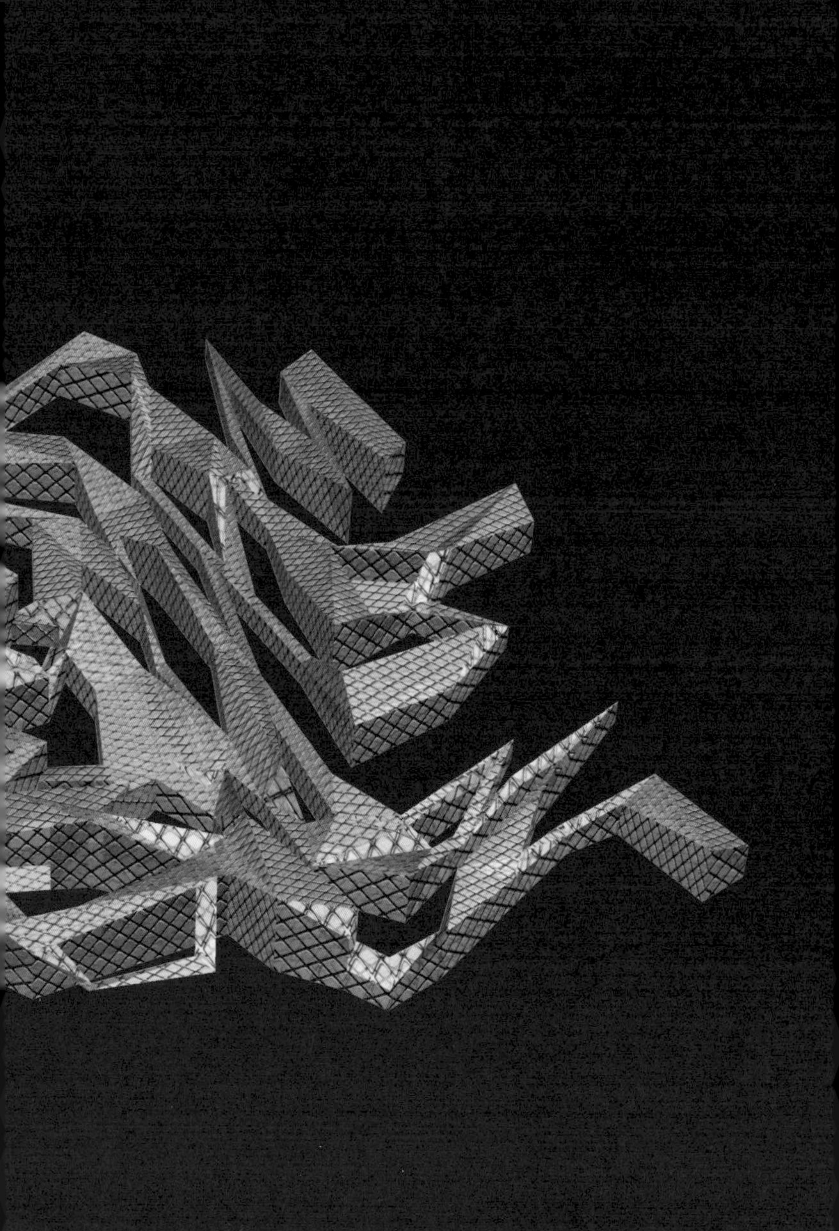

THE FUTURE IS A MULTIPLE OF THREE

"Something has been put in place, and will never stop, despite the sound and fury: the mixing of the world and the individualization of conscience"

MARC AUGÉ

[1] On a leaden morning in March, I made my first visit to OMA (Office for Metropolitan Architecture). [2] Though I didn't realize it, it was something that would radically change my way of thinking and dealing with creation. [3] I was received by a stylish secretary who informed me that the boss was away and that I could leave my resume on the counter. As she nodded, politely bored, I told her about my complicated illegal non-EU status, at a time when Spain was still just a holiday destination for Europeans. In fits and starts, I also referred to my expulsion from England for unrelated reasons, the cost of the train from Amsterdam to get to the office every day, and even something about my passion for two-wheeled vehicles.

[4] Back home again, I found an excited message from Rem Koolhaas on Patricia's answering machine, demanding my immediate return to Rotterdam on the next train, with no argument, whatever the time. That was just a small preview of what was waiting for me during the intense period I spent working in his office.

[5] Well, what can I say, the hope of a young architect is a powerful emotional fuel at times when we sense that our dreams are about to come true. So I ran like the world was about to end, I travelled and I talked haltingly about Chernikhov whom I admired at the time. [6] With superlatives and arrogant words, I tried to put a sheen on the university projects and any competitions where I'd managed to scrape up a prize. [7] From the moral pedestal afforded by knowledge, he smiled pleasantly, looking out the window occasionally.

[8] After a short chat about what was expected from me, he introduced me to the people in the office. Though it was

small, there were people from Holland, Belgium, France, the United States, Germany and Japan. That fascinating environment promised not just an apprenticeship, but the entrance into a world where different points of view intersected. [9] At the time, I thought that his interest for my hand drawings, which I felt were handsome, was what helped me get accepted into that restricted club. [10] But now I suspect that it also had something to do with a hidden collector's ambition,

"I'm really glad to have such an international office and you're my first from Spain," he said.

"Now I just need someone who's black!"

75 [1] Teilhard de Chardin predicted that the future of the human race would be the color of cappuccino. A mixture which would inevitably end up occurring due to the combination of qualities selected by different social and environmental factors, producing a more evolved human alloy. [2] Brass or bronze, which only exist by virtue of artificial processes, were originally mixtures born from human intelligence at the service of their construction in the world. Now we know that life itself is a codified combination, simple and complex at the same time, of a handful of genetic components mixed three by three, which allow for all of our functions.

[3] Everything in our surroundings pushes us in a direction where individuals have to face off against one another in order to grow psychologically and socially. A self-absorbed and autistic sense of self leads irremissibly to mental pa-

ralysis and a flat-lined brain scan. [4] Aristotle maintained the hope of good health in learning to live and to think in the presence of difference. To that end, he proposed that the necessary means should by arranged by the governing parties so that this confrontation of characters could occur habitually in the *polis*.

[5] However, the terrified societies of the globalized world and their territorial reflection provide very little room for this diversity, selecting their communities homogeneously on the basis of race, class and even sexual preference. [6] The contemporary culture of exclusion prefers clear images of itself, and its context is simplified as a result. This leads to paying a very high price in the loss of freedom in the public space we have at our disposal. [7] In order to safeguard the clarity of difference, it is even capable of sacrificing the fruitful mixture of its fragile democracy. [8] The decentralized societies of the future invite participation and do not promote the thematic cohesiveness of their inhabitants, proposing a more fragmentary, mixed organizational character.

[9] Richard Sennett pointed out that this type of society prefers a more polyglot image of itself, inserted into less symbolic hybrid public spaces. [10] The society without a center of power, which is now appearing timidly on all corners of the planet tends to reject the massive and uniform developments of globalization. It recognizes itself better in slower, incoherent growth, proposing a less predetermined image of a spectacular or iconic city.

76 [1] Mixtures are formed through the combination of a number of elements although there is no transformation of their original properties as a new product is shaped [2] There are two clearly differentiated types, depending on the result obtained during the process. [3] On the one hand, the homogenous type, where the elements that make it up cannot be distinguished at first glance, and which display a uniform consistency. [4] On the other hand, the heterogeneous type, where the components can be easily identified, and which maintains a non-uniform composition. In this second type, the subsequent separation of the elements can be undertaken by way of basic methods.

[5] The interest in mixtures comes from the number of states that they are able to produce. This results in the advent of both the most evident aggregates and a number of more complex colloids like emulsions, gels, foams and aerosols. The main difference between them lies in their stability over time, which is defined by the compatibility of the dispersed phase and the dispersion medium into which it is inserted. [6] Lastly, there is the Brownian motion of the particles that make up the mixtures, random in nature, which defines the consistency and the stability of the whole. [7] Some types of sophisticated mixtures like the so-called calibration mixtures are very precise tools for the analysis of variable systems. They are classified using measurements called levels of uncertainty which allow for their traceability throughout the entire process.

[8] Current advances in the technology of mixtures allow for carrying out procedures for the production of states that weren't possible before the novel insertion of catalysts.

The mixture of water and oil, historically heterogeneous in nature, is transformed into a homogeneous state through the addition of palladium nanoparticles. [9] Reactions can be catalyzed on the perimeters of both compounds completely and consistently. The new component from the mixture acts similarly on both sides of the perimeter: the absorbent hydrophilic side and the waterproof hydrophobic side. [10] Likewise, the component can be recovered once the catalysis has taken place, which avoids its presence in the final mixture. [11] Finding the properties that allow for these dual behaviors, given objects with such different characteristics, guarantees the production of amalgamated and stable structures. In them, the initial elements maintain their intrinsic properties, but they make up a new product with unpredictable and multiple uses.

[1] Any territory can be interpreted as a complex mixture **77** of energetic components. The introduction of new uses catalyzes a reaction with the existing conditions, leading to the appearance of potential relationships in terms of repulsion and attraction. [2] This interaction generates seemingly disorganized structures that are free from compositional baggage and urban prejudices.

[3] In order to achieve the Galindo Hybrid City in Barakaldo (1998) in a deindustrialized territory, a process of this type is developed. Percentage distributions of revitalizing uses are produced using a variety of densities with respect to the total surface area of the site. [4] Later, the vectors of reality, or properties of the existing conditions which are

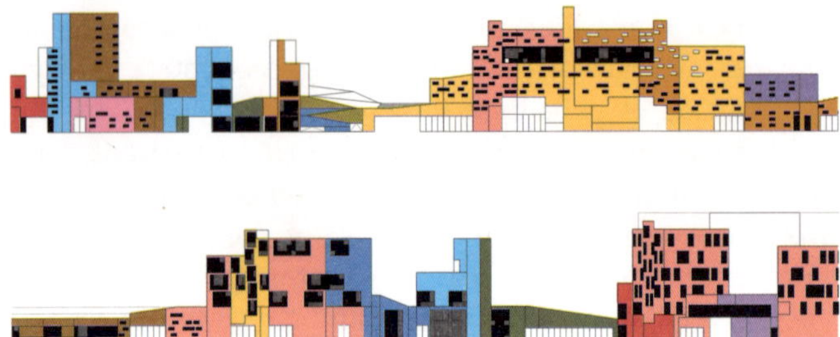

considered fixed or with a permanent presence, are analyzed. [5] Then, the conditions for attraction and repulsion are catalogued from among those properties and the different uses that have been introduced. [6] Mutations in the densities appear as a consequence of this impulse until a balance is reached in their definitive, unpredictable positions in the landscape. [7] Once this balance has been achieved, the uses for building and the ones for open areas are differentiated and grouped together, resulting in the creation of hybrid mixtures in a novel urban structure.

[8] The application of the conditions for accessibility from the public level, the heights for each use and the location of the communication infrastructures transforms the generic embryos into constructive objects. These containers for combined uses uncover surprising and fruitful internal relationships. [9] Promoting the idea of an amiable city that conceals nothing, the urban hybrids express their functions toward the exterior, using codes based on different materials and colors so they can be identified and understood by the public. This generates an urban image,

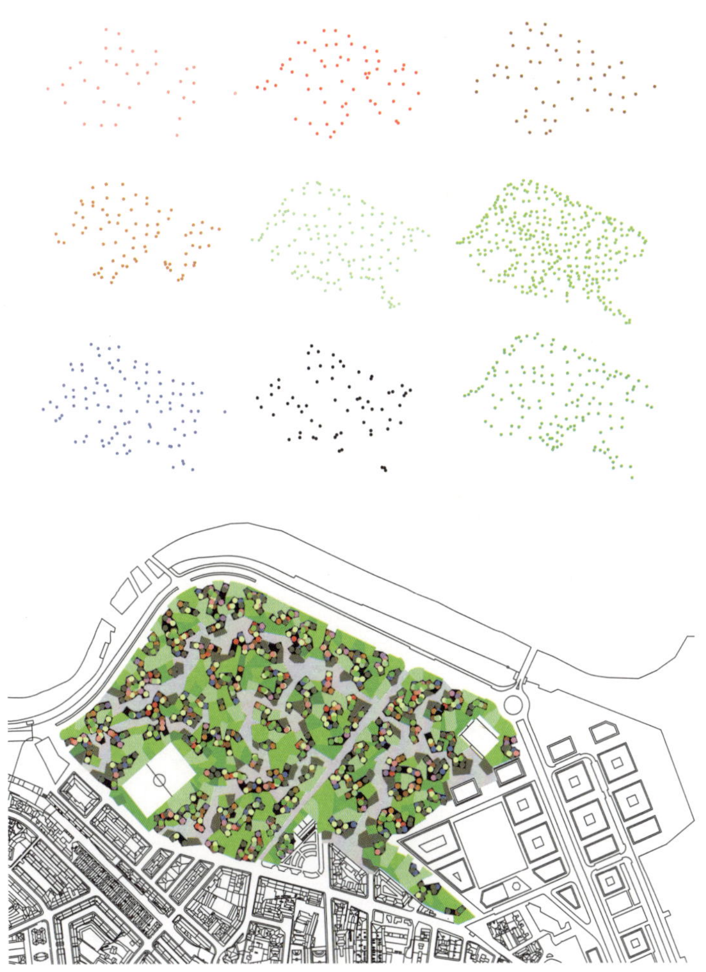

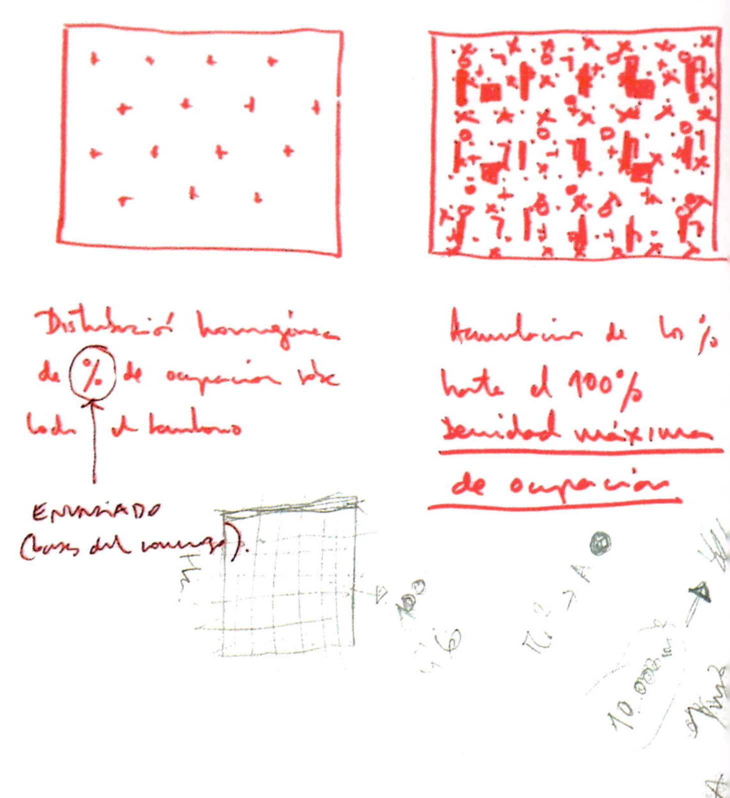

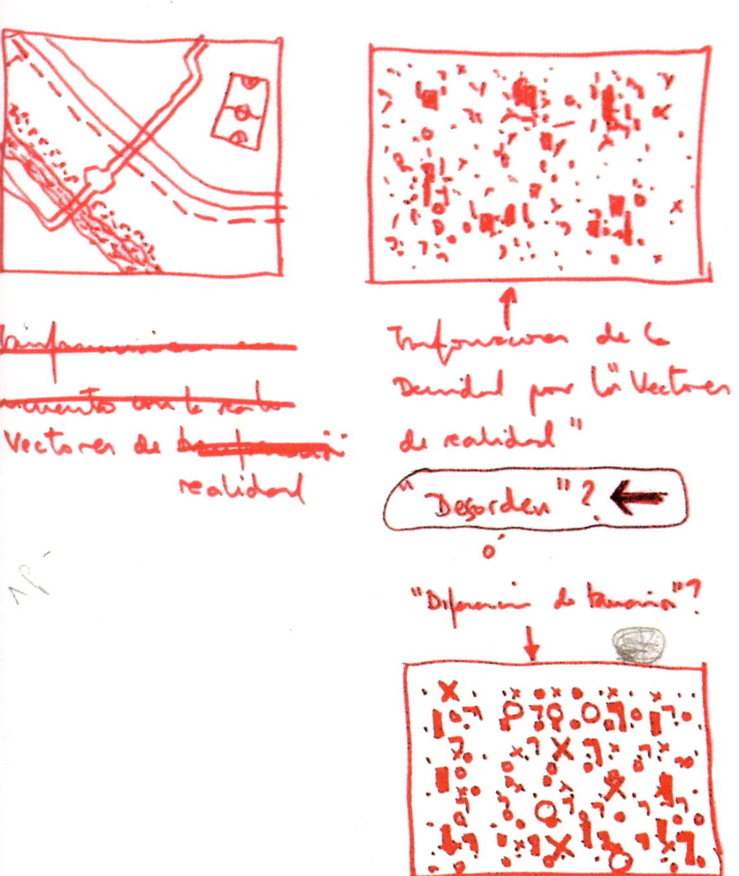
Vectores de realidad
Información de la Densidad por li Vectores de realidad "
" Desorden " ?
ó
" Diferencia de tamaño " ?

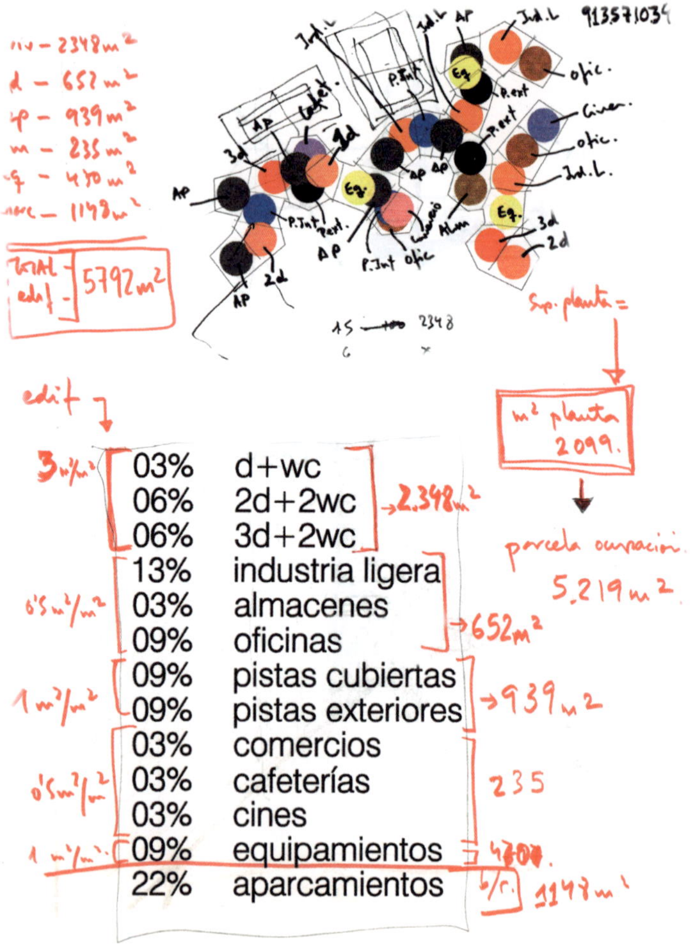

riv — 2348 m²
d — 652 m²
p — 939 m²
m — 235 m²
q — 470 m²
rc — 1148 m²

TOTAL edif — 5792 m²

15 → 2348
6

Sup. planta =

m² planta 2099.

edif

Sup. planta 2099.

porcela ocupación.
5.219 m².

3 m²/m²	03%	d+wc
	06%	2d+2wc
	06%	3d+2wc → 2.348 m²
	13%	industria ligera
0'5 m²/m²	03%	almacenes
	09%	oficinas → 652 m²
1 m²/m²	09%	pistas cubiertas
	09%	pistas exteriores → 939 m²
	03%	comercios
0'5 m²/m²	03%	cafeterías
	03%	cines 235
1 m²/m²	09%	equipamientos = 470
	22%	aparcamientos b/r. 1148 m²

the production of which is removed from a priori conditions of form and design.

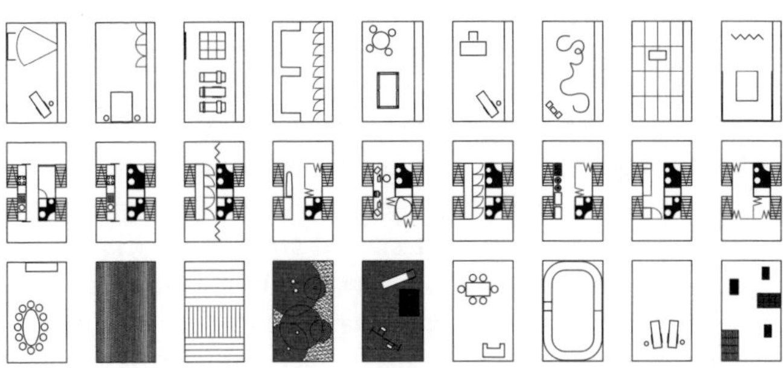

[10] The interior domestic hybridization is also a reflection of the multiplicity of the contemporary individual's character and his atypical characteristics in terms of mobility and communication. This mixture is translated using the identical dimensioning of the spaces that make the dwelling into a place of multiple variations and heterogeneous uses. [11] This gives the user the freedom to interchange the living rooms and recreational areas for bedrooms and areas for relaxation, making maximum use of the lighting and temperature conditions for each season and specific orientation.

[1] The style of language, the typologies and the inherited **78** seductive forms don't convey the need for sharing and enjoying new contemporary public space. The information

that is offered to society is cancelled out by the excess of temporal stability when compared with the variability and unpredictability of inhabitants' behavior. [2] Users resist believing in the permanence of the physical form it promotes, the credibility of which is in question. [3] Reestablishing confidence in creators imposes new factors and new means of transmitting sensory information.

[4] The attraction value of the new public space resides in a possible mix of individualized functions. From this point of view, the information it should transmit initially is a catalogue of the vital and sensory possibilities that it promises for executing the freedom that is longed for by citizens. [5] Sometimes this space is capable of transcending its own construction while uncovering emotions that are traditionally assigned to other arts. This occurs when it clarifies and explains the common man's questions about the world we live in and the reasons we live in it the way we do. [6] It is on par with the paradigms of writing, music or painting, which have evolved in parallel with society in response to questions about the values that help us live together sharing the same space.

[7] But there are not many non-academic descriptions that we can use to clearly transmit this message to society. [8] Creative explanations use a language that sounds strange in the ordinary world and they are sometimes forced to use simplistic metaphors to connect with the perception of the majority, in the search for an innocuous point of dialogue. [9] A less pragmatic reading of place, from the empathetic point of view of a number of combined situations, like the weather or emerging social beliefs, allows for the creator

to backtrack along the path that led to the homogenization of innocuous space, which is not born of life and dies without it. [10] The complex response to these conditions carries with it the implicit requirement that the initial components that went into its creation shall not be discerned when observing the final result. [11] In that sense the creator, as a spectator before a world full of pseudo-poetic references and traditional meanings, should not forget that Kant fled terrified from those who interpreted synonyms as explanations and metaphors as truths.

[1] Public space in the 21st century needs to absorb a multiplicity of behaviors, more than in previous periods, to shape a place of social freedom. It has to be ready to receive collective actions as well as those of isolated individuals absorbed in social networks. [2] This implies the necessity for spatial and ergonomic precision connected with an exhaustive control of landscape based on the creation of spaces of different sizes and atmospheres.

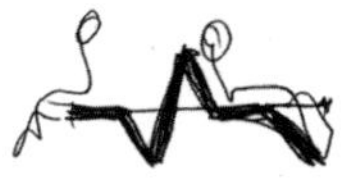 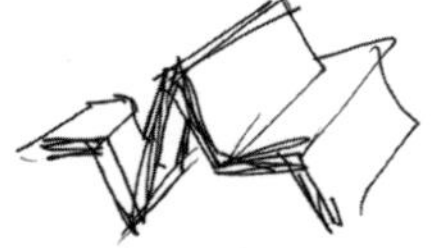

[3] The intention of the new Plaza de Olavide in Madrid (2008) is the homogenization of its structure, providing it with a consistent spatial identity without determining its uses a priori. Different users are left to decipher its func-

tional principles by way of an intelligent and emotional interaction. [4] The size and the ergonomics of the environments guarantee empathy on a personal level or among small mixed groups. [5] The individual dimension is dictated by an object meant to be used in colonizing the space, which can be combined in multiple variations and employed ergonomically for different uses and body positions. [6] The possibility for multidirectional contemplation is explicit in the geometry of this urban colonizing object, thus avoiding the unicity of perspective.

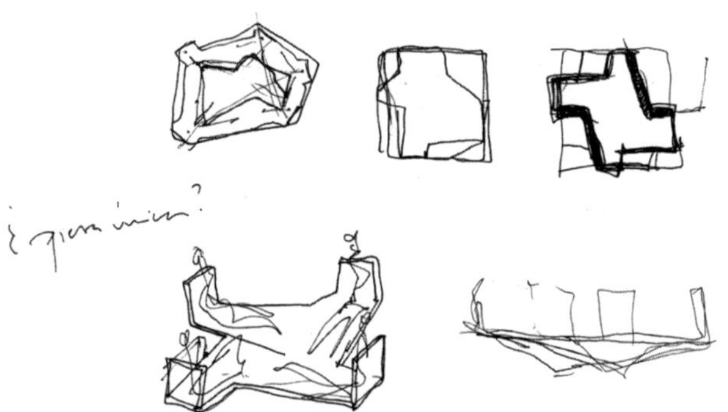

[7] The relationship of this piece with itself, when coupled together and multiplied, creates a matrix of mixed behavior with a whole range of complex structures. Some of these structures act as separators between neutral spaces for individual use, others act centripetally closing off more controlled spaces for group use and, finally, still others adopt a directional nature to place the user into a relationship with the

overall space. [8] Each organization proposes relationships that are bordered by open or enclosed perimeters, which can be larger or smaller, or isolating, accompanied by singularized elements of vegetation that surround and hide them.

[9] The lines of action that serve as a foundation for putting together the chains of colonizing pieces are the result of overlapping different kinds of information. This generates a network based on combining preexisting elements tied in with ventilation and underground accesses, the location of summer terraces or private entrances, the flow of pedestrians, and the seasonal paths of the sun.

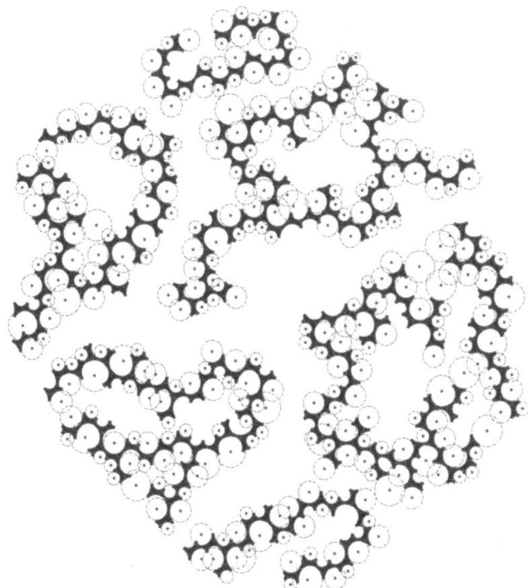

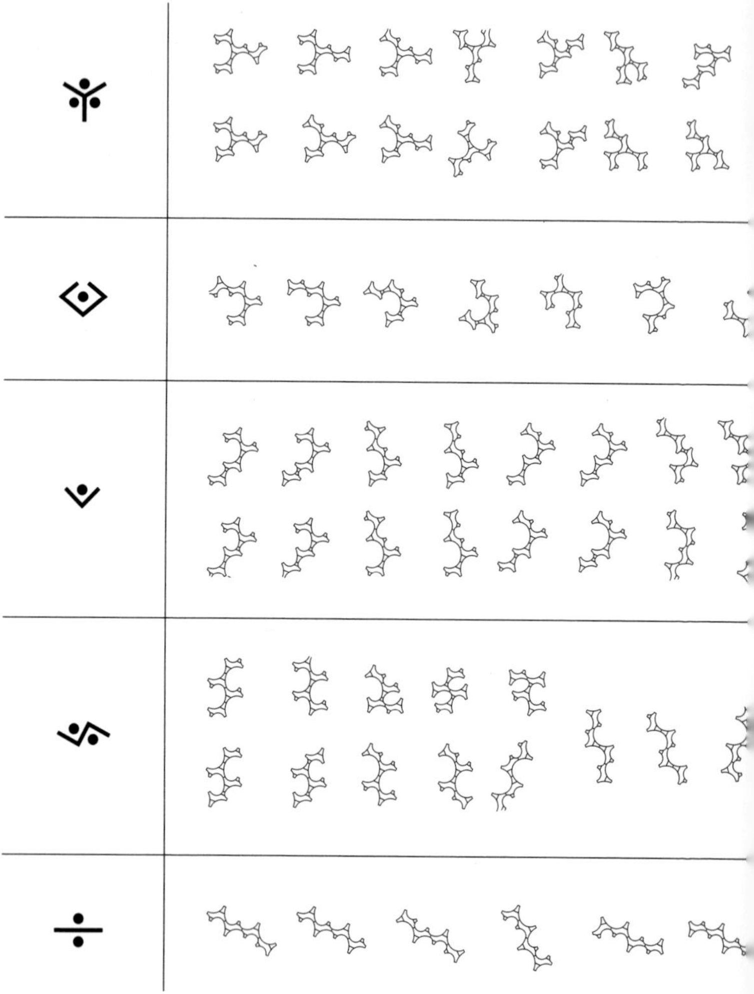

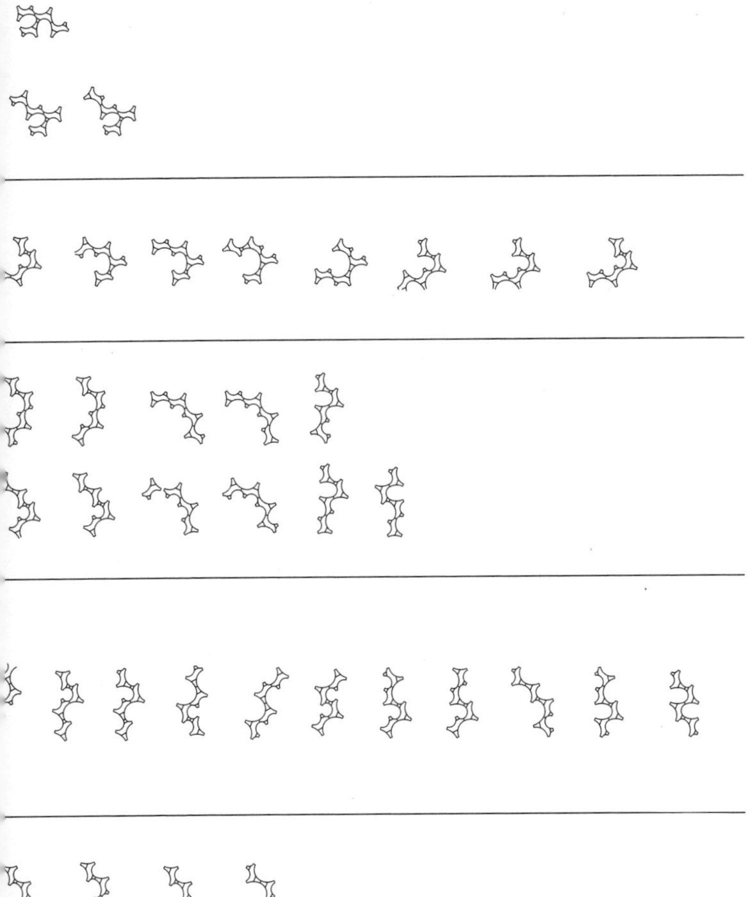

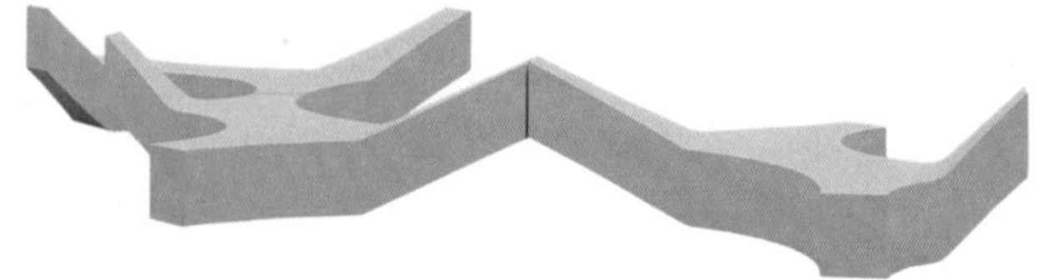

[10] The reading of the final arrangement provides a catalog of spaces that are already qualified by the sunlight, by their size and by their relative positions. [11] This landscape tapestry, which may seem random, acts as a homogeneous foundation for encouraging the discovery of its possibilities for individual and collective use.

80 [1] The totalitarian perception of the city tends to center its gaze on the understanding of place as a stable entity controlled from a place of power. Even so, there are urban elements charged with indetermination in the form of interstitial spaces that cannot be harnessed by speculative planning. [2] Their greatest interest centers on their potential as bordering elements that are capable of absorbing new structuring systems. They are transition pieces between the artificial sectorized city and another possible less segregated one that is more intermingled with nature. [3] These empty spaces, independently of their size, are the driving force for a new shared urban landscape, made up of a mix of programmatic devices and less stable, less closed-off natural elements.

[4] The new urban intensity emphasizes the hybridity of its program, its materials and its circulatory capabilities and it accompanies contemporary Man in the discovery of his communicative affinities and ways of living with the natural world. [5] In this mixture, categories like density or interval, duration or instant, gradient or impulse, threshold or catalyst appear. They are all directed at the elimination of social stratification and the creation and discovery of urban structures that support a combinatorial analysis of the population. [6] Their strength resides in proposing alternative situations that are not found in the traditional city, which raise doubts in the minds of inhabitants as to the urban information they consider habitual in their lives. [7] This acceleration or deceleration of their experiences, together with the recognition of spaces with alternative properties, will spark their desire to penetrate into the unknown.

[8] Participation in a space where the human components are no longer homogeneous, but belong to different creeds, economies or races, requires a generous effort put toward sharing. [9] But again, traditional systems of representation and creating meaning are not useful for defining this new imagined spiritual-ecological sensibility and the timid offers it holds in store. [10] To that effect, the process of creating the hybrid city should be fertilized by disciplines that are external to the traditional practice of urbanism, a fact which is more and more necessary to understanding the transformation of new relationships and hybridization between Man and the space he inhabits.

81 [1] Through the combination of autonomous elements, genetics creates homogeneous fabrics that maintain unaltered properties. [2] This vision allows for contemplating the behavior of urban structures as living textures that can be deciphered as a combination of manipulable information, using systems of a genetic nature. [3] Interventions directed at its intrinsic properties allow for creating mutations in its composition.

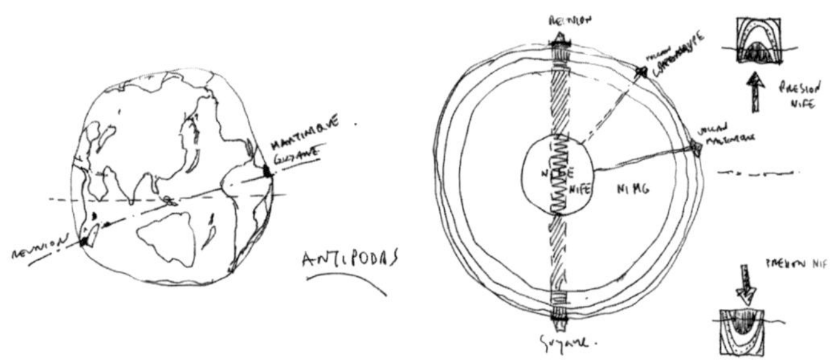

[4] In order to generate the Viral City on Réunion Island (1999) over the existing urban vacancies, we recreated experimental cell farming activities to combine information on the built structure, types of movement, religions and races, or existing uses and materials. [5] The grouping of these cells makes up a generic urban block of aggregated codes that is transformed when it reacts to the existing conditions in each area of inoculation. [6] When this generic cultivation completes its transformation process, the new structures that emerge and their surprising internal mixtures can be read. Promiscuities appear that didn't initially

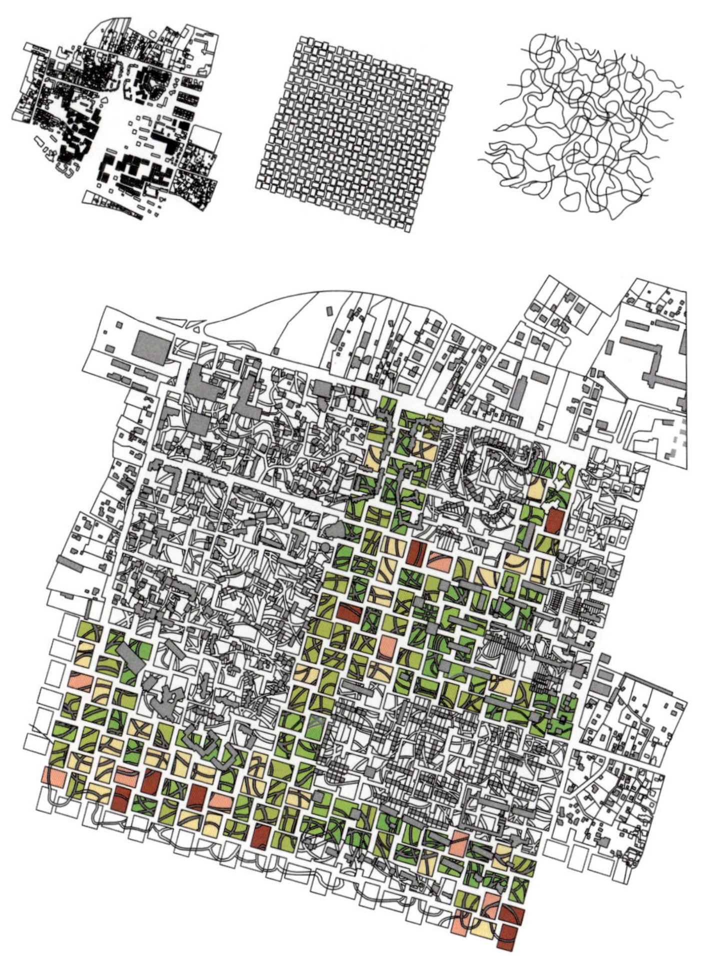

exist, which can be recognized as organizing systems for the astonishing spatial properties. [7] The local materials, from the hard black basalt to the fragile bamboo, are located in the final structure in response to conditions of height, orientation, or proximity to the different speeds of movement. [8] This system of genetic mutation has the following cycles:

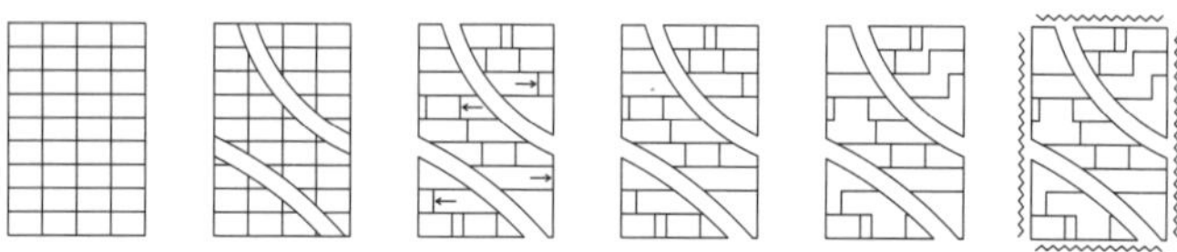

[9] Inoculation of the host cells in the existing urban structure, disseminating the genetic components in each of the replication areas.

[10] Beginning of the pathogenic mutation of the cells using repressors of the existing urban condition; detection of the hybrid formations in the structure.

[11] Defining the continuity of the flow of rapid proliferation of the wheeled infrastructure and the slow transfer of the pedestrian infrastructure.

[12] Analysis and reading of the hybrids involved in the process and the definition of the different densities of built program versus public space.

[13] Reading of the complexity of the new genome, made up of human and material information, in phylogenetic chains.

[14] Analysis of the adaptation sequence of the block and transcription of the mutated nuclei with the appearance of the new spatial mixtures.

[1] "You jerk!" I shout, jumping up toward the sky from my seat.

Makele can't believe it; he starts laughing crazily.

"Seriously, what a day I'm having!" I shout, sitting down in the Jeep again.

[2] As I was opening my sandwich filled with lunchmeat, a bird of mythical proportions swooped down stealthily from above and stole it from me. Since the four-by-four has an open top, the bird put its claws literally in my face and flew off with my food.

[3] I'm beginning to think that Ngorongoro isn't as perfect and self-sufficient an ecosystem as I've been told. We've driven down into the crater at five in the morning to check out the perfect balance among the species. [4] While the driver was sleeping soundly, I didn't catch a wink, with all the zebras kicking our tent. To top it off, at breakfast I got distracted for a second and a giant Marabou stork absconded with the crepes that I had made.

[5] Half starving, I look around to contemplate a world where space is broken up in a very peculiar way. Each animal species occupies a clear-cut area, sharing the water from the interior lake and the existing vegetation. The animal groups and their different densities make up precise limits, but with varying perimeters. [6] In the absence of predators, their peaceful societies share the resources in a balanced way. I imagine that the lions and hyenas have never come up to the summit of the extinct volcano and they have no idea that its perfect cone is full of tasty morsels.

[7] The flocks of pink flamingos appeared some time ago, then the zebras and the wildebeests woke up and a slow group

of hippos came lazily out of the water. They are all moving with such exact timing that we can change position slowly in the four-by-four to watch them appear in the specific places that they occupy.

[8] It's disturbing to consider how the circular shape of the volcano is occupied compactly by groups that attest to its geometry. [9] Time is an important factor in taking in the sight, twenty-four hours of different species alternating, appearing and disappearing, in this living machine. The stable blend of their movements and the particular occupation of space confer it with the image of a closed mechanical system.

[10] And, despite the sandwich, I feel like its perfection nears that of a tourbillon-equipped Jaeger-LeCoultre,

"Finally, a mixture of precision allied with life."

83 [1] There are objects that do not let the internal complexity of how their components are combined show through in their exterior image. [2] Milk, for example, appears as a single product with a homogenous appearance, but a magnified vision reveals a composition of independent particles that do not react in a heterogeneous way. The adaptation of the different-sized particles and the relationships of the tension along their perimeters maintain consistency to prevent break-down. [3] Hybrid compactness within a condensed volume allows for grouping dissimilar programs together while the internal operation remains unchanged and the perimeters of intersection are resolved symbiotically.

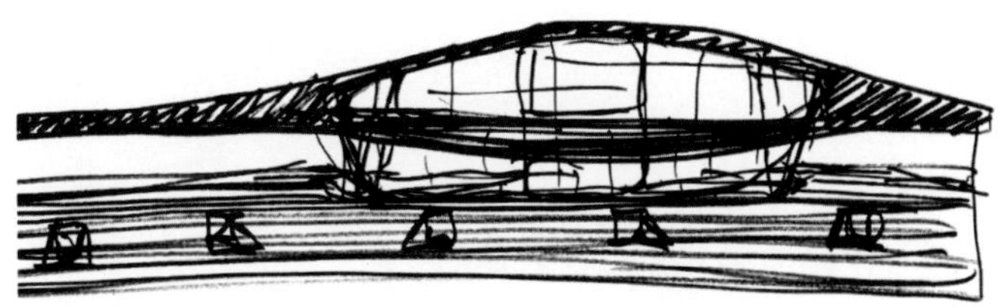

⁴ This course of action combines uses that are apparently incompatible with the Prés-de-Vidy Stadium in Lausanne (2011), like office space, the municipal maintenance group, a hotel, commercial uses and a nursery school. ⁵ This mixture guarantees that the object remains functionally alive within the surroundings even on days when there are no sporting events. The time frames for its different uses enrich and activate the public space around it, maintaining a constant intensity both internally and along the perimeter that breathes life into the new district. ⁶ The decontextualized position of the main volume leads to the appearance of spaces that the stadium walkways feed into counterclockwise. The rotation of the built perimeter with respect to the playing field creates additional deformations on the four sides where the additional uses are situated.

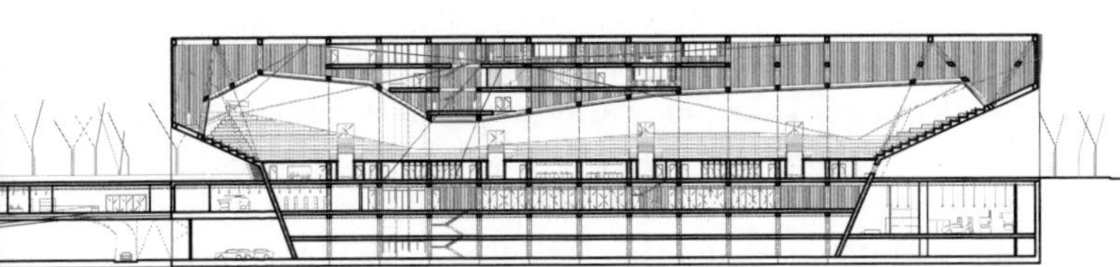

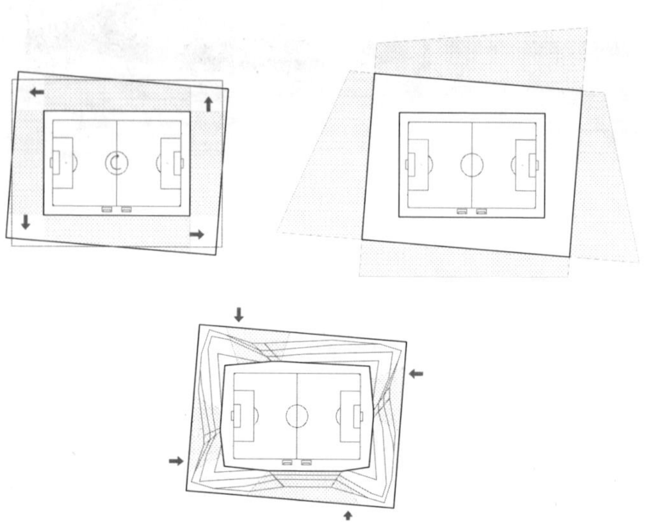

⁷ The manipulation of the enclosure allows for efficient vertical accumulation of the program as well as conditions for private and public accesses and security. ⁸ The variable interior volume provides the building with a peculiar façade inhabited and hybridized by programs that create new atmospheric values. ⁹ The orientation and the privileged location in terms of height promote a transversal relationship between the playing area and the mountainous landscape of Lake Geneva, in addition to resolving the functional perimeter. ¹⁰ The choice of material for the enclosure responds to a combination of logics tied in with energy, maintenance and the durability of the construction

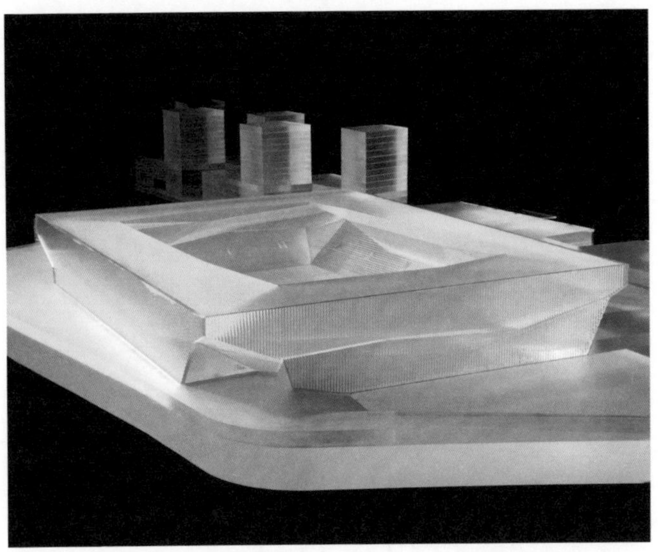

based on a zigzag arrangement that blurs the volume when it is viewed in movement. [11] The distorted amalgam of internal uses seems to transmit the message of a very vague essential compound.

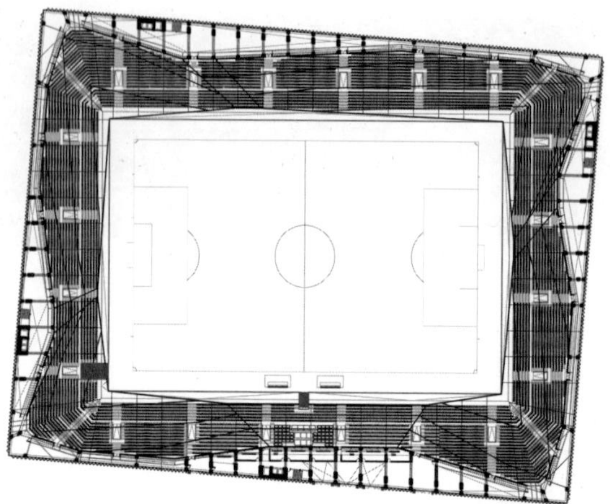

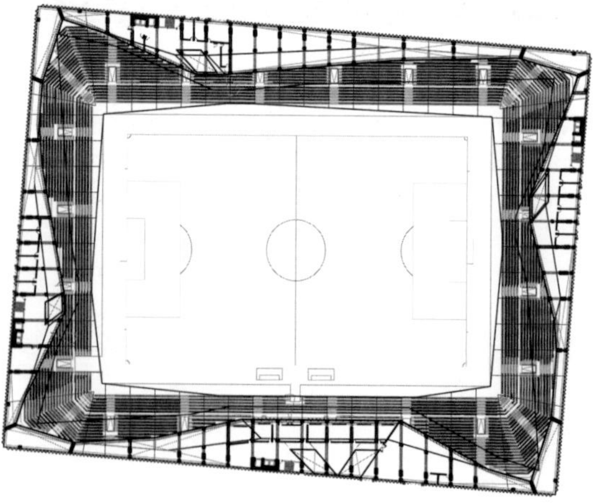

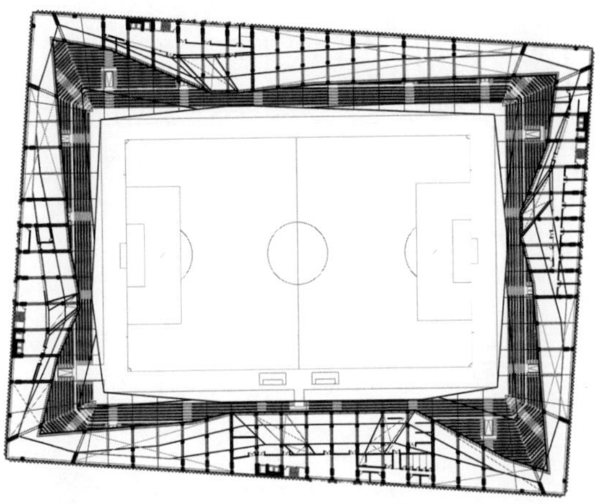

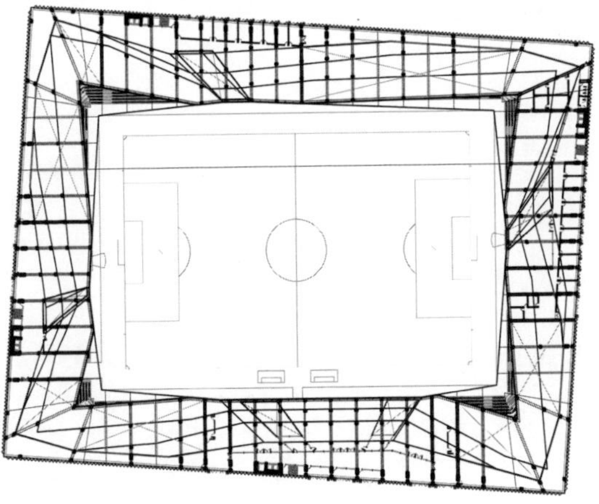

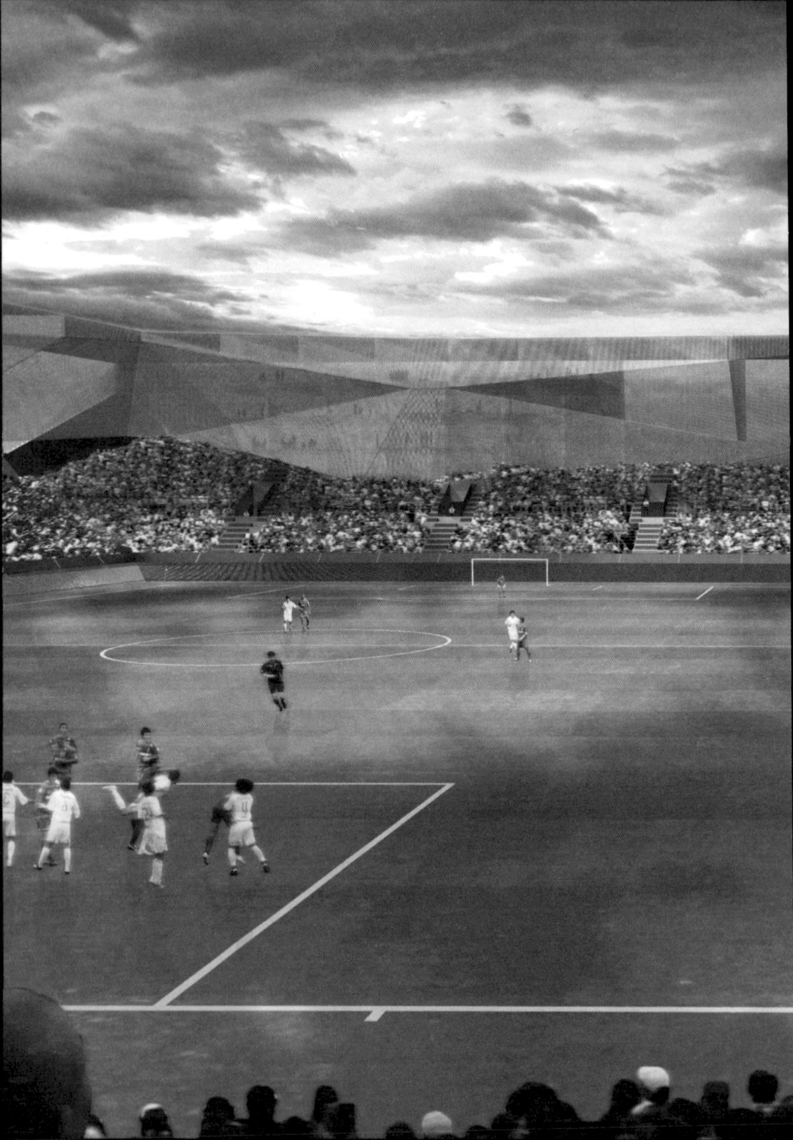

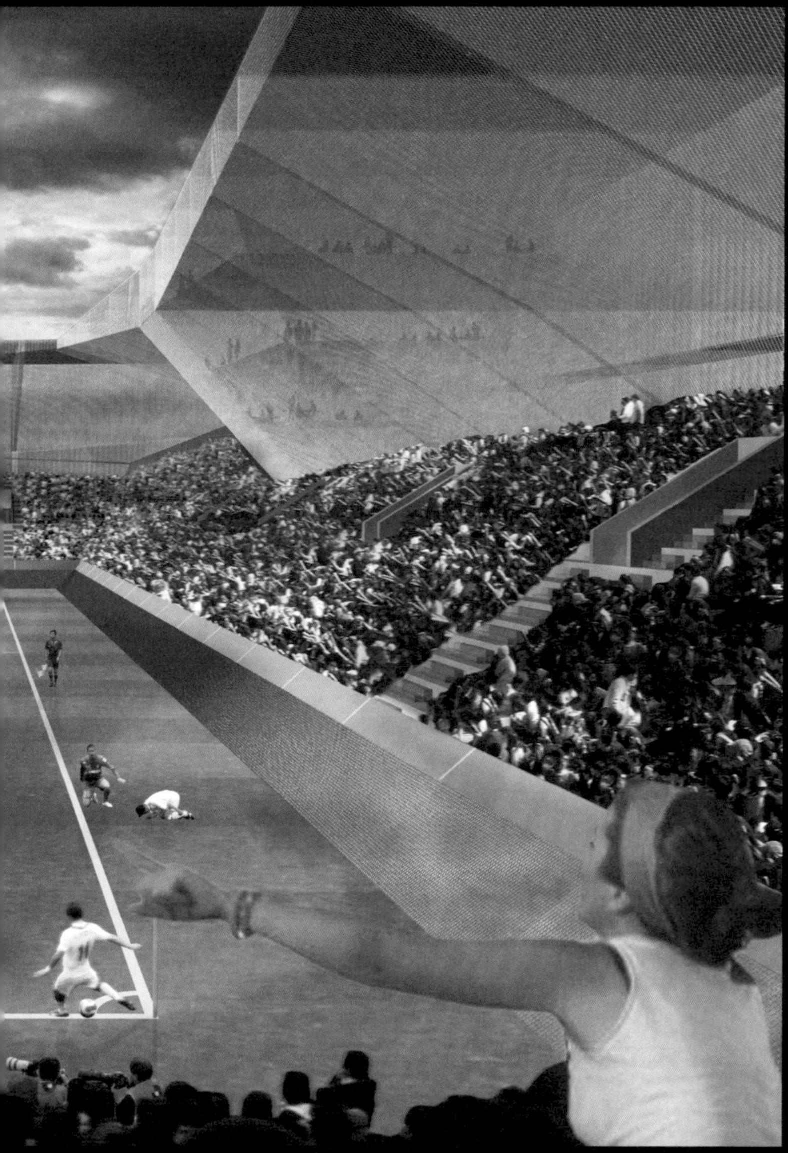

AN EGG IS FULL OF PROCEDURES

"Shall I refuse my dinner because I do not fully understand the process of digestion?"

WILFRED TROTTER ————————————————————

¹ To celebrate my return to life after heart trouble, I decide to gather some friends together for dinner, using recipes from the Futurist Cookbook. ² The drink of the night was an "Alcoholic Joust," from a recipe by Enrico Prampoli, an unshaken mixture of two parts Barbera d'Alba dry red wine, one part lemon juice and one part Campari. I served the chilled liquid with a cube of cheese and a cube of chocolate on a toothpick laid across the cocktail glass. ³ I set out Fillia's "Edible Alphabet" on the circular table, placing each guest's initials on the plates, cut in mortadella from Bologna, thick enough so that they stand upright. Each guest identifies his or her letters and sits in the corresponding chair.

⁴ Then I prepare "Hunting in Heaven", another Fillia recipe, for the main dish, based on hare. The piece is slow-cooked whole in sparkling wine mixed with grated coconut until all of the liquid is absorbed. Then it is soaked for a minute in abundant lemon juice. It is served over a large amount of green sauce made with spinach and juniper berries, sprinkled with anise-flavored silver pellets.

⁵ When it's time for dessert, I serve "Diabolical Roses" with "Mafarka Pudding," two recipes by Pasca d'Angelo. ⁶ For the first, you mix two eggs, a hundred grams of flour, the juice of half a lemon and a teaspoon of olive oil to make a uniform paste. Pull the petals off of a few soft red roses and toss them in. Then slice it thin and fry it in boiling olive oil, like Jerusalem artichokes, and serve hot. ⁷ For the pudding, heat 50 grams of coffee in half a liter of milk with sugar and add 100 grams of rice, cooking it until the liquid evaporates and the rice is al dente. Once it is cool, add lemon

zest and 50 grams of orange flower water. Put it into a mold and chill it in the refrigerator. The taste of the warm roses and the chilled coffee-flavored rice with orange blossoms creates a formidable combination.

[8] For the farewell touch I put together a cocktail created by Barosi called "Fire in the Mouth." Put two cocktail cherries, rolled in ground cayenne pepper, into a collins glass and fill it one-third full with Scotch. Slowly add honey until it creates a waterproof layer a few millimeters thick. Fill in the final two-thirds with equal parts of Alchermes, Strega and Vermouth. [9] The guests smile at me ironically, knowing that they can go home to their beds with a clear conscience.

85 [1] The developmental genes located on chromosome 12 are in charge of the first mutation on an egg's path toward becoming an embryo. [2] This occurs through a process that creates two asymmetries of information in the liquid, a head-to-tail axis and a ventral-dorsal axis. These instructions correspond to gradients and shifts in genes' chemical products and they represent the first adaptation to space on the part of the cells that will become a human being. [3] The egg is full of procedural data concerning positioning, which directs each cell to the place where it can best develop its function. [4] This type of adaptation process implies the establishment of the appropriate guidelines and the minimum instructions necessary to lead to an optimum resolution. During the process, the paradox arises that some of the information and instructions necessary for the operation of the system disappear from the final result.

[5] Fuzzy logic systems are also sensitive to variations in the environment and to the inexactitude of our perceptions. They cannot be defined as problems where the response is 0 or 1. Faced with this restrictive binary solution, they put forward a fuzzier option: "If x occurs, then do y." [6] As such, it is a question of choosing the most precise independent values, never of fusing extreme values. [7] Between black and white we do not find a grey scale, but the colors.

[8] A dive computer manages algorithmic tables to warn us about decompression stop times and calculate the correct speed of ascent depending on water temperature, water density, the possibility of releasing carbon dioxide and the nitrogen permeability rate. There are never two identical combinations in the same surroundings at different times. [9] ABS brake systems also adapt to the environment with instructions like, "If the ground is slippery and the wheels lock up, release the brake," similarly to the autofocus systems on photographic lenses.

[10] These processes involve continuous calculations that take into account unpredictability and the variability of Man's relationship with his surroundings, through the use of fuzzy logic. [11] Many current creative problems require adaptive optimization solutions. [12] The construction of the real requires algorithmic thought that works with data from the territory and from our sensitivity, dictating vague instructions for action that couple together intuition and possibility.

86 [1] Part of Catastrophe Theory is based on a generalization of the problem of maximums and minimums associated with the gradient functions that are generated in a particular state. [2] This leads to the appearance of valleys and mountains associated with the values for each property, which are used to filter reality and the definition of geometric separations in the transitions. [3] The set of places where there is maximum intensity or tension associated with change is used to create a location system for optimum resolution of the question at hand.

[4] In order to generate a new University Complex in Sarajevo (2000), in which inhabitants will perceive a sensory flow but not a contextual one, urban properties are evaluated and selected that tie in with how space is used as opposed to its shape. [5] In this directed reading of the urban environment, which uses thematic maps of topological data, the following concepts are represented:

[6] The density of uses and the quantity of users, which provide its intensity and mixture.

[7] The dynamism of each flow in movement, which contributes the feeling of fluidity in transit.

[8] The potential for development or land use for each program in the city.

[9] The time frames for each use.

[10] Foreignness, as a measure of the races and credos of the people in each area.

[11] Publicness, to measure how the space is integrated into society or how islands of privacy appear.

[12] Permanence or the speed of use, which measures the feeling of the continuity of time in the city.

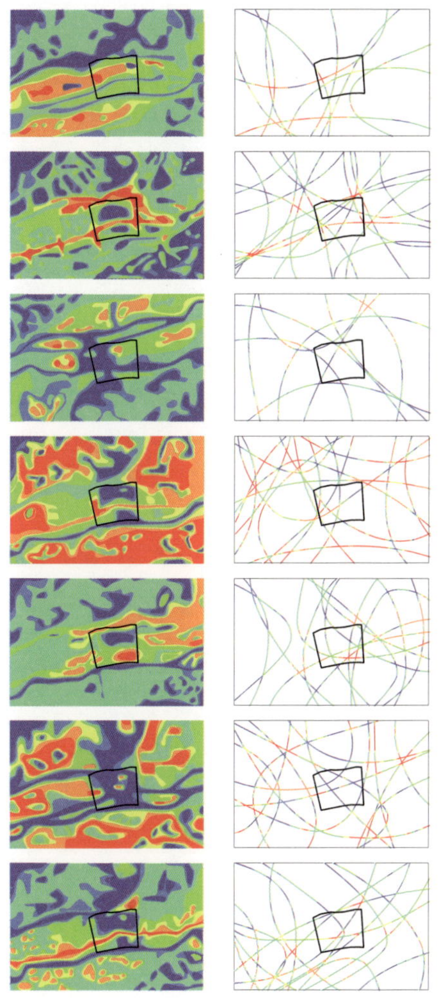

$$MV = M'V' = K$$

QUANTITY OF MOVEMENT ALWAYS CONSTANT... AN ISLAND OF CONTINUITY WITH[IN] THE CITY, AND A ~~WEIRD~~ ~~STRANGE~~ ENCOURAGING FEELING OF PARTICIPATING ON A COMMON MOVEMENT TOWARDS FUTURE!

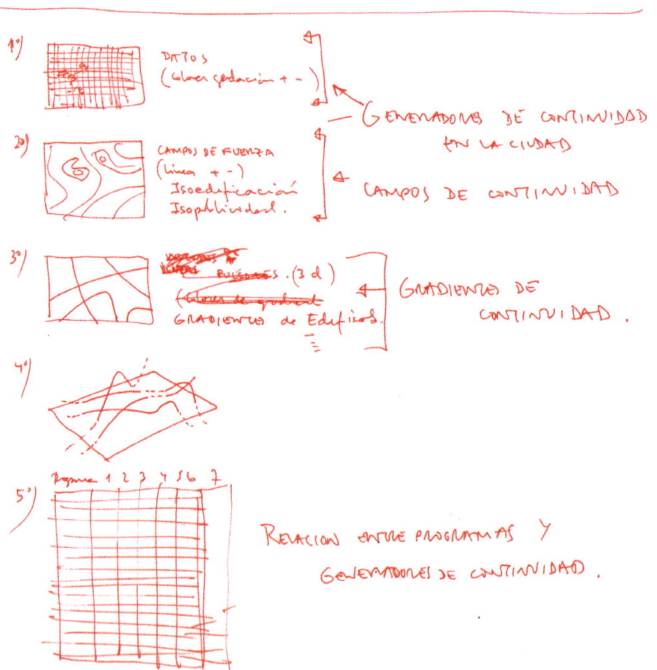

6°/ LOCALIZACION DE PROGRAMAS.

  A – Por Obligación — Zona C
                      — Zona C1

  B – Por Afinidades →

   Programa X → Afinidad — curva generadora 1 {
                           curva generadora 7 {

curva generadora 1

— curva generadora 7

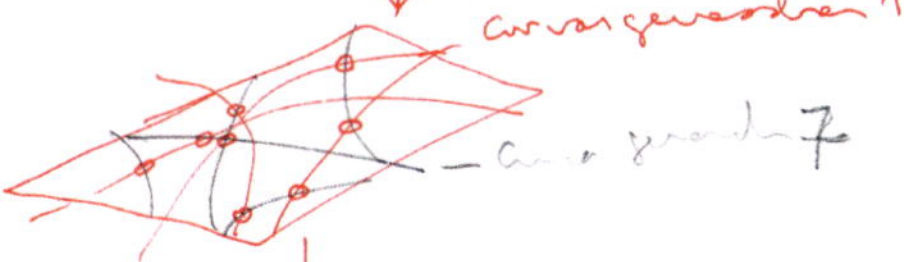

Localización en intersecciones
de Gradiente máximo (OJO)

7) Cuanto mayores son los gradientes mayores
son las alturas? → Gradiente 1 (+5) + Gradiente 7 (+5)

Altura máxima

→ Gradiente 1 (+3) + Gradiente 7 (+4)

Coeficiente de reducción
o deformación.

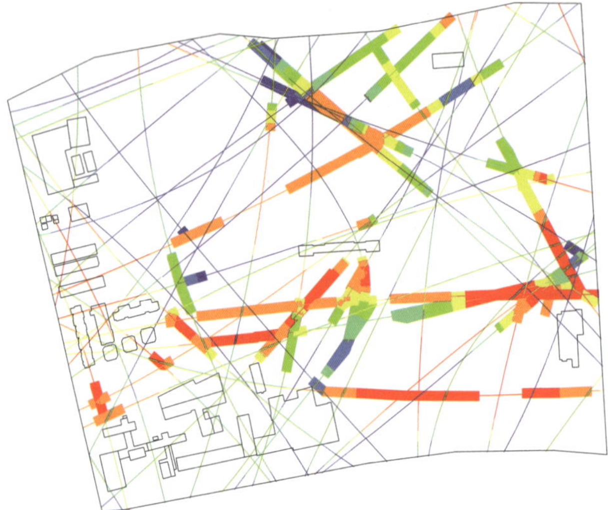

[13] Using the information obtained, force fields are then recreated which provide the variations in each concept as it crosses the area to be occupied. The gradients of those fields reveal invisible lines of hidden data that flow through the city, uniting maximum and minimum values for each of the concepts that generate continuity. [14] The force fields that overlap create a global field that ties them together, defining a map that indicates the optimum locations for the new uses based on their affinities.

[15] A table of these affinities is used to define the behavior of each use with respect to the selected properties, which allows for locating their surface areas to correspond with

the ideal gradient or the most beneficial intersection. [16] The buildings intended to house them appear in their definitive form by preserving the quantity of movement for each use: $M.V=M'.V''$ (number of people in movement per built volume).

[1] Sometimes I ask myself questions like: **87**
"How can we transform reality without hardly touching it? How can we command part of the world from a distance?"
And, directly afterward, I think about the possibility of absorbing those decimals that separate ideas from their connection to the real. [2] Then I ask myself again,
"How can we make a carnival mask that has the precision of a face? or how can we make a shock-absorber that doesn't need oil? or How can we adapt with the precision of a woman's stocking?"
[3] This sense of optimization resides in an invisible world of series that move toward a limit without actually reaching it. They are the key to the strength of any process aimed at adapting to existing conditions. Instructions without excessive definition, which bring together intuition and reality, dreams and possibilities. [4] Between a yes and a no, you won't find a "maybe", but a "which". This ability to choose makes them all the stronger, a range of possibilities as opposed to a binary doubt. [5] Finally, it is a decision of affinity versus agreed-upon appearances.
[6] From this vision of the possibility of transforming reality remotely, I encourage the production of "A Child's Molotov Lantern" to attend the Three Kings' Day parade. The process for its assembly and use is clearly defined.

LAMPARA DE NIÑOS "MOLOTOV".

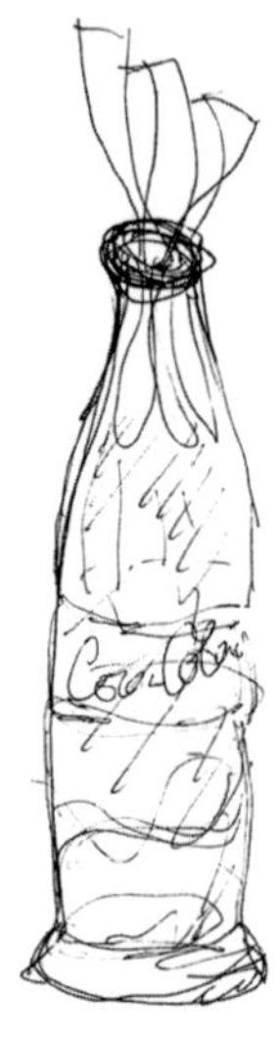

ROBAR A MAMA DEL FUEGO
1- ~~ENCONTRAR~~ UNA BEBIDA EN
BOTELLA DE CRISTAL, ~~DE~~ VACIARLA
EN EL ~~BIDET~~ INODORO SIN DEJAR
2- ROBAR A ~~~~ PAPA UN
PAÑUELO DE LA MESILLA
~~SOLO~~, SIN MOVER LOS DEMÁS.
~~3-ROBAR~~   OBJETO

3- ROBAR A PAPA DEL GARAGE
LA GASOLINA DE LA CORTADORA
DE CÉSPED Y RELLENAR LA
BOTELLA.

4- INTRODUCIR EL PAÑUELO
A PRESION HASTA ~~TOCARLA~~
EMPAPARLO DE GASOLINA

~~5-~~

5- ESPERAR MUY FELIZ EL PASO DE LOS "TRES REYES MAGOS."
ENCENDIENDO EL PAÑUELO CON UN MECHERO SÓLO AL VERLOS.

6- (OPCIONAL) - ARROJAR AL PASO DE LOS TRES REYES MAGOS,
CON PERMISO PATERNO
PROBABLEMENTE EL ALCALDE, ~~Y LOS CONCEJALES DISFRAZADOS~~
EL CONCEJAL DE URBANISMO
Y EL DE VIVIENDA DISFRAZADOS DE BUENOS.

⁷ Steal one of mommy's black drinks in a glass bottle from the fridge. Empty it into the toilet without leaving behind any traces.

⁸ Steal one of daddy's handkerchiefs from the night stand without moving the rest.

⁹ Steal the gasoline that daddy keeps in the garage for the lawnmower and fill the bottle.

¹⁰ Push the handkerchief into the bottle until its soaked in gasoline.

¹¹ Happily await the passage of the parade; light up the handkerchief with a cigarette lighter when they come into sight.

¹² (Optional) Throw the magic lantern in front of the three kings, probably the mayor, and the city council members in charge of town planning and the environment, disguised as good people.

¹ The interest sparked by the manipulation of the genetic **88** information contained in DNA chains allows for a huge number of applications, some of which are still suspect from an ethical standpoint. ² There can be no doubt that these procedures allow for correcting illnesses caused by genetic defects and lead to the appearance of new medical and industrial chemical compounds. But they are also directed at creating new species of plants and animals that enter into the human food chain, with all of the uncertainties that entails.

³ One of the most developed procedures for genetic manip- ulation is based on using a kind of enzyme that is capable

of recognizing specific sequences of information in order to separate them from the rest of the double helix. The use of these Plasmids is the most common method and it allows for a large degree of precision in cutting the exact dimensions of the genetic material. Afterward, a different kind of enzyme is used to reinsert the segmented chain into the organism to be modified.

4 Another manipulation process is undertaken using a replica of genetic material called a Viral vector, which involves cloning in the strict sense of the term. During this process, the information is extracted in the same way as described above, but then it is inserted on the back of an artificially created virus, which allows for interaction with the genetic information of the recipient. The viral material then has to be removed so that the organism does not fall ill, during a phase that is difficult to execute. 5 The problem with this method lies in the lack of precise results, due to the possibility of interfering with healthy genetic material, affecting its proper function.

6 The least precise but most effective technique, especially when it comes to cloning plants, is Biolistics; it consists in shooting micro tungsten particles coated with genetic material into the cell nucleus. 7 The problems with this approach lie in the fact that the inserted genetic material always interferes with healthy information and its alteration can result in the organism's collapse. This is the invasive technique commonly used in the transgenesis of crops.

8 With any of the methods mentioned here there is a component of chance, which can cause the intended transformations to provoke unexpected mutations. 9 Some create

useless aberrations, but others allow for surprising, original discoveries.

[1] The basic difference between a creative procedure that is **89** guided by operating laws and a legislated bureaucratic action lies in the fact that the former personalizes the way we take on the problem without an a priori idea of the result. [2] The latter is always directed toward the achievement of a concrete end and it requires blind faith in ISO standards.
[3] For the creation of a Sports Center in Irun (2001), the procedure for action is based on absorbing the requirements for variable time lengths associated with each recreational use and the erratic rhythms of the public administration

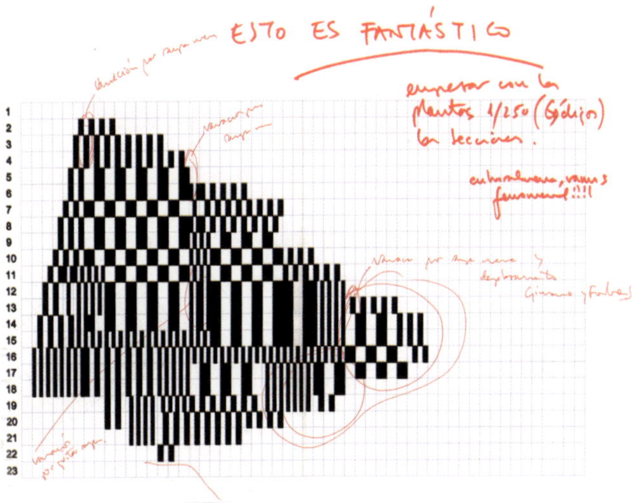

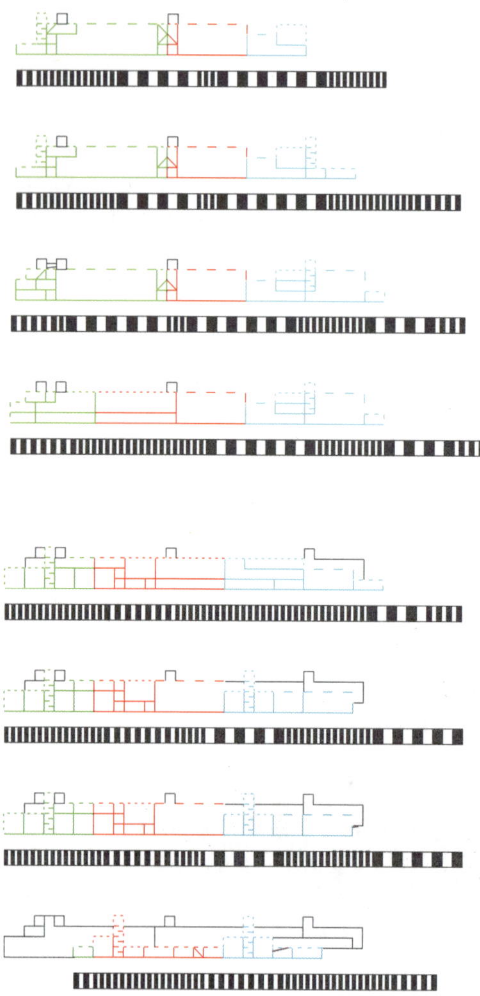

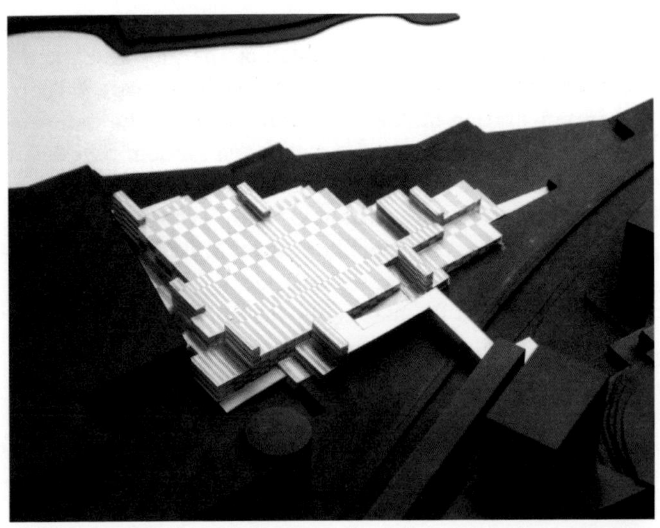

in managing the construction. [4] The sum of these timeframes, added to the energetic conditions, translates into a versatile, generic construction system. Its flexibility allows for responding to the structural specificities and the lighting and temperature requirements for each program individually. [5] The combination of three materials – wood, concrete and glass – according to percentages is reflected in a set of prefabricated elements that can be combined to resolve the practical needs associated with the uses they house.

[6] This generates a series of strings that tie together information, which can be adapted to any unexpected variations in program for constructive or administrative reasons. [7] The set of twenty-three chains, with similar appearances, behave

like a vibrating system that defines the geometry by adapting to the conditions of the perimeter of the plot and the dimensions of the structural voids for each program. [8] There is a fragmentation of the roof resulting from the independent folds of each string, which creates a random pedestrian topography made up of a number of combinations of materials. The gradation of the folds into levels guarantees a smooth continuity of the public space that stretches between the river and the city on the hillside.

[9] The conditions for managing the building in different phases are also absorbed by the system, which allows for building for each use independently based on the necessary length of each string, with complete autonomy. [10] Any incident during the construction or management will result in a new topography which, though it may be different, will maintain the same appearance and usefulness. [11] This wide field of possibilities appears as a result of following the rules for the folding process in addition to the flexibility of the combination of materials.

90 [1] In a world full of machines that calculate, discover and bring reality closer to our perception, it is important to distinguish between probability calculation and fuzzy logic. [2] The former is a numerical representation of the statistical value at which an event may occur or a problem may be resolved, from within a field of possibilities. [3] Conversely, fuzzy logic employs orders that are directed at choosing the optimum value from within that field in order to resolve the occurrence in question.

[4] Fuzzy logic gives machines the ability to make decisions similar to the ones people make, while maintaining an elective role. The intermediate decisions are always located between the affirmation and negation characteristics of a machine that responds to a binary logic. [5] The subtlety of fuzzy logic resides in the use of non-traditional data sets in which a group of objects can belong to more than one set at a time, demonstrating the ambiguity of its properties. These flexible sets reveal a gradient of belonging that is defined by gradual transitions, without clearly defined perimeters. That means we can claim that a bottle is either half full or half empty at the same time.

[6] The systems that handle this type of logic, called expert systems, are capable of making decisions intuitively. In the same way that someone who is very knowledgeable cannot clearly differentiate the specific field of knowledge that informs a decision. [7] In that sense, the system's data base has to be loaded with sufficient previous values to allow for making decisions based on ambiguity. [8] The classification of all that data, assigning it degrees of membership to various fuzzy sets, allows for working with the vagueness of the intrinsic properties of each object and the problem that needs to be resolved. [9] As a result, the fields for the application of fuzzy logic always appear in highly complex situations.

[10] This type of system proves very effective in the analysis of the segmentation of the territory i.e., in the identification of regions with homogeneous properties. [11] The algorithms designed for that purpose create readings of the information by filtering it through pixel matrixes made up of different

kinds of data corresponding to a single property. From the interpolation of those readings, using a fuzzy algorithm, we can obtain the optimum values that respond to the original problem by way of a series of approximations.

91 [1] Adaptive creative processes work with data populations that are codified using a whole battery of parameters chosen a priori according to the type of problem that needs to be addressed. [2] The procedure operators in the system are summarized by the instructions that manipulate and transform the data, activating their exchanges with the surroundings. [3] Their successive application generates new data populations as a result of their adaptation to the reality in which they are being applied. The manipulation of these new appearances, based on the possibilities for cross-pollination between them, generates a consistent and homogeneous hybridization among functions, sensitivities and realities. [4] Studying the adaptation to specific needs requires a prior definition of the orders in the system that will be used, as well as the filtering of the environment according to properties tied in with the question. [5] An adaptive system generates a more optimized, effective and robust result that is specific to each environment.

[6] The relationship that the creator establishes with whatever serves to generate the working system: a thought, a myth, or the properties of a place, defines how he will proceed at any given moment. [7] The success of each procedure depends on the amount of data in the sample that is being used; there is a minimum threshold, under which

procedures shut down and fail to produce results. [8] Then unexpected structures begin to emerge, without pre-established formal values, and the only law of formation is the constantly transforming relationship between what already exists and what wants to exist. [9] They are not looking for a natural mannerism or a high density of scientific confirmations to serve as an excuse, but rather contact with rules that define the optimum evolution of the matter and the energy of an element with respect to its predecessor. [10] This generates urban structures that are adapted to reality, based on the precision of information from the existing city and the new uses and lifestyles of contemporary Man.

[11] The freedom of these creative processes resides in their ability to leave behind compositional limitations through the implementation of original instructions. [12] They absorb dissimilar information from various fields, whether energetic, perceptive or social in nature, something that natural selection already instills in living beings through their innate condition of adaptability in the interest survival.

[1] Creating public space in a place where the city has yet **92** to exist requires a working procedure that combines abstract thought with an understanding of the historic loose ends associated with the place.

[2] On the site of the Plaza del Desierto in Barakaldo (1998–2000), cleared out by deindustrialization, a chaotic atmosphere of memories persists, composed of nocturnal lights, steel tubes, tar-stained railroad ties and rails, charcoal greys and puddles interspersed with overgrown bushes. [3] The

1 ACERO   5 BOSQUE
2 ASFALTO   6 AGUA
3 ARENA   7 PIEDRA
4 MADERA   8 VERDE

INCOMPATIBILIDADES

· AGUA   · VERDE
· PIEDRA   · BOSQUE
· ASFALTO · ACERO
· ARENA   · MADERA

CODIGOS DEFINITIVOS

```
1 2 3 4 5 6 7 8                    1 2 3 4 5 6 7 8
        5       8 —                        5       8 —  VERDE | BOSQUE
      4         8 —                       4         8 —  VERDE | MADERA
    3           8 — |piedra| — 8
1       5       8 —       — 5     1                 8 —  VERDE | ACERO
      5   7     —                     5   7         —  PIEDRA | BOSQUE
          7 8 —                           7 8 —  PIEDRA | VERDE
1   3           —                 1   3             —  ARENA | ACERO
1     4         —                 1     4           —  ARENA | MADERA
        6   8 —                             6   8 —  AGUA | VERDE
    3 4   7   —        — 7            3 4           —  ARENA | MADERA
      5   7 8 —                      ( 5    7 8 — )
        6 7   —                             6 7     —  AGUA | PIEDRA
      4 6     —                           4   6     —  AGUA | MADERA
    3       7 —                       3         7   —  PIEDRA | ARENA
1         6   8 —      — 6
          6 7 8 —    [scribble]           ( 6  7 8 — )
    3   6   8 —       — 8 — 6
      4 5   8 —       — 5
 2      5        —    — 5
    3   6        —    — 6
      4     7   —                     4        7    —  PIEDRA | MADERA
      4 5        —    — 5
    3   5        —                 3   5             —  ARENA | BOSQUE
 2          8 —                   2             8 —  ASFALTO | VERDE
1           8 —
      4 6 8 _        — 6
    3     7 8 —      — 8
    3   5   8 —      — 3                   [scribble] —
```

creative system attempts to maintain the presence of this hidden atemporal order in the new public space, as a link between past and future. [4] To that end each existing material, identified using a chromatic code, is quantified according to units of surface area which are grouped into densities in relation to the total dimensions of the space. [5] These

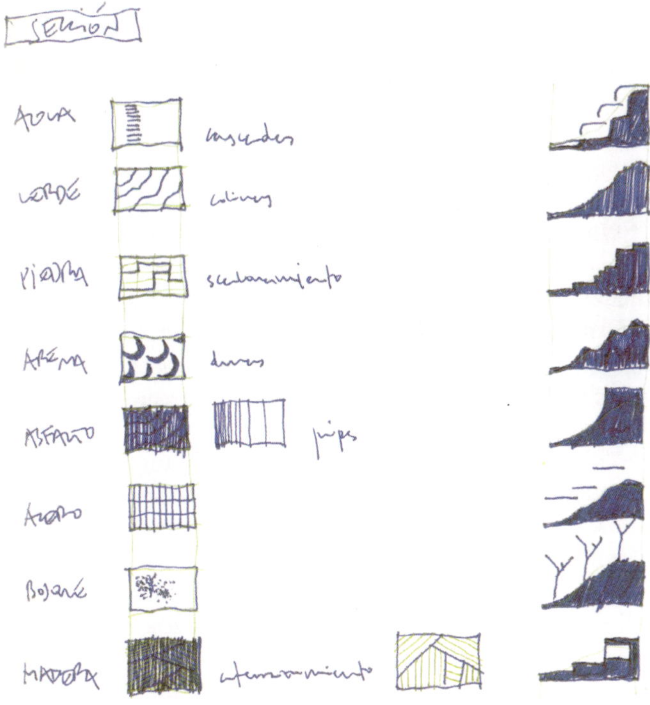

units of surface area are referred to as urban rooms and are equivalent in size to the living room of a house.

[6] In order to act on an area surrounded by future buildings and variable shadows, traffic noise, firefighters' accesses and visual axes taken from the master plan, a series of rules of fuzzy logic for each material are established. [7] They are behavioral rules of the type, "If there is a fire truck crossing, then there will be no water," or "If there is a visual axis, there will be no trees," and so forth, until there are enough orders to allow for the process to operate smoothly. [8] The displacement of materials in accordance with these incompatibilities results in a distribution based on new mixtures of rock and trees, water and stone, concrete and steel, among others, which are translated into spatial and constructive realities.

[9] Where steel appears by itself, the topography is characterized by elevated rooms that allow for discovering the hidden order. Knotted tubular structures rise above these deformations, scrawling across the night, while providing light. [10] The vegetation also takes on specificity through densities, pruning, heights and colors that underscore the degree of privacy that corresponds to each room.

[11] This creates a grid of multi-material lounges, with no instructions for their use, which promote empathy among users. [12] This self-generated space forms a game board that provides a multitude of opportunities and an intense kaleidoscopic vision: lovers in hidden rooms, old men meeting to tell their stories or children with their toy boats, watching the ethereal skateboarders. [13] It is the reflection of the complexity of abstract action in the service of life.

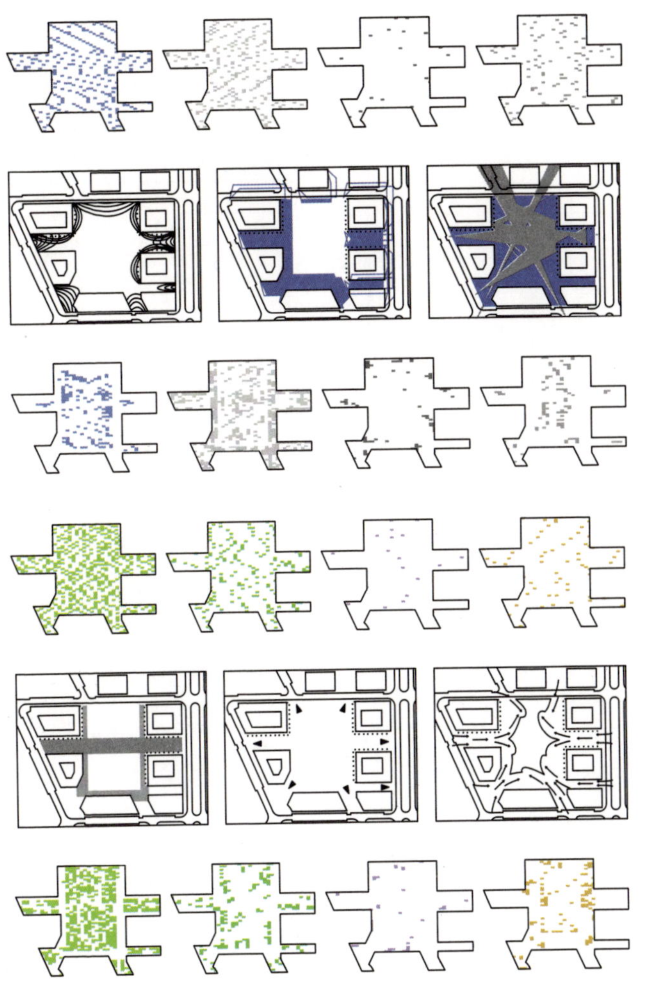

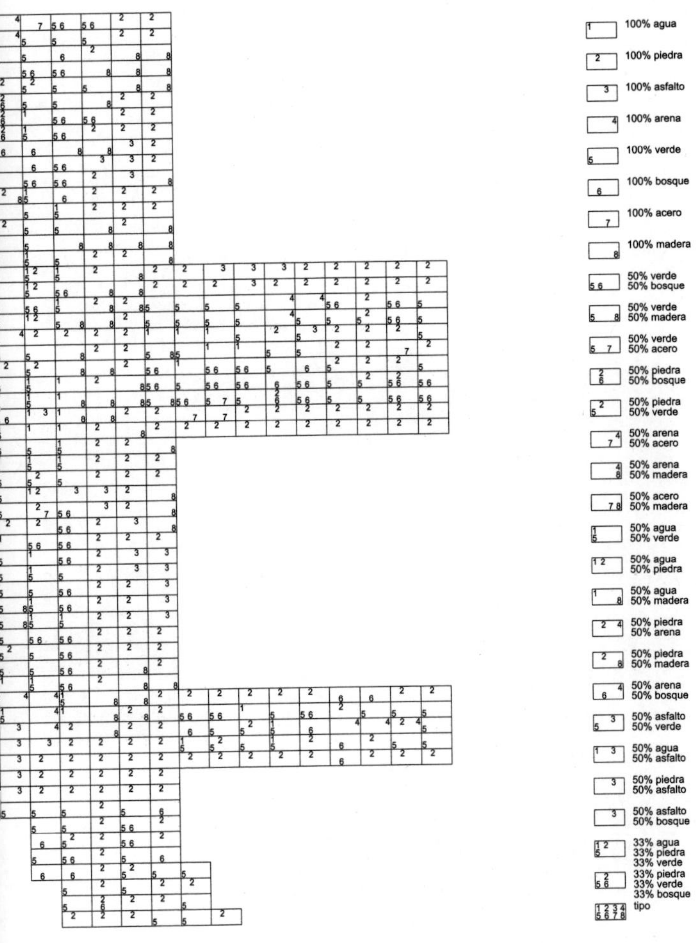

1   100% agua
2   100% piedra
3   100% asfalto
4   100% arena
5   100% verde
6   100% bosque
7   100% acero
8   100% madera
5 6   50% verde / 50% bosque
5 8   50% verde / 50% madera
5 7   50% verde / 50% acero
2 6   50% piedra / 50% bosque
2 5   50% piedra / 50% verde
4 7   50% arena / 50% acero
4 8   50% arena / 50% madera
7 8   50% acero / 50% madera
1 5   50% agua / 50% verde
1 2   50% agua / 50% piedra
1 8   50% agua / 50% madera
2 4   50% piedra / 50% arena
2 8   50% piedra / 50% madera
6 4   50% arena / 50% bosque
5 3   50% asfalto / 50% verde
1 3   50% agua / 50% asfalto
3   50% piedra / 50% asfalto
3   50% asfalto / 50% bosque
1 2 5   33% agua / 33% piedra / 33% verde
2 5 6   33% piedra / 33% verde / 33% bosque
1 2 3 4 5 6 7 8   tipo

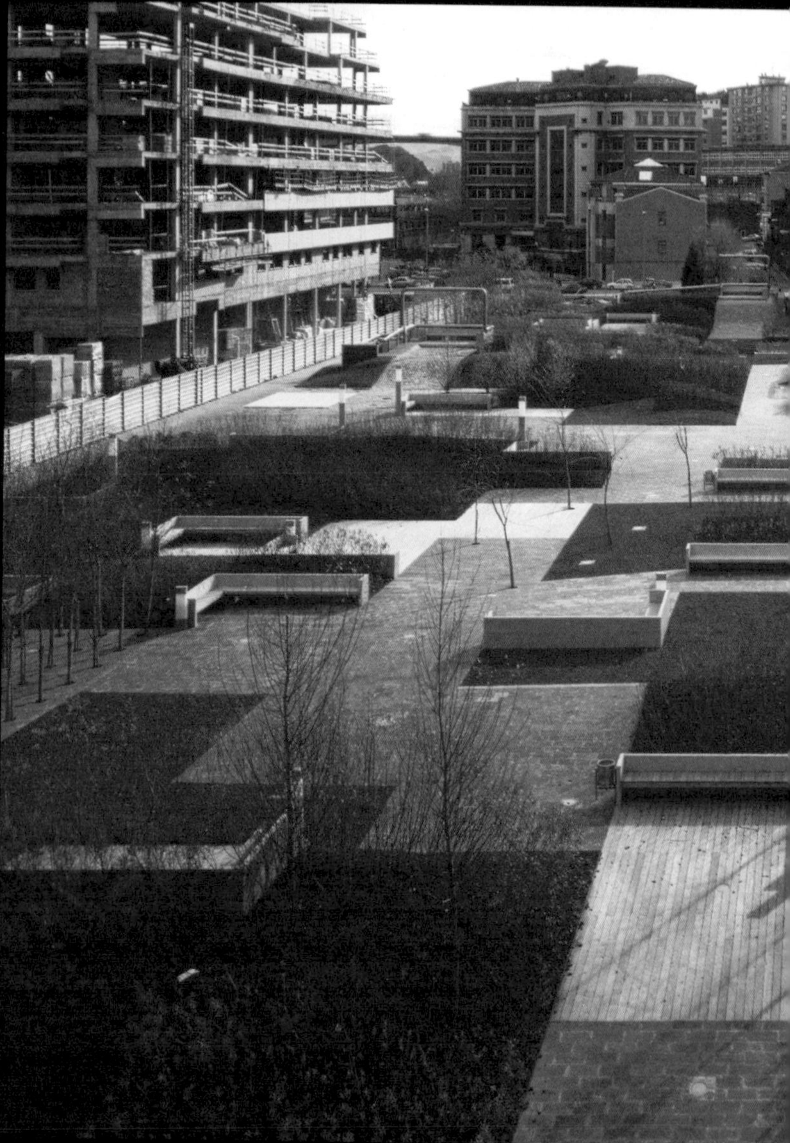

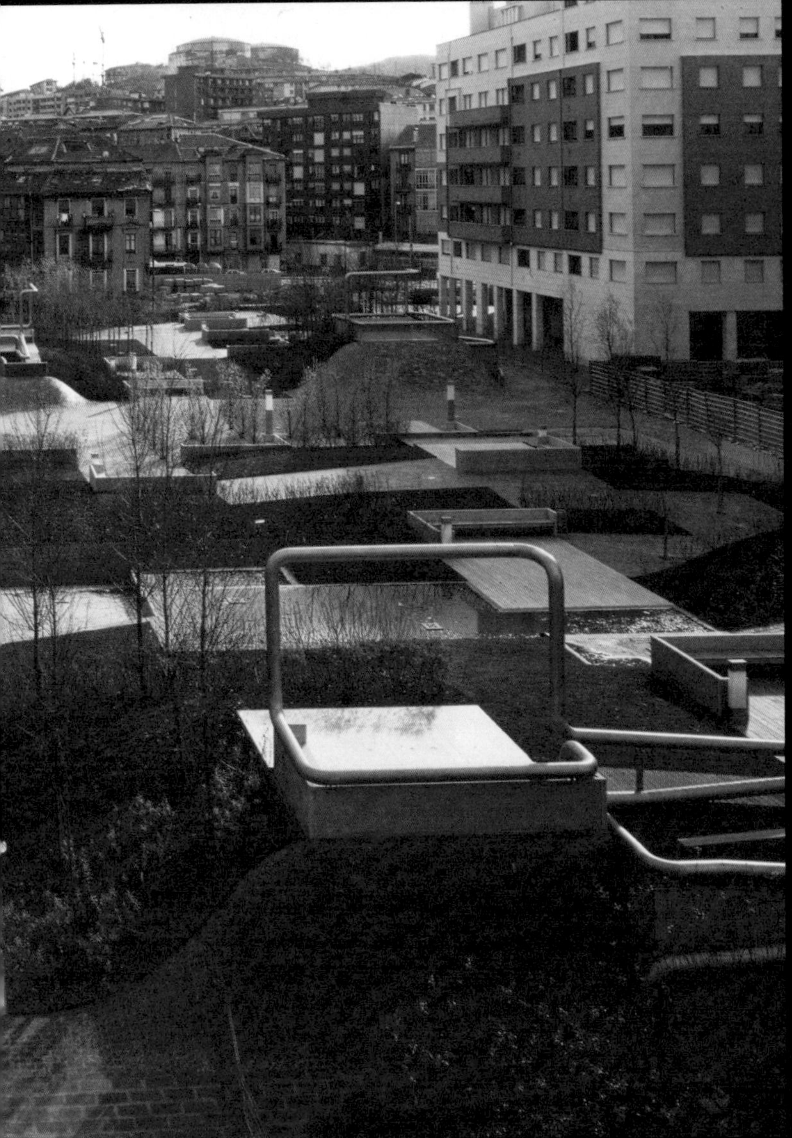

PRESENCE MARKS THE DIFFERENCE

"Everyone sees what you appear to be,
few really know what you are"

NICOLÁS MAQUIAVELO ——————————————————

¹ I've just read in a newspaper that slides will cease to exist **93**
and that we won't be able to find slide film to load into
mechanical devices that are destined to become obsolete.
² Finally, the digital energetic world has colonized everything
and is unrelentingly substituting the world of matter and
its analog manipulation.

³ Standing on the balcony, with my Leica resting on its
powerful tripod, somewhat dispirited, I sense that this
adventure in transformation is coming to an end. It was
in that same position, faced with the perception of the
changing views of Madrid's Gran Via, that I was struck with
desire to capture what we feel exists, although we don't know
how to perceive it.

⁴ Day after day, new elements have invaded the identical
field of vision. Though it is difficult to make out exactly
what they are, the presence of sensory novelties is certain.
Their temporary nature crossed fleetingly through the stable
reality, endowing it with hidden presences. Light, weather,
traffic, advertisements, people's movements and changes in
the sky, ungraspable aromas, in combination or separately,
subtly transform the permanent aspects of the world.

⁵ In order to decipher these unperceivable variations of
what remains constant, yet with an altered presence, I decided to take the same picture, without a fixed time period,
until I was able to catch a glimpse of that essence. ⁶ It's been
a little over ten years and thousands of similar, yet varying
images are gathered in worn out photo albums. Straight
frames, shots that are volumetric, heroic, blurry, artistic,
raw or colored, reveal subtleties in a single form that are
tied in with the extraordinary aspects of everyday life. ⁷ No

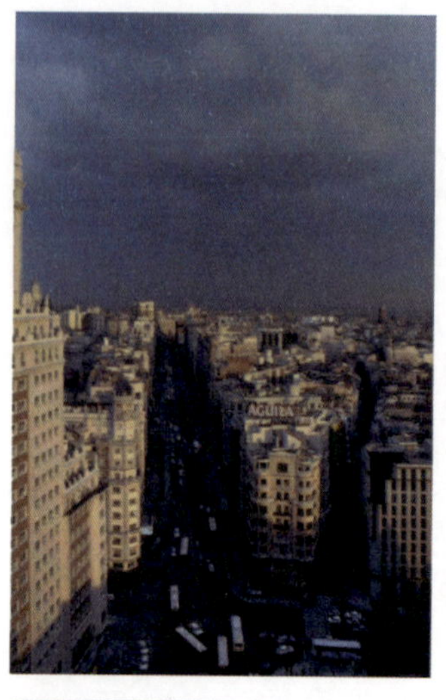 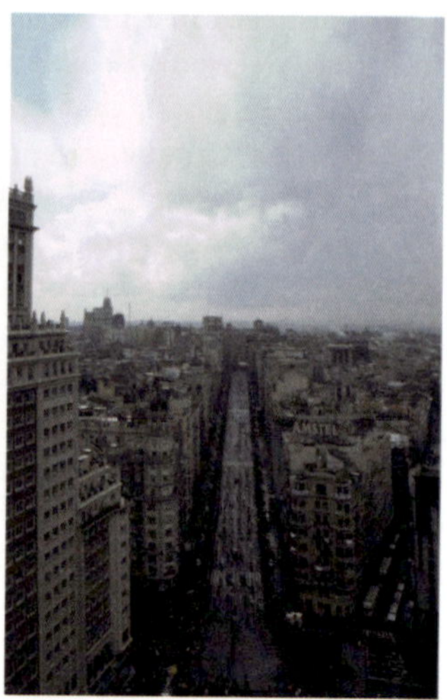

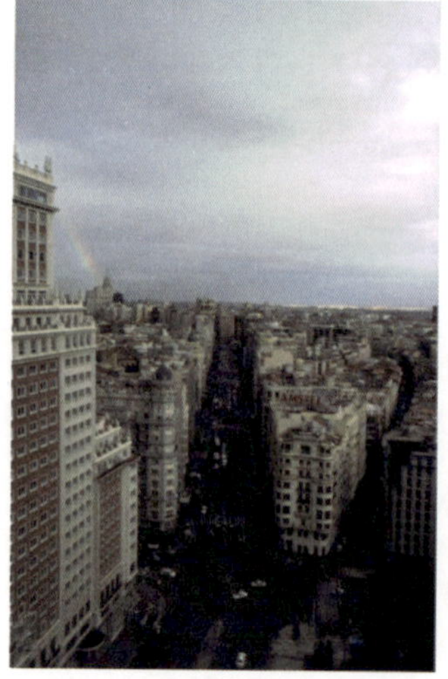 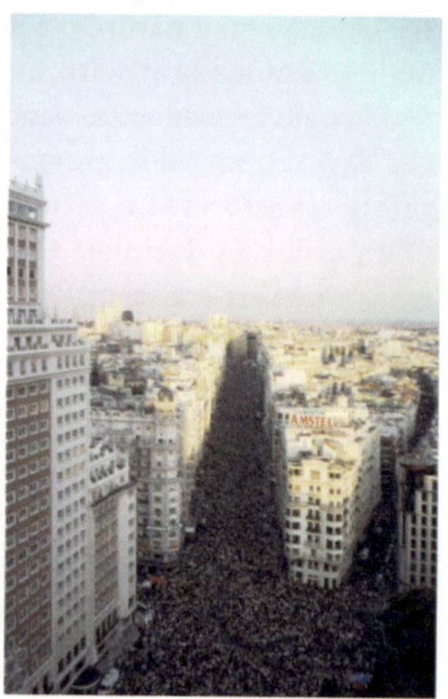

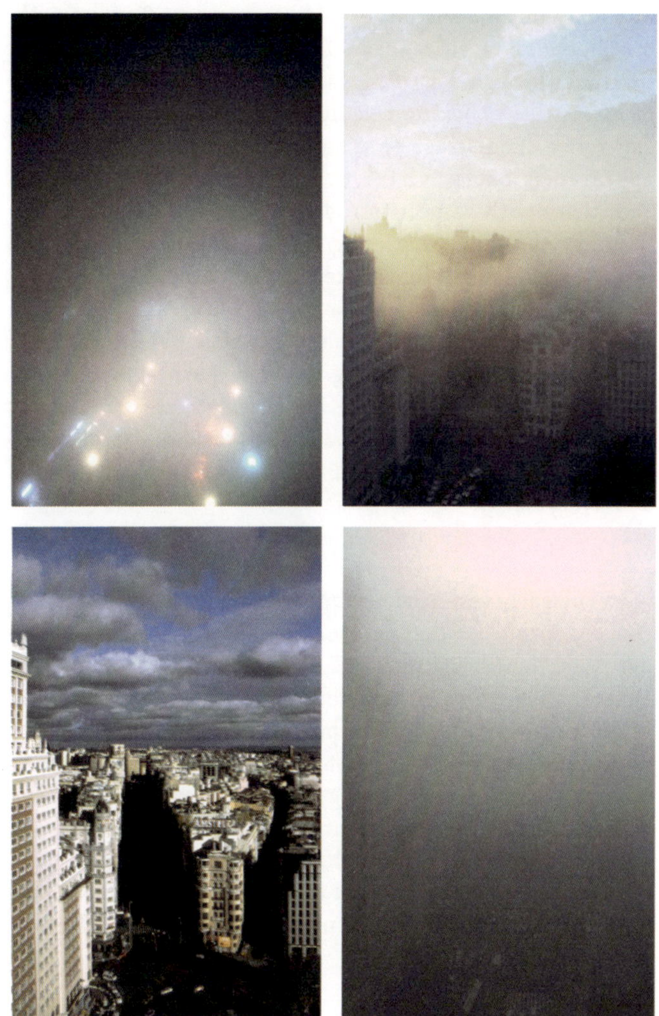

one of them, individually, holds the secret of what really occurs, but all together they tell of presences that are chained together through a passing gaze, which reveal the mystery of existence. [8] Looking fixedly through this kaleidoscope I can relive the passage of time, not through the superficial appearance, but by virtue of what gives each of them its specificity with respect to the rest, their presence.

[9] Today there is a dense fog and I think that there is no better way to finish up this technological assault on the gelatinous look. The message-empty nothingness erases the memory of all the intense moments that have occupied a city that, today, isn't talking. [10] Before pushing the button on the shutter-release cable, I've understood compellingly that something has ended and that a world of extreme sensitive precision is disappearing. This is my final slide. Nothing and everything.

94 [1] In the early seventies, Jacques Monod developed the idea that evolution is the result of a chain of errors and accidents during life's attempt at copying itself. [2] He surmised that chance was a pre-established internal order in the replication of nature for the purpose of progress in the face of the environment, and not a series of acts of free will. [3] From this point of view, it seems reasonable to believe that Man's attempt to copy himself, maintaining the same identity and constant thought, is the worst service he can do. Hence, Monod's proposal of a constant search for positive accidents directed at progressing beyond what we already know.

⁴ Reproducing and copying objects through cloning is then revealed to be useless, since as an object develops with respect to its predecessor, evolutive actions occur that alter its presence with the appearance of new properties. ⁵ Within this chain of discoveries, the way the creative journey takes place always hides the dizziness of failure, but it promises an unknown path for reveling in the appearance of the unexplored. Each different working system tied in with an initial idea or object displays along the way both the initial potential properties and their evolution. ⁶ These properties bring about a series of rules that connect the abstract thought that encompasses all of the possible variations of an object with the conditions of reality that affect it. ⁷ When they are confronted, differentiated but vaguely similar structures appear; their recognizable familiarity originates in dynamic or unforeseen accidents.

⁸ In the creative world, the age of turning a quick profit has led to cloning objects from other existing ones, eliminating the subtlety that is conferred onto them by their adaptation to the properties of their surroundings. ⁹ Overall, in the mountain or on the beach, in the city or in any town, public buildings or housing, far from representing the diversity that is present in any act of adaptation, are exhibited as autistic-natured copies. ¹⁰ Multiple objects are manufactured serially and marketed as open to personalization to hide their inability to adapt, providing the illusion of individuality. ¹¹ This world of identical spaces drives people to share the same generic information, without any capacity for becoming rooted in a place.

95 [1] Seeing people or objects with a clone-like appearance is a peculiar event in routine life, and it is still surprising to see two identically dressed twin sisters walking down the street. [2] A well-used situation of this type can be a more powerful reivindicative mechanism than archetypes or models of traditional beauty.

[3] In this regard, the creation of an enchanting landscape through the visual presence of clones hopes to cancel out the slovenly appearance of the installations for the Wasterwater Treatment Plant in Sestao (2007). [4] To achieve this, a series of totemic towers are put up to hide the systems that deal with the smells from each treatment pool. [5] This symbolic device manages both to divert the gaze from the large area of muddy pools and to filter and eliminate the offensive odors that result during the treatment process.

[6] Although these vertical structures belong to the same geometric and material families, they are equipped with a specificity that makes them unique, generating modified

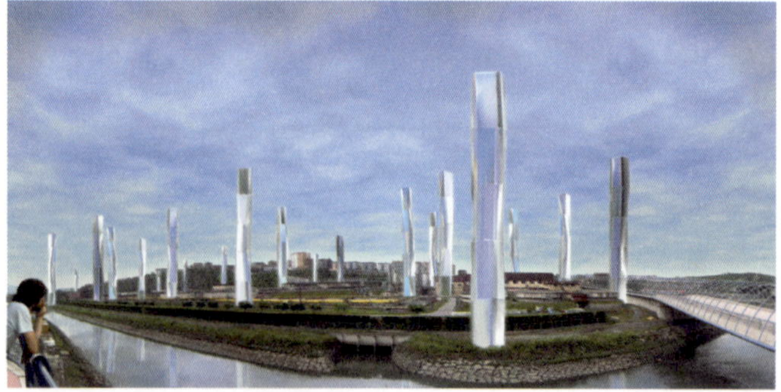

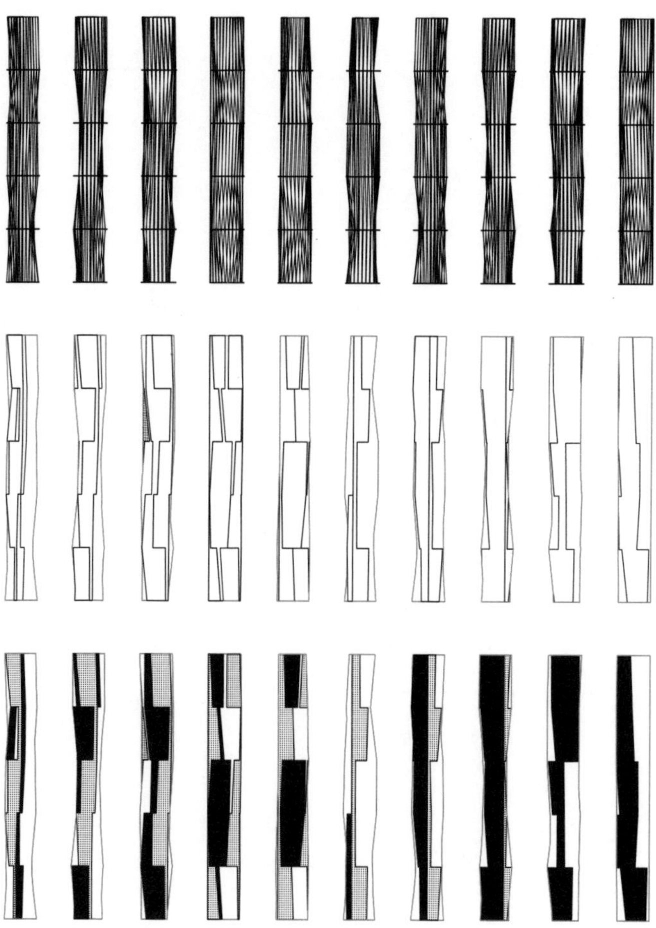

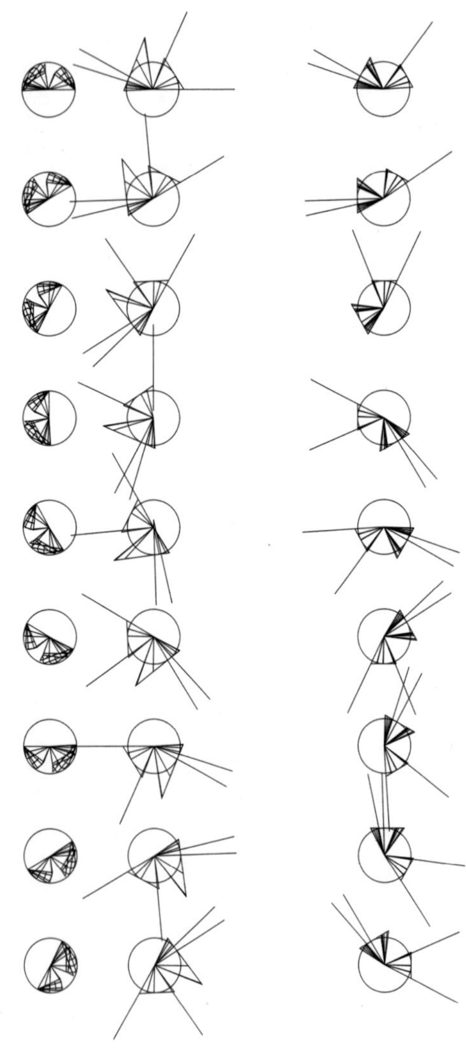

presences. The arrangement of each punctuates the ends of the sightlines from the city streets and its wheeled ring road, perceptively tying the new landscape of the treatment plant to the urban surroundings.

[7] The mirrored metallic material that covers them is arranged into different, nearly imperceptible inclines which create reflections and rhythmic glimmers in response to the movement of passers-by and drivers. [8] This creates an interaction between spectators and their positions in relation to the totemic landscape, through a haze of nearby and far-off dynamic gleams which are only recognizable through movement. [9] At nightfall, the interior lighting is projected out toward the territory, transporting us into another landscape of rays of light that break through the darkness. This light network connects the towers, revealing to pedestrians the surprising hidden geometry of their positioning.

[10] Between the changeable and flickering gleams, which weaken the gravity of the towers during the day, and the luminous vibrations that vanish into the darkness of the night, appearances blur before the eyes of the bewitched spectator. [11] A new presence appears before the inhabitant, who stands astonished once again by the grandeur of the apparently useless.

[1] Twins are a kind of subtle variation in the configuration **96** of human beings. Their appearance alone cannot permit us to decipher whether they come from one or two eggs, and even less to determine whether the exterior differences

between them are genetic or environmental. [2] The study of the factor of heritability makes this distinction recognizable through the analysis of their genetic code.

[3] Of the two existing types, monozygotic twins arise as the result of the division of a single fertilized zygote and they are always the same sex. Their genetic similarity is exact and the differences between them after they are born are due exclusively to environmental factors. [4] On the other hand, dizygotic twins appear through the fertilization of two separate eggs by two different spermatozoa. Their degree of genetic similarity is the same as non-twin siblings, and their differences are due both to genetic diversity and the environment in which they develop.

[5] The appearance of dizygotic twins is influenced by the mother's age, nutrition or race, indicating an important genetic component, whereas the appearance of monozygotic twins is constant in any human population and the causes are random and accidental. [6] Even triplets that carry the same genetic information can transform their personalities in different ways as they adapt to diverseenvironments. Three identical children could turn out to be a doctor in Alaska, a gay man in San Francisco, and a serial killer in the Bronx, with the same outward appearance.

[7] With the current capabilities of computers, we have been able to retrieve the genome that defines Man and distinguish its one hundred thousand chains of information. Based on this achievement, non-uterine human cloning is now a possibility. [8] This manipulation leads to the creation of a world full of doubt, which preserves only those properties that are considered useful for a directed evolution

that is no longer adaptive and, as such, is independent from the surroundings.

[9] However, this deciphering of genetic codes also makes us a part of the world; it transforms us into beings that are nearer to physical matter, which means that we can begin to think of ourselves in terms of place. [10] Understood as entities that are produced using the same components according to the laws that control them, the space we inhabit is prefigured more as an amplifier and definer of our emotional character than as something meant to repress it.

[1] The vision of a variable and adaptable world shines through in a short animated film developed to effectively tell the story of architecture's adaptation to its environment. [2] It includes a soundtrack based on the behavioral rhythms and mutations of the clone protagonists as they come into contact with different kinds of surroundings. This visual opera "Castaluna" (2002) is divided into three acts with an accompanying libretto in which a powerful Mediterranean region forces its beautiful capital city to go to work colonizing unknown territories:

[3] **Prologue. A Place in the Mediterranean.** Castaluna is of unparalleled beauty, with cities that used to look out over the sea, but now prefer to be close to the valleys. Its unblended, low-density territory provides a high degree of naturality, which its cities no longer possess.

[4] **Act I. Waking the Sleepers.** The city's buildings, overwhelmed by the density and the absence of nature, organize themselves to leave in search of new places. The sleepers

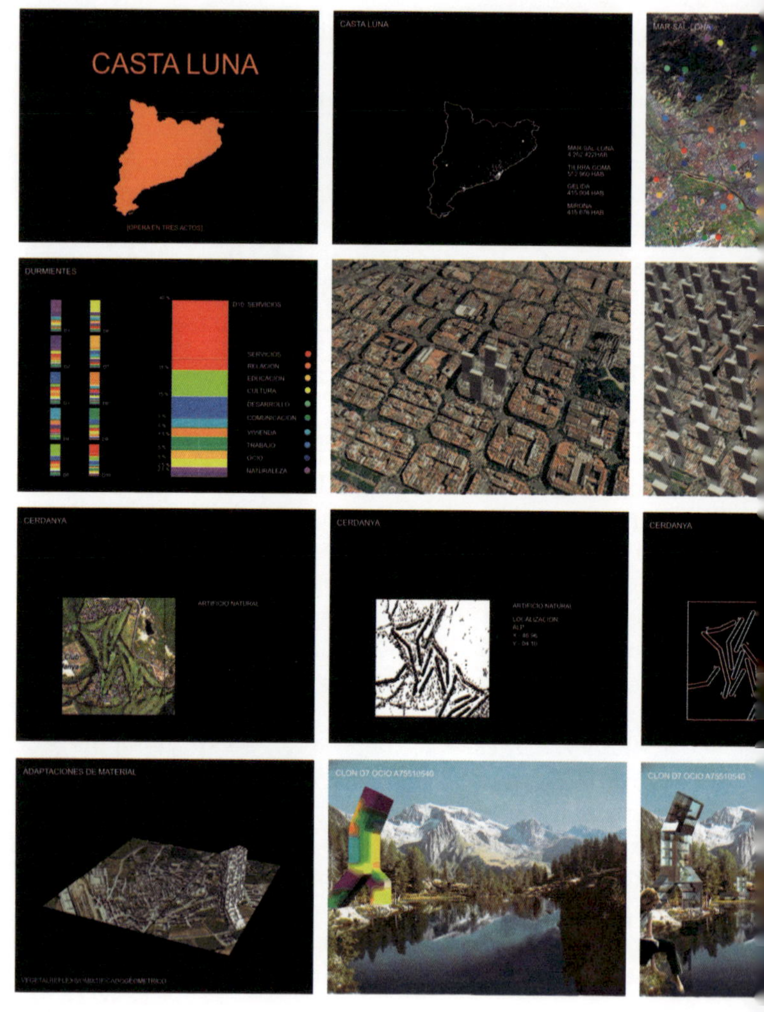
CASTA LUNA
[OPERA EN TRES ACTOS]
CASTA LUNA
MAR SAL LUNA
TIERRA GOMA
GELIDA
MIRONA
MAR SAL LUNA
DURMIENTES
D10 SERVICIOS
SERVICIOS
RELACION
EDUCACION
CULTURA
DESARROLLO
COMUNICACION
VIVIENDA
TRABAJO
OCIO
NATURALEZA
CERDANYA
ARTIFICIO NATURAL
CERDANYA
ARTIFICIO NATURAL
LOCALIZACION
CERDANYA
ADAPTACIONES DE MATERIAL
CLON D7 OCIO A75510540
CLON D7 OCIO A75510540

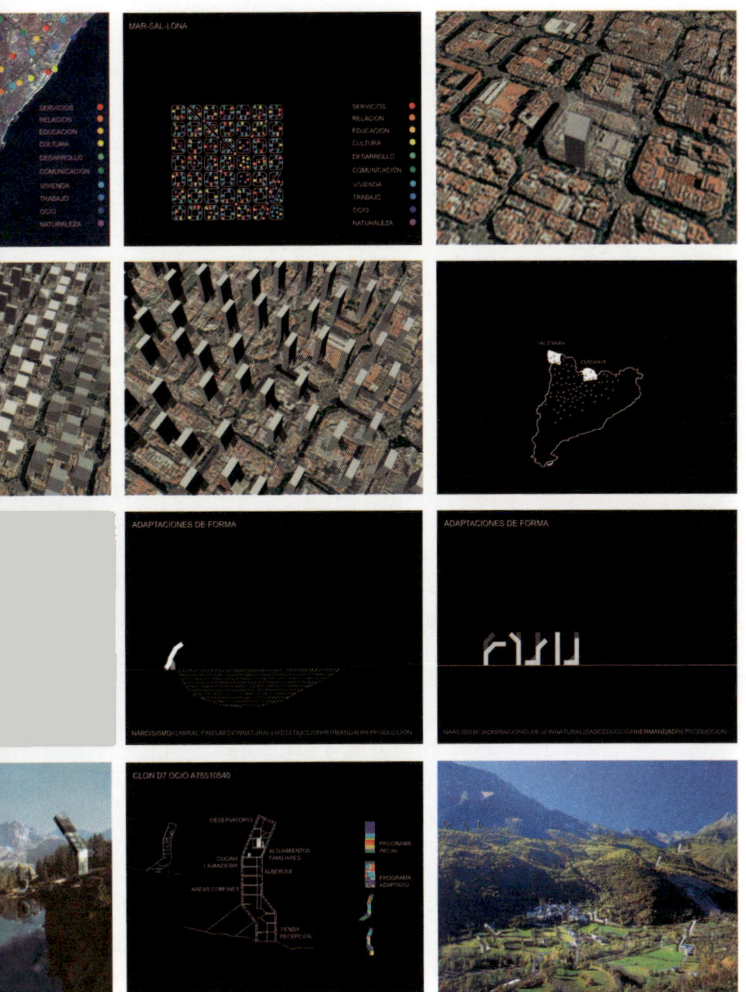
MAR-SAL-LONA
SERVICIOS
RELACION
EDUCACION
CULTURA
DESARROLLO
COMUNICACION
VIVIENDA
TRABAJO
OCIO
NATURALEZA
ADAPTACIONES DE FORMA
ADAPTACIONES DE FORMA
CLON D7 OCIO A75510540
OBSERVATORIO
COCINA
LAVANDERIA
ALOJAMIENTOS
FAMILIARES
ALBERGUE
AREAS COMUNES
TIENDA
RECEPCION
PROGRAMA
INICIAL
PROGRAMA
ADAPTADO

are organized with surface areas and urban uses, cloning themselves with a predominant program that makes them unique behind their similar appearances. The city is set in motion.

[5] Act II. Advancing toward Nature. As sad Marsalona, bored with its lovely architecture, turns into a vanity fair, the clones silently study new territories to take over in Val d'Aran and Cerdanya. There, they discover places with unique properties, which they absorb into their new behaviors to guarantee their adaptation.

[6] Act III. Emancipation of the Clones. Weary of wandering and fed up with urban servitude, the clones find their final locations and adapt their forms, uses and materials to their new homes. They optimize their shape in keeping with the landscape, making the most of the properties of the scenery, and they generate presence by absorbing the material conditions of each place. The temporality of each of the uses they house benefits from the location on the interior, establishing an intimate relationship with the surroundings.

[7] Epilogue. Naturban Castaluna. 3,019 clones are settled along the mountains and valleys, providing the population with a programmed naturbanity. The inhabitants perceive new ways of living in the hybridization of urban programming and nature within exciting landscape structures.

98 [1] I'm going to be late for the meeting on Portland Place. I'm trotting nervously through Candem toward the underground station when I catch sight of a spectacle that stops me short.

[2] On the opposite sidewalk a pair of punks are embracing affectionately. Their slim intertwined bodies are much more appealing than the messages of repudiation scrawled across their clothes. They are staring at a large-scale shop full of wedding dresses and accessories. [3] There are a dozen manikins in the store window, dressed in all kinds of men's and women's clothing; different colors, fabrics and beads.

[4] The young man's head is covered with a black cap, crushing a yellow mohawk that hasn't been put up, but can be made out under the edges. His studded black leather promotes his heroes from GBH, atop a pair of carefully worn-out pants. The girl is rhythmically nodding her straight-up neon green mohawk. Part of her carefully ripped fishnet stockings are hidden under a very tight black miniskirt. Her sophisticated image is completed by Doc Martens boots and symbols of the Soldiers of Destruction.

[5] They are both looking at the most elegant of the couples of brides and grooms. The girl is wearing a long dress made of silk and organza with a multi-tiered tiara and an embroidered veil. Her head is resting lovingly on the groom's shoulder, her arms around his impeccable black tuxedo and white dress shirt with ornate frills. He is wearing Ray Ban Wayfarer sunglasses, staring off into the distance as though he expected sun on his wedding day.

[6] Suddenly, the young girl slides her arm under companion's. Mimetically, she leans her head on the stud-covered shoulder that brushes through her styled hair. [7] I imagine that the real people are hankering after the fictitious happiness suggested by the advertisement, imitating the posture of the publicity for a long while.

⁸ Unexpectedly, an astonishing thought hits me: the tidy manikins are the ones who envy the urban savages, fed up with being locked up in their perfect glass box. They no doubt miss that disobedient freedom, which they can't enjoy. ⁹ Time stops for a moment and two apparently opposite worlds overlap into one. Their energies are transferred through the glass as though a double teleportation were about to take place. It is captivating, and I don't care about missing the train anymore.

99 ¹ Generally speaking, it is assumed that an object with a specific use and stable appearance does not need to vary its conditions of form and use when it is introduced into new surroundings. ² However, the particular conditions of a place may be strong enough to produce slight variations in the object that optimize its use, while the difference in its presence is nearly imperceptible. ³ From this standpoint,

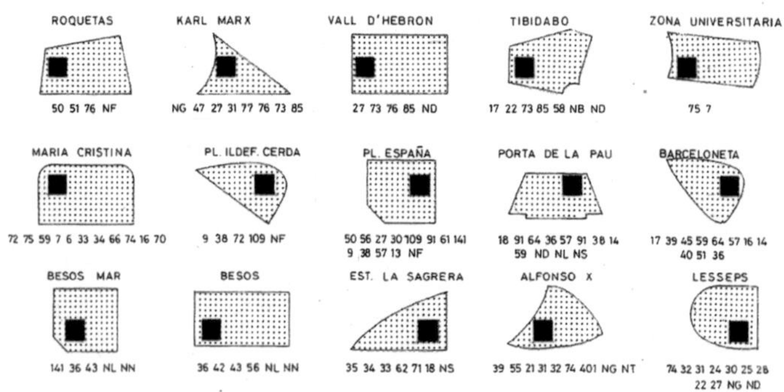

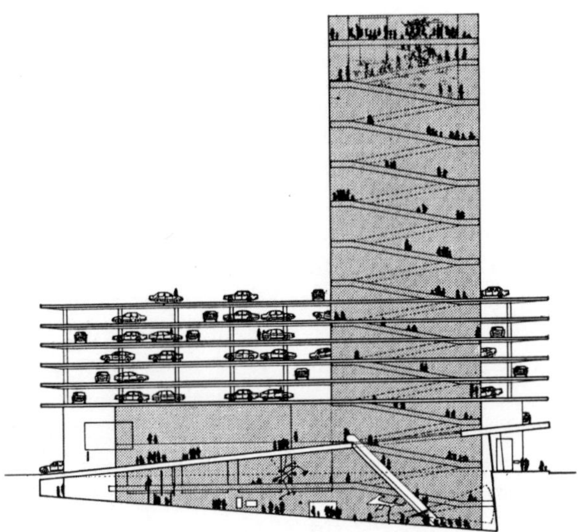

we can also suppose that the distribution of quantities of identical uses in the same city creates a predisposition toward repetitive thought with respect to the buildings that house them.

[4] Given this absorbent vision, and in order to dissuade inhabitants from taking their cars into the city center, a Parking Structure System is generated in Barcelona (1990), consisting of nodal buildings to be used for leaving cars behind and switching to various methods of public transportation. [5] A series of constructions with a similar appearance are developed on strategic plots along the ring road to act as metropolitan interchanges. [6] In addition to the uses associated with vehicle storage and transfer to the metro

and bus system, accompanying leisure uses are also included. These new programs are located in ample spaces that provide panoramic views of the city. This allows for people to relax while they wait or to meet up before or after work.

[7] The new generation of cloned buildings defines their parking structures using successive static levels combined with a volume that houses the dynamic routes and the leisure uses. [8] The system for storing vehicles is optimized, adapting its variable form to the different geometries of the perimeters of each plot, while its interior nucleus remains unchanged. This provides each structure with an individualized presence. [9] The invariable internal volume allows for panoramic spaces all around, absorbing transitions through the use of gradual ramps which are conducive to relaxed enjoyment of the distant views. [10] A range of recreational programs and spaces for temporary exhibitions can serve as a setting for meetings or chance encounters during peak times for vehicle pick-up.

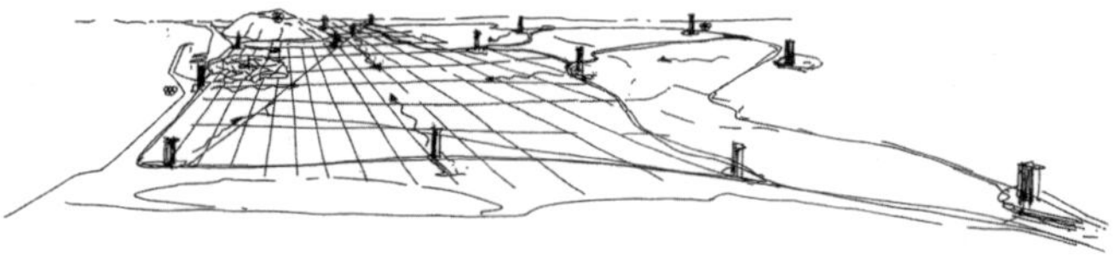

[11] This group of buildings, distributed concentrically throughout the city, creates an iconography of urban clones, which can be recognized as a permanent landscape of memory in movement.

[1] The double helix of DNA is one of the most popular and iconic scientific discoveries in recent history. But, beyond this iconography, many of the causes of transformations in people lie in its hidden properties. [2] Its structure, made up of two intertwined strands of nucleic acid, is formed by a combination of four seemingly random elements, which nevertheless maintain strict laws of configuration. [3] The most important condition is that Adenine can only bond to Thymine and Cytosine can only bond to Guanine, which means that the quantities of each are always constant. This pairing is what makes the system for copying or replicating genetic material possible.

[4] The large quantity of genetic material we possess is partly due to the double-stranded structure, which prefigures a security system against the possibility of its destruction. That is to say, we are basically redundant. [5] All of this material is nothing more than information, a hard drive that can be transmitted through time, though not precisely, but with subtle variations. [6] The four-letter alphabet that is used to compose the complete genetic code is also written using combinatorial phrases made up of those same letters, and it is those elements that alter its meaning.

[7] The replication process is truly ingenious: RNA appears to keep the DNA intact, transmitting the encoded messages and producing the synthesis of the proteins that serve as the foundation for an organism's functions and growth. [8] During that process of transmission and replication is when the erroneous tragicomedies of the mutation of information take place.

[9] On the one hand, the natural process of evolution contains an implicit system of mutations at a continuous rhythm, as though there were an order within the information itself to refrain from replicating itself absolutely identically. That is what is called spontaneous mutation. [10] But on the other hand, and much more interestingly, there are also induced mutations. These are variations to the replication system influenced by external environmental agents, such as climate and radiation, the intake of food, or the emotional conditions generated by the inclusion in a social group. [11] These transformations are responsible for generating adaptability to the environment and, in any case, they are what leads a living being to change its interior essence in response to its surroundings.

101   [1] In contemporary societies, ever more conscious of their decision-making power, systems for choosing from personalizable catalogs allow for arriving at strange degrees of individual or collective creativity.

[2] In order to find a simultaneous solution for a number of sports centers in Hadsten, Naestved and Frederiksberg (1999), we set up a fictitious mail-order company offering the sale of that specific type of building. [3] We created a catalog of images that include the different material footprints for each sporting use, the necessary infrastructures for their operation and multiple types of roofs, based on the use of diverse materials and structures. [4] This appeals to the illusion of independence and choice on the part of the collective, so that they can organize a specific building

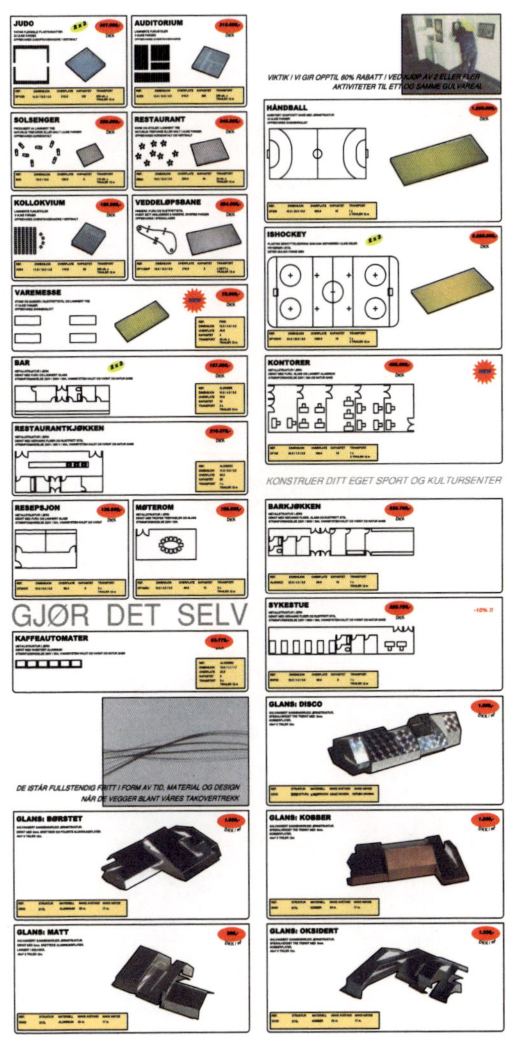

JUDO
AUDITORIUM
SOLSENGER
RESTAURANT
KOLLOKVIUM
VEDDELØPSBANE
VAREMESSE
BAR
RESTAURANTKJØKKEN
RESEPSJON
MØTEROM
KAFFEAUTOMATER
GJØR DET SELV
HÅNDBALL
ISHOCKEY
KONTORER
BARKJØKKEN
SYKESTUE
GLANS: DISCO
GLANS: BØRSTET
GLANS: KOBBER
GLANS: MATT
GLANS: OKSIDERT
VIKTIK / VI GIR OPPTIL 60% RABATT / VED KJØP AV 2 ELLER FLER
AKTIVITETER TIL ETT OG SAMME GULVAREAL
KONSTRUER DITT EGET SPORT OG KULTURSENTER
DE ISTÅR FULLSTENDIG FRITT I FORM AV TID, MATERIAL OG DESIGN
NÅR DE VEGGER BLANT VÅRES TAKOVERTREKK

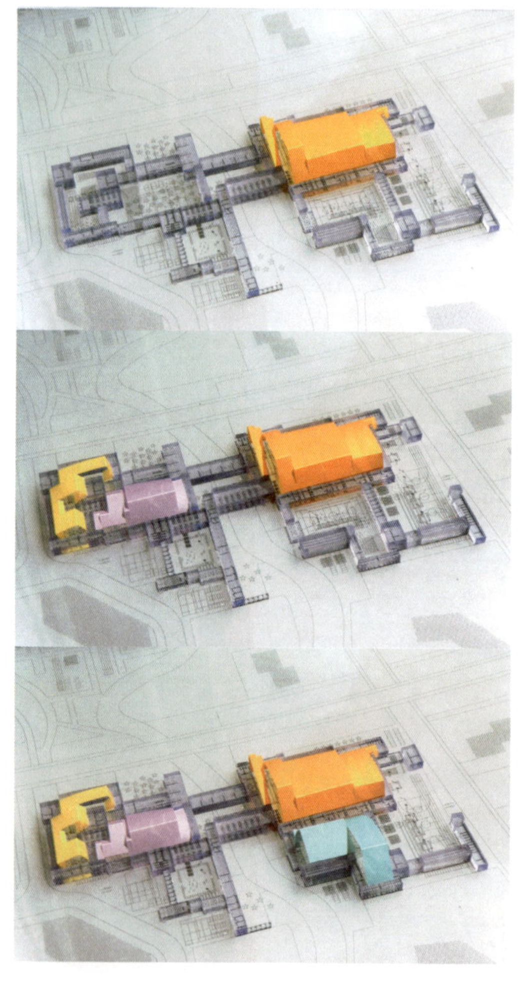

all by themselves, based on their economic and spatial needs. [5] The specification of dimensions, consumption and costs of the production system, which is modular, allows for coupling together all of the components on any of the municipal plots of land, adapting them precisely to the management schedules and physical perimeters.

[6] The selection and subsequent disposition of the playing fields produces the initial occupation of the site. The technical infrastructures and the necessary uses for their operation are displayed around them. [7] As such, combinations and arrangements appear that are already specified for each plot of land.

[8] Each function corresponds to a time of use with a maximum occupancy and a specific spatial configuration. A number of different programs that occur during different periods of time can share the same sports venue, alternatively. [9] Different activities may take advantage of the same spatial possibilities or they may take place at the same time, but never both situations. [10] With the selection of the materials for the different roofs, the creative cycle of the building is completed, which has been defined by a democratic will taken to the extreme.

[11] The result of applying this mechanism for selection and adaptation to different places generates buildings that look like clones. They all maintain a familiar image and similar operations and they can only be differentiated through a detailed look at their presence in their differing surroundings.

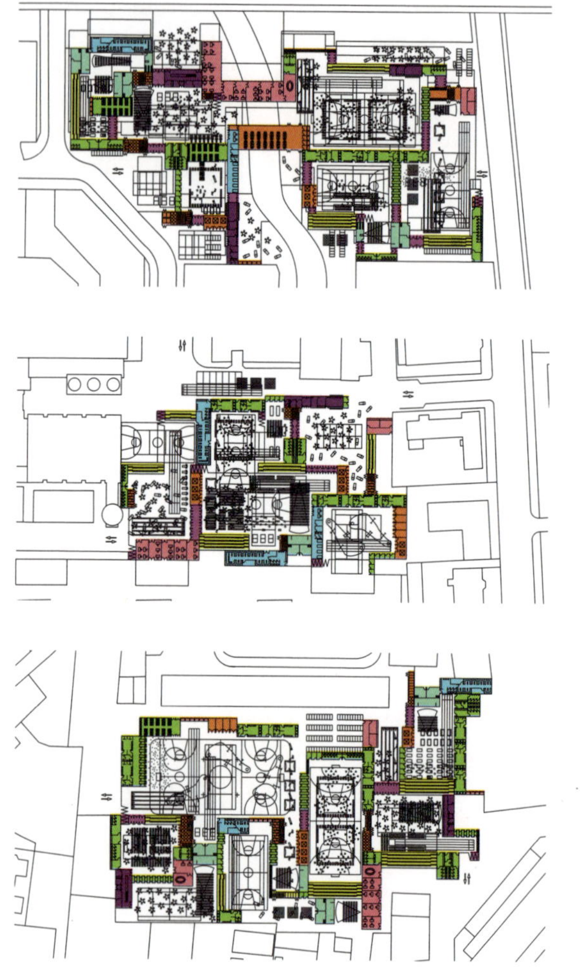

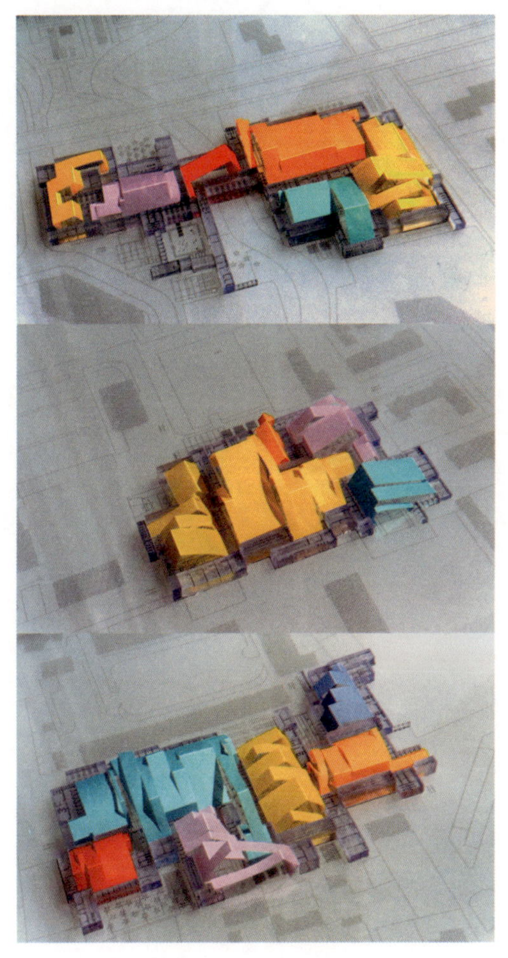

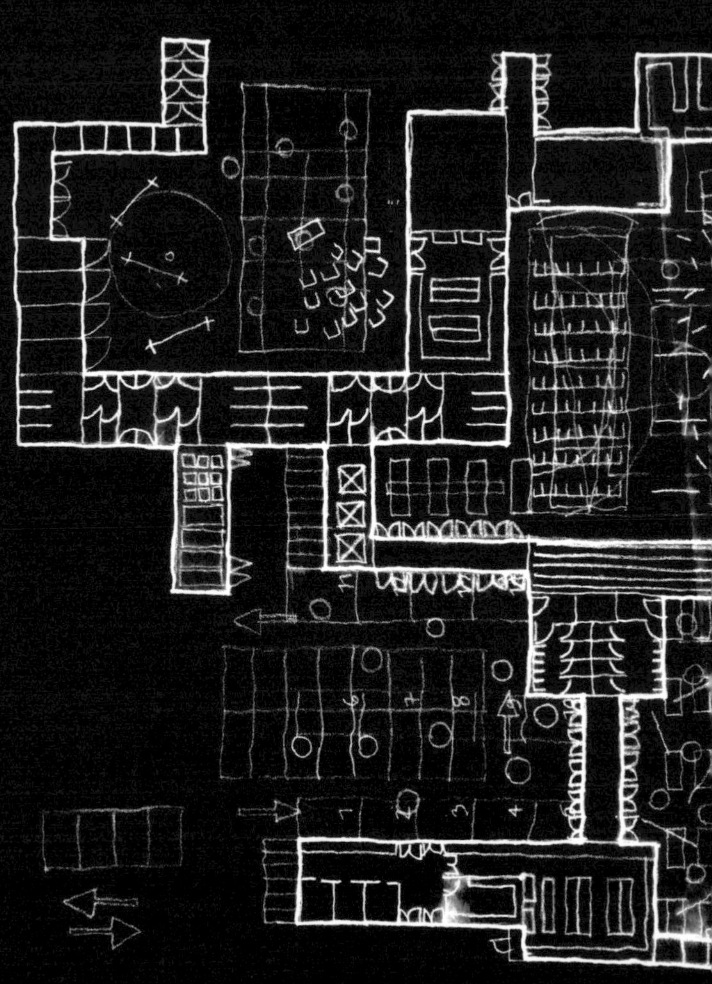

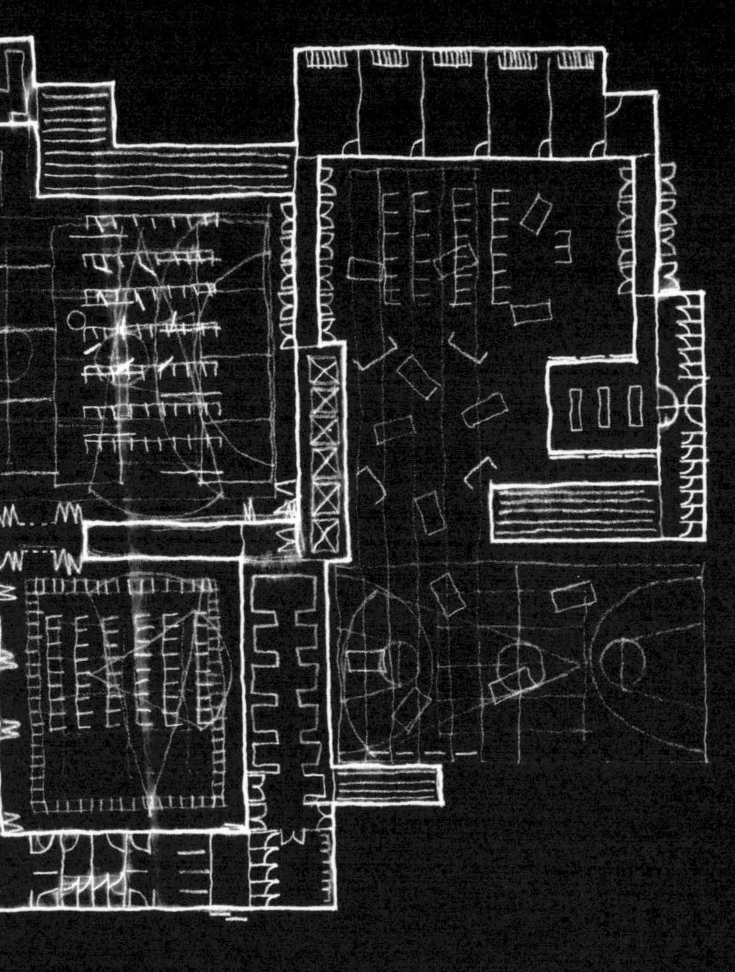

ENTROPY IS AN INTUITION

"Clearly, life is just a continuous process of destruction"

F. Scott Fitzgerald

¹ The Chrysler flew a few meters. The blast wave lifted us into the air, coming through the open windows with a re-sounding punch. ² I rub my aching neck as I watch a police officer jump out the back door of the van next to us, shoot-ing bursts from his CETME rifle. In the midst of the con-fusion, I start up the motor to get out of there when I hear Julio shout,

"Hey, stop! Stop, they'll kill us!"

³ For an instant, we sit facing the wrong way on the Ma-ria Cristina bridge, amid the chaos of a hectic mess of burn-ing cars. The explosion hit the first police van full on and no one has come out of it yet. ⁴ We climb slowly out of our car and Julio tells an officer that he's a doctor, in case he can be of any help. The officer turns his gaze hysterically to his surroundings and, grabbing Juilo by the arm, drags him running, head down, toward the site of the attack. Meanwhile, I can't stop looking at so much irregularity, resting my trembling hands on the car's golden fin.

⁵ Then I see a uniformed officer run up, pointing his weapon in my direction. At a few meter's distance he stops and, petrified, I look into his shaken face, red with rage, and his damp and irritated eyes. Naively, I'm thinking that it's because of the smoke and the heat of the burning vehi-cles, to keep from thinking that it might be from pain and fury. ⁶ He screams at me for my ID, but I'm not carrying it. Nervously, without really knowing what I'm doing, I hand him a credit card. Without taking his finger off the trigger or lifting the hand that is unconsciously manipulating the safety, he glances at the information but I sense that he doesn't really care.

7 At that moment my friend appears, his face twisted up, moaning,

"They're all dead, except the driver, but the steering wheel is embedded in his stomach."

His eyes are welling up and he is leaning disconsolately on my shoulder, dejected at the powerlessness of all his knowledge. It strikes me that it could be the salty breeze from the Cantabrian sea that has wet his eyes. 8 With my arm around the back of his neck, I look out at the disaster in front of me. 9 In the wake of so much destruction, I contemplate the laws of the expansion of matter, its thermodynamic effects and the chemical processes with physical orders and strict combinations, understood and manipulated by the terrorists too. 10 I realize that my analytical mind is trying to protect me by preventing me from recognizing the inevitable presence of death and suffering, "I'm sick."

103 1 Nearly all human beings live as prisoners of a constant terror and an existential despair caused by the fear of a scenario of physical or economic decline. 2 Faced with a possible rebellion directed at their personal transformation, it seems they are only left with the possibility of ordering, defining and containing the world around them under the stable appearance of immutability and harmony.

3 The fear of the unknown spurs the need for order, which is revealed to the consciousness as the only life line in the face of an unstable existence. It is camouflaged behind designations such as historic, style, tendency or global like space-time barriers that absorb anything novel they find

in their path, except for certain concepts that are useless from that point of view like chance, love or courage. [4] Man's weakness for the appearance of order is something observable throughout history. From the beginning of his opposition to nature, he has confused order with rigidity, regulations with prohibition and memory with the past. [5] This confusion is maintained in contemporary creation and is born from the scant reflection given to the difference between acting freely according to clear-cut rules and acting randomly. The diverse degrees of order that we can access appear with our ability to process multiple variables and giving them to a child to work with is not the same as giving them to a quantum physicist.

[6] From this point of view, there is an attempt at disguising and imposing clichéd thinking under a singular order that responds to the comfortable appearance of Cartesian geometry. That geometry is, however, the Platonic space of our fear and it represents our will standing petrified in the face of the unknown. [7] Order, in the strictest sense, is a state of equilibrium that rarely has to do with a law of an aesthetic nature, but rather a topological one.

[8] As such, the discovery of any order based on the manipulation of conditions and original properties intended to resolve a specific problem has to be understood and accepted as optimum. Order generated in this manner, independently of its appearance, responds specifically to all of the information at hand and, as such, the consistency of its operation is guaranteed. [9] This disordered stability demonstrates a larger importance than any temporary aesthetic prejudice endorsed by the group.

104 ¹ When a place that has been forgotten by collective memory returns to daily routine, its structure does not have to obey the order of the city that has been consolidated along its perimeter, which has learned to live without that inaccessible territory. ² The opportunity for autonomous creation promotes a powerful collective self-esteem with a novel spatial character that is no longer permitted by the rhythms and obligations of the traditional city.

³ From this standpoint, the values that are latent in the geography of the surroundings lead us to promote the creation of a Geo-routes System in Benicàssim (2009) with an ambition on a territorial scale. The system is based on the appearance of a continuity of perceptive movements that place an intense value on the potential of the mountainous and maritime landscape. ⁴ A large ring is programmed for leisure uses which leads to the appearance of a slow urban rhythm, opposed to the hustle and bustle of the existing city, directed at promoting slow attitudes toward social relationships. ⁵ The perception of the landscape in movement

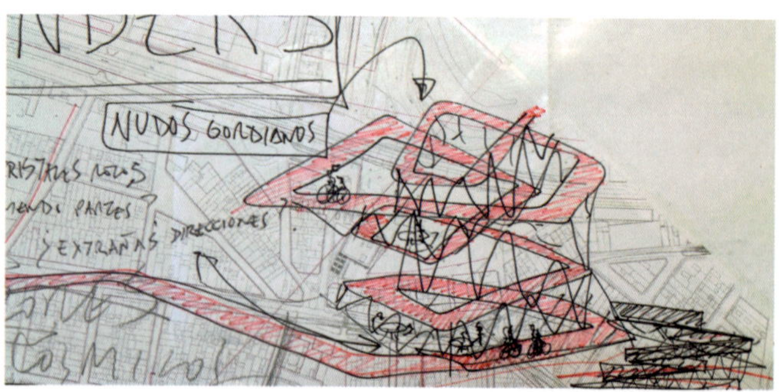

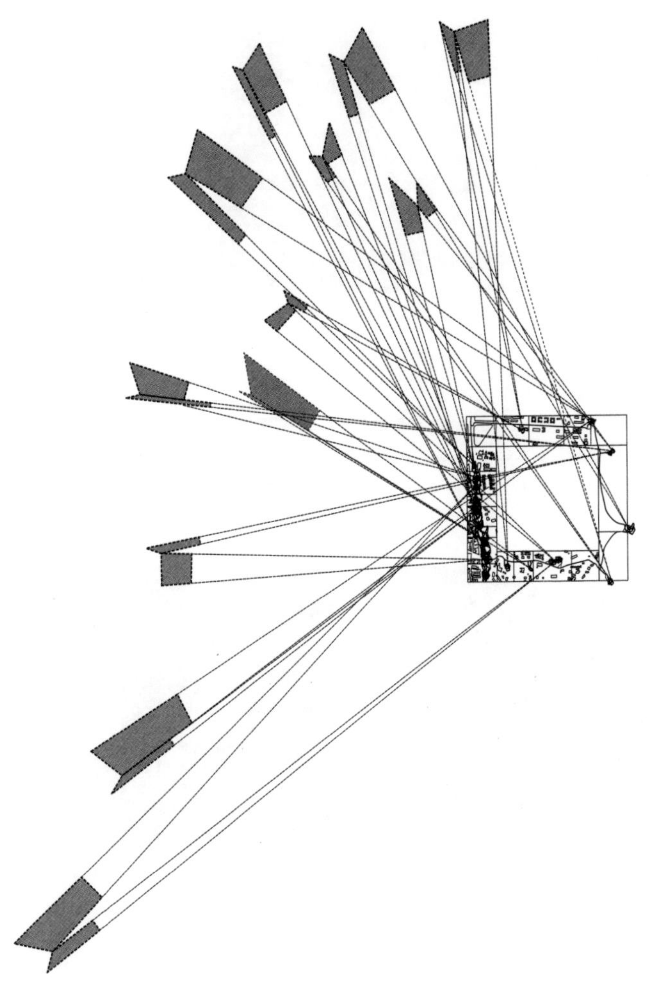

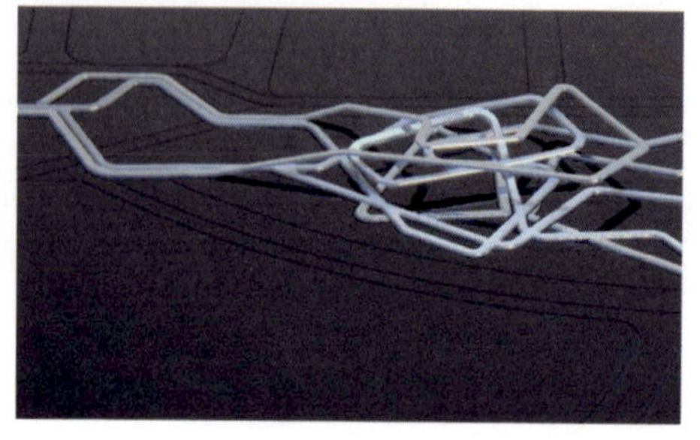
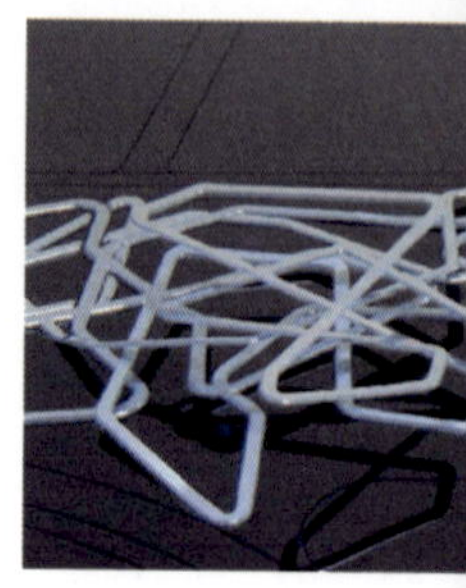
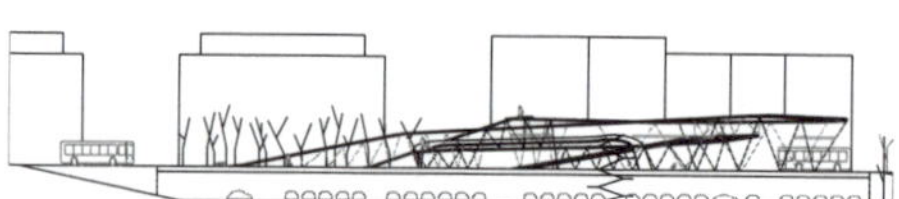
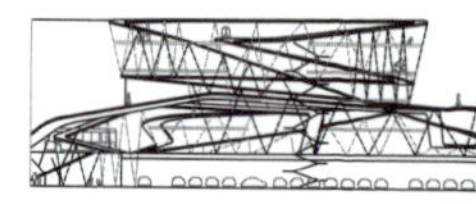
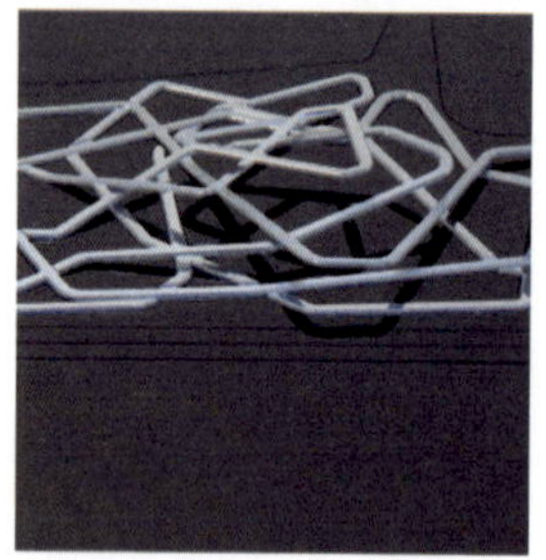
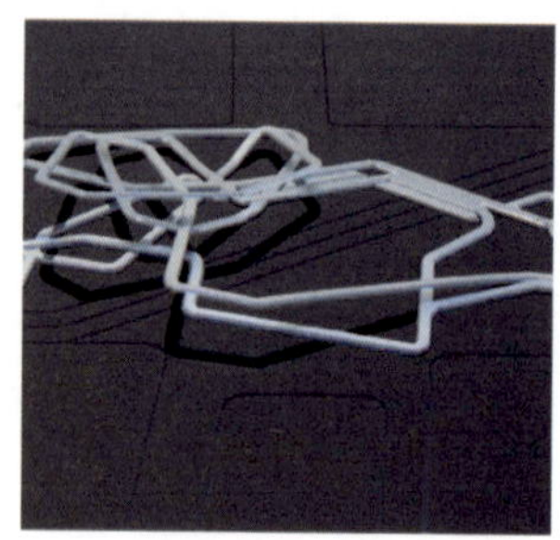

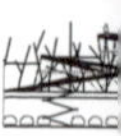
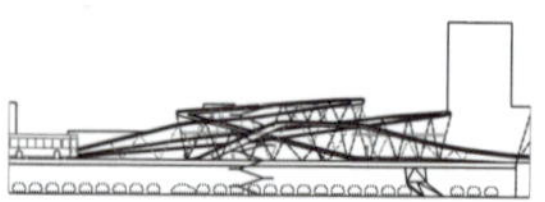
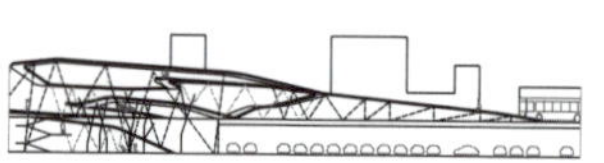

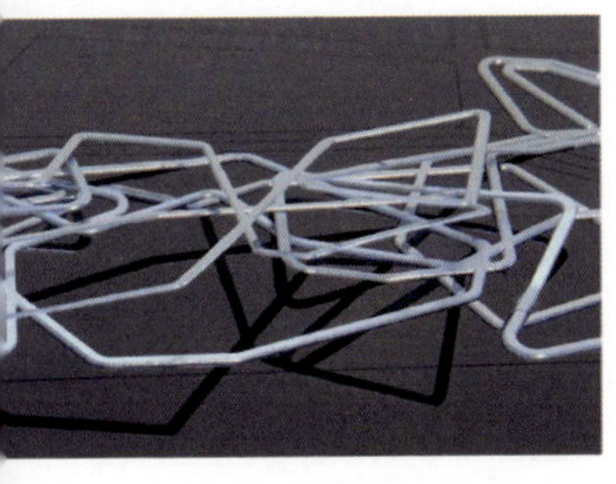
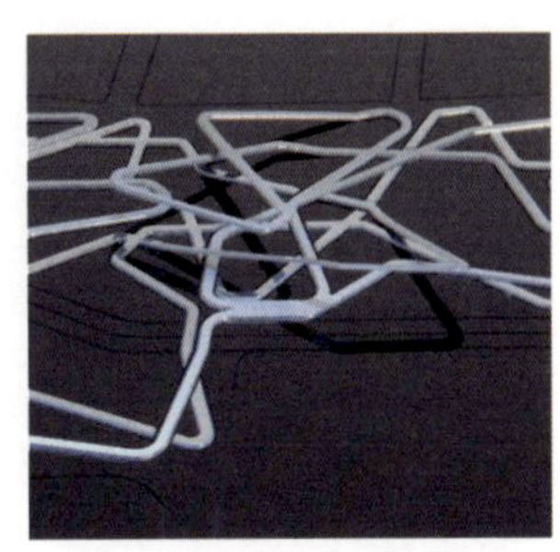
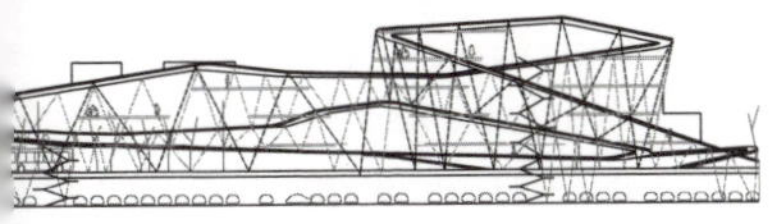
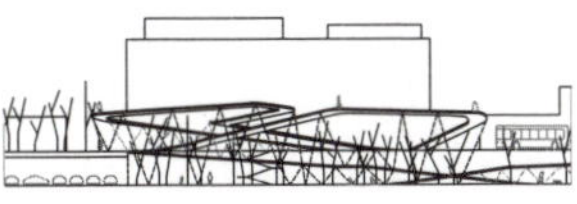
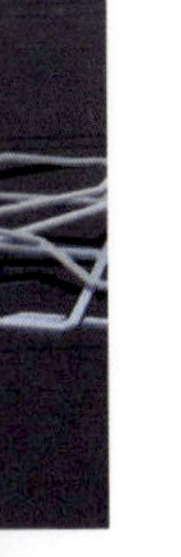
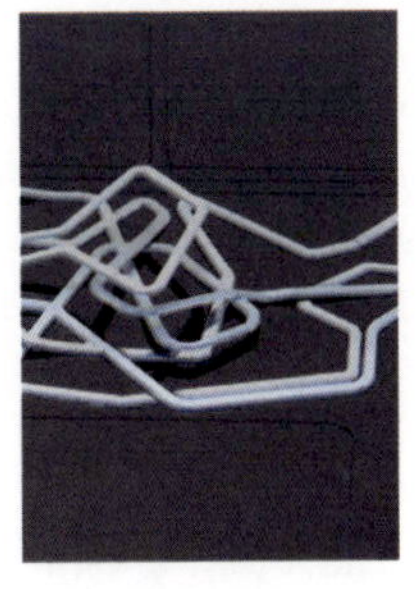
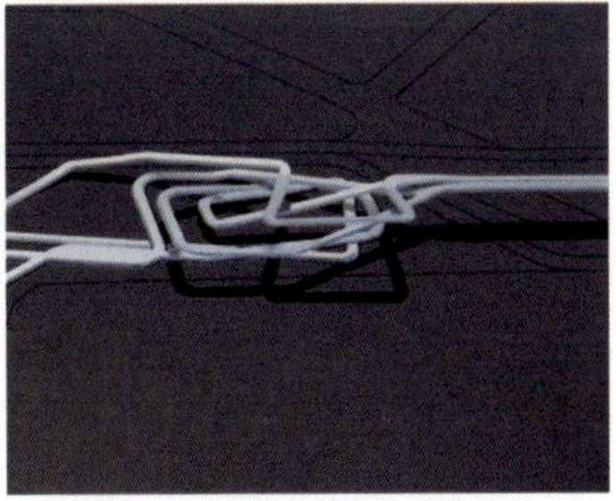
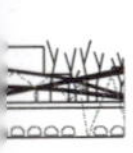
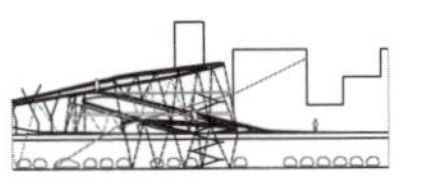
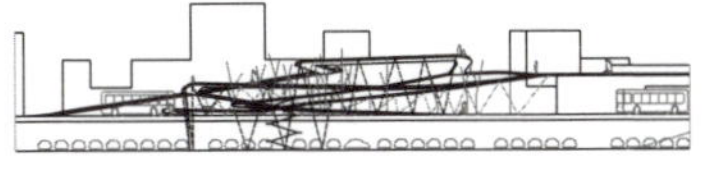

on the part of walkers and cycling tourists and their speed in relating to the mountains and the shoreline defines the geometry of the entire operation. This new geometrically autonomous environment is tied in with central points from each sector of the ring, generating intensities of use and places where there is a more concentrated presence of population.

[6] The different curvatures of the outline behave in accordance with the speed of pedestrians and cyclists, generating specific responses for each perceptive moment and the conditions for access from the existing roads. [7] Each sector is shaped by parameters that slow down the speed of our lives. This allow for enjoying places that have complex sensibilities, along routes that become panoramic once they are free of obstacles along the perimeter. [8] This knotted development of the movements, with the unexpectedness of the intersections and the elevated location of some of the collective uses, creates an unambiguous desire to mix contemplative living spaces with dynamic experiences. [9] It is organized as a system for the decompression of the built limits of the existing city and its rhythms of use in a new buffer characterized by relationships and surprising discoveries.

105　[1] Ludwig Boltzmann's tombstone in the Vienna cemetery is inscribed with his formula for entropy as a kind of farewell. Engraved on a block of stone under his bust, we can read that entropy is the product of Boltzmann's constant multiplied by the natural logarithm for the number of possible atomic organizations or microstates of matter. [2] From this master formula, which sums up a whole life dedicated to the pursuit of the laws of Thermodynamics, comes the famous fact that disorder never decreases. In other words, disarrayed matter will never be ordered spontaneously; an exterior effort will always be needed for that to occur.

[3] The degradation of the world left to its own devices happens as the result of the expansion of atomic matter and, as such, it has a spatial character. [4] We always take matter into our charge in a specific state of order; controlling it through external means determines the moment in which its disorder is halted. [5] The effort to return that material to a previous or more utopian organizational state will require more effort the further we move away from the reality that surrounds us. [6] Dealing with actions that only serve to control disorder allows for more accessibility to reality with less energetic effort toward its conservation.

[7] Similarly, we cannot forget that any action of ordering matter is not an isolated system and always leads to a proportional compensation of chaos in another place. [8] This entropy always occurs from solid orders to gaseous ones; not for nothing, the word gas, invented by a French scientist, has its etymological roots in chaos. That is the origin for the calming sensation produced in the population by any solid construction in the classical style, as opposed to the ethereal creations of the contemporary world.

[9] We live in a highly entropic and gaseous creative moment, accompanied by the distressing awareness that there

are no evolutionary states following gas. This intuition of the end of a cycle generates a reactionary attitude, accompanied by creative paralysis in the face of the unknown. [10] Boltzmann asked himself, shortly before he committed suicide, if behind any constructive act there is not an implicit intuitive battle against a world that we feel is rapidly collapsing.

106 [1] In places where there are objects with a large mass, electric potential or other powerful properties, new objects that enter into their field of influence gravitate around them in an apparently haphazard way. [2] Their related trajectories complete cycles of approach and distancing with the resulting accelerations or detentions in their velocities. They behave like the strange attractors that define the movements of particles, by way of orbits that combine different types of complex geometric curvatures like the trifolium, or the rose.

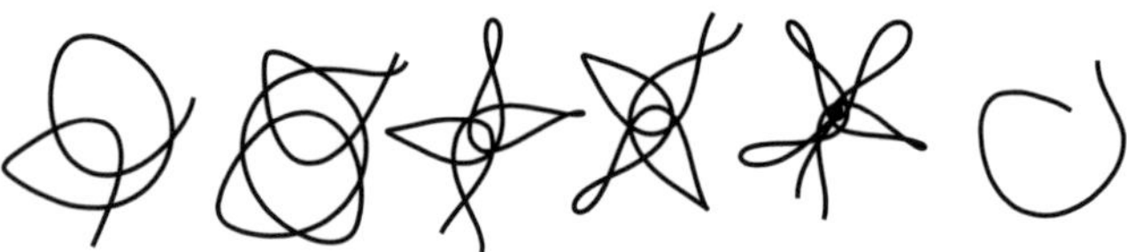

[3] From this standpoint, stable groups of existing trees are used as centers of attraction to define a gravitation system for visitors to a large forest. [4] Subsequently, a system of lines of movement is created around them, fol-

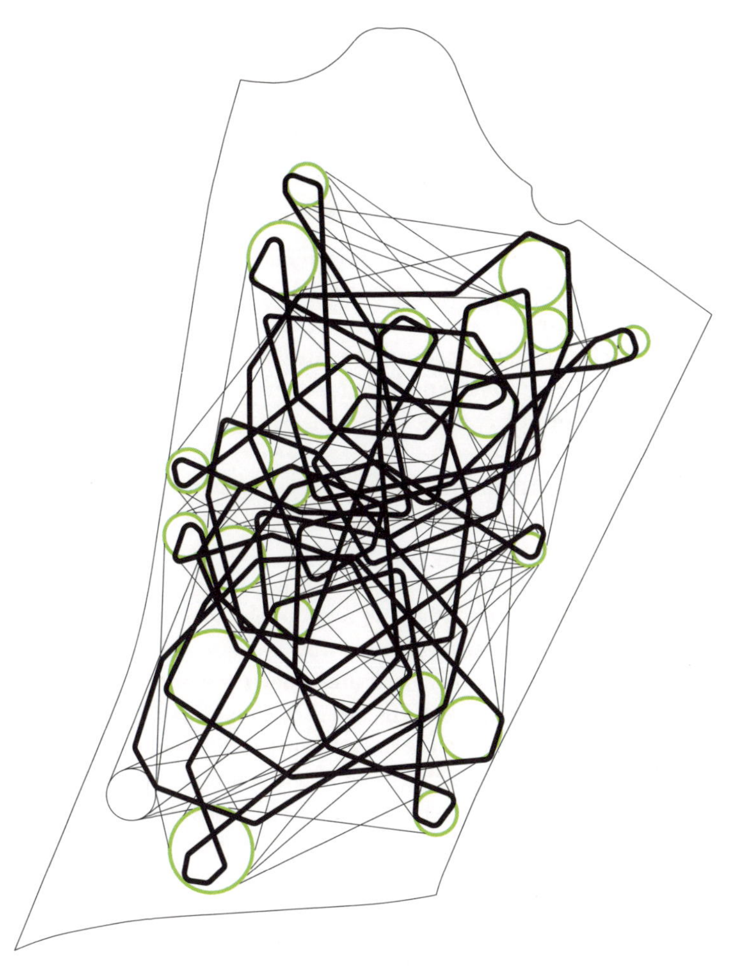

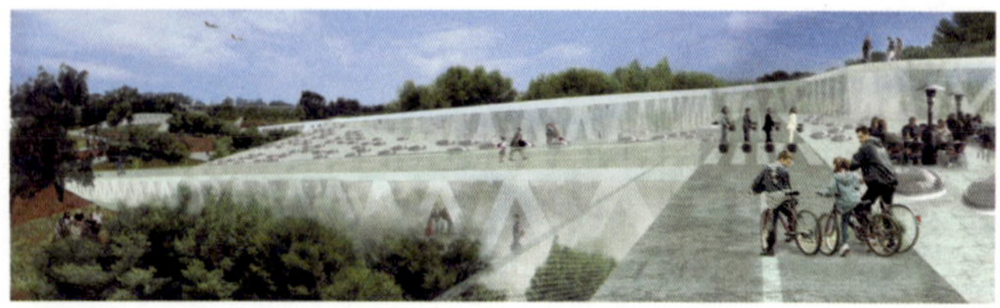

lowing a behavior like the one defined for strange attractors. [5] Though they conserve a random appearance, they keep to precise rules for movement which generate a network of circulations across the entire surface of the park. Its complex and homogeneous character allows for lending an atmosphere of continuity to the whole, within its diversity.

[6] These cyclical itineraries are generated using two types of movement in relation to the groups of trees. [7] The first promotes inroads with paths that cross through the group and back, creating an internal loop. [8] The second type has an enveloping character, circling around the group of trees, continuing along a different one-way trajectory. The linear non-planar character of the routes allows for choosing between elevating one above the other or simply having them cross at ground level. [9] These two repetitive systems allow for enjoying unrecognizable circuits without tending toward immutable conditions. The possibility of dealing with the routes vertically also creates locations underneath them for the various park services that are necessary for visitors and the open-air museum.

[10] The Málaga Transportation Museum (2007) is located in the spot where the most trajectories are concentrated.

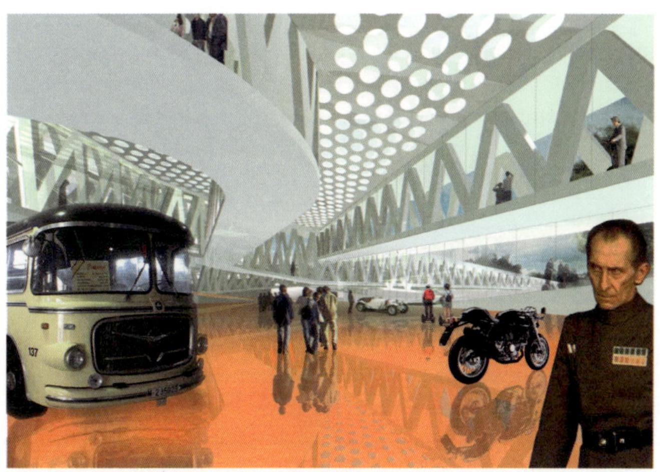

¹¹ The reading of this complex geometry of inertias at different heights uncovers the internal operation of the exhibition space. Likewise, it guarantees the perceptive continuity of the entire terrain through a common topology that cancels out the presence of a massive construction therein.

¹ Every evolving creative process develops over a fixed **107** period of time where there are always more disordered states than ordered ones. ² Contrary to the idea of a puzzle where one single arrangement results in the finished image through infinite incomplete variations, what begins with a very high degree of order always tends toward disorder. ³ This is the psychological arrow or the subjective direction

of time, defined by Stephen Hawking, which leads us to a more intense perception of the passage of time depending on the increase in disorder. An order that is identical to a previous state in time enters into direct contradiction with memory's systems of recall. [4] According to the entropy principle, an increasing amount of energy will be required to maintain it over time or to advance one small step in its direction.

[5] As such, processes have moments of maximum entropy when they slow down and the effort needed to move forward becomes noticeable. They are not isolated instants; they are periods of time that coincide with more stable results than the ones immediately prior to them. [6] It is impossible to define one of these states completely, as seen in Heisenberg's Uncertainty Principle, which leads to accepting the impossibility of specifying their material and energetic characteristics at the same time. An intelligent combination of properties, similar to a quantum state, provides temporal statistical information from among an infinite number of possible states. [7] Those spatial-temporal moments can be read in their complexity by counting up the variables that support them, such as use over time and spatial drive or their position in their surroundings. As such, they can specify a possible acceptable state as a mixture of the information contained at the time of the reading.

[8] From this point of view, chaotic systems are not random and their definition in chaos theory presents them as ordered by their mathematical condition. [9] Despite the presence of this internal order, we cannot predict a particular result due the interaction of the different causes that appear from

the outset. [10] This phenomenon of the reflexivity of information demonstrates that a specific action has an influence on the conditions for the next one, transforming small effects that appear during the process into large causes that are no longer connected to the origin.

[1] Lewis Carroll drew the sea as a large empty square in **108** *The Hunting of the Snark*. His invisible message transmitted the impossibility of representing the intensity of the variable properties of the sea: its depths, the roughness of the wind-swept surface, the directions of the currents, or all the shades of blue. [2] The abstraction of the perimeter of his drawing also accepted the need for putting together a generic framework as a focal point to allow for the discovery of the hidden order of those properties.

[3] In the same way, the study of the conditions that bring about the transformation of the earth's interior in the case of karst caves needs an abstract framework so it can be understood and represented. [4] The surprising sensitivity of these cave spaces is revealed through the conditions that produced the three-dimensional and homogeneous erosion of the soluble material in all directions of the space.

[5] Taking a generic sample of karst terrain, big enough to hold the entire program of the Neanderthal Museum in Piloña (2010), the different geometric properties of its internal erosion are studied. [6] Based on hollowed-out spaces directed toward different landmarks in the landscape, perceptive relationships are established with the possibilities for situating the internal program. The apparent

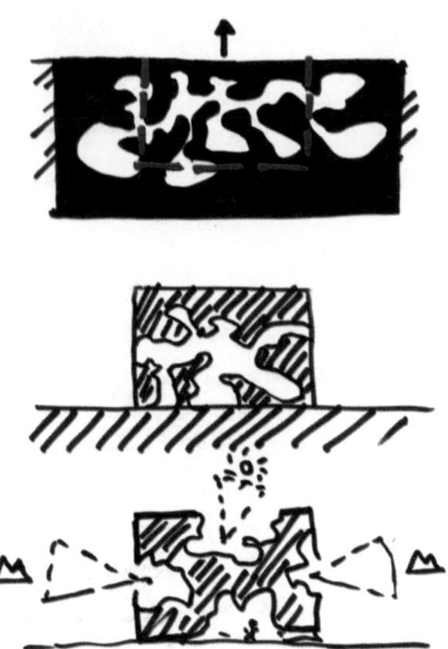

disorder laid out in this way defines a continuous space of cavernous characteristics, which is lit up in all three directions. [7] The interior stimulation transforms the compact envelope, creating the cavities that provide the object with a presence that affords information on what can be expected from the visit. [8] The interaction of each use with the perimeter determines a variable geometry that houses surprising relationships with the landscape and the sky from within each exhibition space. In this way, the areas with natural light are defined, associated with the visitor's routes past the exhibition areas, where there is more lighting control.

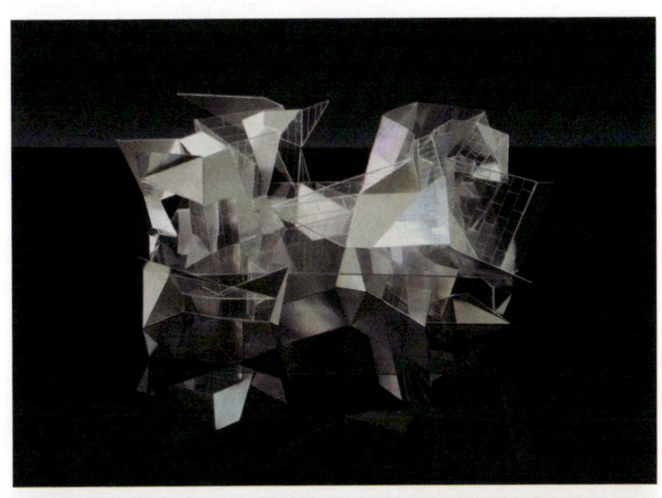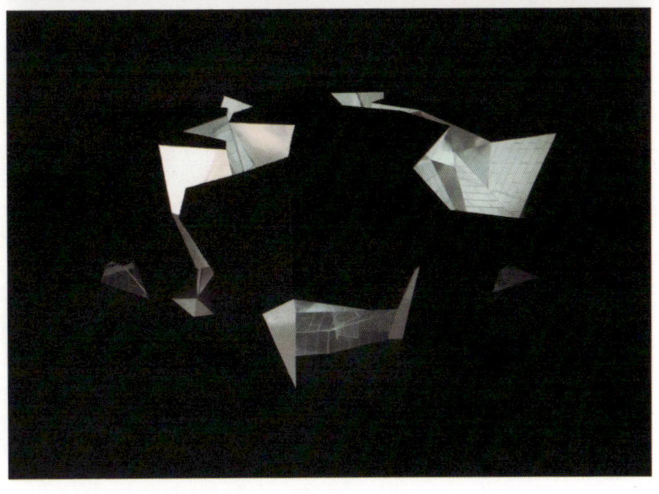

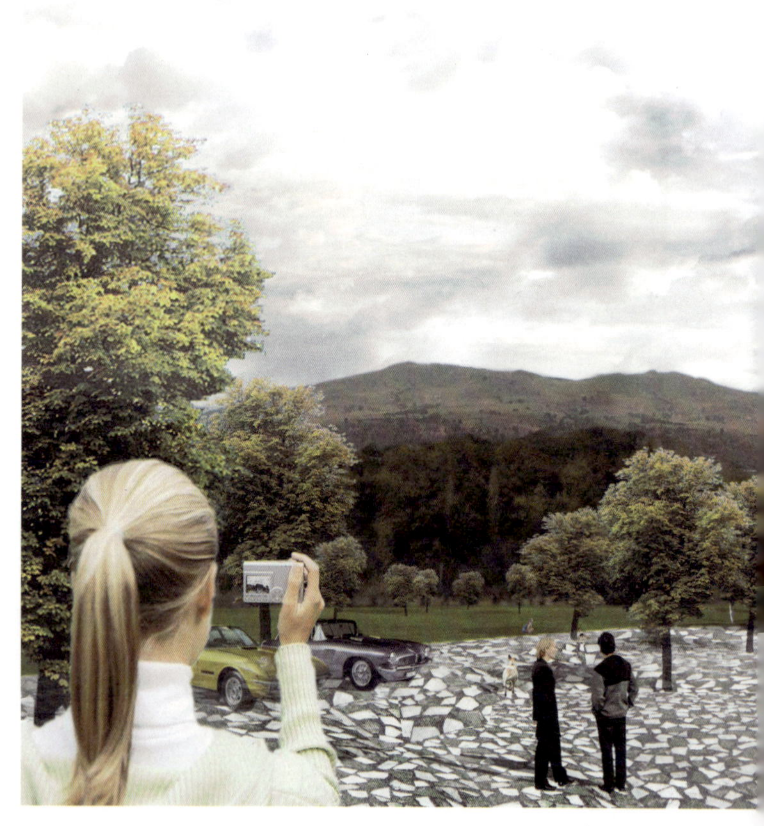

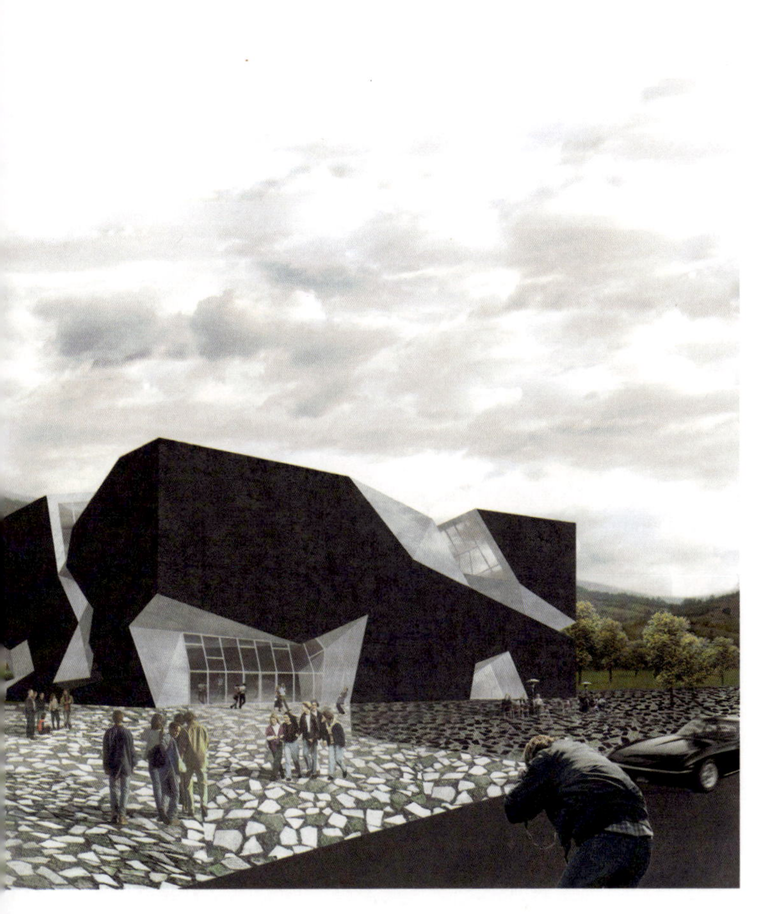

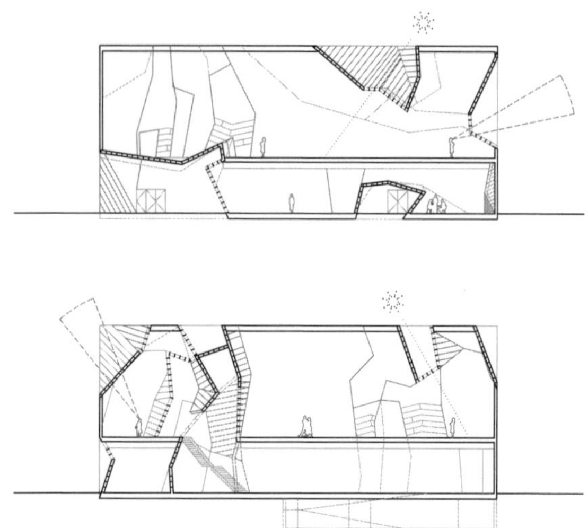

⁹ The route through this empathetic-cavernous system characterizes the entire visit, framing fragments of the landscape temporarily from small lounge areas between the exhibit rooms. ¹⁰ The final complexity of this continuous spatiality is defined by its entropic geometry, yet it does not allow for reading the parameters that led to its appearance.

109 ¹ We've taken one last picture before the dive, just in case. That's how we conjure the demons that take over us before we descend into the darkness. Unconsciously, I lower my voice to ask the divers to check their lighting equipment, like I might wake up the sharks in these waters. ² Among them, there is a couple participating in their first night dive. They are petrified in silence and their faces are turned toward the ground as I study them discreetly. ³ Once I've given the final instructions about how to communicate in the darkness using our spotlights, we put on our equipment. Without thinking too much, we jump systematically into a blackness that is so deep that the impact with the water's surface is always a surprise.

⁴ As we descend, a dozen beams of light dance randomly, outlined against the nothingness. ⁵ Then I think that I've done so many dives in Silver Gardens, I'd rather look at the spectacle of lights. The green chemical light sticks secured to the diving tanks follow a much quieter rhythm than the fumbling arms. A constellation of distracted comets and phosphorescent particles has formed in front of me and I feel like I'm floating in a weightless universe that is out of order to amuse me.

⁶ Multi-colored circles appear across the coralline sea bottom, changing position by the moment as they look for octopuses and lobsters. I can make out who is holding each light just by the steadiness of the hands that direct them. Their speed across the bottom, their tension and even the way they float indicate the experience of the divers. Attentively, I follow the trembling circles and the ones that distort into ellipses as they point out into the distance.

⁷ Suddenly, some of the lights start to fail and I wait impatiently for the divers to activate their emergency lamps. Their yellow color serves as an added spectacle, but I'm picking up on the chaotic vibration of the divers that are

frightened. [8] The circles have disappeared from the coral seabed as they try to light the way for one another, blinding each other and forgetting the emergency instruction. I try to get the group to pay attention, signaling with my light, but they're lost in a monumental chaos. I sound my air horn and send everyone up to the surface. During the ascent, some of the flashlights run low on batteries and begin to flicker.

[9] Fascinated, I contemplate the beauty of all that luminous disarray, created by the laws of the nervous system in panic. Without a doubt, that's my favorite kind of dive.

110 [1] Inserting the Zafra-Uceda house in Aranjuez (2006–2008) into a place with an inanimate order because of its speculative character, involves eliminating possible contaminating relationships with the environment. The selection and promotion of strict conditions of visibility and accessibility allows for controlling the absence of deterioration in the new family life. [2] The essential outline of the building's volume does not pursue any relationship with the sur-

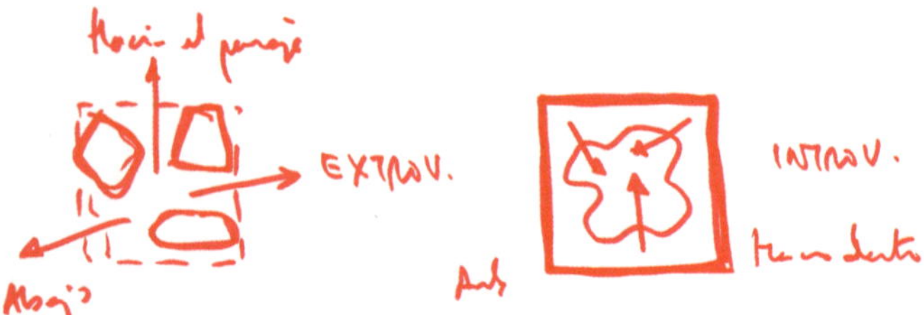

roundings that are lacking in character, so that the use of the dwelling is related with the only objects in the far-off landscape of Aranjuez that are worthy of interest.

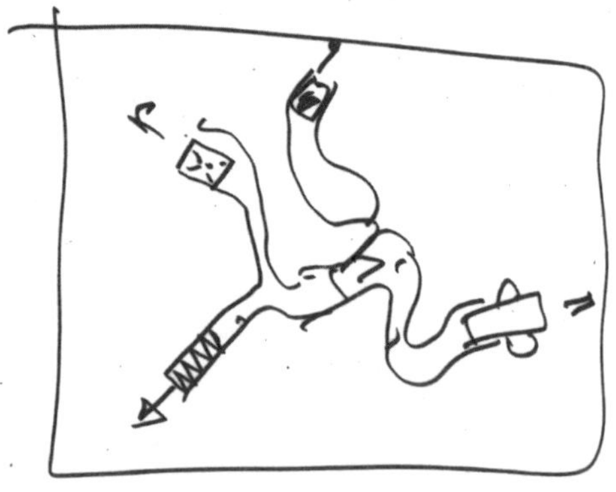

³ To that end, the perimeter of this innocuous parallele-piped is stimulated using directional conditions linking icons in the landscape with the internal possibilities for use. In this way, objects on the horizon are recognized and framed like interior images and their positions and dimen-sions are defined in relation to the programs for each floor. ⁴ This focus on landscape, together with the needs for pedestrian and vehicular accessibility from the street, pre-shape a series of protective empty spaces in the volume. ⁵ When the angles of these particularities are related, a three-dimensional geometry is revealed that governs the spatial properties like a high-precision construction net-work. Its random appearance does not prevent the recog-nition of a hidden order that carries multiple perceptive

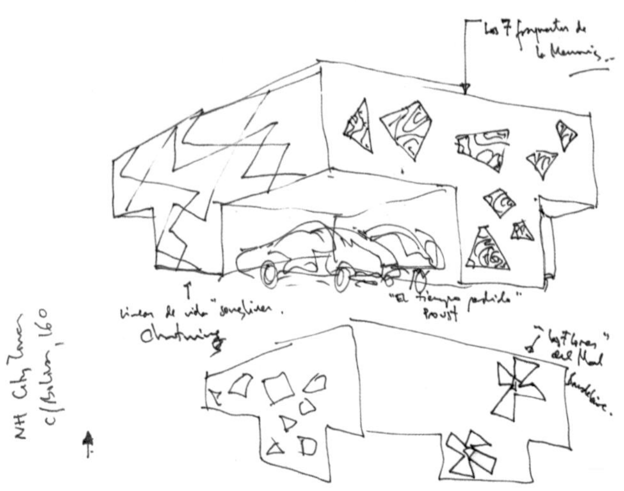

possibilities. [6] The set of internal diagonal visual relationships that this geometry proposes becomes a three-dimensional landscape that is capable of absorbing every function
in an exciting way.

[7] The separation between uses is achieved by way of a
twisting laminar element which follows the overall network,
defining the limits of each program around a double-height
space. [8] This fragmented object that houses the stairs, installations and building services, exhibits the two specific
interior material properties on its parallel faces. [9] On one
side, the iridescent skin that varies with the changing light
and, on the other, a mirrored skin that disrupts and mul-

tiplies the perception of the stability of each space, drawing the landscape into the interior. [10] The linear structure is also perforated with holes at different heights according to the guidelines of an invisible order. They allow for visual relationships among the different uses, demonstrating a hidden organization under the random appearance.

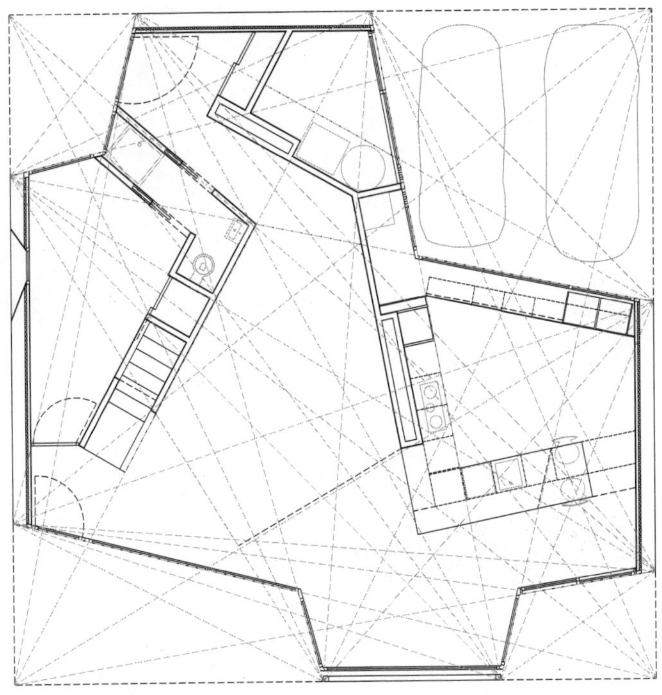

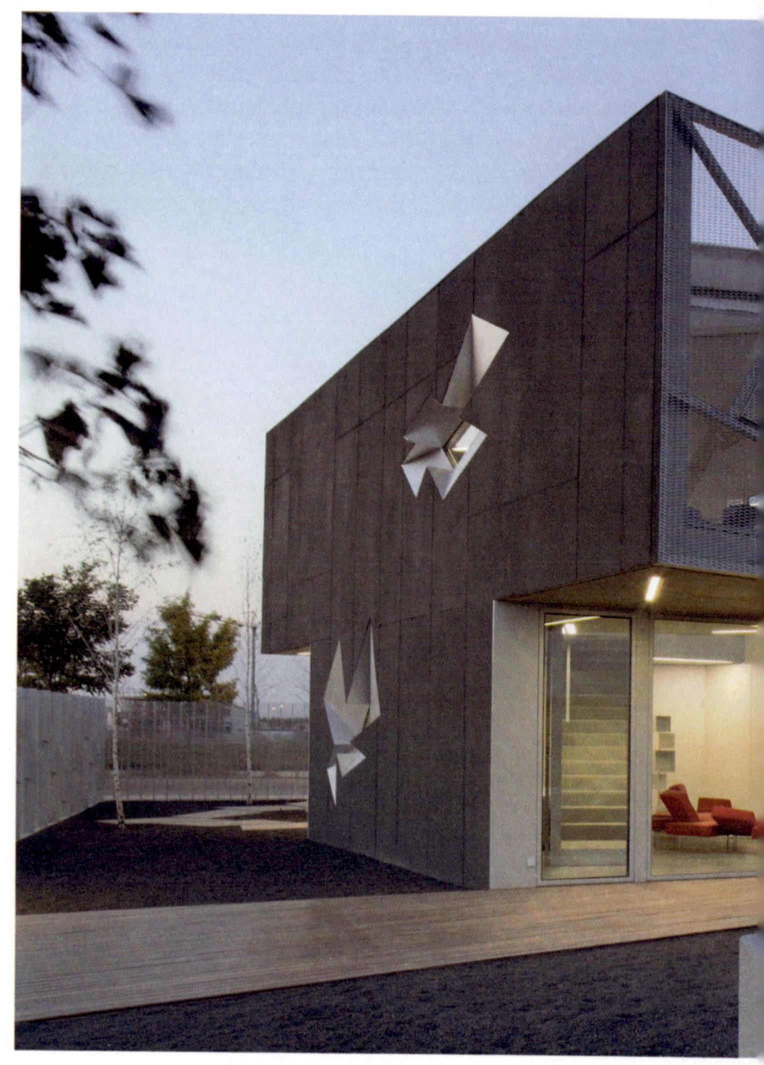

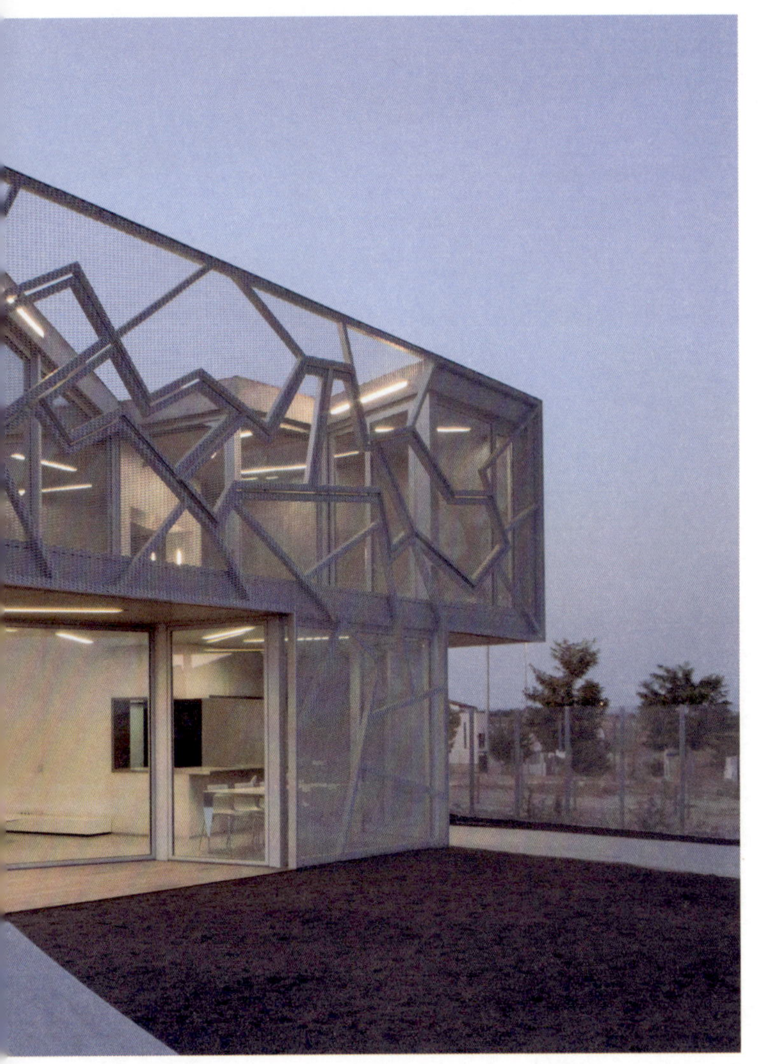

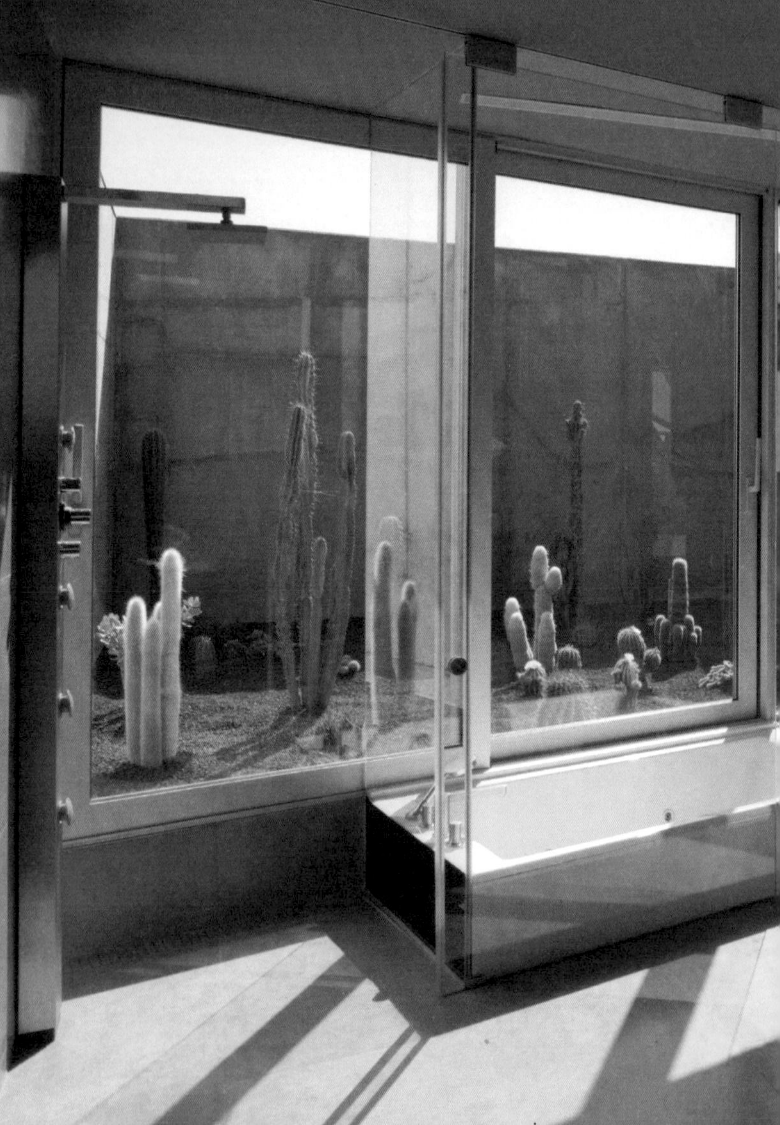

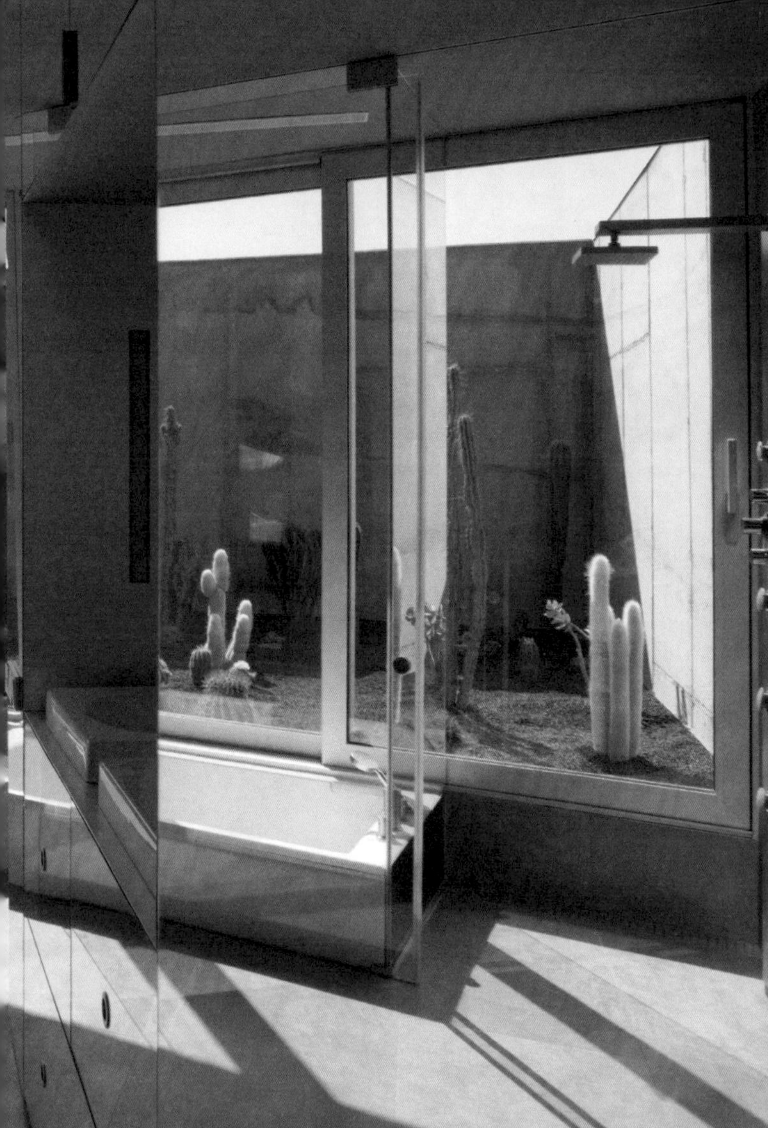

THE ESSENTIAL IS INVISIBLE TO THE EYE

"No matter how many facts are told,
no matter how many details are given,
the essential thing resists telling"

PAUL AUSTER

[1] His movements respond to an unusual tempo. Sometimes easy, then energetic. Even the geometry of his gestures seems strange when unrelated to each moment and tool used during the production process. [2] A number of glass and metal apparatuses are arranged along the bar, each one with a precise shape responding to its evolution over time.

[3] My face is fragmented in the mirror at the far end, reflected through the Loos Bar's neat arrangement of bottles. As I wait for my drink, I try to delve into the mysteries of the décor to find out whether there are any secondary elements, any redundancies, but I can't find any. I give in to the charms of the contours of the reddish marble multiplied in all directions by the reflections that enlarge the tiny space.

[4] As I walked in the door, the Viennese waiter smiled at me and picked up his instruments.

"You know, Herr Arroyo, the Dry Martini is the story of invisible precision," he says to me. And he continues,

"You never get tired of perfecting it; as though there were no limits to its preparation."

[5] I reflect on the certainty that, beneath its transparent boring appearance, as opposed to other flashier cocktails, there lies an infinite subtlety. It may have looked the same for over a century, the iconic cone-shaped glass, no ice, crystal clear gin and an indiscernible twist of lemon. [6] There is no information that our senses can use to anticipate the experience. Only in the instant of contact can we catch hold of the properties it hides. Even then, they never taste exactly the same, and its only through non-visual senses that we can appreciate its ever-changing essence.

[7] "Today's is special. I put in a tiny drop of Lagavulin because you looked angry when you came in," he says winking.

I realize that I'm not hiding anything. I've just come from a site visit and the lack of precision in the details has put me out of sorts. [8] The first sip changes my mood as I think that every master imprints his own personal signature onto seemingly identical glasses. And, it is these minuscule properties, which lash out from the invisible, that transform us instantly. [9] Then I let go, relaxed, rambling about the possibility that almost nothing of what we see contains authentic information,

"The essence never lies in what 'just' seems."

112 [1] At the beginning of the 1980s, Fred Brooks established a distinction between Essential Complexity and Accidental Complexity in software engineering. He asserted that most engineers were no longer concerned with the essential; that was why all of the reduction work on the big programming problems wasn't producing consistent improvements. [2] In his reflections, he defines Accidental Complexity as referring to the problems we create, like the details of code writing or the optimization of its assembly. [3] On the contrary, Essential Complexity is described as caused by the problem itself as it is resolved and is understood as something essential to the solution, which cannot be avoided.

[4] In this search for the essential, he advocated for the organic growth of software through incremental development. This kind of programming, also called agile software

development, provides a different working system for each stage in the design, organizing its writing as a creative process in successive independent phases. [5] From this point of view, one technology that represented a significant improvement in the realm of the essential was the invention of high-level programming languages, like Fortran. At present, new languages, like C++ or Java are only seen as accidental improvements, independently of the effectiveness and popularity of their use.

[6] When applied to a creative vision of urban space, essential complexity does not deny the complex nature of life. As such, it is directed toward selecting and reducing those factors to the indispensible minimum for the resolution of particular problems. [7] The reality of contemporary urbanity requires an open point of view that identifies the precise problems that need to be addressed, making use of essential complexity. [8] It is true that creation can go on being falsified with reassuring elements, like simple-looking instantaneous sedatives. However, time will cut off this analgesic property and the illness will come back in all its virulence. [9] The attitude of concealing urban complexity using pieces of political candy without any active properties but momentary popular fascination is like taking an aspirin when what is failing is your heart.

[1] One of the great discoveries of hidden properties that **113** were already at work before we turned our questioning gaze toward the world is the double helix of DNA. Its complex structure is, however, an example of the essential: nothing

can be eliminated without damaging its properties. Its energetic materiality is essentially complex.

² On the other hand, among the objects designed to resolve existing problems in tangible reality are watches, which help us relate to our surroundings in a more controlled and precise manner. ³ A watchmaking complication is any indication that is added beyond that of the time of day, the minutes and the seconds: for example, the phases of the moon or different time zones. However, an automatic winding system or a tourbillon, used to cancel out the differences in speed caused by the force of gravity, does not provide an indication, as such. ⁴ These mechanisms solve problems without adding new functions and are considered complexities. ⁵ Complications add layers of information and additive functions, whereas complexities increase and resolve the precision of existing functions without adding information.

⁶ The tourbillon was created to compensate for the fluctuation of the balance wheel and hairspring, and escapement in watches under the effects of slowing and acceleration caused by the pull of the Earth. This precision is made possible by enclosing the balance wheel in a gyroscopic case which carries out one rotation each minute, adopting all of the vertical positions in succession.

⁷ In the same way, the automatic winding mechanism solves a dynamic problem of energy loss in the watch, transforming the user's kinetic energy into accumulated static energy. That energy is then released in a constant manner to be consumed by the spiral mainspring.

⁸ A watch that only tells the hour, minutes and seconds, with a tourbillon that allows it to remain independent from

Earth's gravity is an object that can go anywhere and is almost entirely independent of the environment. [9] Precision that is based on the use of autonomous complexities resolves fundamental problems, eliminating complication. Organized in this way, nothing can be removed without harming its function, which defines its mechanism as an essentially complex object.

[1] In an apparently barren landscape there can be hidden **114** forces that cannot be perceived at an initial simple glance but, given a deeper reading of its properties, they can be helpful when it comes to introducing objects into that territory.

[2] As such, the axial forces that appear in the desolate landscape between two lakes encourage the preservation of its essence during the introduction of the volume intended for the new National Museum in Tartu (2005). [3] The elevation of the built volume allows for defining a public space under it, protected from the arctic climate, which

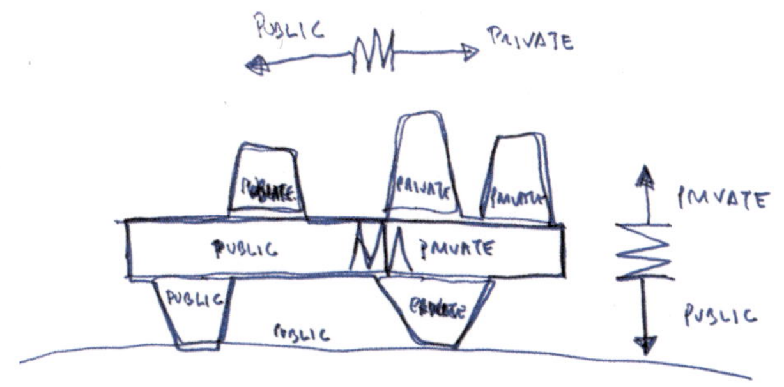

emphasizes its collective character with multiple centrifugal and fragmentary visions out toward the broad sheets of water. Resolving the continuity of the territory defines a place that mixes together nature and artifice between the volumes that house the museum access and the auditoriums that keep the new construction elevated.

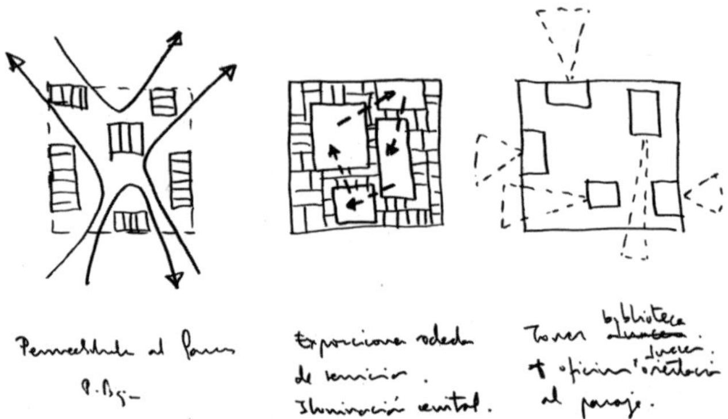

⁴ On the other hand, the different types and storage conditions for the collections that include art, textile, leather, metal or wood, encourage separate locations in independent elevated towers with self-sufficient operations. The offices and library are also housed in independent volumes of similar construction, located so that they take maximum advantage of the relationships with the landscape through the views between the other towers. ⁵ Their different sizes and self-sufficient operation intertwine on a high-ceilinged intermediate level made up of an elevated

base with an abstract and essential presence. That is where the museum's exhibition rooms are located, with natural lighting and perforated visions of the surroundings along the perimeter and the roof.

[6] The lack of vertical coincidence between the storage towers and the lower access volumes is resolved on the inside using an internal coupling geometry which, though apparently haphazard, stems from the requirements of the whole. [7] This geometry for the accord produces the deformation and adaptation of different mechanisms, which take on their synchronized form as a result, lending the building its original presence. [8] The museum, born from the exist-

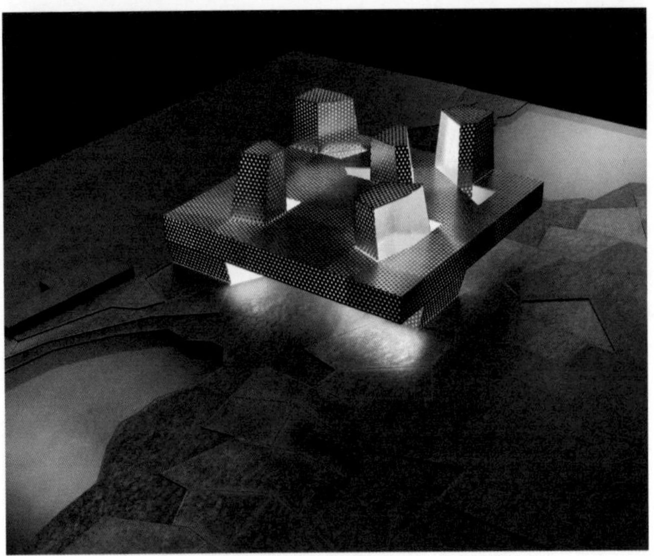

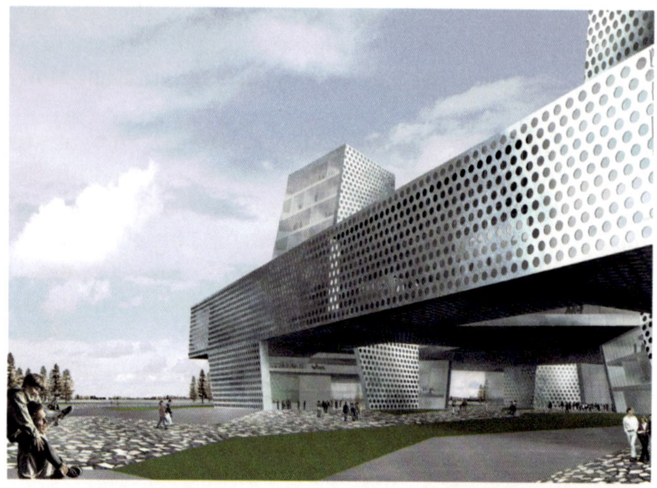

ing forces on the site, gives the resolution of its program back to the surroundings, expanding its geometry in the form of platforms at different levels that prepare future visitors for its surprising hidden spatial structure.

115 [1] The richness of the lexicon in certain languages allows for differentiating words that have a similar meaning in daily use, whereas under a less superficial gaze they define opposite characteristics and properties. [2] Complex and complicated, or simple and straightforward are used interchangeably in a colloquial register, but using them as adjectives applied to people lends them a deeper meaning. There is no doubt that we can differentiate a simple person from a straightforward one and a complicated person from a complex one. [3] It is easily understood that simple and complicated are negative personality traits, whereas straightforward and complex, though they are still opposites, are positive traits associated with interesting people. These properties can be extrapolated and understood in creative terms.

[4] From this standpoint, simple objects can be produced, vulgar in nature, that try to camouflage themselves as straightforward; there can also be complicated objects that don't possess any hidden legible properties behind their complex appearances. [5] The primordial labor of the contemporary creator resides in knowing how to differentiate them using the arts of a detective, recognizing the presence of complication as opposed to the discovery of complexity, and in the same way, the degrees of reduction of straightforwardness, instead of the harmlessness of simplicity.

[6] Complexity is seen, therefore, as a sum of collaborative properties that make up a whole, pushing it to transcend toward something more elevated. It also appears as the solution to a specific problem by means of enquiry.

[7] Complicatedness, however, is formed through the addition of different non-complementary properties which generate unfocused and incoherent objects. Likewise, it is identified by the appearance of new problems while we are attempting to solve the present ones. With complication, one can always perceive a superficial use of images and it brings with it an absence of complementarity in its operating characteristics. The form it proposes is its fundamental vocation and it never appears associated with properties guided by interior principles.

[8] On the other hand, the straightforward is what is detached from the unnecessary, preserving its intrinsic properties and it is arrived at by subtraction. It is not surprising that this is the most difficult of journeys for building up a personality and, by extension, for creation.

[9] In contrast, there is no evolution in the simple and it is defined as a static system, in which nothing new appears and no existing problems are resolved because it is pure temporary appearance.

116 [1] There is no doubt that people and objects sometimes have to give up part of their own interest to respond to the forces of the common good. Behaviors that appear in this way transform their intrinsic properties and sometimes even their physical form. [2] From this standpoint, the vocation for making a private art collection accessible to the public for pedagogical reasons is not sufficient to lend meaning to its container. Removed from the exterior conditions, it could

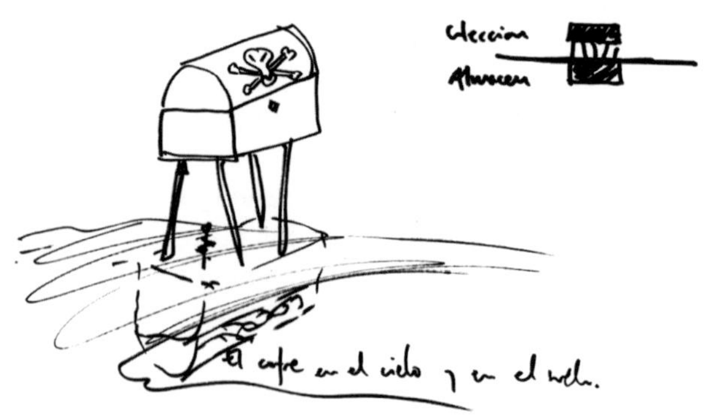

end up becoming a mere pirate's chest full of treasure, with an autistic nature.

[3] In order to absorb external forces, in a consolidated environment in the city, the outline of the new Art Foundation building in Lleida (2009) appears referenced to a relational geometry hidden in the urban structure. From a clear desire to create and protect spaces with a collective vocation, the volume responds by freeing up a generous park space through its compactness. [4] This public determination is also revealed in the appearance of three large hollows, with urban dimensions, at the base of its volume. With their configuration, they protect a series of large-scale terraces over the park, while they maintain a disturbing weightlessness in the eyes of the curious citizen.

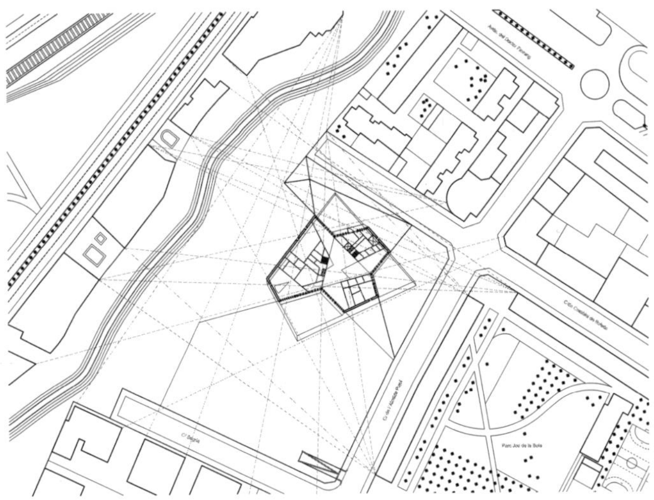

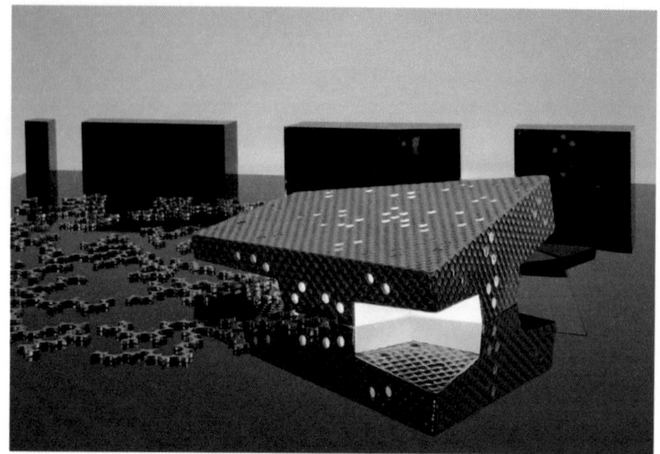

⁵ The volume, subtly inclined, organizes the building, situating the exhibition spaces on a peculiar upper floor. The space, of variable height and surprising construction, consists of a continuous hall that allows for housing large-scale contemporary pieces. ⁶ The internal geometry is born as the resolution of the external incitement from the large hollows with a central space that has a centrifugal character. ⁷ The exhibition space is seen as partially compartmentalized through arms with different uses.

⁸ These protuberances are projected from the center toward the perimeter and they house the communications and the projection areas, generating the expository continuity of different but unified atmospheres. ⁹ The perimeter is equipped with illuminated circular perforations on all sides which are located along the transitions between the exhibition

spaces and the circulation areas. [10] The relationship between the neutral continuity of the exhibitions and the excited central hollow proposes complex leisure experiences through elevated observation decks. They allow for contemplating the collection and the building from points of view that are different from what everyday passers-by usually see.

[1] I've gotten lost during a winter hunting expedition on the **117** border with Sweden. In the faint blue light, I can discern a vast white world without points of reference. [2] I've walked for hours and, worn out, I drag myself through the snowy silence until I fall, exhausted. Lying there, my body sunken a few centimeters into the snow, I can hear my camouflage suit crackling with the slightest movement. The white camo suit lets me move freely through the landscape, but it also erases me: I'm invisible.

[3] Suddenly, I spy an impressive moose about six hundred meters away, smelling at the tops of the buried trees. I turn over awkwardly, my snowshoes smacking against my legs. The specimen raises his head then, sniffing at the air as though he senses danger, but he can't see me.

[4] My hands are protected by a pair of Hestra gloves like the ones worn by the Norwegian army, with a sophisticated hole made for the right index trigger finger. Silently, I stretch out my left arm across the cold powder, firmly grasping the Browning Bar MKII 338. The handcrafted butt of the gun is covered with obscene motifs, as though it were an attempt to counteract the frailty of its precision mechanism with a bit of humanity.

5 Positioned for shooting, I feel the cold lens of the gun's sight caress my pupil. My breath, faltering from fatigue, makes the crosshairs dance about in space, quivering drunkenly. Knowing that I will only have one chance, I inhale deeply to steady my pulse and I hold it for an instant.

6 My bullet hits the animal and he falls motionless, his forehead thrust into the snow, kneeling as he draws his last breath. 7 With a savage sensation of violence I run toward him, my snowshoes crunching under the weight of the rifle. I pull out my Aitor hunting knife and slice through his belly, which lets out clouds of hot steam like a pressure cooker.

8 Overpowered by the frenzy of survival, I lean my frozen body and face in closer to his tepid entrails. A feeling of comfort comes over me and quells my fear. 9 I think about how his death, such an essential and extremely simple act, saved me. Leaning against his dark flank, I am visible again, as I hear the distant sounds of the rescue party's motor. I know that I'll never go hunting again.

118 1 Just as the resolution of the internal precision of a watch is closely tied in with the exterior gravitational forces, the precision of the internal program of a building is directly related to the form in which it resolves the city's problems.

2 From this perspective, the essential compactness of a Public School in Vienna (2010) solves the structure of a complex node in the city with its presence. 3 The limits of its functional mechanism absorb the park and the roads, providing specific solutions for each situation along the perimeter. Following the geometric relationships from the planning,

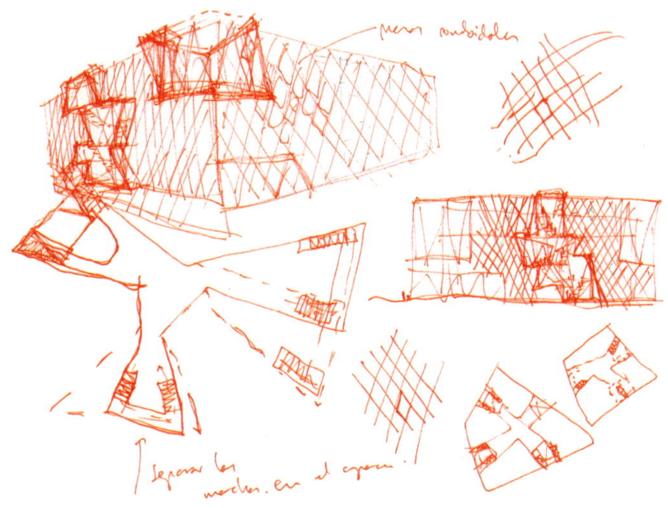

it creates an extensive square in the shape of a diabolo as a decompression zone leading toward the large park. The student access is located on this wide square, which guarantees their safety because it is closed to traffic. [4] On the other hand, its alignment with the main avenue creates a singular perspective along the curve. [5] Lastly, the compact character of the program allows for freeing up land, creating an open space to house the school playground with extensive views of the park.

[6] The pedagogical uses are associated with the uneven perimeter, determining its length. [7] Each educational area is located on a different floor and they are organized independently, acting like a series of mini interior worlds. [8] The

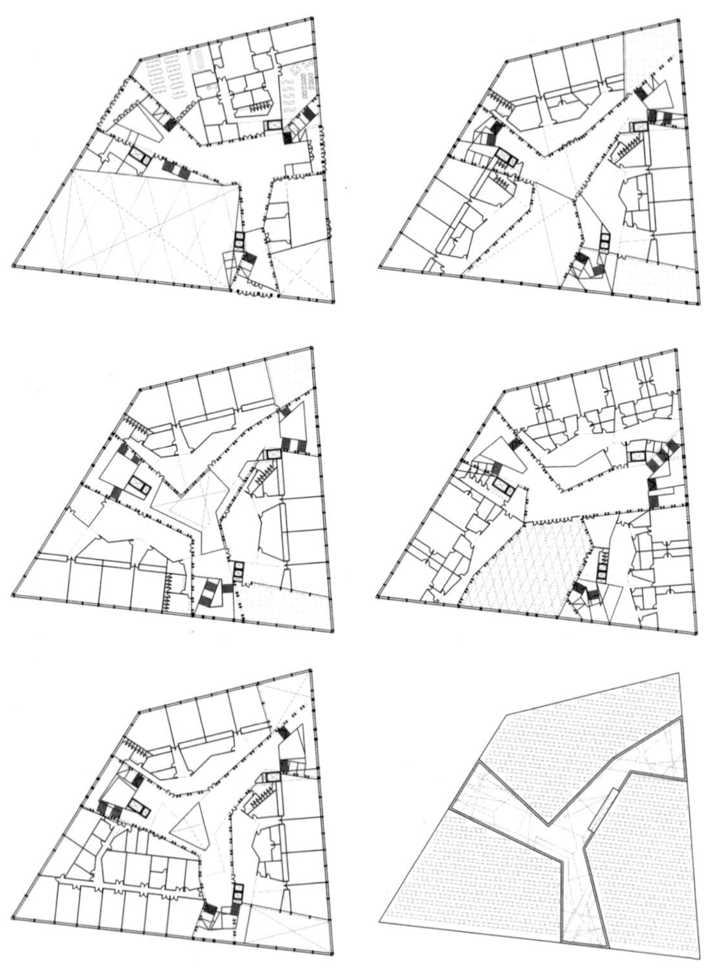

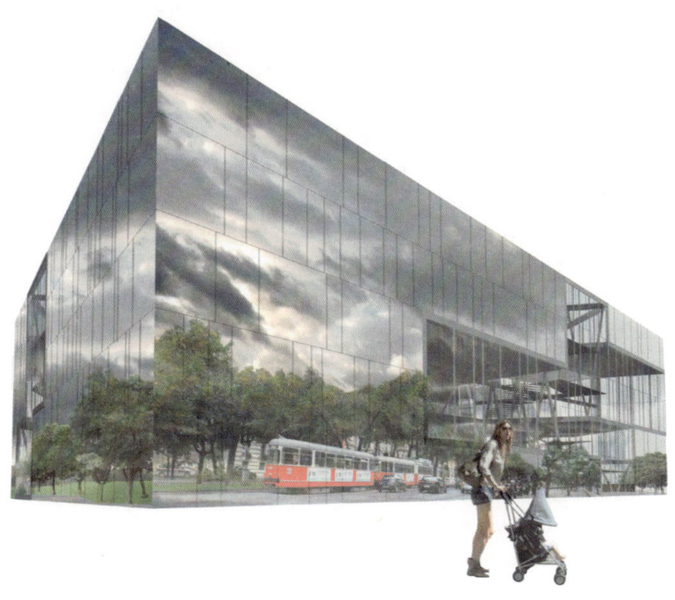

size differences among the various groups of classrooms produce distortions in the space, which leads to a non-coincident geometry between the different levels.

[9] The circulations are funneled through the interstitial space that appears between the different educational areas. This defines a mechanism that absorbs and resolves the accessibility of urban forces into the internal organization through the abstract perimeter. The vertical hollowing out creates surprising visual relationships involving complex spatiality, guiding the students through urban-scale pano-

ramic spaces with natural lighting. [10] Likewise, it promotes a variable set of focalized visual relationships, from the core out toward the park and the city. [11] The essential character of the enveloping form allows for catching glimpses of the frenetic movement of the students, through the large hollows that are cut into the mirrored façade as it intersects with the circulation area. [12] This dynamic depth, together with the system that creates mutable reflections of the clouds, trees, streetcars and people along the perimeter, provides a feeling of changeability and sophisticated instability.

119 [1] Learning to differentiate the essential requires a certain isolation from routine and from constant external demands. To some extent, it supposes a degree of introspection that is necessary in order to resolve problems from the inside. [2] Revealing essential complexity entails a kind of behavioral autism and an operation based on more self-sufficient properties. From this position, we can respond to exterior stimuli, categorizing them by assigning them a particular status of importance. [3] The idea is to carry out a selection of priorities, by virtue of which everything that we consider to be accessory or accidental is eliminated. An incorrect hierarchization means that some issues get mixed into the mechanism for resolution, provoking a defective operation. [4] The acceptance of internal complexity allows for discovering the degree to which it can be reduced to the limits of its essence. The object must then house a mechanism to resolve the profound problems that originate in the surroundings, releasing the perimeter from the responsibility for solving them. [5] This entails an abstraction and distinction of the form in its relationship with external pressures. Its function and its protective perimeter are then organized separately; the resolution of their intersection is what produces the coupling between the two. [6] The limit of the object is defined as an element that is charged with abstract information which only allows for intuiting something of the essence of its interior complexity. As such, form is displayed as unity in difference.

[7] This duality between internal system and the abstract containment perimeter encourages thinking about the non-existence of limits for the mechanism. It is prefigured as something expansive toward the territory, the size of which is defined by pragmatic conditions of quantity, either in terms of surface area or in economic terms. [8] In this way, system and environment appear as an unbreakable unity that crosses the material condition of the perimeter. [9] Only the internal mechanism of resolution remains tied to the exterior properties, whereas the perimeter response supposes self-referentiality on the part of the object that provides it with presence. [10] This reduces complexity to a minimum, since the limits not only define the dimensions of the system but its direct relationship to the surroundings.

[1] In places where there are no nearby urban traces and **120** there is a large presence of farming activity, reducing the land consumption allows for the present activities to continue. [2] As such, the installation of an object in the agri-

cultural landscape is carried out by minimizing its footprint, which allows the topography of the vegetation to continue with its productivity between the mountains and the meadow.

[3] Two organizational structures support the building using a pair of variable volumes with dimensions that increase from the ground up. They come together at the top, creating a larger compact volume. [4] This dual character of the CSIC Research Building in Brañas del Sar (2010) allows for dividing the uses, assigning one of the volumes with the programs dedicated to theoretical research and its transmission in auditoriums, classrooms and office space. [5] The other volume houses uses dedicated to practical experimentation, with workshops, laboratories and testing areas.

[6] This vocation for programmatic compactness localizes the uses with longer occupation times, like offices and laboratories, on the upper floors, which are related directly with the landscape in an enriched atmosphere. The essential volume of the building brings about a homogeneous relationship to the surroundings, without favoring any one direction. Its extensive development along the perimeter allows for all uses to enjoy natural light.

[7] The inclined rise of the two thematic structures sets up a truncated opening in the central intersection made of transparent material. That is where the pressures of the program are resolved in terms of interior lighting and circulation. [8] The geometry leans over, seeking out the optimum orientation and the largest amount of light, creating exciting variations throughout the day. The resolution of the interior mechanism for growth can only be seen

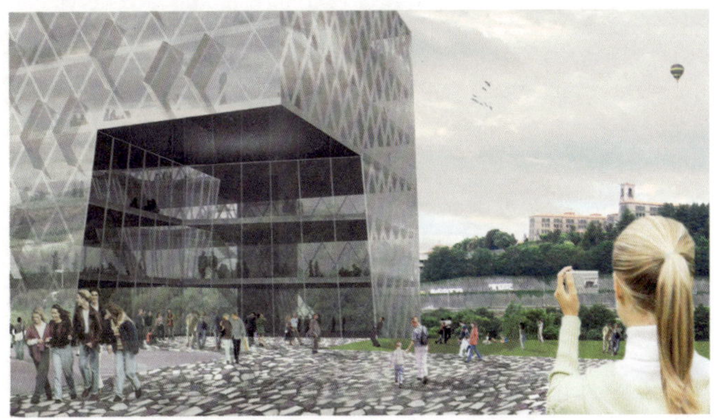

through the transparency of this intersection. [9] The variable spatiality also establishes an effective energetic system that ensures the ventilation and cooling of the building.

[10] On the top floor, the volume is resolved with a relaxation level where the library and the panoramic lounges are located. A number of exterior terraces encourage relating both with the landscape and the hollowed-out space. [11] The discontinuous elements that create shade, located along the perimeter, are fitted with mirrored material that introduces a disturbing vibration into the essential stability of the volume in the form of fragmented visions of the surrounding territory.

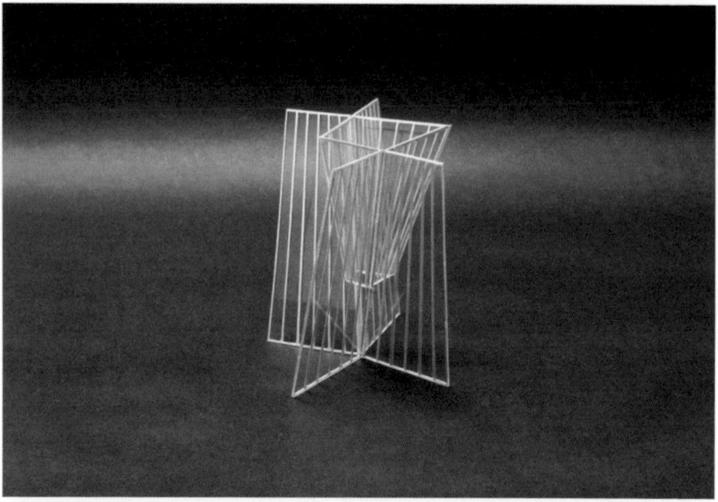

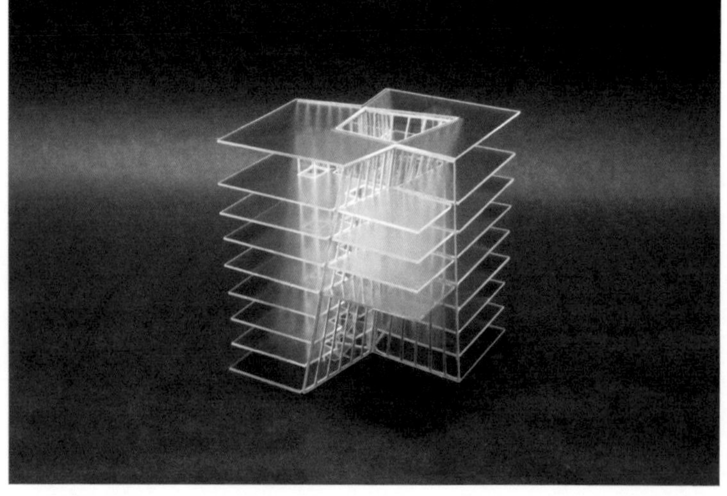

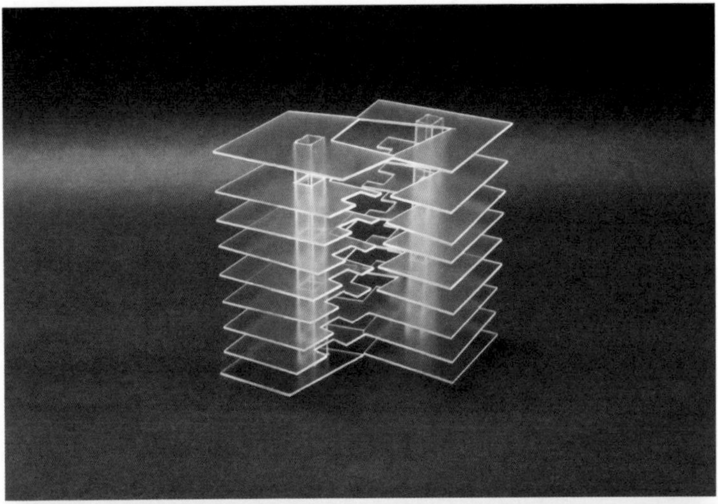

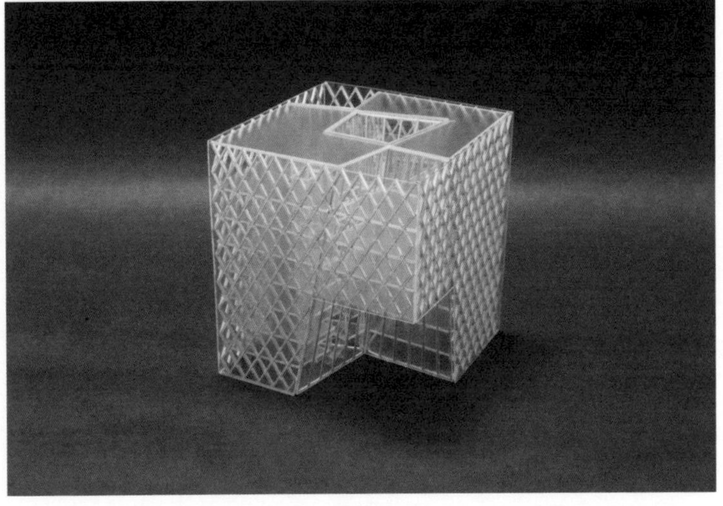

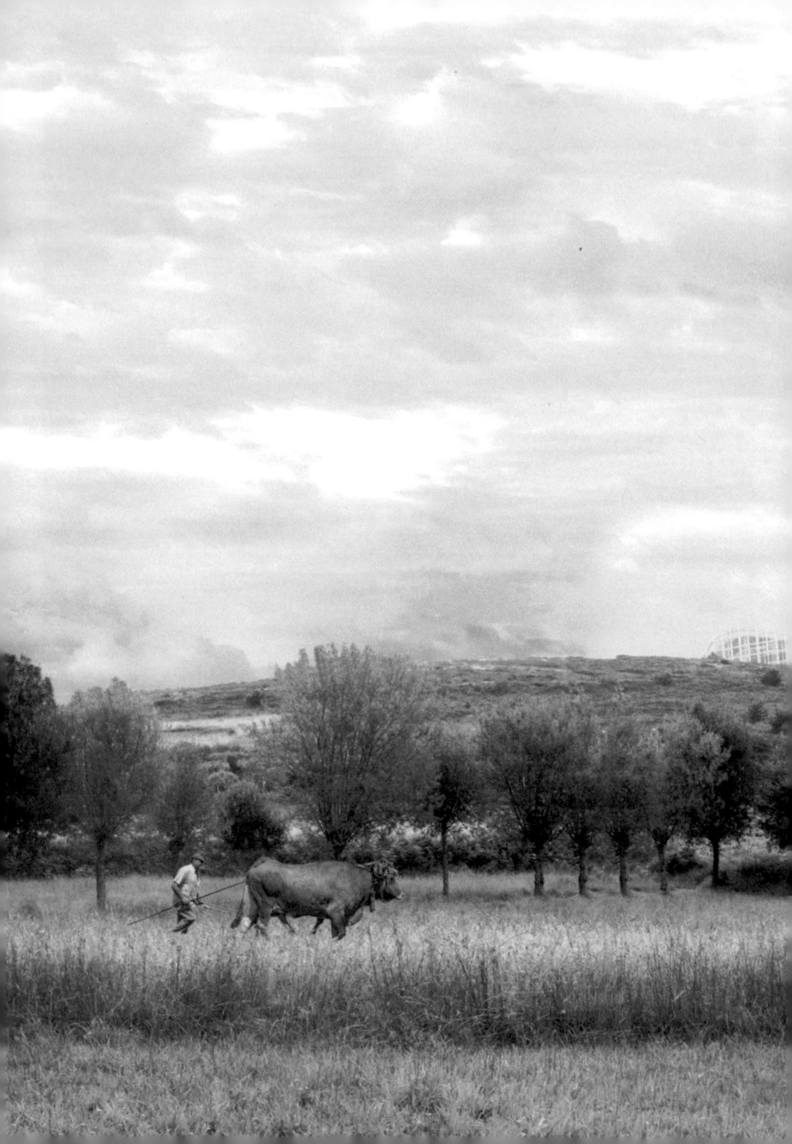

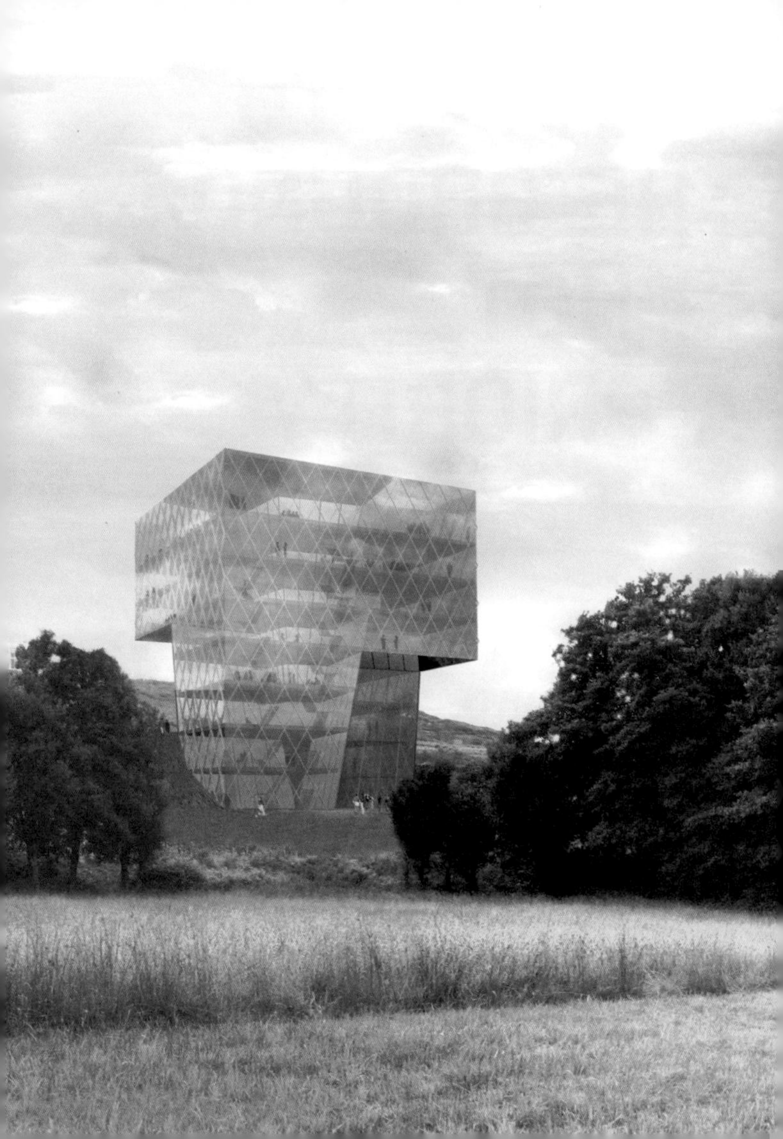

GETTING TO THE GROUND IS NOT A PRIORITY

"You're sure to get somewhere, if only you walk long enough"

LEWIS CARROL

¹ The noise of the helicopter prevents us from communicating clearly. Toby points at my equipment, making gestures with the final instructions for the jump. We are flying in the only helicopter in Utila; the owner uses it to go on outings in the keys. ² Today is the final test before I can be certified as a rescue diver and I'm pretty excited.

"Don't forget! The most important thing is to enter the water perpendicularly," he reminds me before we stand up.

Eight meters above the surface, I realize that height is something largely relative. ³ The depth meter is anchored to my Dive Rite BCD wings and I use my right had to hold the Poseidon regulator firmly against my mouth. ⁴ As the door slides open, my will falters and I look toward my instructor. Smiling, he shouts,

"You first, fearless!"

Without thinking twice, I take a large step and start to fall. Instantly, I push the fins firmly together, pushing the tank forward so that it doesn't flip me over.

⁵ "It's very important to keep gravity from adding to the surface tension of the water or you'll break something," I hear in my head as I pick up speed.

A powerful force tries to bend my web-footed legs as I pierce the thin surface. I forget to tip my head forward and the air tank hits me in the back of the head. ⁶ Floating there, half stunned, I wait until the instructor jumps, elegant and light, hardly stirring the water, as though he were weightless.

"How's it going, hot-head?" he asks.

⁷ Immediately, we dive to twenty meters to start the orientation test, with just a compass, toward the ship's

coordinates. A clear view for dozens of meters brightens up this final training session. [8] When the dive computer reads half a tank, I see a shadow the size of a yacht outlined against the sea bottom of giant sponges. It's doubtful we've been able to reach our destination in such short time. As I turn over to look up, I see a fifteen-meter-long object moving elegantly, gravityless. It's Big Utila Tom, the whale shark that lives in these waters.

[9] Toby signals me to swim up and we grab on to his large dorsal fin like lazy suckerfishes. As I look at my compass again, I realize that the whale is taking us in the right direction. Out of the corner of my eye, I can see my companion smiling under his regulator.

[10] We float for a long time in perfect zero gravity, sailing through stalactites of sunlight. Suddenly, and with suspicious precision, the shark swims a few concentric circles around the keel of the ship. Then I'm blown away by an astonishing realization:

"He's asking us to let go!"

122 [1] All solid objects have an objective mass but, as far as their equilibrium within their environment is concerned, they behave as though all of their mass were concentrated in the virtual point of their center of gravity. This point in space determines whether their balance can be maintained. If the object is symmetrical, the point will fall along the axis of symmetry though it does not necessarily have to correspond to the object's geometric center. [2] In the case of the human body, the center of gravity is in constant movement and the distortion of muscle mass produces the necessary efforts to counteract the effect of a loss of balance. 3 Clearly, equilibrium is the product of the adaptability of our structure and its flexibility.

4 With inert objects, equilibrium depends directly on how they are supported on the ground and on whether the center of gravity remains within the vertical with respect to the contact zone. Likewise, the forces that act on them have to be controlled so that the effect of rotation does not cause them to fall. 5 Regardless of their weight, objects with a center of gravity outside of the support area will fall if there is no exterior force applying pressure in the opposite direction. The fall implies a shift of the center of gravity to a lower point. This equilibrium, by means of forces that are complementary to the object's weight, is always unstable in nature. 6 In contrast, in the case of a stable equilibrium, if the object is subject to pressure from the exterior, its center is lifted in an attempt to recover its original position. 7 When, despite the fact that the center of gravity changes location in space, its location within the object does not change, the equilibrium is referred to as indifferent.

8 Recent research has uncovered that there are objects that float optimally when they have more mass on the top half and, therefore, a higher center of gravity. 9 This contradicts the common notion that, the lower that virtual point is and the more homogenously the mass is distributed, the greater the equilibrium. This fact represents great progress in terms of the definition of stability. 10 Therefore, the evaluation of the type of structures that maintain their equilibrium better depends on the air flow around the

volumes they define. [11] From the analyses undertaken up to the present it can be deduced that objects with a higher center of gravity generate turbulences beneath their geometries, automatically adjusting the balance of forces toward a vertical position.

123　[1] The different arrangements of matter are produced on an atomic level. Gases appear without a recognizable order and metals have a very regular one. [2] However, there are elements like water or glass that have an order that is only maintained over short distances. [3] The material networks made up of atoms are ordered in repetitive patterns with a coordination number or a quantity of closely related atoms.

[4] Even so, most structures never follow an ideal pattern and they present defects that are a manifestation of the conditions in the surroundings. These internal adaptations have an isolated, superficial or planar character, displaying different geometries in each case. The imperfections always emerge in the areas of long-range or granulometric ordering.

[5] On the one hand, temporary defects create discontinuities in the structural network, which generate displacements due to external heating or, artificially, due to the introduction of new objects. This leads to the appearance of gaps that distort the original network, which then readapts spatially. Returning the network to its original state requires a large amount of induced strain that will increase the network's resistance.

⁶ On the other hand, dislocations are processes that appear in the properties of certain materials and that explain many of their attributes of hardening, resistance or elasticity. They are linear deformations and they can emerge or be created artificially through torque or filling at cut areas. These dislocations have a fundamental importance, since they confer matter with ductility when it would otherwise be fragile and break.

⁷ A volume always defines an exterior surface, the structure of which does not have the same compactness or spatial properties as the three-dimensional properties on the inside. It is the result of a different material grouping and it signifies that more spatial and energetic instabilities arise, generating planar defects. ⁸ The structure's orientation at each point on the surface then takes on increased importance, since it will define the optimum interface between the internal and external tensions. ⁹ Finishing the structures abruptly in contact with the exterior generates an adaptive deformation that is closely related to the surrounding conditions.

¹ The search for an adaptive equilibrium refers back to the **124** possibility of small-scale calculations and transformations in space and time. ² One of the emblems of this type of infinitesimal adaptive calculation is the Segway, which is fitted with five gyroscopes to maintain it in constant unstable micro equilibriums. By managing information on its location in space, the forces of gravity and the passenger, it establishes the necessary calculations to create an instantaneous

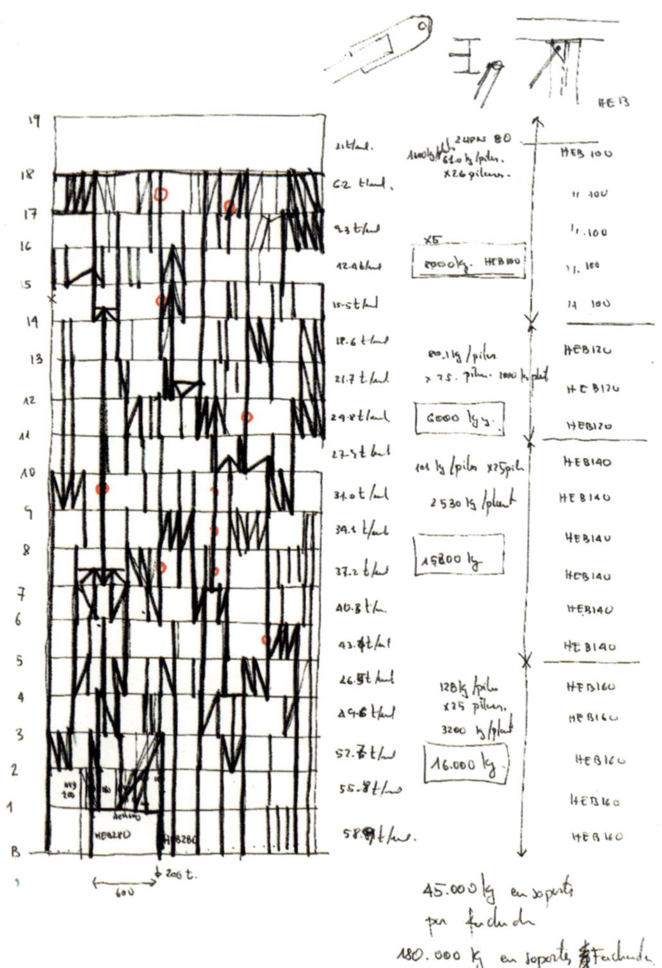

19
18
17
16
15
14
13
12
11
10
9
8
7
6
5
4
3
2
1
B
600
200 t.
HEB280
HEB280
21 t/ml.
62 t/ml.
23 t/ml
12.9 t/ml
15.5 t/ml
18.6 t/ml
21.7 t/ml
24.8 t/ml
27.3 t/ml
31.0 t/ml
34.1 t/ml
37.2 t/ml
40.3 t/ml
43.4 t/ml
46.5 t/ml
49.6 t/ml
52.7 t/ml
55.8 t/ml
58.9 t/ml.
24 PN 80
61.0 kg /pilar.
X 26 pilares.
X5
8000 kg. HEB100
80.1 kg /pilar
x 25. pilar. 1000 kg plat
6000 kg.
101 kg /pilar x25 pilar
2530 kg /plant
15800 kg
128 kg /pilar
x25 pilar.
3200 kg /plant
16.000 kg.
HEB 13
HEB 100
" .100
" .100
" .100
" .100
HEB 120
HEB 120
HEB 120
HEB 140
HEB 140
HEB 140
HEB 140
HEB 140
HEB 140
HEB 160
HEB 160
HEB 160
HEB 160
HEB 160
45.000 kg en soports
per fachada
180.000 kg en soports fachada

partial equilibrium. [3] Using the application of fuzzy logic, it also generates an individualized response for each spatial position of the user.

[4] That kind of one-time response, which is, nevertheless, part of a general system, is used as an adaptation method by spatial structures in random or highly variable situations. [5] The apparent randomness that is present in the façade of the Social Housing Building in Durango (2005) is resolved by means of a similar approach. Using a system of small-scale triangulations, the vertical discontinuities, created by the inequality and variety of the different open spaces, are absorbed.

[6] In the case of the Zaragoza Stadium (2002), the structural variation absorbs the different particularities that appear in its geometry. The inclines and varied forms of the bleachers and walkways are interconnected, with individual responses for each of them, in a vertical gradient in terms of the rigidity of the structural pieces. [7] Shaped using X, V, Y or Z layouts, the exact resolution of the nodes couples the transfers of stress independently. At the same time, it provides the building with a homogeneous vibration, yet an unstable presence.

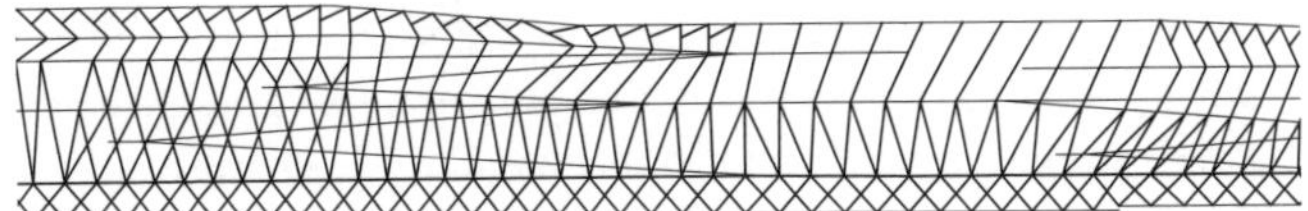

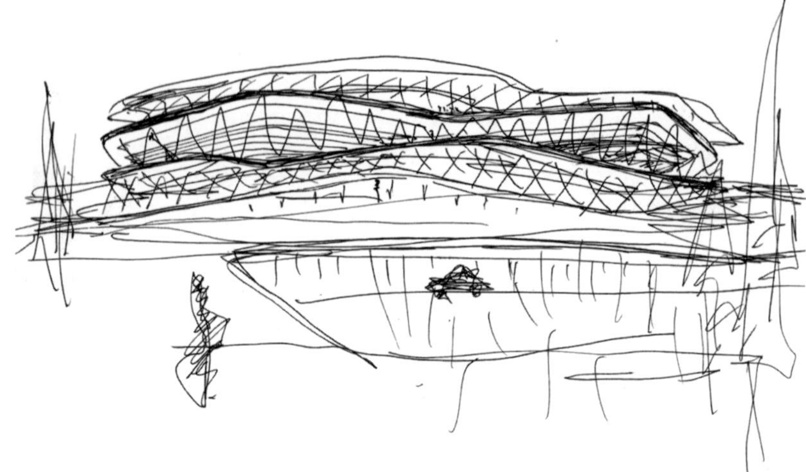

[8] When the factors that participate in the structural adaptation go beyond resistance, its configuration takes on surprising values. [9] That is the case with the Nam June Paik Museum in Seoul (2003), where a non-directional structural geometry appears deformed by qualities tied in with the orientation, lighting needs or security needs of each interior program. The relationship between each use and its location demands a shapeless structural system with multiple variations to resolve the demands of each situation. [10] This filter applied to the relationships between use and exterior nature makes up an envelope characterized by gradual behaviors in terms of density and permeability, which speaks to the user about properties as opposed to forms, and experiences as opposed to images.

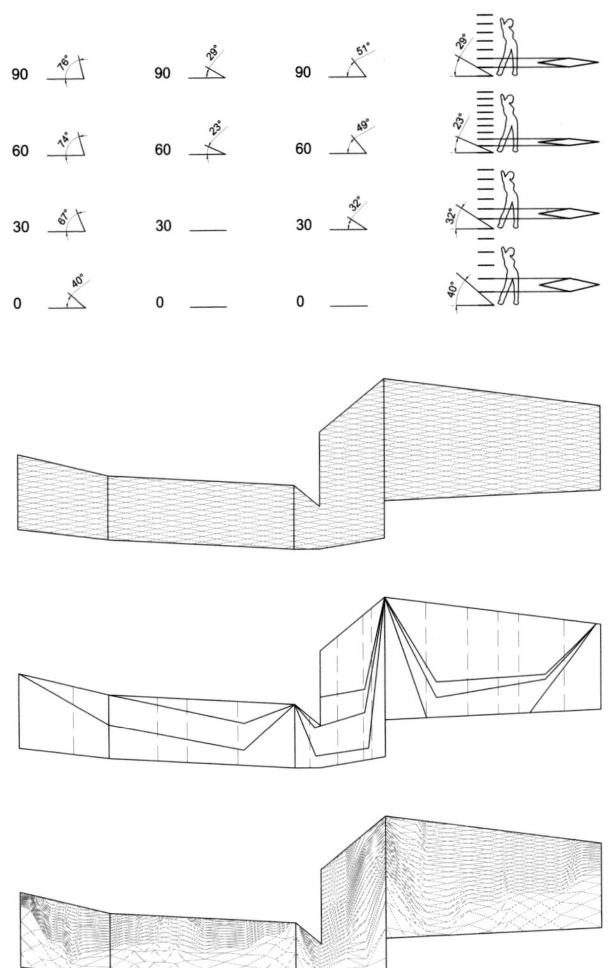

90
76°
90
29°
90
51°
29°
60
74°
60
23°
60
49°
23°
30
67°
30
30
32°
32°
0
40°
0
0
40°

125 [1] Topology was developed by Henri Poincaré as a branch of Mathematics to deal with certain properties of objects: more specifically, the qualities that remain after the object has been distorted, without breaking it or adding anything to it. [2] It is based on the study of the continuities and deformations of geometric figures in multi-dimensional space. [3] As such, it is a science in which only the qualitative properties are important, not the quantitative ones. The objects it is concerned with, called topological spaces, are obtained from other objects by deforming them in a continuous or homeomorphic manner, without creating any singularity. [4] In a troubling way, topology considers a polyhedral volume and a sphere to be equal, since one can be obtained from the other through the simple distortion of its material.

[5] Its studies make use of a collection of instructions that, when coupled with a set of tools and techniques for manipulation, allow for modeling geometric or thematic relationships with a high degree of precision. [6] Its direct application to the creative process allows for grouping together entities that share the same geometry, spatial relationships and other characteristics in an integrated way. As such, their transformation and variation always guarantee continuity in the system to which they belong. [7] For an effective operation, they are represented in planar graphics which store the properties and the relationships between each of the topological primitives: faces, nodes and edges. They are used as elements for analysis that allow for the addition and dissolution of the limits between various objects and their edge properties.

[8] The development of complex systems for handling topologies has mainly been focused on geographic and urban information, but it is also applied to the structural continuity of entities formed by points, lines or areas and their associated properties. [9] The use of systems for storing coordinates: databases with instructions for the relationships between entities and clustering algorithms, work toward recognizing these shared properties among objects in order to be able to act on them. This allows for isolating each property and monitoring its continuity independently, guaranteeing an effective assembly. [10] Given any scale or object it is applied to, topological analysis allows for dissolving the physical links of material in favor of an interested reading of the continuity of its properties.

[1] The Théâtre de la Ville is in total silence. Despite the **126** crowd of spectators packed into the hall, there is something that foments a compulsory stillness. [2] The final piece of the dance is called Shijima and it's my favorite. I've brought Dagmar to see Sankai Juku's performance.

[3] When the curtain goes up, the master Ushio Amagatsu appears, floating four meters high against a golden background cut out of stone. Faint lighting on his face and torso increases the feeling of weightlessness. The long pleated skirt that covers him down to his feet moves gently in the air that circulates through the theatre, hiding the support. He raises his arms slowly, stretching up into infinity, creating the sensation that there is a force working against gravity to keep him in the air. [4] Dagmar holds tightly to my

arm, which is also tense, secured against the armrest. I imagine that everyone sitting there is in the same situation of induced stress.

5 Four dancers come out of the wings, contorting their bodies silently like marionettes controlled by invisible strings. Their brusque movements, legs and arms moving identically, prevent onlookers from discerning clearly up from down. A carefully choreographed lack of synchronicity maintains them in a strange harmony.

6 On the floor of the stage, out of sight, a fine layer of sand transmits a symphony of friction, instrumented with lightness and pressure, sliding and rotation, framing silent moments of emptiness. 7 Suddenly, I realize that the random distortion of the dancers responds to the orders of the guide floating above them. Each intermittent movement of his arms produces a different adaptation in each dancer's body.

8 The rhythm picks up frenetically, transforming the stage into a crackling tornado of impossible shapes. The ground lighting, at the back of the stage, outlines their figures with violent intersected shadows. I can see the audience members in front of me shifting anxiously in their seats.

9 Then the lights go out and a dark heavy silence returns the room to its normal gravity. As the house lights come on, I find myself contorted in my seat. My companion is in an unpredictable posture and the rest of the audience is visibly unsettled and uncomfortable.

10 Like illusionists, they manipulated our bodies, bending them from a distance. During that interval, we stopped

believing in our own weight and body structure. Even our polite composure. It was disturbing and brilliant.

[1] Charles Darwin, introduced the term adaptation into his **127** ◼▶ theory of natural selection as the interaction between the internal workings of a living being and its environment. [2] The adaptive mechanisms are exhibited in different ways and their mechanisms allow for gathering them into groups as functional, behavioral or morphological. Most of them have to do with genetic persistence, instinct or changes in form.

[3] Tropisms and nastic movements are among the morphological adaptations that organisms present in their structure. [4] The first consist in deformations or movements caused by a property or an exterior stimulus that divert the typical form of the original. The exterior stimuli that condition these adaptations can come from different sources: such as gravity, which causes geotropisms; light, which causes phototropisms; or water, which causes hydrotropisms, among others. When the movement that is generated is an attraction toward the source, the tropism is considered positive. Thus, any structural adaptation in the direction of gravity is positive.

[5] Evolution considers that responses which are assimilated genetically, or innate learning, increase the complexity of living beings and, as such, their capacity for survival. A being that escapes from so-called stereotypical responses will therefore have a stronger duration system.

[6] On the other hand, nastic movements are a temporary response to a stimulus that is fleeting and vague. They produce a reinforcement of the beings' structures with the variation of its volume and resistance. This type of adaptation is independent from the direction of the source of the stimulus received and exhibits a reversible character.

[7] It is clear that any adaptation of form in a living being produces conditioning in its internal organization. According to the complexity of the individual, the reconfiguration of its interior happens more or less effectively and rapidly. [8] The combination of a number of simultaneous stimuli can, however, create a more subtle adaptation, which does not reproduce any of the responses that might occur given any of the stimuli independently. Many of the adaptive behaviors that are developed are transmitted as innate and no longer depend on the external environment. [9] The paradox can arise, in which some of the behaviors persist despite alterations in the external stimuli.

128 [1] Scoliosis is an adaptation system to create a balancing adjustment to body structure in response to a lack of symmetry. Far from the aesthetic prejudices that are the consequence of the ideal body, that adaptation allows for continuing to resist gravity instead of losing balance. [2] The systems for correcting that deformation operate in two very different ways. [3] The first, more traditional way uses the application of a constant pressure over time, against the deformation. [4] The other, more sophisticated way, involves the creation of a body mold with an anti-form opposite to the formal mutation. [5] The necessary pressure in the second case is much lighter and the time for action is reduced, lending the readjustment a more spatial character. [6] The necessary structure is then defined as an envelope that responds directly and precisely to the efforts and the variations of the internal form.

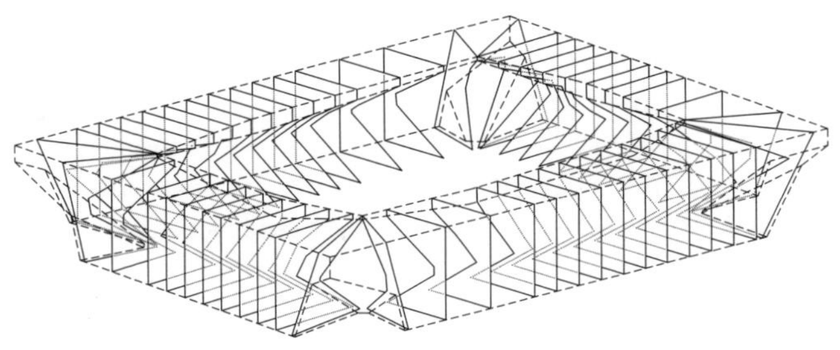

[7] From this point of view, the structural resolution of complex spatial programs requires systems that are capable of evolving formally through their adaptation. [8] In the case of the Prés-de-Vidy Stadium in Lausanne (2011), the distribution of uses across the habitable roof leads to the preparation of a variable structure that absorbs the deformations resulting from the uses it houses. Its geometry is defined as it envelops the program, through the use of portico structures which are diverse, though they belong to the same topological family.

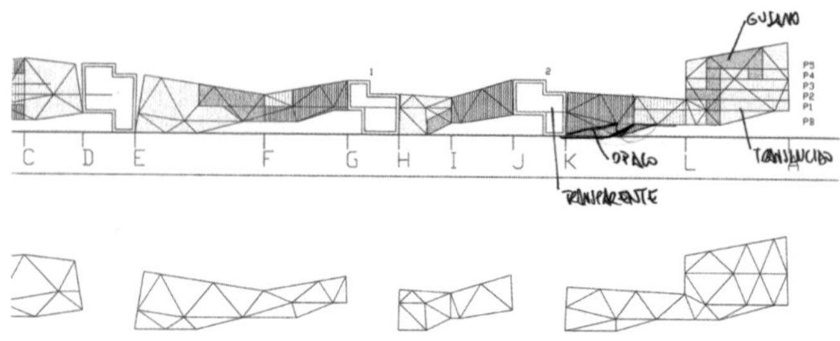

⁹ This adaptation to the scale of the building is also exhibited in the Train Station in Durango (2004), through a structural concept that avoids the train tunnel underneath. Supported like a lizard on four limbs, it keeps its body elevated using a series of large triangulated beams that absorb its changing form. The apparent randomness of the triangulation that emerges informs the variability of its stress state toward the exterior.

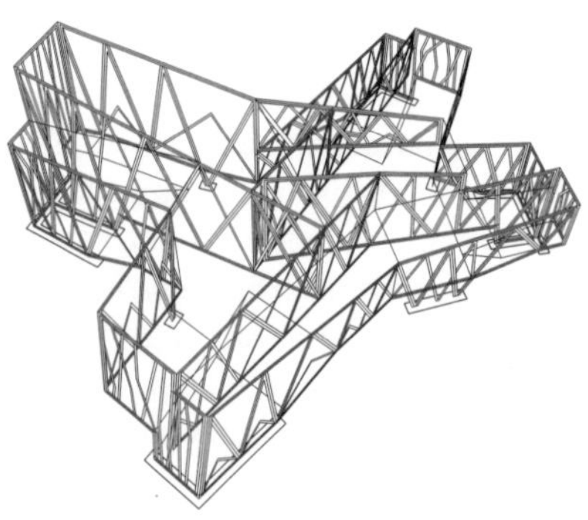

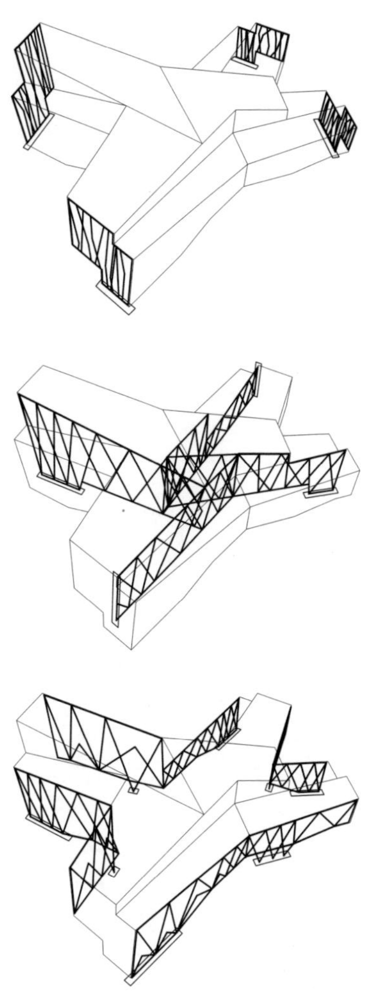

[10] In a similar way, the Oslo Art Museum (2009) precisely adapts its structure to the interior space transferring the requests of the terrain indirectly, guided by the geometric particularities. That geometry responds to the extreme climate conditions, absorbing the flow of the streets in a hollowed out volume with a covered square. It makes up a series of cantilevers that protect the exterior public space from the inclemencies of the weather along with a number of courtyards to let light into the central square. The structure that supports these spatial specificities is resolved, on the one hand, with a ring around the perimeter that holds up the cantilevers and, on the other, through the use of an interior core defined by the courtyards.

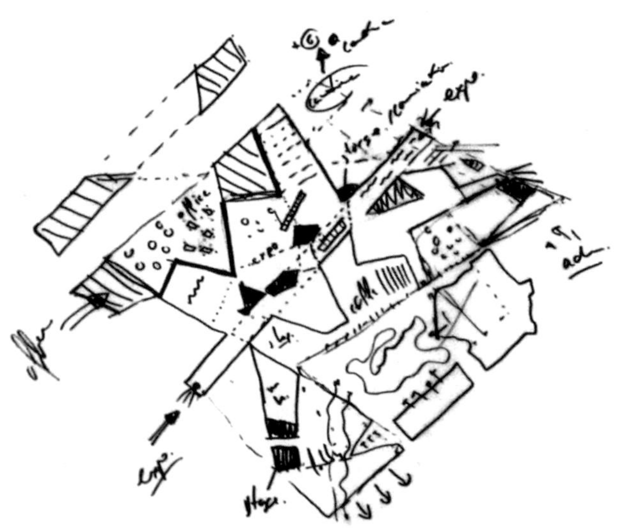

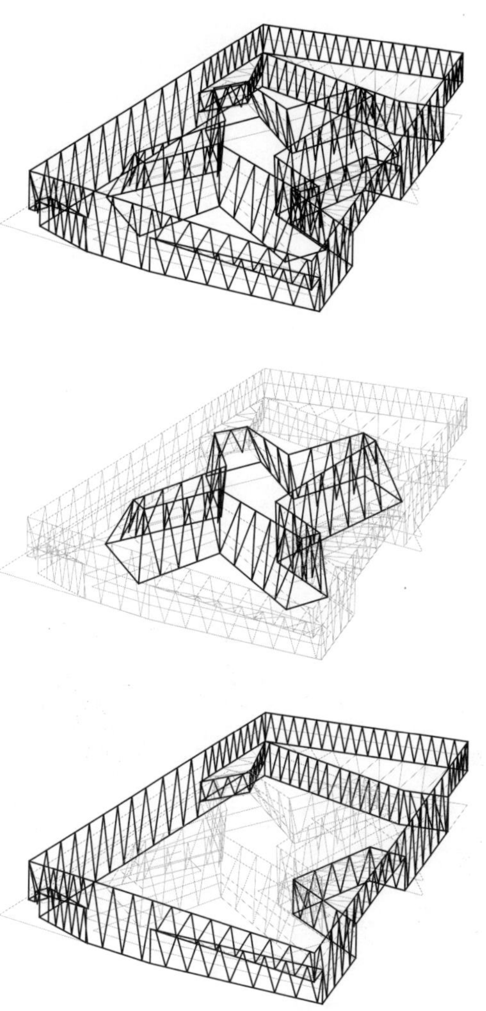

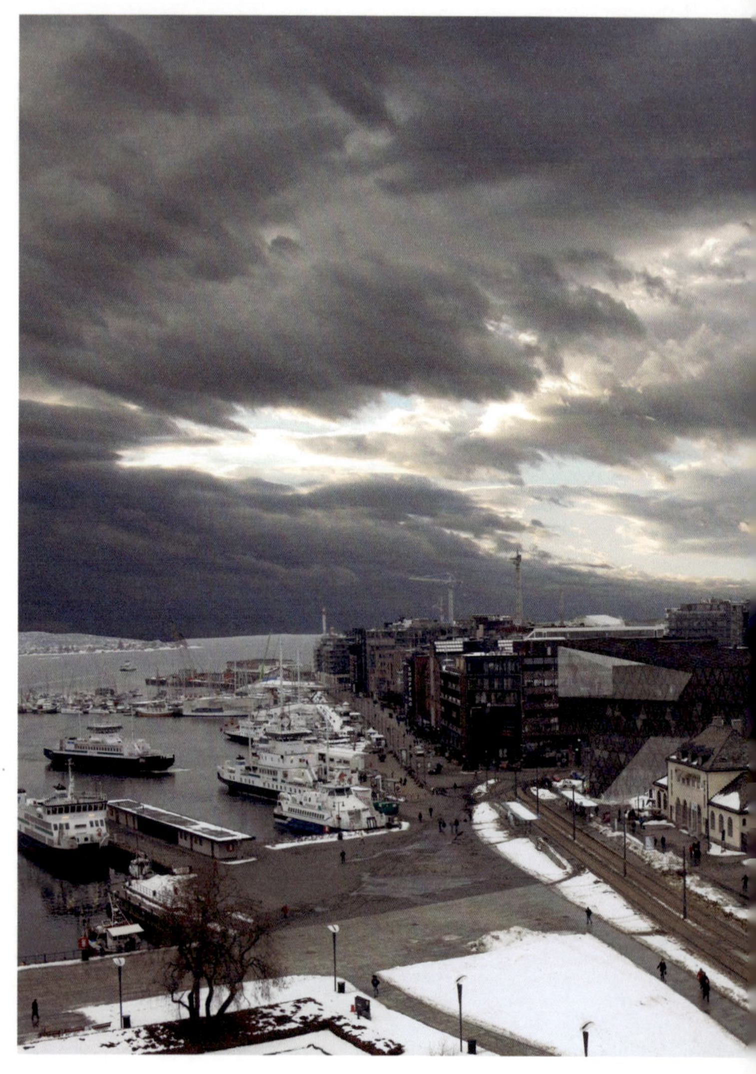

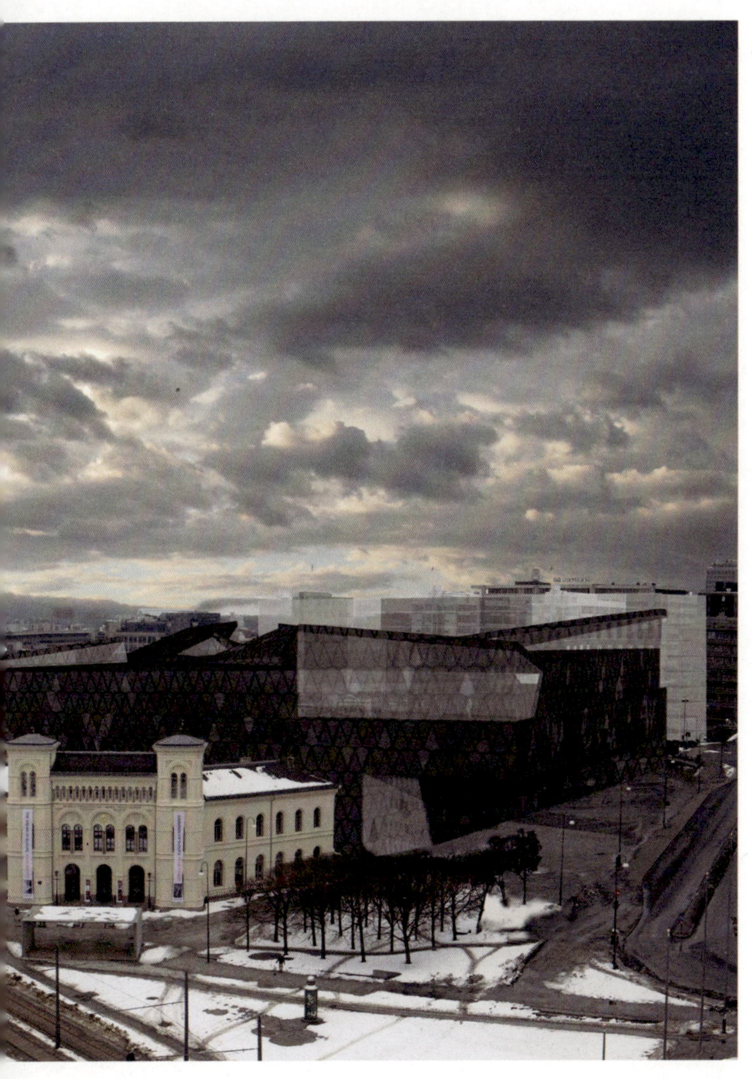

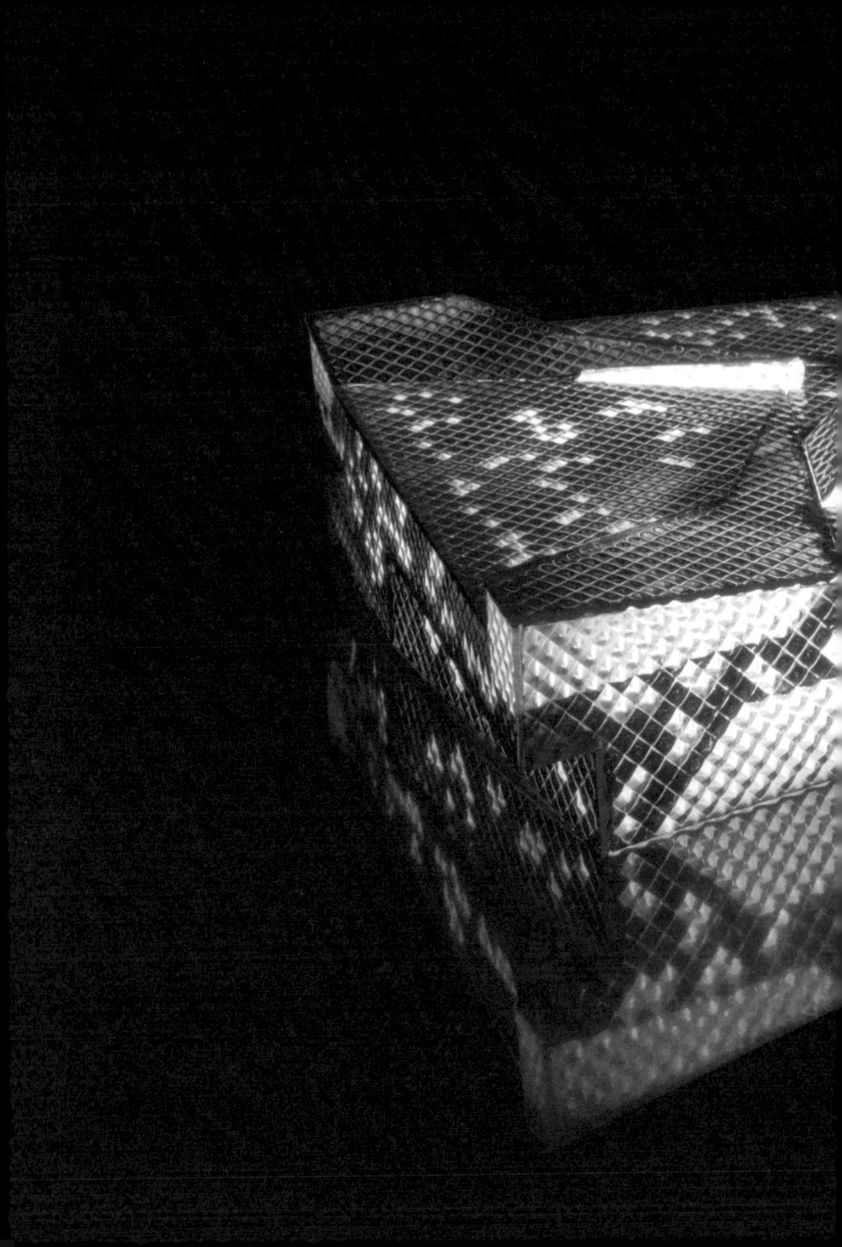

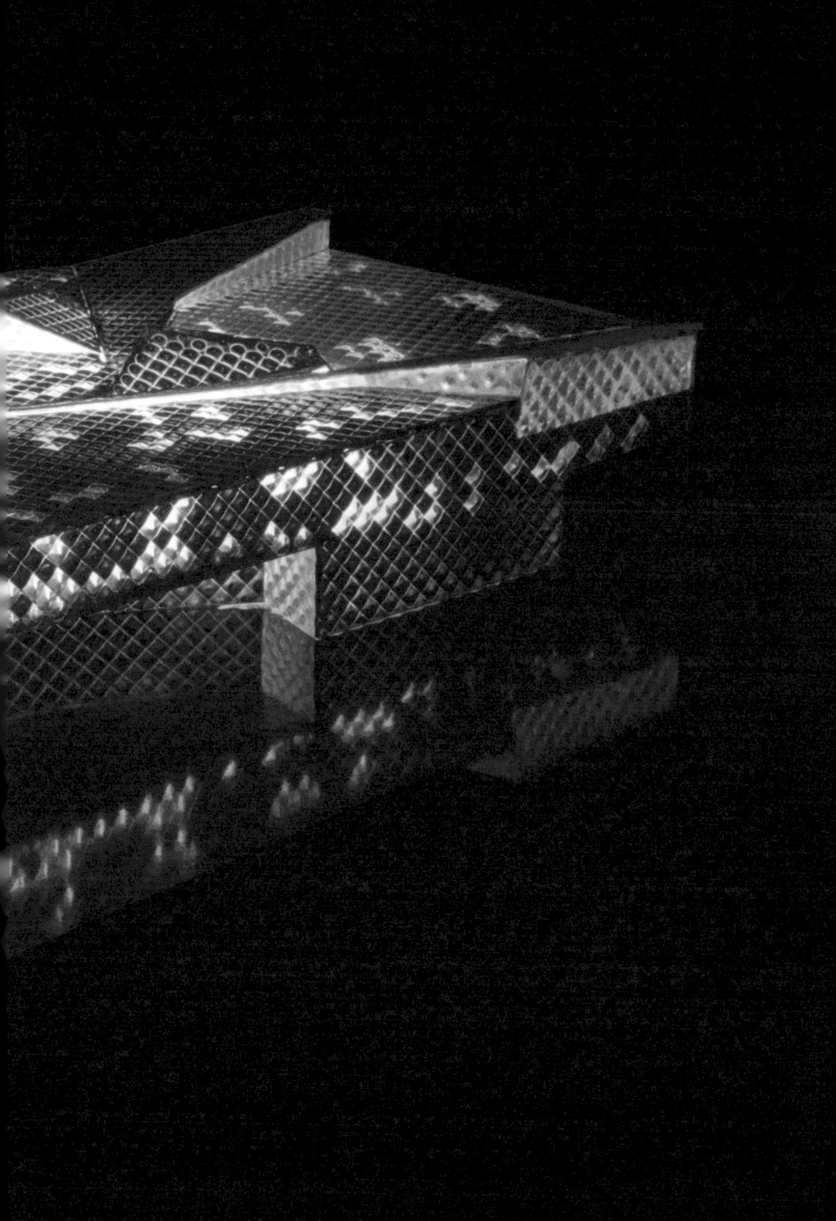

DOES A MIRAGE EXIST?

"Change alone is eternal"

Arthur Schopenhauer ——————————————————

[1] "Don't worry, big man. It's a piece of cake!" the surgeon says to me, relaxed.

I have a feeling that he's smiling under his mask, but I'm just imagining it. [2] I'm lying on a gurney in some kind of green cape tied with a type of knot I've never seen. Without warning, an industrious nurse sticks an IV needle into my left arm at wrist level and connects it to a large transparent bottle. She's injecting me with something and, given the amount of symbols on the label, it doesn't exactly look harmless.

[3] My vision blurs and a pleasant sensation of well-being and optimism washes over me. I'm not nervous anymore.

[4] Two big orderlies wheel me toward the OR as I count the lights going by on the ceiling. Then I feel someone take a firm hold of my hand with warm, rough, strangely large fingers. [5] I'm pretty out of it, but when I turn my head to look up, I recognize a young man, about thirty years old, with tanned skin, clear eyes and blondish hair. He's smiling beside me as though he's known me for some time, but he doesn't say a word. He is wearing a burgundy sweater with a white dress shirt and dark green trousers; all pretty worn out. He walks without lifting his head, as though he's also gliding along on wheels. [6] He has a translucent consistency, which varies in intensity as he moves. A knotted rope stands out, encircling his waist. I blink my eyes that won't focus, but I can clearly perceive his golden, bewitching gleam.

[7] With a sharp blow, the gurney enters the OR and I feel that he'll have to let go of my hand. The pressure is still there, though, and somewhat confused I turn my head in his di-

rection again. He is still there and I'm not quite sure how he got in.

8 Lying under the spotlights, the anesthesiologist looks at me intently and I hear two phrases at the same time,

"You're going to feel a bit dizzy" and "Give my love to your father."

9 In the recovery room, two hours after the operation, I open my eyes when a telephone rings. Sluggish and dry mouthed, I try to move my heavy arms. I am still hooked up to a number of machines, but my mysterious companion has disappeared. I look down at my left hand, flushed with blood, still connected to another bottle printed with unfriendly symbols. 10 As I raise my right hand, where my ID bracelet is, I realize that it's covered in a whitish dust. Intuitively I slowly touch it to my lips. It's flour! Flour from Grandfather Amos, the miller.

130 1 Radiation travels through space as electric or magnetic energy. Sometimes this energy acts as a wave; other times is behaves like a particle or a photon. 2 Energy understood in this way is defined with respect to its wave length, which can vary: from kilometers, in the case of radio waves, to millionths of millimeters, in the case of x-rays. 3 The interaction between radiation and matter is described in terms of a function of the wave length, which is the object of study for spectrometry. 4 The relationship between them is fundamental outside the field of vision since it allows for defining the chemical composition and the physical properties of objects with invisible radiation. It also helps measure their velocities based on the Doppler effect of their light spectrum. Therefore, what Physics understands as light, in a broad sense, defines the entire field of electromagnetic frequencies.

⁵ However, the visible light that can be perceived by the human eye occupies a very small band comprised between 380 and 780 nanometers. ⁶ These radiations are registered by receptor cells located in the retina that transforms the energy into electric impulses. ⁷ They form codes that are sent to the brain through the nervous system where the sensation of color is made. It is an extremely complex neurophysiological process. The selection of the color with each light radiation is defined by its intensity or quantity of energy per unit of time and its chromaticity.

⁸ Thus, an object has a specific color when it reflects or transmits the radiations that correspond with that wave length. Therefore, a surface is seen as blue when it absorbs all of the radiations except the blue ones, which are bounced back or pass through it. If it reflects all of the light, it will be seen as white; on the contrary, if it absorbs it completely it will be seen as black.

⁹ Most of the colors we experience, however, are mixtures of wave lengths that originate in a fragmented absorption of light. ¹⁰ That way, any color can be reproduced using radiations that are different from those of its own wave length, through the addition of a specific quantity of the primary colors: red, green and blue. A mixture of red and green radiation with controlled intensities is similar to the yellow light on the spectrum although it does not contain the wave length associated with that color. ¹¹ As such, color is not an

intrinsic property of the objects or the matter from which they are made, but originates in the electromagnetic radiation they receive.

131 [1] Johann Wolfgang von Goethe developed a theory of color in 1810 that expanded on the postulates defined by Isaac Newton two centuries earlier. He inherited the physical principle that light is color along with the definition of the color spectrum, from red to violet, with its breakdown through a prism.

[2] In his theory, he revealed the degrees of complementarity of colors in his famous closed circle and he added those that don't belong to visible light: extra-spectral colors, like magenta. Likewise, he defined a clear position with respect to the color black, which was defined as an active color, as opposed to the absence of light, as it had been considered up to that point. [3] Goethe also established that colors have an empathetic function with respect to the perceiver's spirit; he even went further, indicating that they carry conditions for moral behavior in society.

[4] His question about the acceptance of what we see through our eyes as what truly exists led him to reflect on those colors that are not present in light. The colors that belong to the light spectrum are defined by the corresponding wave length, but the ones that don't have an associated wavelength, because it does not exist, are manifested as a perceptive product of the brain. [5] It is our eye's retina that is in charge of distinguishing and classifying each wave length of light that reaches it and is automatically trans-

mitted to the brain, which interprets within the range of colors.

[6] Goethe realized that all colors, except greens, have complementary colors, and it is the brain that combines the different wave lengths to form the intermediate colors. [7] But if violet and red, located on the extremes of the visible spectrum, are combined at once, the brain does not have any intermediate wavelength to recognize that color. Instead of retracing the spectrum to reach the midpoint between them, which would lead to green, it invents magenta.

[8] There is a whole range of colors that are a product of this neurological mechanism and that, because they don't have a definite wave length, are built using two other existing ones. [9] This manifests that colors are an experience of the mind, a way of selecting and relating with the exterior world.

[1] The variability of our gaze, combined with the transformation of our surroundings over time, creates an exciting instability in the city. [2] This variation in the image of objects can occur as the result of their material properties, internal transformations in their spatial structure or interaction with the movement of perception from the outside. In any of these situations, there is an intense attraction between object and spectator, which is rich in transitions of information and is highly empathetic. [3] From the belief that color is capable of producing different moods, any manipulation thereof directed at the urban environment, will no

doubt cause a collective effect that is worth experiencing. [4] But, given a fixed multi-colored or multi-material image, the possibility of variations allows for establishing exchanges of variable data over time with respect to what is happening inside a building. This constant change in its image is then directly related with the intermittence in its operation.

[5] In the case of the Pamplona Congress Hall (1998), the façades act as interactive panels that relate with curious inhabitants. The system that controls the lighting for each internal use displays a chromatic code that identifies it and, when it is activated, speaks toward the outside about its lapses in use. The combinations of all of the colors make

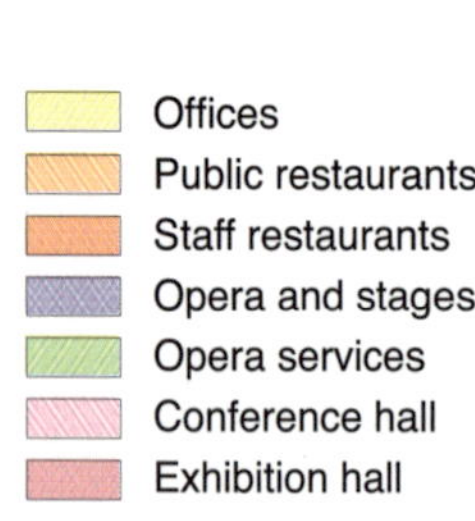

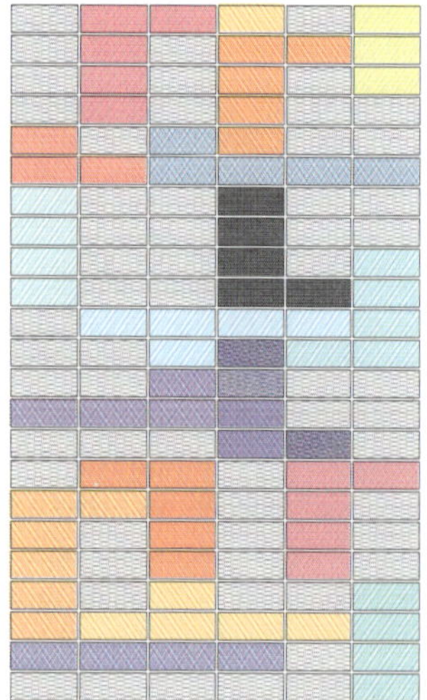

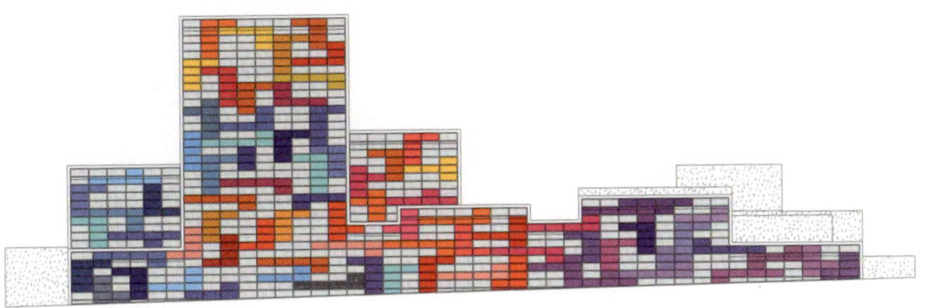

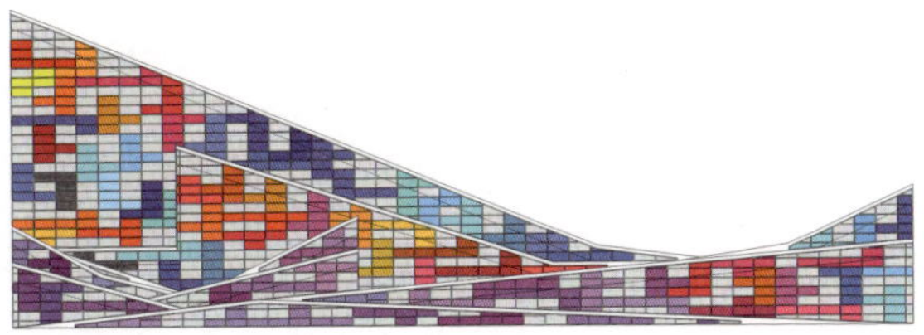

up a singular moment in the building's presence, shifting it as the different spaces are activated or switched off.

[6] This relationship between the object and the spectator goes a bit further for the Hotel-Parador in Alcalá de Henares (2002), where the users of the hotel rooms can change the external presence at will by way of their activity. [7] Given the degree of visual and light protection necessary for each use, a variable field of opaque densities is generated that filters its relationship with the surroundings. To that end, a number of lines of mobile sunshields are installed along the perimeter with a double color condition, one color on each side.

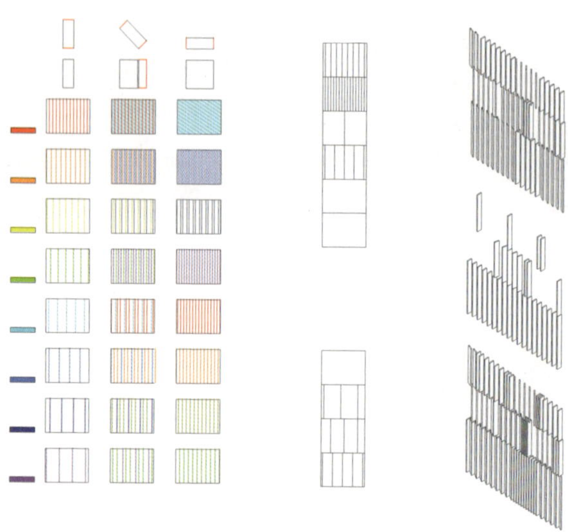

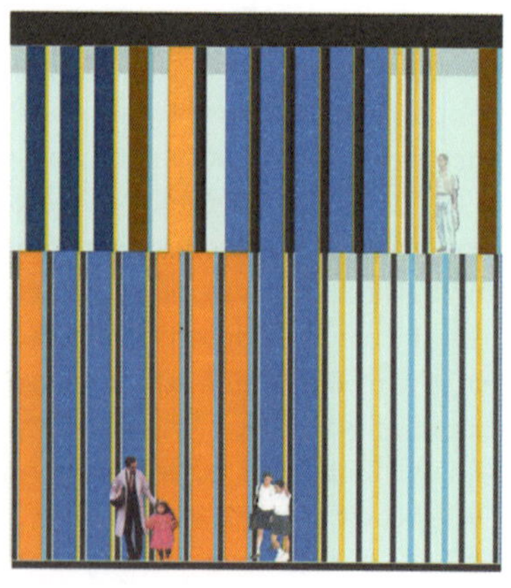

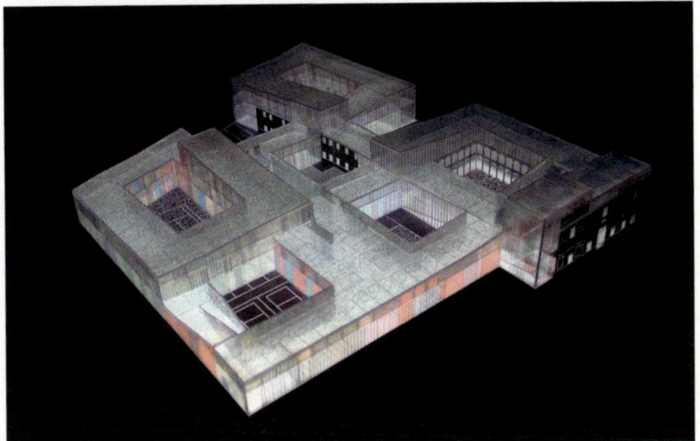

[8] The times of use for each room and the collective spaces determine a codified image of the building, which is variable and has a different duration at each moment. [9] To a certain extent, this kind of system sets up a platform that reveals information about user behavior, both in terms of decisions and random actions.

[1] The vision of what exists in the world and the images **133** that are generated artificially are not constant for all living beings. This perception implies an adaptation system defined by the speed of the vision and its colorimetric spectrum. [2] In the case of bees, the vision is quicker, since the eye cells that are in charge of detecting light can capture five times as many frames as the human eye in the same amount of time. This lets them identify flowers in shaded areas,

but they consume a lot of the energy that they need for flying in discerning the colors so they adapt by taking them in half as fast, in black and white. [3] On the other hand, dogs don't process greens or red, but they can see more types of blue and ranges of grey. They have more photoreceptor cells that pick up on black and white, which helps them see better in the dark. They also have a smaller range of three-dimensional vision, which means they see the world as flatter.

[4] In the case of artificial television images, they are formed using lines in a process that is invisible to the human eye. [5] The frequency at which the operation takes place is measure in hertz and, whereas conventional televisions run at fifty images per second, latest generation sets can run at two hundred. With this frequency, the human eye does not perceive flickering in objects as they move rapidly along the horizontal. However, a dog's perception of movement begins at seventy hertz, which means that they perceive any image on an old television in slow motion.

[6] When we notice a flickering in the image on a screen it is due to a low screen refresh rate, which decreases the clarity of the image. [7] Technology resolves this problem by increasing the frequency, generating intermittent artificial images, with more fluid transitions in their movement.

[8] In the case of movies, the twenty-four images per second allow for fooling the brain, rendering it incapable of detecting the black spaces between each frame. [9] This effect, known as persistence of vision, is the minimum rhythm

necessary to generate the illusion of movement through the use of fixed images. Similarly to the refresh rate in television, movies are also beginning to use forty-eight frames per second, with surprising effects in terms of image fluidity. [10] In any case, perception is shown as an adaptive reflex tied in with the speed at which our vision processes information.

[1] Among the special phenomena that occur with respect **134** to the behavior of light energy, we find diffraction, which splits up light; refraction, which causes mirages; and elastic plasma, which creates aurorae.

[2] The diffraction of light waves creates patterns of interference through the physical networks that already exist in nature. Butterfly wings and certain feathers include diffraction nets that generate special colors that change according to the angle from which they are viewed. [3] That type of net is made up of identical and equidistant parallel lines, with spaces between them which are equipped with optical properties of reflection and transmission. The light that reaches it is separated into diffracted beams with respect to the original; its different angles depend on the separation lines of the net and the wavelength of the incident light.

[4] On the other hand, the refraction of a ray of light is defined in Snell-Descartes law as the decomposition created during its trajectory as it passes from one medium to another of lesser density. If the incident ray's angle with respect to the surface is too small, it cannot penetrate the surface and

is reflected. [5] Scuba divers know all about the effect of the water's surface as seen from the depths, acting as a gigantic mirror. [6] Warm air also has a lower refractive index than cold air, and it can act as a mirror if it is seen from far enough away and at an acute angle. That is how mirages are formed, which can be seen above certain overheated surfaces that seem to shine. [7] But when the air is much hotter than the water, there is a thermal inversion and the mirage appears in the sky. This can lead to seeing ships upside down amid the clouds or towns lit up in the night before they are visible on the horizon.

[8] Finally, when the energy from solar wind enters into contact with the Earth's magnetic field it stretches elastically, creating an accumulation of energy within. When the distorted network of magnetic field lines closes again, it releases all of that energy, launching the electrons toward the Earth. [9] Those energy particles collide with the atmosphere, creating the bright flow of plasma called an aurora. Its breakdown into multiple glows and colors that vary over time confirms the universe's capacity for surprising our befuddled senses.

135 [1] The desire for objects to get closer to the processes that deal with their light energy variation moves us to work with their material and geometric properties. [2] From this point of view, the variation in perception generates non-conventional images that animate an increasingly more homogeneous world. The pre-meditated arrangement of filters to distort or diffract requires a subtle selection for the configuration of the materiality and its layout, in keeping with the message to be transmitted.

[3] The seductive value of what we intuit faced with the evidence of transparency is expressed in the Train Station in Durango (2004). Its envelope, made up of different gradients of plastic translucidity, responds to the orientation and the type of internal programming. [4] The grading is varied using more or less dense folds according to the need for privacy. The rich range of uses and the different orientations produce a vibrating image that speaks of movement and variability of light, at the same time that it provides a specific roughness.

[5] On the other hand, when a building's opacity is obvious for functional reasons, the distortion of its image becomes

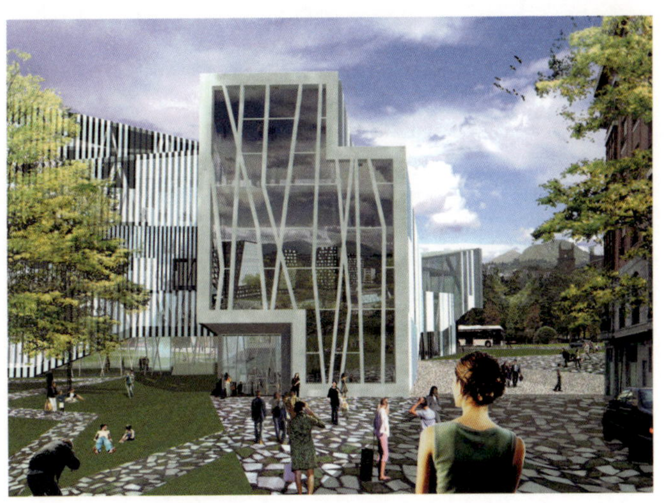

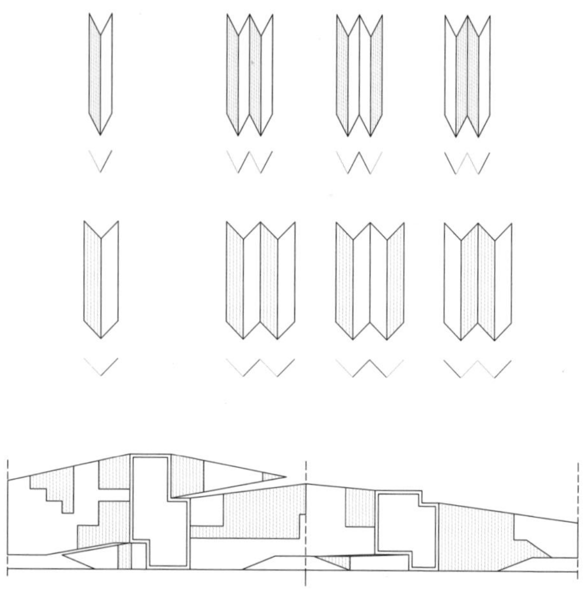

a value in the relationship between the object and the urban spectator. [6] In this way, the central volume of the Art Foundation in Lleida (2009) acts with a surprising sensibility toward the surroundings, through its fragmented epithelial structure. The skin is formed by concave semispheres of mirrored steel embedded in the concrete walls, transforming its bulky volume into an object of fragmented luminosity. [7] Each spherical form absorbs the park, the city or the sky, distorting them into micro-images that bounce back an upside-down, instantaneous and changeable vision.

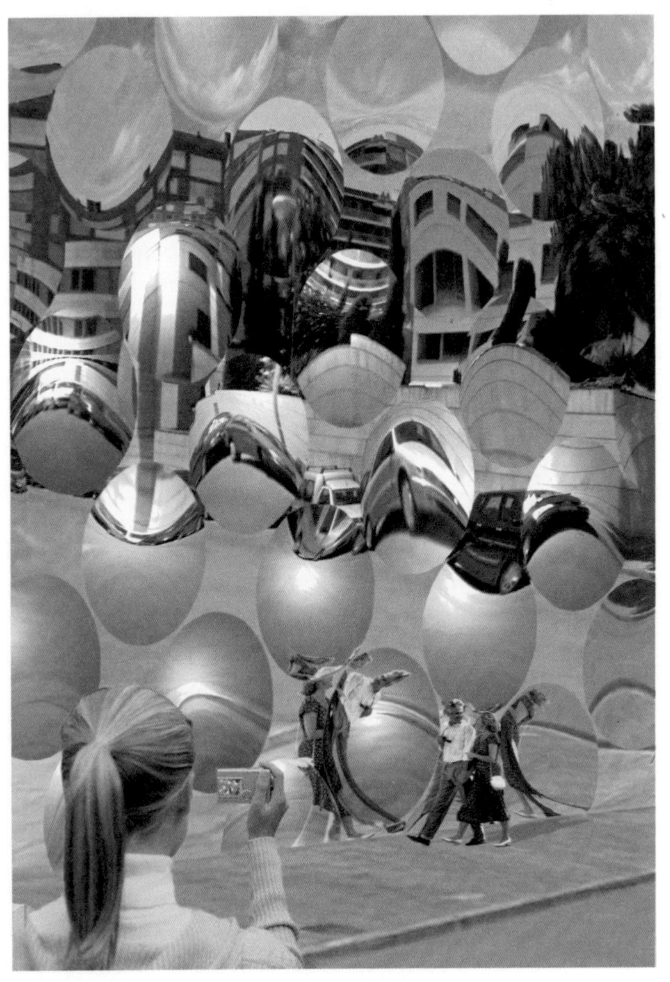

Mutability — 135 : 7

[8] In some special cases, when the objects are supplied with the possibility of movement, the variation in their ability to reflect the light lends them a unique appearance. [9] That is the case with the Floating Stage in Miami (2011), with an undeniable playful character for its ability to move along the bay, with multiple uses and positions. This object, which rotates freely with the winds and tides, changes its appearance and orientation throughout the day. Its non-coplanar geometry allows for the sunlight to reflect off its different faces at any moment. [10] In order to increase this reflective capacity, the covering is made up of faceted tetrahedral pieces of stainless steel that create a variable constellation of shining glimmers.

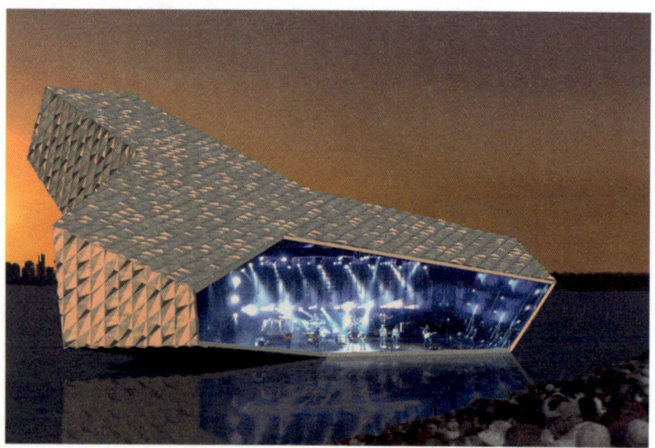

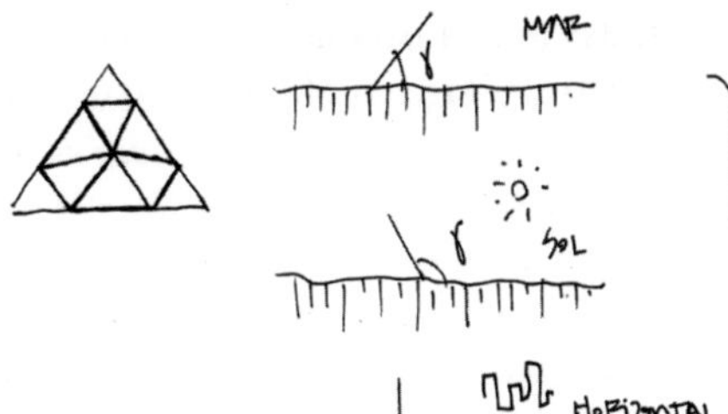

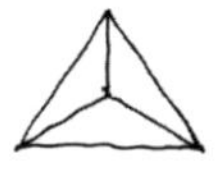

2 opciones → EN CADA PIEZA EXISTEN 3 planos, refiriéndose cada uno a cada tema (mar, sol, horiz...).

o... 3 tipos de piezas.

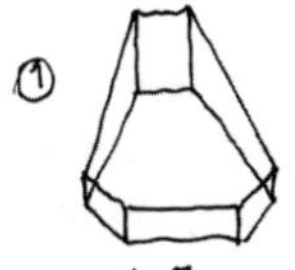
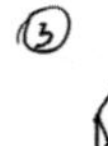

TENDREMOS 2 TIPOS de FACHADA

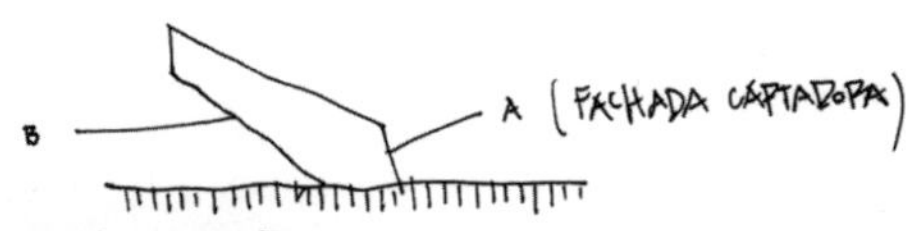

FACHADA REFLECTORA

136 [1] "Daddy, it's the most beautiful thing I've ever seen!" Ada shouts, in a tone that is not totally absent of irony.

[2] I glance at her smiling and it occurs to me that, at eight years old, she hasn't seen all that much yet, but it doesn't matter. I see in her attentive gaze that she's understanding something deeper than even she can imagine. I wonder where this intuitive sensitivity, which some children possess from a very young age, comes from. Inevitably, I think that some of it is lost with the transition into adulthood, and it saddens me a little.

[3] The thermometer outside the cabin reads fifteen degrees below zero on a pointillist night full of every star imaginable. [4] That afternoon we cut tube-shaped pieces of ice from the chain-gutters hanging from the roof. They are all different sizes, since the shovel blows made uneven cuts. They are hollow in the middle and their transparency is obscene. Looking through them, everything is distorted into intense temporary images.

[5] I carved the hard snow into a large table a few meters long and a solid bench in front of it. Sitting on the reindeer pelts that cover it, we are silent attendants to the depth of infinity. [6] Sitting atop the table, twenty-some tubes of ice light up the night with changeable brilliance. Set inside them, flickering candles blur the boundaries of their frozen confinement. In some ways, they look like a medieval cathedral organ, vibrating to a luminous score.

[7] As we contemplate the sound of the ice lights, the lively child shouts excitedly,

"Look, look! What's that?"

Green-toned northern lights have begun to form, extinguishing some of the stars. Before long, an explosion of color floods the darkness, crying out with new pinks and violets. Its rhythmic movement sketches variable sensual shapes that hold us in silence for several minutes. [8] I think then that the violent battle between energy and magnetism is frighteningly beautiful. It's immortal presence reigns over time and looks down from on high to contemplate the defenselessness of two astonished beings.

[9] I look back at the lit-up tubes that we liked so much and I become aware of the artificial effort they enfold, full of futility. I instantly understand that any attempt to make our creative force resemble the true energy of the universe is an act of pure desperation.

[1] Matter is the scale of energy that we can see and which **137** becomes accessible through the way we evolve sensorially in our environment. [2] A closer look at the equation of energy shows us that what we call matter is energy in its pure state, organized and more or less compact. As such, we work with energy in movement, with all its internal conflicts.

[3] But, not all matter is compatible, since all states of energy are not either. Therefore, this strange consciousness that is sometimes present in the lack of dialogue between materials may have more to do with their incompatibility in terms of energy than with cultural questions. [4] When we make use of the characteristics of a specific material, like its resilience, color or shine, we are dealing with internal electromagnetic properties. It is these properties

that finally produce the perception of their individual effects for its optimum use. [5] This means that there may be something more sensitive in the relationship between the senses and energy than we can understand without entering into aesthetic-esoteric realms. These properties, some of which are perceptively highly effective, can be used to produce spatial atmospheres that transmit intense emotional information.

[6] From this perspective, an environment of distorted transparency is created as a hidden message in a Bank Office in Bilbao (2007–2008). [7] This blurry image is managed with a diffracting glass skin that generates privacy and brightness, at the same time that it maintains visual separation between the public and the work spaces. A feeling of brilliant subtlety and variable points of view invades the operations courtyard, qualifying waiting areas and zones for information or enquiry.

[8] The partition is made from tubes of borosilicate glass so that its diffracting property is transmitted vertically. It geometric layout stems from avoiding the existing structure on the premises, creating a spatial continuity that supports different scales of distortion depending on the distance of perception. [9] The interior atmosphere that is generated provides the space with a dynamic blurriness that surrounds the public during their visit. [10] The access to this continuous wrapping occurs through two mini bamboo forests which take root in the depths of the lower floor, imposing a mysterious atmosphere of discovery from the very first moment.

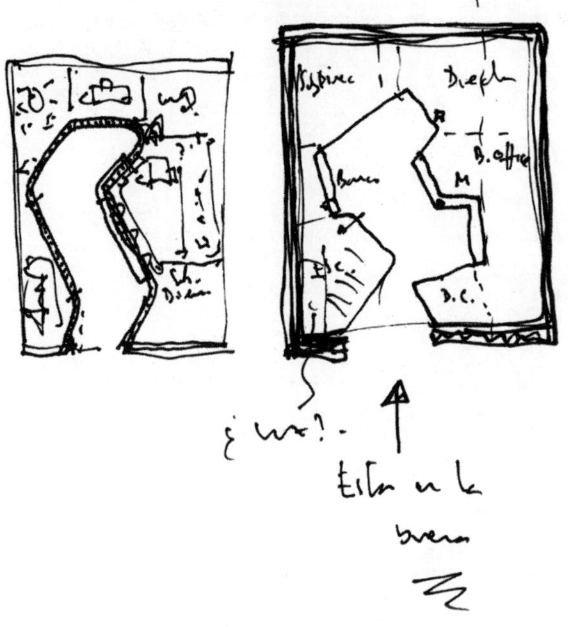

Subdirec
Direcph
B. office
Barres
M
P.C.
D.C.
¿ uno? -
Esto no la
buena

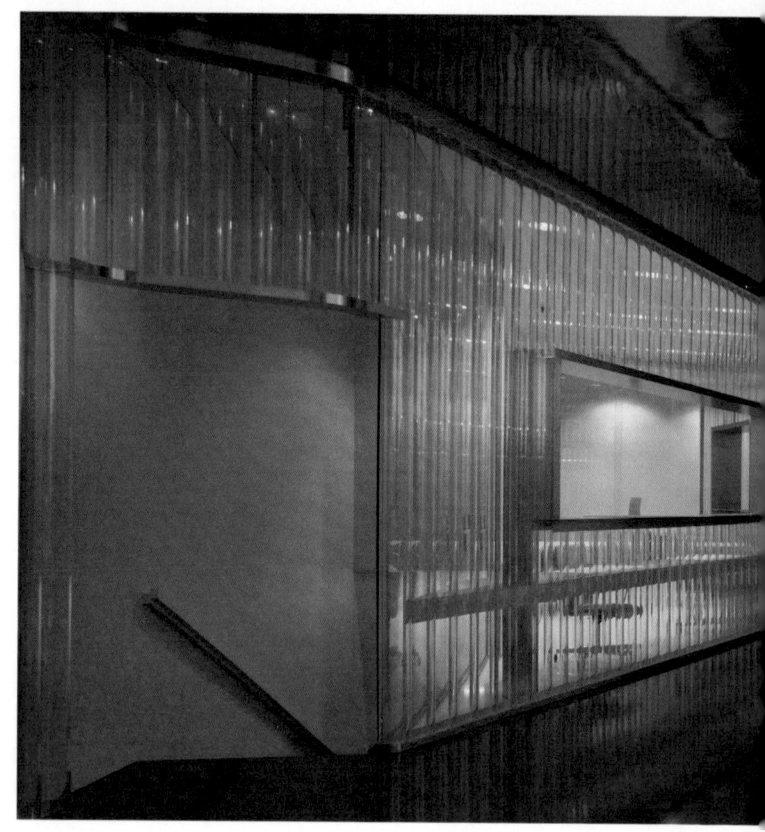

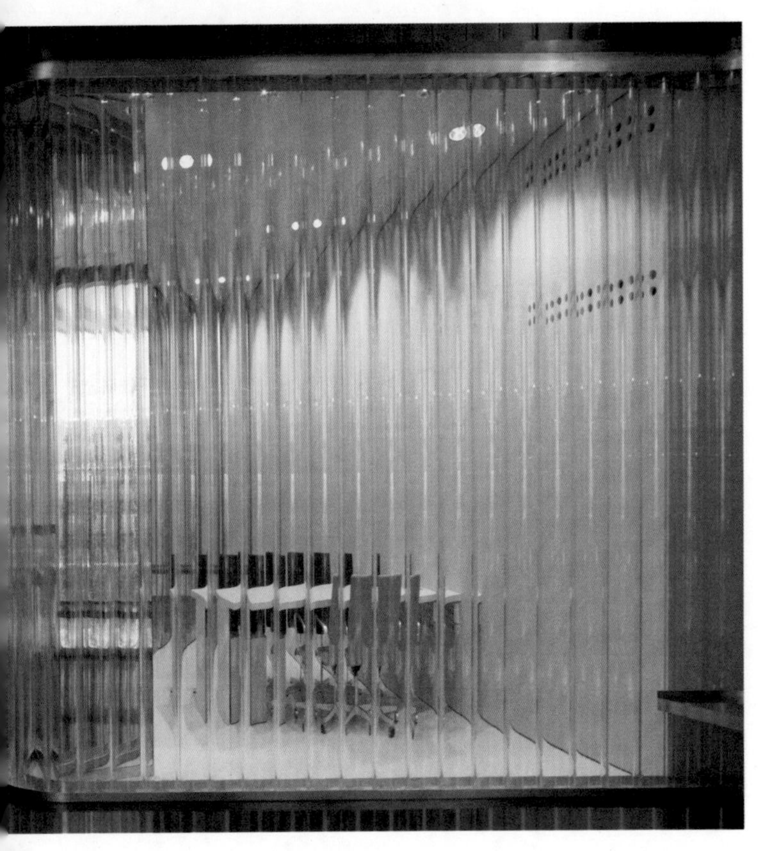

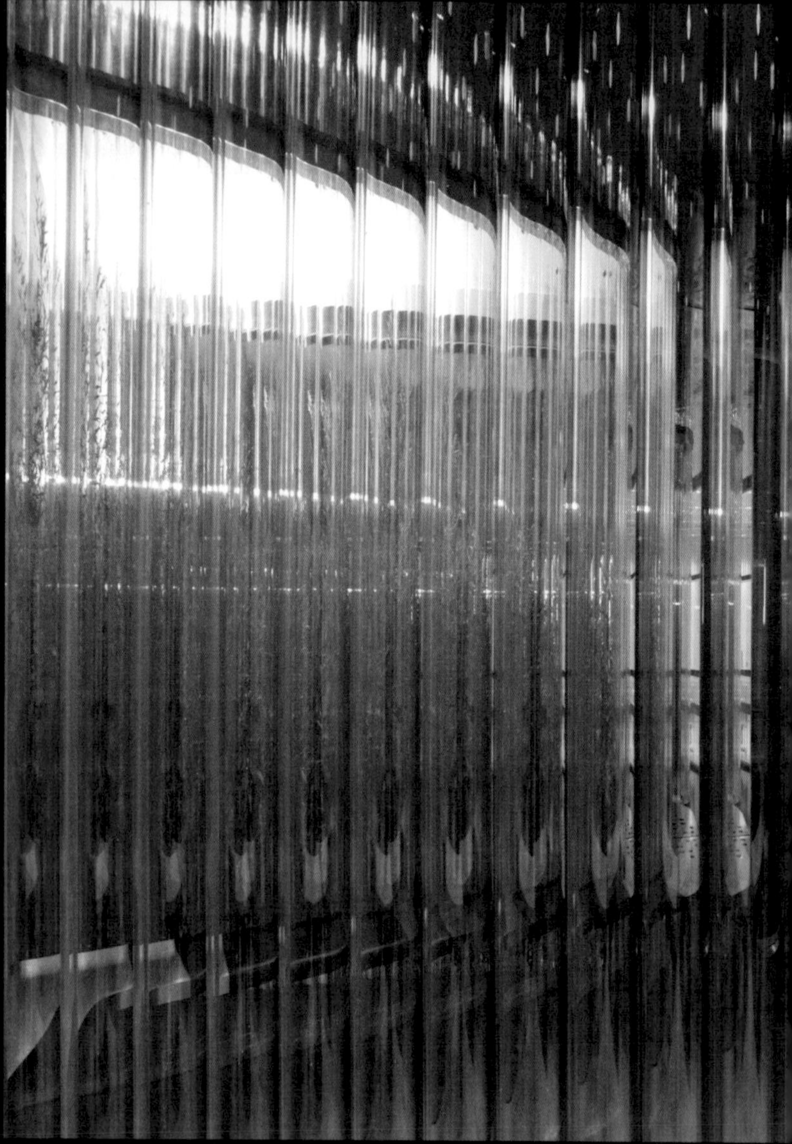

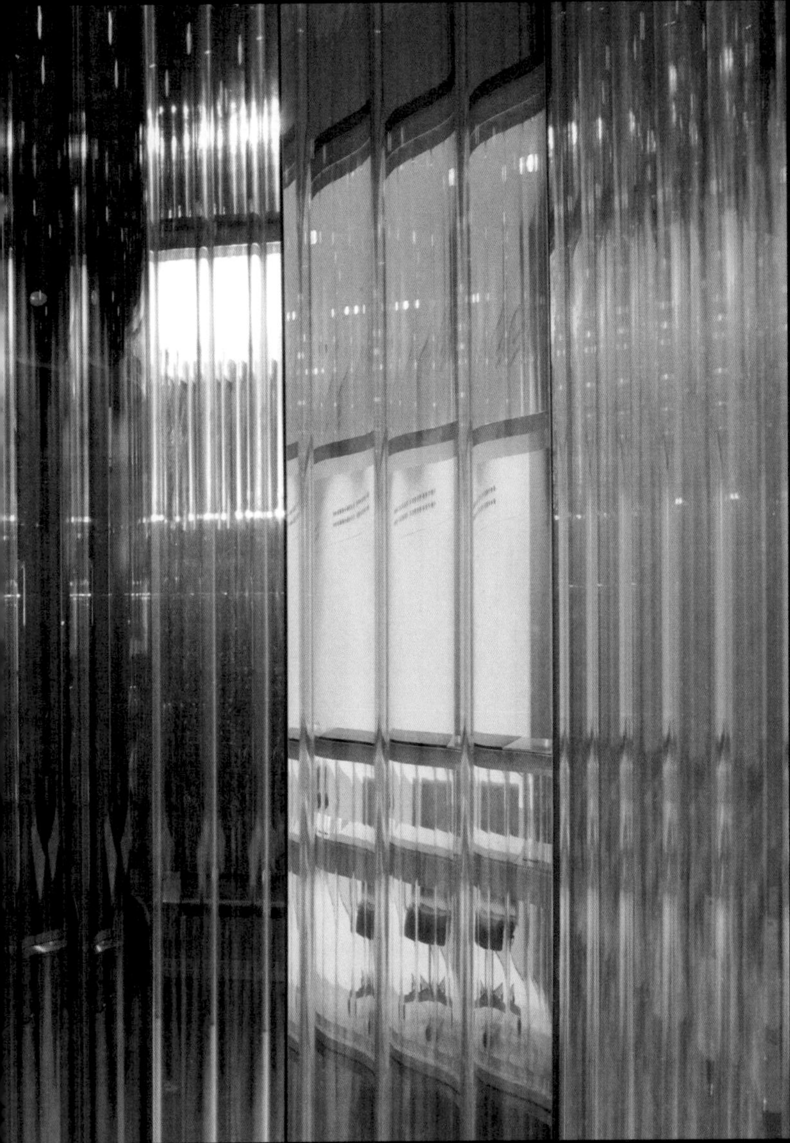

MATTERGY ELIMINATES PREJUDICES

"Any sufficiently advanced technology is indistinguishable from magic"

Arthur C. Clarke ───────────────────

[1] "Ouch, damn it! I nearly electrocuted myself!" I shout
desperately, alone in my room.
The lash of electricity has made me drop the scissors on my foot. [2] As I pick them up with my left hand, I see that one of the blades has two symmetrical holes in it.
[3] We've been given a high school assignment to build an object that moves using electricity and, obviously, I'm designing a motorcycle. It's a pretty special machine, because the two motors, which I stole from coffee grinders, are set along the wheel axels. When I cut one of the grinder's cables to disconnect it from the transformer, I didn't realize that it was still plugged in. I sliced it cleanly in two with a pair of metal scissors as a loud bang knocked out all the lights in the house. I nearly made a real mess of it.
[4] When I turn the power back on, the Meteor's "Wrecking Crew" starts up, as though the turntable and the amplifier hadn't noticed anything suspicious during the time they were without power. [5] With psychobilly playing in the background, I look over the scissors again, focusing on the strange holes that have appeared in one of the blades. The holes have the exact same diameter as the bipolar cable, like a tiny pair of glasses. [6] So I ask myself,
"Where did the missing metal go?" and Why is it only missing on one side?"
I sit thinking about it for a long time, regardless of the scolding I know I'm going to get from my mother,
"What about the material? Did it melt? Was the missing piece cut free and it flew off into a corner of the room? Or did it turn to smoke?
The fact is, the scissors were cold when I picked them up.

7 Pondering the matter, I'm struck by the idea that it may have been transformed into energy and has disappeared into the outlet in the opposite direction toward an electrical substation.

8 I try out the motor to make sure that I won't be left without the rear wheel drive and I see that it still works. I put together the aluminum frame using the tubes from the Cohibas my father smokes and I use cylindrical batteries of up to twelve volts as ballast so that its center of gravity stays as low as possible. The starter switch has a silver skull on it, which I push to test whether it works. Truth be told, the sound could be better, but it runs perfectly around the living room.

9 It is an essential apparatus – nothing is missing, nothing is superfluous – and I don't care if it looks good or bad. I put it into a cardboard box to take it into class, sure that it will be a great success. 10 But what I really want to talk to the physics teacher about is the question that's eating at me,
"Where did the material from the scissors go?"

139 1 Robert Pirsig made his most luminous journey through the Dakota mountains at the beginning of the seventies. Riding on the back of a motorcycle with his son, he reflected on the conflict between different visions of reality and the fundamental dissociation between what things mean and what they are. 2 He established the difference between perceiving an object rationally and using a more intuitive method.

3 As such, he delves into the world of underlying form as

a reading of the invisible forces that support any object, beyond its image. [4] He defends that a direct reading always appears more imaginative and creative, producing our inspiration. [5] And, on the other hand, that a reading of the invisible is governed by operating laws that have their origin in technique and are foreign to the common man. Travelling for kilometers on the back of a motorbike can be vitally moving, whereas its operation is measured in terms of objective knowledge. He concludes his thoughts by determining that free and natural aesthetics reside in visible form, whereas the invisible hides the oppressive world of technology where everything is constantly measured and tested.

[6] For contemporary society, riding a motorcycle is a frivolous and irrational act of untrustworthy people. [7] However, the mechanics who bring order to the internal entropy of their motors elicit a blind confidence that stems from a lack of understanding. [8] The basic problem outlined by this perspective is that there is no a point of view in which the two positions come together.

[9] The analytical description of a motorcycle highlights the set of its technical components, its energetic and mechanical parts that participate in a closed sequence. Understanding the cycle of transforming energy into work is shown to be removed from any intuitive discernment of the object. [10] A motorcycle described in this way is nearly impossible to evaluate, since the only objects and functions that exist are independent from the observer. Nor can a judgment be emitted or an opinion be generated about the suitability of its use.

[11] On the other hand, a superficial or epithelial vision of it, which is also very contemporary, moves us away from the profound understanding of the wherefore of what we perceive. The overwhelming presence of the aesthetics of the object then generates a whole host of fleeting opinions rife with moral prejudices. [12] This divisive discrimination of the object into separate parts avoids the necessity of a vision to explain it unitarily: its underlying form.

140 [1] In his memoirs, Mark Twain wrote that, after he had dedicated himself to dominating all of the analytical knowledge about navigation and the necessary laws to be a riverboat pilot on the Mississippi, he realized that the river had lost all of its mysterious beauty. [2] So it is that the hierarchy of the importance of certain knowledge with respect to other knowledge in an airtight manner results in the elimination of creative sensitivity in the face of the technology of the invisible.

[3] This tension can only be cancelled out at the moment when both the perceptive image of the object and the opacity of its working move into the background in terms of importance in the face of a unified way of "understanding" it. It will be the way that immediately explains, to our sight, the creative intuitions that are inseparable from the understanding of its energetic and operational laws. [4] Then, energy, matter, resistance or use will no longer prevail one over the other and, finally, the expert compartments will no longer have control over a consistent whole with no loose ends.

[5] But, the division of the world into increasingly more hermetic parts and functions is very contemporary. It creates the illusion that a group of specialists working in their defined, impermeable fields is more effective and trustworthy. [6] Likewise, this fragmented selective process becomes legally less vulnerable, since it can apply a more specific particularization of civil responsibility. The fear this entails on the part of the expert means that their field of action curbs the other in the possibility of enriching objects.

[7] From this point of view, part of the lack of entity in contemporary architecture resides in its evident dissociation from the engineering calculations that were traditionally a part of it. This fragmentation, which has its origin in the discredit of creators, produces a whole series of constructive subspecies and kinds of numeric management that generate new market niches for innocuous professionals. [8] Like the watertight compartments on a large ship crossing savage waters, the fear of sinking in our society produces a preference for the loss of spatial richness in our habitat in favor of the credibility of its energetic qualification. [9] We will need to accept that, for the moment, the dignity of an object resides more in its class-A energy rating than in the emotions it can evoke in the user, even if it implies a loss of meaningful perception of the world around us.

[1] It is highly probable that the unifying resolution between **141** sensibility and thermodynamics is derived from the relationship between matter and energy itself. [2] The capability of new materials to incorporate perceptive and energy prop-

erties simultaneously refers to a possible combined thermodynamic and spatial use in the future. On the small scale of medical prostheses and technological apparatuses, they already appear as homogeneous entities in which it is impossible to dissociate their properties from the form that carries them.

³ As such, multifunctional wrappings and coverings make of metamaterials, porous hybrid materials or biomaterials, need to figure out their constructive and functional dimensions on the scale of building. The scarcity of a desire to invest in this direction makes a profound investigation into the possibility of its large-scale production unviable, for the time being.

⁴ Artificial metamaterials have electromagnetic properties in their components, which provide them with certain behavioral conditions that are not present in reality. The most interesting conditions in their present development are acoustic and material invisibility as well as acoustic ultra resolution. ⁵ One example that has appeared recently is graphene, built with a crystal layer only one atom thick. Its structure in the form of a hexagonal mesh generates an unimaginable resistance in everyday materials. It also possesses surprising optical properties since its light absorption is always constant, which opens up exciting possibilities for spatial and atmospheric applications.

⁶ On the other hand, hybrid materials that combine others of a distinct nature, organic and inorganic, also possess properties that are far superior to those of their constituent elements. They tend to be composed of a base material that provides stability and solidity, to which some type of fiber

is added which provides flexibility. [7] Kevlar is a commercial example initially developed by the military industry.

[8] Hybrid materials also allow for porous preparations with applications in membranes and catalysts. This kind of material is essential for capturing and storing carbon dioxide or hydrogen. [9] There is no doubt that they all have a promising future in the possibility of interaction between their fascinating properties and their possible spatial layouts, directed toward emotional pleasure in dwelling.

[1] The creation of new artificial properties of matter in **142** laboratories is always developed on a nanoscale or the smallest scale. [2] As such, their application still responds to an energetic character, or to micro-resistance, which makes their creative application to objects from a sensory perspective difficult. [3] Their cost and the efficiency of their production means that they have to be used as an overlay, like skins attached to traditional objects to disguise their appearance technologically. Thus, they guarantee an informative propaganda for their contemporary correction.

[4] The systems for thermal control through vegetation, solar panels or inflated laminates made of plastic materials or polymers then become transmitters of an epithelial image that has a scarce influence over the transformation of interior space. [5] The creator, powerless before the abstract pressure of energetic calculations, does not possess novel construction systems to provide an imaginative spatial response that integrates the sensitive problems of habitability and energetic requirements.

⁶ Within that panorama, the Lausanne Art Museum (2004) attempts to add other capabilities, related to the sensitivity toward internal use and the structure of the landscape, to certain techno-energetic construction systems. The new building absorbs each situation in its surroundings with individualized responses. ⁷ On the one hand, the topography of the vegetation continues the green belt of the riverbank folding over to house the museum's program and to create an overlook for contemplating the Alpine landscape. The constructive system allows for controlling the loss of energy and for recycling water. It is also sensitive toward passers-by with the creation of artistic images in the form of interchangeable vertical plantations of flowers. ⁸ On the other hand, a thermal curtain wall responds to the docks on the lake, creating the conditions for energetic

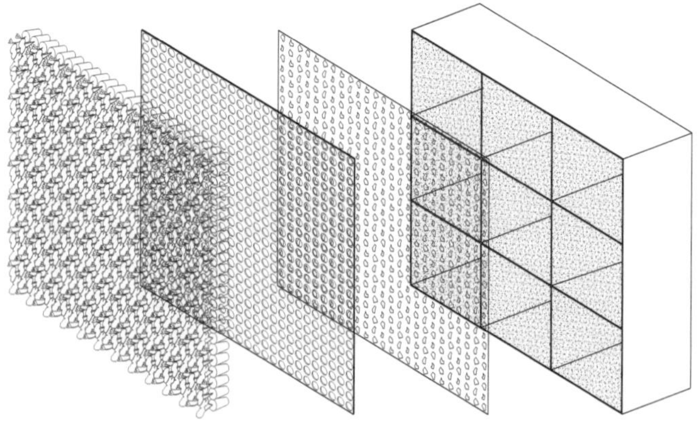

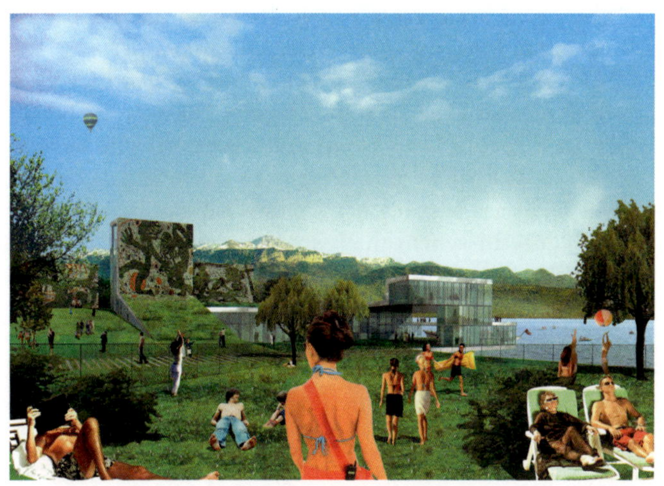

comfort in the exhibition spaces. Their composition using micro solar panels also generates added energy to the system. The grouping of these elements into diverse densities provides sun protection and different degrees of privacy with respect to each use.

[9] It is true that the set of constructive systems used does not participate in the formal production of the building. However, the properties that are added which belong to the realm of the sensible cause them to lose their exclusively energetic condition, since they collaborate in the perception of the continuity of the landscape.

143 [1] "These guys are savages"! Farhad says, as though it were all foreign to him.

[2] Our vehicle is trapped in the center of Isfahan by a crowd of men in a trance state, flogging themselves shamelessly in a spectacle of blood and devotion. The heat is unbearable and we've moved into the shade of a building, but the walls are burning hot. Endless rows of bare-chested men shudder in synchronicity, dealing well-placed lashes with each step. [3] The leather strips fitted with chains, spikes and hooks at the end leave ulcers, cuts and wounds that dowse their faithful backs with blood. Under a burning sun, the solely masculine presence transmits the anxiety of being immersed in an unknown punishment facility.

"Let's go somewhere else. Now," I say, somewhat bothered.

[4] We abandon the car in the crowd and my friend suggests going someplace to cool off, but I have serious doubts about his imaginative proposal. After walking along the narrow boiling streets for a while, we stop in front of a small door cut into an adobe brick wall. [5] Just inside, we discover a large pool made of white marble and a sudden gust of cool air caresses us delightfully.

"Wow! This really is incredible," I shout cheerfully.

In the wake of so much scorching lashing, a little fresh sweetness relaxes the tension of our tempestuous arrival. [6] At the far end of the pool, we can see a dwelling with a strange geometry and no windows. There is a large impassable opening at the base and a blind half apse that hollows it out. At the top, a number of chimneys can be seen that disappear in the distance.

"Weird! I didn't know that people built fires here to keep warm," I say ironically, pointing toward the roof.

[7] Those aren't chimneys for heating, they're for cooling!" Farhad exclaims.

Then he explains that these century-old constructions were built with the idea of lowering the searing temperatures of the local landscape. And that their incomprehensible curved shape and cavities in exotic places work together in an invisible geometry of conduction and thermal cooling. [8] Once the air temperature has been lowered by the layers of water, it is pushed along through the cavities into the basement. Then it is drawn through the holes into each particular room, where it enters, cool and humid, before escaping through the adiabatic maze of chimneys. [9] Astonished by the intelligent simplicity and the technical perfection of what stands before me, I ask my friend,

"And, are the people who thought of this related to the ones out there?"

[1] A closed thermodynamic system is characterized by the **144** lack of exchange of matter, only carrying out transfers of heat or work. [2] However, in an open system, the most important aspect is the quantity of energy that penetrates into the system with respect to what is released, measured in the quantities of mass that are transferred per unit of time, or mass flow rate. [3] Thermodynamics establishes that a system of this type is only in equilibrium at maximum entropy. That is where the concept of irreversibility appears, meaning that any exchange process will never be indiffer-

ent to the passage of time. [4] To put it differently, there is a continuous tendency toward energetic disarray.

[5] From this point of view, the City of Wind in Cordoba (2002) is born from seeking out conditions of comfort using energetic exchanges that make use of the wind as a material for urban cooling. [6] To that end, the territory is fragmented using a grid of principal mobility, in a series of mini-cities with individualized energy management. [7] The distribution of traffic within each city is undertaken through a second-tier road network, which responds to conditions of thermal exchanges in the air and a respect for the environment in lake zones and existing woodlands.

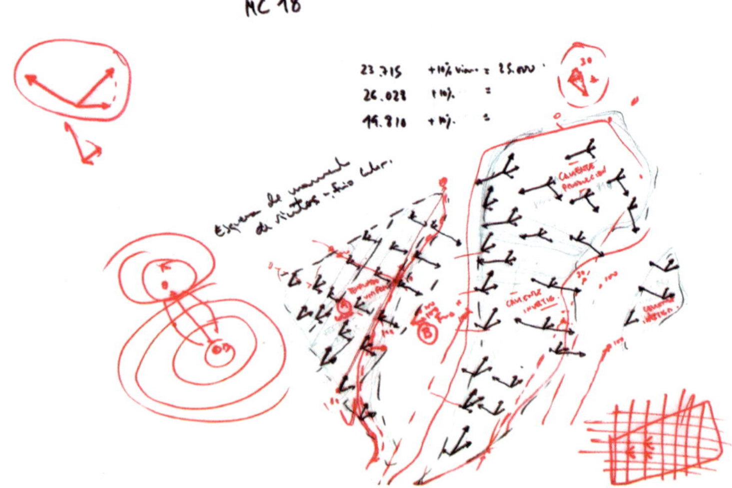

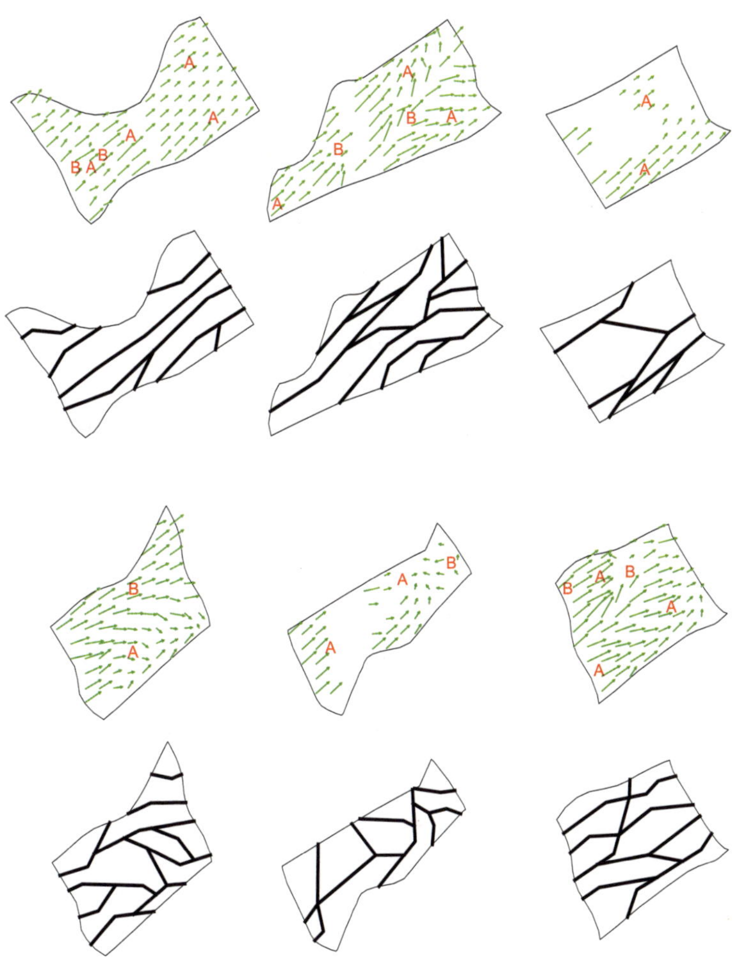

N
W
E
S
ABREGO
VENDAVAL
58°
28°

[8] Their geometry proposes a system to control the directionality of the winds and creates optimum ventilation and cooling for the city. In the definition of these guidelines, the seasonal nature of the territorial winds, south-west and south-east, and the daily local breezes created by heating of the built areas with relation to the green zones and cooler aquatic areas are combined. That creates thermal differences with low and high pressure, which produces local air movement.

[9] The precise control of the direction of the wind is developed on two levels. [10] On the one hand, using the geometry of the road network that responds to the combined results of the different winds and, on the other, using elements that are built vertically and dense, large-scale groups of trees. These large magnitude objects work like aerodynamic wings that redirect the currents of air that are generated. [11] This creates differentiated structures for each mini-city, which guarantee cooling and their particular morphology responds to the specific thermal results.

[12] The refrigeration roads associated with the wings ensures an exciting architecture-landscape. It is variable in its spatial characteristics, but homogeneous in terms of the conditions for climate conditioning and comfort. As such, and again, the breeze makes time its prisoner.

[1] Matter and energy are two ways of expressing the same **145** thing using different languages and both manifest scientific behavior. [2] But, when we work with them in the

realm of visible reality, life, the former takes on aesthetic prejudices and the latter, political prejudices. Although physics understands that matter and energy identify one with the other, the prejudices applied to them are different.

[3] On the scale of the visible, we still don't have a language that can simultaneously define spatial configuration and energetic conditions. We know that the physical behaviors of matter and energy are fundamental to the structure of the universe, but something different happens with the shaping of habitable space. [4] If we only account for behavior of a scientific nature, the language we use to explain them, ironically, is not precise enough to respond to Man's sensory and perceptive needs.

[5] From this standpoint, the immersion of thermodynamics in creation has brought the study of the energy transfers produced during physical processes onto the front lines. Attention has been turned away from the unsolvable and volatile problems of agreement between creators to place architecture within an objective system with a scientific nature, permissible as true without any cracks. [6] The analysis of those energy balances is always developed abstractly and anything that cannot be reduced to formulas and calculations tables is omitted. [7] In a system with these characteristics, only the quantifiable values of the exterior universe are taken into account, but the ones that belong to the realm of the sensible are difficult to justify.

[8] Any built reality is a closed system of exchange, since if it were imaginary it could be understood as open. Therefore, the thermodynamic properties of the materials that make

it up respond to a strict assessment of the quantities of heat needed to raise or lower the system's temperature by one degree centigrade.

⁹ Thus, the thermodynamic analysis requires a clear definition of the limits and surfaces of the object being studied, as well as its relationship with the exterior. The makeup of its internal structure goes nearly unnoticed, understood as an innocuous volume of masses of air, which relegates its spatial sensitivity to a plane of secondary importance.

¹ When a complex atom with a specific internal geometry **146** is bombarded, it tends to divide and organize itself into smaller atoms through a readaptation of its geometry, which releases energy. The only thing that varies in the process is the atomic spatial structure of the matter, which implies that the energy expulsion is the exclusive consequence of the change in geometry and, as such, it is of a spatial nature. ² This new four-dimensional organization then appears as a different language that can be used to talk about exchanges of energy.

³ Geometry can then be looked at not only as a component of the original definition of form but also as something that guides adaptation and energetic optimization processes. This provides a glimpse of the possibility for "geometric savings" through spatial-temporal discoveries that result from its interaction with the outside world. ⁴ The structures used in the construction of form are not an end in themselves; they are a means to discovery. ⁵ Similarly,

form is a single appearance among all of the geometric possibilities captured into a four-dimensional creation that responds to the conditions that are dealt with at the outset; it is never aprioristic.

[6] Creative acts undertaken in this manner don't provide a cultural appearance of order, since they simultaneously generate a dose of disordered appearance that increases their formal entropy. [7] A hidden presence can be intuited in these objects, that don't possess an immediately recognizable language, which does not respond to acquired aesthetic criteria. [8] Their form no longer pursues a function or a material independently, or even energy as a contemporary paradigm of correction. These objects are guided by material and energetic properties associated with a combination of internal functions and sensibilities.

[9] The more variables the creator is dealing with, the more they lead him toward sophisticated and unrecognizable orders, reaching the intimate union between the essential problems of production, use and consumption. [10] By eliminating the sensationalist idioms of a scientific-aesthetic appearance from the outset, there is a unification that inevitably generates an entropic informality. From this point of view, the order that represents the recognizable is always left out of the equation. [11] To activate the creative combination that is defined in this way, the prejudices about form need to be eliminated in order to immerse ourselves in the alternative guided by the conditions of this new "mattergy".

[1] In times of energetic panic, there have been attempts to define an architectural paradigm using replicating mechanisms from the natural realm, the incorporation of genetic algorithms using computers or thermodynamic exchanges. [2] But, evolution through the use of new tools for analysis reroutes toward forms that are judged based on aesthetic values and the economy of systems. The non-personalized use of shared computer programs, without adding individualized spatial or functional values, leads irretrievably toward homogenization.

[3] Something similar happens in automobile design; their production is defined by the results of the drag coefficient in the wind tunnel and its influence on consumption. This same detection is valid for commercial programs that calculate energy ratings. [4] Guided by an insensitive parameterization, their results return to the creator the need for similar constructive conditions that define professional homogenization.

[5] In an experimental attempt to combine the internal uses and the systems for geometric discovery in the processes of energy exchange, the Administrative Building in Seville (2008) emerges. Its development begins with a generic volume that houses the compacted program. [6] Then the uses are displaced toward the best orientation and height according to the optimum needs for lighting, sun protection and lengths of stay. On each floor, they swing toward different orientations, placing the programs with less lighting needs toward the interior of the volume. [7] The programs with stay lengths of eight hours seek out north-east orientations, and the public uses with shorter stay times are oriented toward the south-west.

[8] This leads to the appearance of a new volume with a non-recognizable geometry. [9] Its sloping facets create a whole range of shadows that fall one on top of the other on different timetables. The analysis of its complexity allows for deciphering specific places between adjoining floors that are enlarged using ramps and openings as relaxation spaces with panoramic views over the city. [10] This unprejudiced protective form is added to the passive systems created by the circulation along the façades and the traditional active energy-related systems. [11] The geometry that provides self-protection for the volume acts simultaneously as a tool that generates surprising promenades, interior comfort and energy savings.

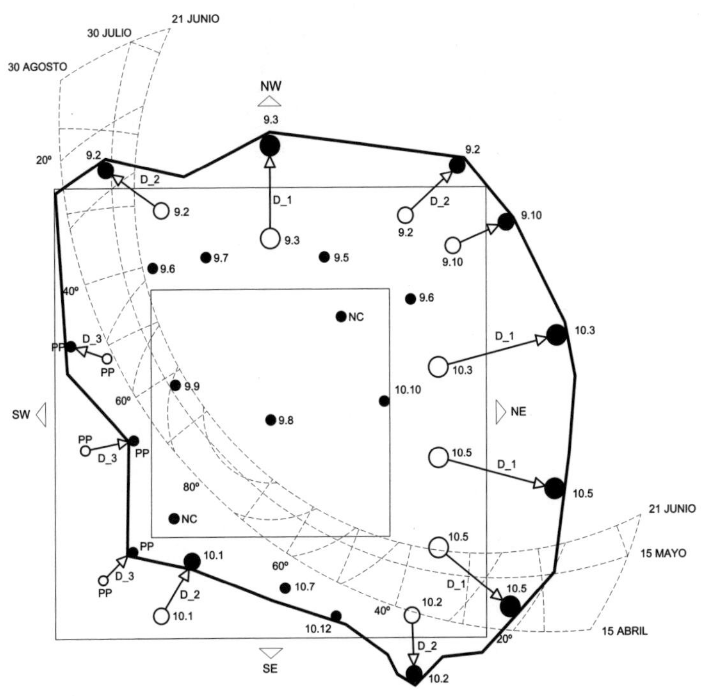

30 AGOSTO
30 JULIO
21 JUNIO
NW
9.3
20°
9.2
D_2
9.2
D_1
9.3
9.7
9.5
9.2
D_2
9.2
9.10
9.10
9.6
40°
9.6
NC
D_3
PP
PP
60°
9.9
D_1
10.3
10.3
SW
NE
10.10
9.8
PP
D_3
PP
10.5
D_1
80°
10.5
NC
10.5
21 JUNIO
PP
15 MAYO
D_3
PP
10.1
60°
D_1
10.5
D_2
10.7
10.2
10.1
40°
10.2
10.12
20°
15 ABRIL
SE
D_2
10.2

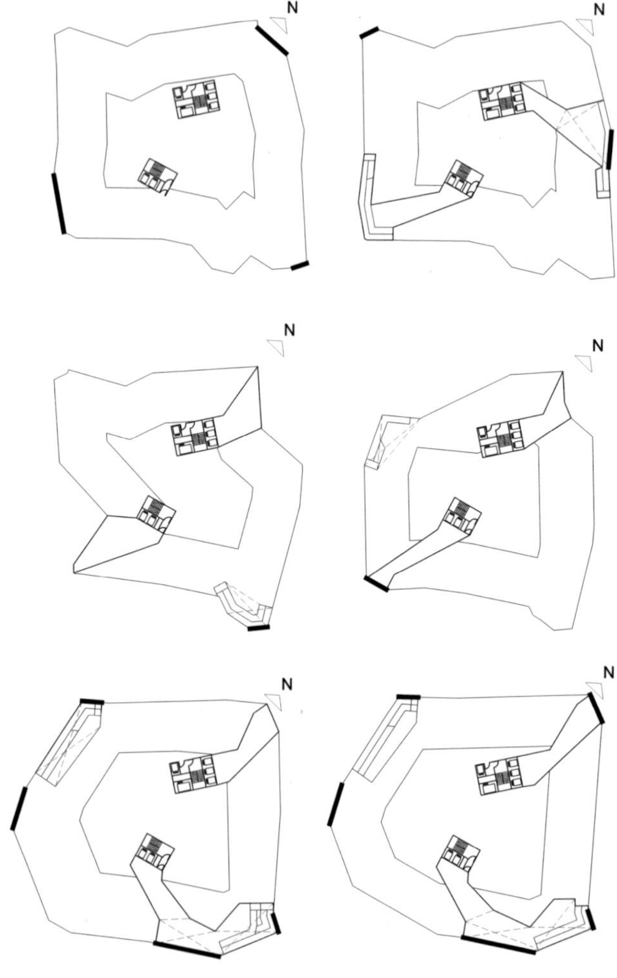

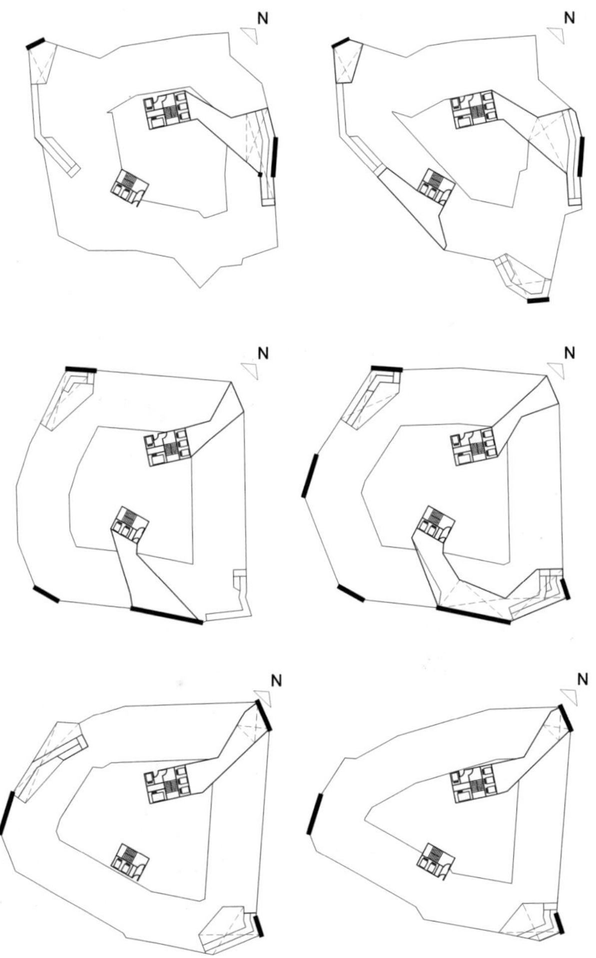

N
N
N
N
N
N

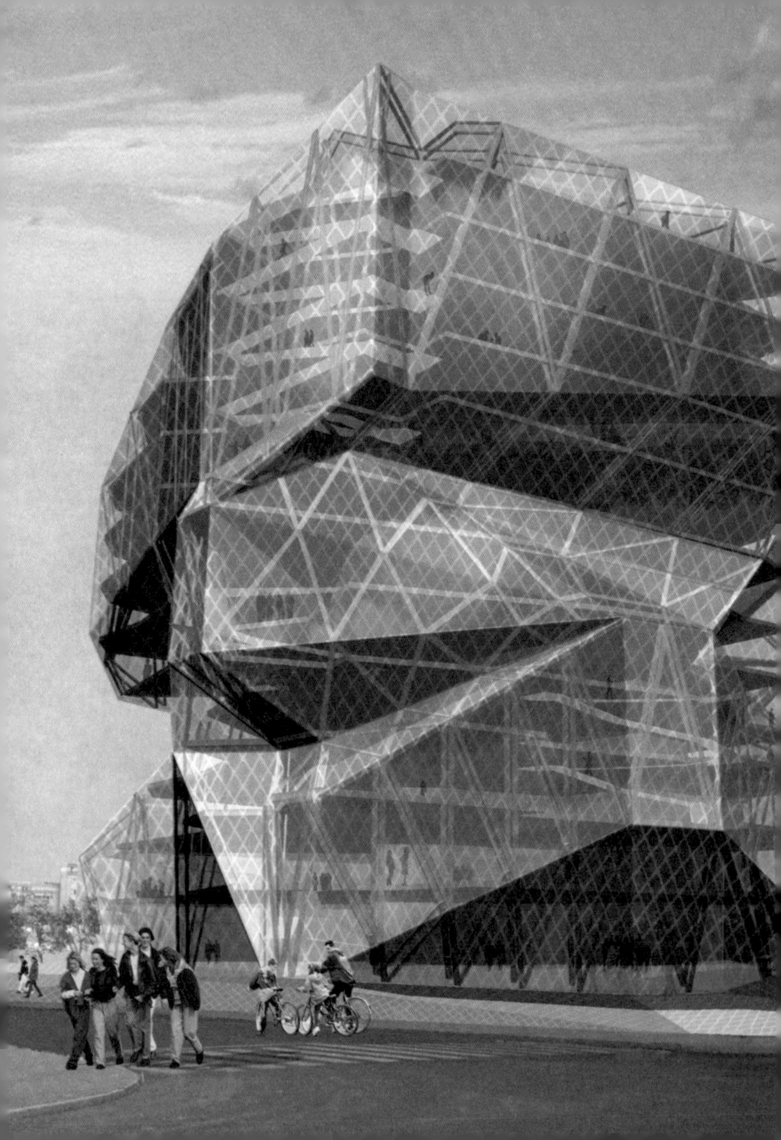

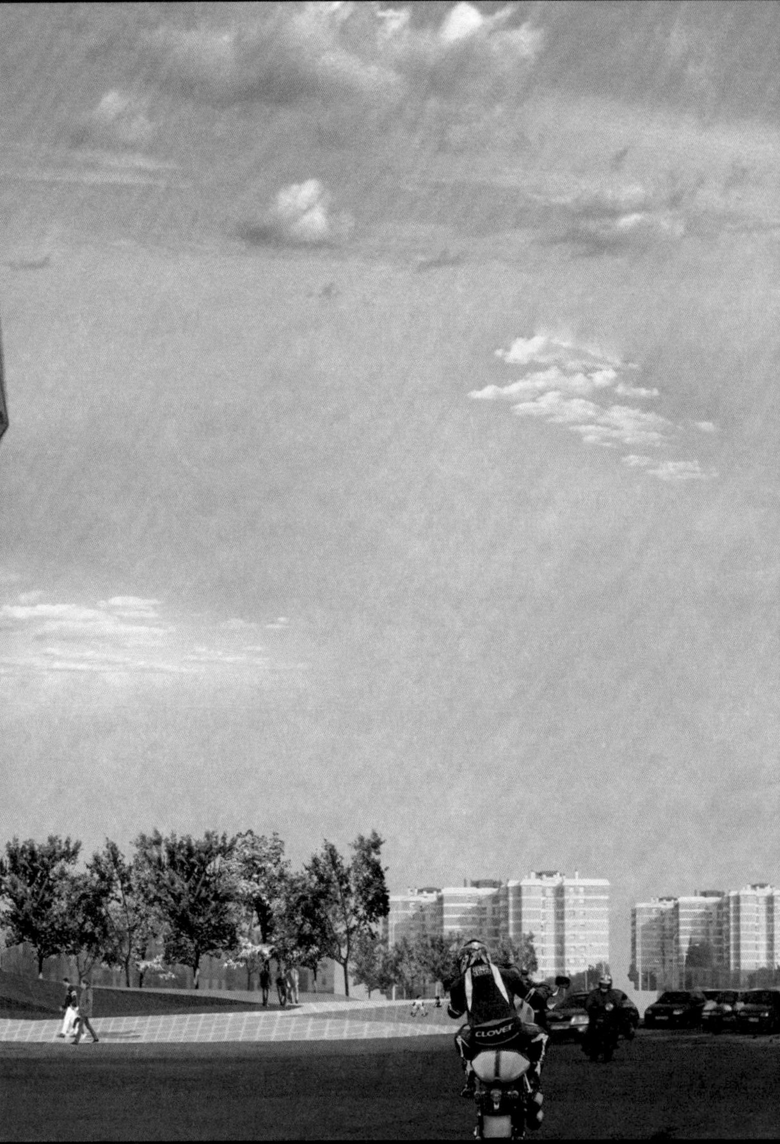
CLOVER

ENTHUSIASM AHEAD OF RISK

"Where there is danger some Salvation grows there too"

Friedrich Hölderlin

¹ I'm flying in a Mustang P-51, a skittish airplane. It's **148**
painted in IKB and there are some aggressive shark's teeth
stenciled on the nose. ² I don't quite know where I am and,
despite the fact that I've been trying to decipher the clouds
for a while, I can't get oriented. I trace risky rolls, spins
and barrels, even a tailspin with a geometry that it seems
like I won't be able to come out of. But, it looks like I'm
having fun.

³ At two thousand meters I see a luxurious Falcon, an elegant silver color, fitted with panoramic windows. It's flying lazily while it eats up an insulting amount of kerosene
and I notice the thick slime of pollution it's leaving behind.
⁴ There is a major party going on inside and, strangely, I
can see all the people. I make out a number of well-known
Spanish architects, a critic or two and their political connections. There are half-naked women dancing sensually in
the arms of the smiling passengers, who are sweaty with
champagne. I see piles of yellow envelopes, some of them
open, spilling out magenta colored bills uncontrollably. I
can even hear the nightclub music mixed in with the mo-
notonous purr of the reactors.

⁵ I signal to them with my lights in Morse code, though
they don't understand, as they look back with mocking
smiles when they recognize me. I tell them they're about
to fall and that they need to stop the party with high-end
prostitutes because their plane is worthless. But they continue their mindless merrymaking and I speed up, knowing
there's nothing I can do. ⁶ They don't want to hear that
there's no pilot in the cockpit!...

⁷ Then, I wake up with a start. My hands are sweating

and, incomprehensibly, I can still feel the vibration of the fighter plane's controls.

"It was so real!" I repeat to myself over and over.

[8] Still half asleep, I'm trying to figure out what it means when, suddenly, it all makes sense in keeping with a decision I made the night before. [9] It began with the feeling of exclusion when I arrived at a party where everyone spoke the same language, which, it so happened, wasn't mine. As a naïve guest, I had two options: stay and pretend like I understood everything while I got drunk on foolish words and suspicious alcohol; or, on the contrary, go out quietly to the corner to buy cigars and enjoy the honest company of the woman at the tobacco shop. [10] I imagine that the party continued just the same when I opted for the second option, but the human quality around me lost their vacuousness, appearance, insecurity and corruption of character.

[11] More relaxed now, I think that there's no doubt that we can choose the piece of the world we want to live in. [12] And that leaving a bad party just in time has proven to be the highest art in life.

149   [1] The firefighters' brigade uses a breathing mask attached to their helmets which, without creating a hermetic seal, prevents unbreathable air from getting in. [2] The continuous flow of air from the bottle toward the exterior, at a higher pressure than the atmosphere, guarantees this non-hermetic airtightness. There is maximum visibility between eyes and safety glass, whereas the world loses color behind an asphyxiating smoke that dilutes reality into something shapeless and meaningless. All this decomposition tries to penetrate between the skin and the neoprene seal, clawing at the folds with destructive disdain.

³ A soft fresh breeze, hissing with compressed air, pushes in the opposite direction, cancelling out the toxicity and blindness. The clean air in the protected chamber applies positive pressure, with the centrifugal flow around the perimeter, providing protection from the degraded surroundings. ⁴ If it relaxes, it will let intellectual death seep into our pores like a high-end virus.

⁵ On the opposite pole of this vision of protection against the surroundings, Arnold Toynbee maintained that, without the pressure of the environment, societies cannot be born; they are cut short or they die. ⁶ But also that, throughout history, ease has always been the enemy of civilization. The external condition, then, is the support for determination; the stimulus of the hardness of edges is what hovers over the subconscious of grand creative acts.

⁷ At the same time, biologists define human beings as a gregarious life form that needs the protection of the group. And, the charm of collective protection is demonstrated in a contemporary way, not only in politics and in professions but also in the realm of pedagogy. ⁸ The obligations and debts of the group that are contracted over time are then organized as an internalized pressure that promises glory in return for obedience.

⁹ In present-day societies the pressure of nature has been substituted by the pressure of interest groups and this negotiated world of groups shouldn't be confused with the

cooperation between equals. [10] The appearance of security expresses the unique search for tranquility which, as Tolstoy expressed, implies moral turpitude. Keeping up this mirage requires an enormous amount of acceptance and mediation, which are incompatible with the effort in an attempt to discern something of the origin.

[11] The door that opens to dissidents is not on solid ground, but in a state of fluid resistance and its key is in the shape of "No". [12] Having arrived at this situation, the only possible conclusion lies in putting enthusiasm ahead of risk.

150 [1] Baruch Spinoza, somewhat restless in his tomb, reminds us that society made the promise of a job well done translated into dignity. [2] And that achieving a more just society lies in the cooperation between multiple individuals who aspire to a kinder world. [3] The excuse of correction, as a guarantee of protective adaptation, deflates creative bravery; then it is only from a shared place of opposition that emotion and life can be brought together. [4] So with your permission, Baruch:

[5] Proposition: Correct architecture is useless for life

[6] Corollary:

[7] Axiom I   The opposite of correct is incorrect.
              If what is correct is what is accepted as a norm, then it is not unpredictable.

[8] Axiom II   What excites us is not what is established by norms, but what is unpredictable.
              What excites us, therefore, is not what is correct, but what is incorrect.

⁹ Axiom III   Architecture serves life.
          A full life gives rise to emotions.
          Therefore, life has to be exciting.

¹⁰ And if architecture is for life, it necessarily has to be exciting.
¹¹ Which demonstrates that if architecture is exciting, it is unpredictable (Axiom II) and, therefore, necessarily incorrect (Axiom I). Q.E.D.

¹ "I want one too!" shouts a little girl as I hand out the manifesto I've written for when they're old enough to read.

Since it's written on multicolored cardboard, they've pounced on me like I'm holding a new toy. ² Today is the official opening of my first building and I endure the admiring words of the parents, knowing that they are being polite. ³ The director has gathered the children, who have only been at the Nursery School in Sondika (1998–1999) for a month, into a circle; she tells them that I'm the architect. She has asked me to talk to them about the space where they spend so much time playing, eating, napping and even learning.

⁴ "Let's see, who knows what a kangaroo is? Take one step forward," I say with authority.

Most of the children take a timid step forward, coming closer and I can tell by their fascinated expressions that they'll understand what I have to say.

"Well, this is the same thing, right!" I exclaim, clowning around a bit.

⁵ When I see them all smile, I realize that I've reeled them in.

There are places where you can play and the grown-ups can't see you; there are others where you can play while you watch your friends playing outside in the garden," I whisper softly.

⁶ Then I turn toward a little girl with eyes like saucers and I ask her,

"What's your favorite place?"

The girl answers almost without thinking, in a soft voice,

"The bathroom with the little doors."

I can't hold back a resounding burst of laughter, which startles them a bit, but I go back to my questions,

"Why is that?"

The little girl hesitates for a second, but she answers,

"Because the teacher can't follow me through them."

⁷ As all the children applaud and shout energetically, I can't but admire such an act of independence from a little person.

⁸ So I take heart and, even though I know they won't understand any of it, I read straight through the Exciting Manifesto for Brave and Generous Children:

⁹ Trust in your intuition despite your teachers

¹⁰ Follow the light inside you despite the fireworks

¹¹ Devour things with your mind despite your stomach

¹² Recycle with your imagination despite the effort

¹³ Speak with conviction despite the opposition

¹⁴ Use your irony, despite what grownups do

¹⁵ Trust in your creativity, despite negotiators

¹⁶ Insist on simplicity, despite luxury

¹⁷ Look into the distance despite your family

¹⁸ Believe in your nature despite religion

[19] Half way through my histrionic recitation, some of the kids are yawning, some have even gone off to jump about somewhere else, but they've made me realize that enthusiasm and surprise far exceed the predictability of the profession. As I pick up my motorcycle helmet, I realize that some of the parents are scowling at me. [20] Even so, I take leave of their little ones, blowing kisses as I shout from afar:

Whenever you're faced with choosing between protection and freedom, choose freedom!"

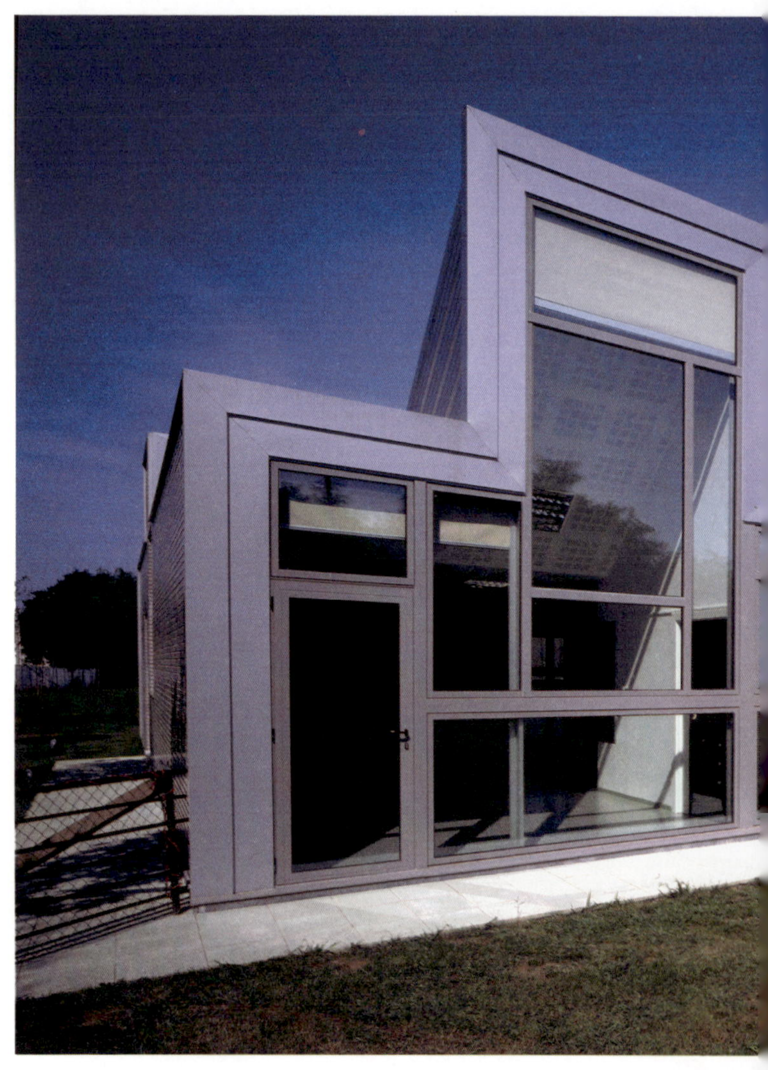

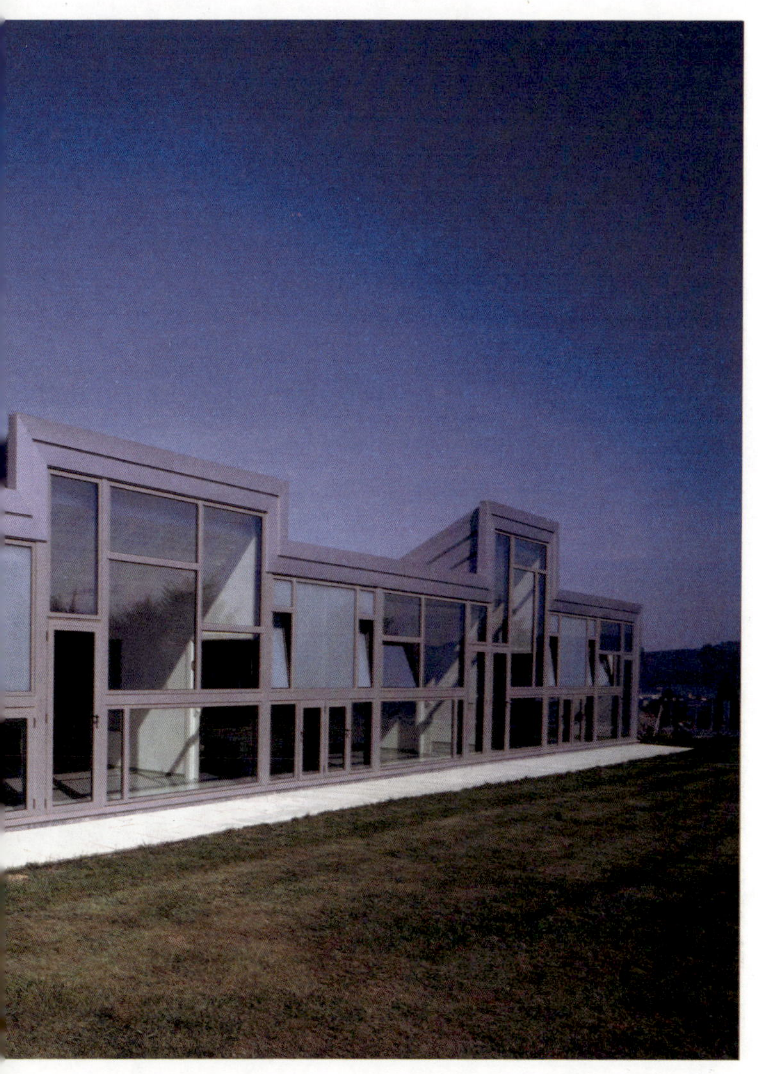

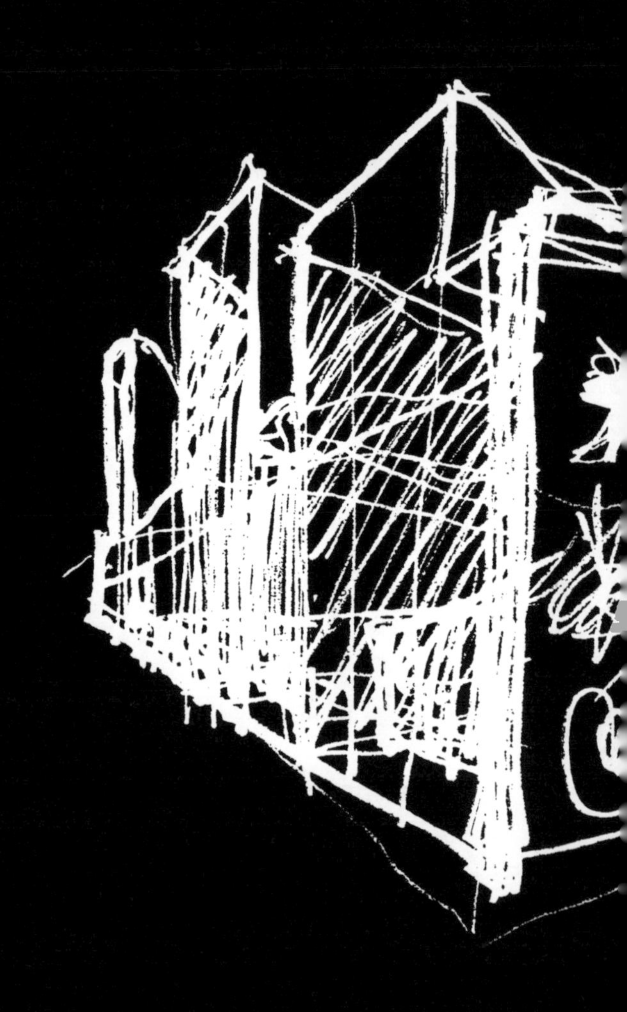

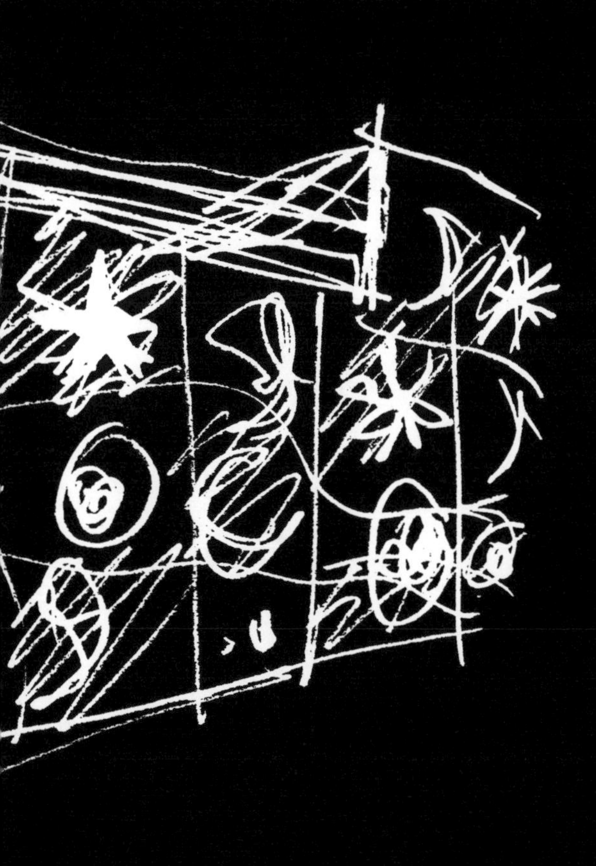

GENEROUS PEOPLE

My thanks to everyone who has accompanied me with any of their personal attributes throughout the process of preparing this book. Special thanks to Amadeu Santacana for his sharp editorial eye in selecting the texts and the images. To David Rodríguez and Esteban de Backer for their precision and sincerity in making choices and decisions about the publication. Also to David Lorente and Tomoko Sakamoto for their contributions in elegance and graphic essentiality. To the entire team at Actar Publishers and especially to Ramon Prat and Ricardo Devesa for their enthusiasm and organization. To Luis and Elvira for passing along a few brilliant genes that have driven me in life. And, above all, to Pia and Ada for their infinite patience and understanding with my disappearances, both physical and mental.

This book would also not have been possible without the collaboration of everyone who has been a part of NO.MAD at some point and has contributed, sometimes unwittingly, something of their thoughts or attitudes toward life to our creative commitment.

CREATION ——————————————————————————————

Paisajes de bolsillo (short film). Madrid: Fisuras de
Cultura Contemporánea, 2000. Francesco Monaco,
Simone Muscolino. —*see* 11 : 1-13

BARZUN, Jacques. *From Dawn to Decadence*. London:
Perennial Edition, 2001.
CAMUS, Albert. *L'Homme révolté*. Paris: Éditions Gallimard,
1951.
LAXNESS, Halldór. *Sjálfstaett fólk*. Reykjavík:
Landnámsmaður Íslands, 1934.
MONTAIGNE, Michel de. *Essais*. Paris: Ed. Marie de
Gournay, 1592.
RUSSELL, Bertrand; NORTH WHITEHEAD, Alfred. *Principia
mathematica*. New York: Cambridge Press, 1913.

MEMORY ——————————————————————————————

Bilbao Fine Arts Museum, Bilbao, 1997. —*see* 16 : 1-8
Floating City of Zorrozaure, Bilbao, 1994.
Juan Calvo. —*see* 19 : 1-5
Abandoibarra Business Center, Bilbao, 1993.
Juan Calvo. —*see* 20 : 1-4
Prado Museum, Madrid, 1995. Santiago Alarco, Miguel
Ángel Alonso, Luis Arroyo, Alejandro Gaspar, Ramón
Hervas, Juan Sádaba. —*see* 22 : 1-9

ARGULLOL, Rafael. *Territorio del nómada*. Mexico City:
Ed. Fondo de Cultura Económica, 1987.
CHATWIN, Bruce. *The Songlines*. New York: Viking Penguin,
1987.

Eliade, Mircea. *Le mythe de l'eternel retour.* Paris: Éditions
Gallimard, 1951.

Precision

Levene House, El Escorial, 2002–2005. Francesco
Monaco, Javier Tamer Elshiekh, Cristina Fidalgo,
Joaquin Antuña. Photos: Roland Halbe. —*see* 27 : 1-10
WU Executive Academy, Vienna, 2008–2013.
David Rodríguez, Esteban de Backer, Michael Rabold,
Frank Müller. Photos: Roland Halbe. —*see* 32 : 1-10

Of Hippo, Augustine. *Confessions*, 398.
Du Sautoy, Marcus. *The Music of the Primes.* London:
Harper Collins, 2003.
Musil, Robert. *Der Mann ohne Eigenschaften.* Hamburg:
Rohwolt, 1952.
Yanagi, Soetsu. *The Unknown Craftsman.* Tokyo: Kodansha,
1972.

Chance

Zaragoza Stadium, Zaragoza, 2002. Francesco Monaco,
Javier Tamer Elshiekh, Cristina Fidalgo, Carlos Martín.
—*see* 36 : 1-10, 124 : 6-7
City Hall, Bolzano, 1999. Federico Soriano and Dolores
Palacios, Sergio López-Piñeiro, Alessandra Abbruzzese,
Carlos Arroyo, Manolo Pérez, Dan Budik, Isabella
Pasqualini. —*see* 39 : 1-10
Social Housing, Durango, 2005. Cristina Fidalgo, David
Rodríguez. —*see* 41 : 1-9, 124 : 4-5

Monod, Jacques. *Le hasard et la nécessité.* Paris: Éditions de Seuil, 1970.
Prigogine, Ilya; Stengers, Isabelle. *La fin des certitudes.* Paris: Odile Jacob, 1996.
Sheliepin, Leonid Alexándrovich. *Lejos del equilibrio.* Moscow: Editorial URSS, 1987.

Empathy ──

Congress Hall, Pamplona, 1998. Nerea Calvillo, Sergio López-Piñeiro, Daniel Valle. —*see* 45 : 1-9, 56 : 1-10, 132 : 5
Social Housing, Valencia, 2006. Francesco Monaco, David Rodríguez, Lars-Sebastian Dillner, Esteban de Backer. —*see* 47 : 1-10
Therapeutic Housing, Valencia, 2003. Paloma Cañizares, Enrique Moya-Angeler. —*see* 50 : 1-10
Lasesarre Stadium, Barakaldo, 2000–2004. Nerea Calvillo, Sergio López-Piñeiro, Héctor Mejía, Francesco Monaco, Raúl Ortega, Santiago Mazorriaga. Short Film "Yellow fever": Simone Muscolino, Francesco Monaco. Photos: Roland Halbe. —*see* 52 : 1-11

Bergson, Henri. *La Conscience et la Vie, le Possible et le Réel.* Paris: Magnard, 1911.
Sloterdijk, Peter. *Sphären.* Frankfurt am Main: Suhrkamp Verlag, 1998.
Wittgenstein, Ludwig. *Logisch-Philosophische Abhandlung.* Leipzig: Wilhelm Ostwalds, 1921.

EVENTS ───────────────────────────────

Congress Hall, Pamplona, 1998. —*see* EMPATHY
National Hotel-Parador, Alcalá de Henares, 2002.
  Francesco Monaco, Javier Tamer Elshiekh, Cristina
  Fidalgo. —*see* 58 : 1-10, 132 : 6-9
Train Station and Euskotren Headquarters, Durango,
  2004. Francesco Monaco, Javier Tamer Elshiekh,
  Cristina Fidalgo, Enrique Moya-Angeler. —*see* 61 : 1-11,
  128 : 9, 135 : 3-4
Saint-Denis Olympic Village, Paris, 2000.
  Francesco Monaco, Nerea Calvillo, Malca Mizrahi,
  Raúl Ortega. —*see* 63 : 1-11

BACHELARD, Gaston. *L'intuition de l'instant*. Paris:
  Mediations, 1932.
BAUMAN, Zygmunt. *Liquid Modernity*. New York: Cambridge
  University Press, 1999.
PROUST, Marcel. *À la recherche du temps perdu*. Paris:
  Éditions Gallimard, 1919.

PROPERTIES ─────────────────────────────

Visitors Center, Fabriano, 2003.
  Francesco Monaco, Cristina Fidalgo. —*see* 66 : 1-10
Isla Chica Urban Center, Huelva, 2004.
  Francesco Monaco, Javier Tamer Elshiekh, Cristina
  Fidalgo. —*see* 70 : 1-12
Nam June Paik Museum, Seoul, 2003.
  Paloma Cañizares, Javier Tamer Elshiekh, Cristina
  Fidalgo, Enrique Moya-Angeler. —*see* 73 : 1-9, 124 : 8-10

Coveney, Peter; Highfield, Roger. *The Arrow of Time*.
London: Harper Collins, 1991.
Goethe, Johann Wolfgang von. *Die Wahlverwandtschaften*.
Munich: Dt. Taschenbuch-Verlag, 1808.
Harman, P.M. *Energy, Force and Matter*. New York:
Cambridge University Press, 1982.
Popper, Karl. *The Open Universe*. London: Hutchinson, 1982.

Hybridization

Galindo Hybrid City, Barakaldo, 1998.
Nerea Calvillo, Sergio López-Piñeiro. —*see 77 : 1-11*
Plaza de Olavide, Madrid, 2008. David Rodríguez,
Margarita Martínez. —*see 79 : 1-11*
Viral City, Réunión Island, 1999. Sergio López-Piñeiro,
Nerea Calvillo-González, Héctor Mejía. —*see 81 : 1-14*
Prés-de-Vidy Stadium, Lausanne, 2011. David Rodríguez,
Esteban de Backer, Frank Müller, Ander Rodríguez,
Estefanía Mompean. —*see 83 : 1-11, 128 : 7-8*

Sennett, Richard. *Together*. New Haven: Yale University
Press, 2012.
Teilhard de Chardin, Pierre. *L'Avenir de l'Homme*.
Paris: Maurice Blondel, 1959.

Procedures

University Complex, Sarajevo, 2000. Nerea Calvillo,
Francesco Monaco, Raúl Ortega, David Casino, Ignacio
Toribio. —*see 86 : 1-16*

Sports Center, Irún, 2001. Francesco Monaco, Cristina
  Posadas. —*see* 89 : 1-11
Plaza del Desierto, Barakaldo, 1998–2000.
  Sergio López-Piñeiro, John Garcés, Nerea Calvillo,
  Teresa Galí. Photos: Geraldine Bruneel. —*see* 92 : 1-13

Kosko, Bart. *The Fuzzy Future.* New York: Harmony Books,
  1999.
Mandelbrot, Benôit B. *The Fractal Geometry of Nature.*
  New York: W. H. Freeman and Co.: 1977.
Marinetti, Filippo Tommaso. *La Cucina Futurista.*
  Milan: Viennepierre Edizioni, 1932.

Cloning

Wastewater Treatment Plan, Sestao, 2007. David
  Rodríguez, Margarita Martínez, Alfonso Navarrete.
  —*see* 95 : 1-11
"Castaluna" Visual Opera, Vall d'Aran, 2002.
  Francesco Monaco, Cristina Hidalgo, Javier Tamer,
  Simone Muscolino. —*see* 97 : 1-7
Cloned Parking Structure System, Barcelona, 1990.
  Patricia Woldring. —*see* 99 : 1-11
Cloned Sport Centers, Hadsten-Naestved-Frederiksberg,
  1999. Sergio López-Piñeiro, Daniel Valle, John Garcés.
  —*see* 101 : 1-11

Ridley, Matt. *Genome: The Autobiography of a Species in
  23 Chapters.* London: Fourth Estate, 1999.

Invisible order

Geo-rutes System, Benicàssim, 2009.
David Rodríguez, Esteban de Backer, Frank Müller,
Michael Rabold. —*see* 104 : 1-9
Transportation Museum, Málaga, 2007. David Rodríguez,
Margarita Martínez, Alfonso Navarrete. —*see* 106 : 1-11
Neanderthal Museum, Piloña, 2010. David Rodríguez,
Esteban de Backer, Estefanía Mompean, Ander
Rodríguez. —*see* 108 : 1-10
Zafra-Uceda House, Aranjuez, 2006. David Rodríguez,
Lars-Sebastian Dillner. Photos: Roland Halbe.
—*see* 110 : 1-10

Carroll, Lewis. *The Hunting of the Snark*. London:
Macmillan Publishers, 1876.
Lindley, David. *Boltzmann's Atom*. New York: Free Press,
2001.

Complexity

Estonian National Museum, Tartu, 2005. Francesco
Monaco, Cristina Fidalgo, David Rodríguez. —*see* 114 : 1-8
Art Foundation, Lleida, 2009. Esteban de Backer, David
Rodríguez. —*see* 116 : 1-10, 135 : 5-7
Public School, Vienna, 2010. David Rodríguez, Esteban de
Backer, Frank Müller, Michael Rabold. —*see* 118 : 1-12
CSIC Research Building, Santiago de Compostela, 2010.
David Rodríguez, Esteban de Backer, Ander Rodríguez,
Estefanía Mompean. —*see* 120 : 1-11

Brooks Jr., Frederik P. *No Silver Bullet.* Boston: The
  Mythical Man, 1986.
Wagensberg, Jorge. *La Rebelión de las Formas.* Barcelona:
  Metatemas, 2004.

GRAVITY ——————————————————————————————————

Social Housing, Durango, 2005. —*see* CHANCE
Zaragoza Stadium, Zaragoza, 2002. —*see* CHANCE
Nam June Paik Museum, Seoul, 2003.
  —*see* PROPRERTIES
Prés-de-Vidy Stadium, Lausanne, 2011.
  —*see* HYBRIDATION
Train Station and Euskotren Headquarters, Durango,
  2004. —*see* EVENTS
Art Museum, Oslo, 2009. Esteban de Backer, David
  Rodríguez, Babak Rostamian, Frank Müller, Michael
  Rabold. —*see* 128 : 10

Darwin, Charles. *On the Origin of Species.* Oxford: Oxford
  University Press, 1859.
Poincaré, Henri. *La Science et l'Hypothèse.* Paris:
  Flammarion, 1902.

MUTABILITY ——————————————————————————————

Congress Hall, Pamplona, 1998. —*see* EMPATHY
National Hotel-Parador, Alcalá de Henares, 2002.
  —*see* EVENTS
Train Station and Euskotren Headquarters, Durango,
  2004. —*see* EVENTS
Art Foundation, Lleida, 2009. —*see* COMPLEXITY

Floating Stage, Miami, 2011. Ander Rodríguez, Estefanía
Mompean, David Rodríguez. —*see* 135 : 8-10
Arquia Bank Office, Bilbao, 2007–2008.
David Rodríguez, Luis Arroyo, Margarita Martínez,
Alfonso Navarrete, José López. Photos: Miguel de
Guzmán. —*see* 137 : 1-10

Goethe, Johann Wolfgang von. *Zur Farbenlehre*. Tübingen:
Cotta, 1810.

Mattergy ——————————————————————————————

Art Museum, Lausanne, 2004. Francesco Monaco,
Javier Tamer Elshiekh, Cristina Fidalgo. —*see* 142 : 1-9
City of Wind, Córdoba, 2002. Francesco Monaco,
Sandra Martín, Marion Michaut. —*see* 144 : 1-12
Administrative Building, Seville, 2008.
David Rodríguez, José López. —*see* 147 : 1-11

Pirsig, Robert M. *Zen and the Art of Motorcycle Maintenance*.
London: Harper Collins, 1974.
Twain, Mark. *Chapters from My Autobiography*. Boston:
North American Review, 1907.

Epilogue ——————————————————————————————

Nursery School, Sondika, 1996–1998.
Photos: Cesar Sanmillán. —*see* 151 : 1-20

Spinoza, Baruch. *Ethica ordine geometrico demonstrata*.
The Hague, 1677.
Toynbee, Arnold J. *A Study of History. Abridgement*.
Oxford: Oxford University, 1946.

Published by **Actar Publishers**
151 Grand ST, 5th Fl., New York, NY 10013, USA

Author **Eduardo Arroyo**

Editor **Amadeu Santacana**

Graphic Design **Tomoko Sakamoto & David Lorente,**
(www.spread.eu.com), with the collaboration of
Claudia Parra

Editorial Coordination **Ricardo Devesa,** Actar Publishers

Digital Production **Núria Sabán,** Actar Publishers

English Translation **Angela Kay Bunning**

Collaborators **David Rodríguez** and **Esteban De Backer,**
NO.MAD

Printing and binding **Grafos S.A., Barcelona**

ISBN 978-1-940291-05-5

Printed and bound in the European Union

Distribution

Actar D, Inc.
151 Grand ST, 5th Fl.,
New York, NY 10013, USA
www.actar-d.com

North America & Asia
Innovative Logistics
575 Prospect Street
Lakewood, NJ 08701, USA
orders@actar-d.com

Europe, Middle East & Japan
Marston Book Services Ltd,
160 Milton Park, Abingdon
OX14 4SD, UK
trade.orders@marston.co.uk

A CIP catalogue record for this book is available from the
Library of Congress, Washington D.C., USA.